The Psychology of Women

VOLUME TWO

MOTHERHOOD

The Psychology of Women

A PSYCHOANALYTIC INTERPRETATION

By

HELENE DEUTSCH, M.D.

Associate Psychiatrist, Massachusetts General Hospital
Lecturer, Boston Psychoanalytic Institute

VOLUME TWO

MOTHERHOOD

GRUNE & STRATTON

NEW YORK

1945

First printing, January 1945
Second printing, April 1945
Third printing, September 1945
Fourth printing, July 1946
Fifth printing, June 1947
Sixth printing, March 1948
Seventh printing, July 1950
Eighth printing, February 1954
Ninth printing, February 1959
Tenth printing, April 1963
Eleventh printing, September 1967
Twelfth printing, December 1971

GRUNE & STRATTON, INC.
111 Fifth Avenue, New York, New York 10003

Library of Congress Catalog Card Number   44-5287
International Standard Book Number   0-8089-0116-8

Preface

With this second volume of *The Psychology of Women*, my attempt to draw a picture of the psychologic life of the normal woman in our society is completed. In the course of my discussions I have frequently used pathologic material and historical illustrations, but this has been always in an endeavor to light up more clearly the normal and contemporary psyche.

The psychosomatic interdependence of the psychologic and physiologic processes is nowhere so clearly demonstrated as in the female reproductive activity. Examination of the psychologic aspects of motherhood makes it inevitable to consider the disturbances not only in the one sphere but also in the other. The related physiologic disturbances are so common that it is entirely justifiable to maintain that there is hardly a woman in whom the normal psychic conflicts do not result in a pathologic distortion, at some point, of the biologic process of motherhood. This explains why abnormal manifestations such as sterility, abortion, and many kinds of difficulties of pregnancy, delivery, lactation, etc., have been included in the discussions of this book. However, since my intention was never to move too far from the normal, the pathologic aspects have only been touched upon, and will be treated in greater detail in a future volume.

The same can be said as regards consideration of the cultural and social factors that influence the shaping of the feminine psyche. Occasionally these factors have been mentioned both in this and in the earlier volume, chiefly to illustrate my views on the constancy of certain psychic phenomena in woman's life, occurring as they do in all cultures. Still another volume will be devoted to a thorough discussion of these problems.

I wish to acknowledge my thanks to Dr. Stanley Cobb, who has enabled me to continue my clinical observations in the Psychiatric Department of the Massachusetts General Hospital.

I also wish to thank all those social workers who in the course of many years of collaboration have given me opportunity to acquaint myself with the social background of the psychologic conflicts of their clients. I am especially indebted to those who have contributed to the enrichment of my material through the discussion of social case records in consultations and in seminars. I am indebted to Mrs. A. Barrett and Mrs. L. Fine for having helped me in the editing of my manuscript.

HELENE DEUTSCH

Boston, April, 1945

Contents

CHAPTER ONE

Social and Biologic Aspects

MAN can experience his relation to his environment in two ways. First, there is the individual ego experience in which he perceives all the events of the environment only in relation to his own ego, and which unifies the immediate impressions of his senses and gives them content only in so far as he can relate them to his own life. Second, there is that mode of experience which is rooted in the fact that every human being and his whole existence are a link in the long chain of historical evolution, a part of the eternal life stream. In this type of experience, existence is no longer defined by the personal past; instead, the impersonal past creates for the individual experience a timeless background, a perspective of "eternity" and "immortality."

In motherhood woman is given the wonderful opportunity of directly experiencing this sense of immortality. The female reproductive function is not merely a single or repeated individual act on the biologic level. On the contrary, the biologic events as such can be conceived as individual manifestations of the universal human fluctuation between the two poles of creation and destruction, and as the victory of life over death. Such a sense of these biologic manifestations is expressed in primitive feelings, in religious cults, and in the most advanced philosophic thought. We can explore them directly and individually in woman's reproductive tasks.

On the other hand, motherhood as an individual experience is the expression not only of a biologic process, but also of a psychologic unity that epitomizes numerous individual experiences, memories, wishes, and fears that have preceded the real experience by many years.

In the psychologist's laboratory, the individual experiences are observed and analyzed as they appear to him subjectively. The insight into life that we thus gain is not free of contradic-

I

tions. But a large number of such observations can perhaps
enable us to draw certain general inferences. Two questions
arise here. The first is: Are there psychologic events free of
the accidental features of the individual event, enabling the
observer to draw objective conclusions? And conversely:
Are the individual psychologic aspects of woman's reproductive
function grounded on universal biologic or social determinants?
We can leave this question to the biologists and sociologists.
The biologists must decide to what extent the events observed
by the psychologist are subject to general laws, that is to say,
are determined biologically; the sociologists must decide to
what extent they are determined by cultural influences. The
psychologists' task is to observe and report certain spatially
and temporally limited psychic facts.

Some psychologists, however, believe that they can contribute much to the understanding of psychologic phenomena by
bringing in cultural factors and trying to prove that the psychologic element depends exclusively upon a given social-cultural
structure. Some of these psychologists have dealt with woman's place in a given social order, her role in the family, and
the influence of these factors on the psychology of motherhood
conceived as a social phenomenon. Others emphasize the
influence of social institutions and ideologies on the psychology
of the biologic functions of motherhood.

The first type of sociologic approach to the problem of
motherhood can be illustrated by the role of woman in present
day society and a comparison between the prewar situations of
the European and the American woman. For certain well defined historical reasons, the American woman is much more
"emancipated," that is, her social rights and duties are not as
sharply differentiated from man's rights and duties as in most
European countries. But if this state of affairs, which is
gratifying in itself, is examined more closely, it will be seen that
it is not the result of progress made along a straight line, but
that it constitutes a holdover from a past epoch, from which
there have been retrogressions. In the early nineteenth century, when America was won for civilization, her women were

forced to overcome their biologic tendencies in order to fulfill important pioneering tasks at the side of their men. They were expected to display courage and an active spirit of conquest, they fought along with their husbands and brothers against the tremendous difficulties of life on the newly won continent. In their sexual role, because they were less numerous than men, they were a scarce and therefore extraordinarily highly valued element. Thus various factors contributed to securing for American women equality and even dominance. Nevertheless, from the beginning of American colonization, currents opposing woman's high social position and differentiating the two sexes were also operative. These currents, barely perceptible at the start, grew gradually stronger. By the end of the nineteenth century the role of the American woman was more and more similar to that of the European. Her extraordinary value decreased along with her rarity as a sexual object, but the old attitude persisted for some time in the special, sometimes ridiculously exaggerated "gallant" protection with which she was surrounded because of her alleged "helplessness"; her social role was still connected with certain cultural privileges, and she had a dominant position in the family. At that time American men engaged in a ruthless struggle for new conquests of wealth in a rapidly developing civilization and had little time for family, religious, or cultural problems. They willingly left these to woman, recognizing her moral and to some extent cultural superiority. The American woman might have achieved even greater social and political advantages than she did, although, as we have said, women in America had more rights than those of most European countries. Especially strong was woman's dominant position in the family. The matriarchal type of woman (cf. vol. I, p. 283) is more frequent in certain strata of American society than in Europe.

We might regard our observation on the position of American women as conclusive. But if the perspective is changed, and the facts are examined more closely, we discover that this global comparison applies only to certain social strata, and that the same type of woman has long been common in several European countries in well defined social classes, although her cultural manifestations were different (for instance in certain orthodox Jewish circles, among some Slav nations, etc.). We may also note here that the role of women in the German middle classes before the war was different from that in the French middle classes, although the social and cultural conditions were similar.

Our example suggests other questions. Is the effect of social causes, such as we have observed in America, constant? Or is this effect eliminated by subsequent social developments? Does progress always continue in one direction, and if not, why? Do psychologic and biologic factors come into play to counteract the effects of social developments? And assuming that the domineering woman is a result of social development, does every woman make use of this socially acquired position in the same way with regard to herself and her environment? The domineering woman in New England, for instance, plays a great part in forming the moral personality of her children. Because of her characterologic features, she often sets up an excessively high ideal for herself and for them, an ideal that involves so many obligations that it frequently becomes a burden to the children. Furthermore, the part she assigns to the father in the family depends upon her tact. If she devaluates him and reduces him to insignificance, she will certainly create profound psychologic conflicts for her children, and she herself will be unhappy and unfulfilled as a woman. But if, despite her social position, she possesses the feminine qualities of intuition and emotional warmth, her influence will have a quite different effect.

Another type is the domineering woman who uses her position to gratify her aggressions and is unable to develop a warm, feminine emotional life. When this occurs, social equality seems a curse, and one is inclined, even at the risk of appearing reactionary, to wish that she might be deprived of her position of authority in the family. It must be stressed that this type of domineering woman is not found only in America.

On the other hand, the domineering matriarchal woman in Jewish families is usually distinguished by excessive tenderness toward her children, and her love often has a primitive character that inspires her constantly to seek to satiate her children.

We might cite many other examples of identical socially determined situations producing reactions that are psychologically opposite.

Despite this variation in reactions to identical social influences and despite similarities of reaction under different cultural conditions, some emotional relationships between mother and child are so deep and primitive that they transcend all social and individual differences. In 1933, when racial hatred was at its height in Germany, I happened to travel from Vienna to Switzerland in an overcrowded train. Most of the passengers were women, many of them orthodox Jews fleeing from Germany; there were also two working women who were probably politically suspect, and two German women with swastikas on their sleeves, typical fanatics of the Germany of that day. They had an attitude of contemptuous disdain toward the other passengers. At daybreak, when the train pulled into a big station, someone brought in a morning paper. The headlines reported that a well known young Nazi leader who had gone skiing in the mountains had been buried under an avalanche. Then followed a description of the searching party, organized by the boy's mother, who had wandered in the blizzard and struggled against the snow and ice until she collapsed in exhaustion. One of the women read this news story aloud; ten minutes later there were no Nazis, no despised Jews, and no Marxist proletarians in the compartment; there were only mothers moved by their common maternal feelings to weep over the fate of another mother whom they did not really know.

American soldiers in the present war, whenever they are seized by homesickness or are forced to suffer bitter privations, often speak of their mothers' pies. Similarly, the German soldiers of the first world war used to talk about their mothers' dumplings or other favorite national dishes, which were symbols of their deep childish longing for their mothers. Whenever a strong man faces danger or death, on this or any other continent, he calls to his mother, no matter under what cultural and social conditions his deep, powerful mother tie was formed.

In every case, we have on the one hand individual reactions to a given social situation, and on the other a deeply rooted, universal human component, independent of environment, amenable to the psychologic point of view. Nevertheless, the conscientious psychologist knows that frequently a deeper understanding of the problems confronting him can be achieved only with the help of information gained from the related fields of sociology and biology.

When we turn to the writings of the anthropologists for data on the history of motherhood as a social phenomenon, we discover two fundamental methods of approach in conflict. One represents the patriarchal theory, built upon the long prevalent hypothesis that the male, thanks to his superior bodily strength and mental ability, has always been the ruler of his species. This hypothesis was, if not refuted, at least undermined by scientific investigations. It was discovered that among several peoples all family rights stemmed from the mother, not from the father. From various old laws the pattern of so-called matriarchy (mother rule), which supposedly preceded the patriarchy (father rule), was reconstructed. Bachofen maintained that the original type of the primitive community was that of a group of blood relations stemming from the same tribal mother.

This hypothesis, according to which matriarchy preceded patriarchy and the rule of women represented the earliest stage of human society, was energetically disputed. While it was readily admitted that under certain social and legal systems the woman as mother held a high position, Bachofen's assumption of a period of general female domination, which was only later overthrown by the patriarchal family, met with the greatest skepticism and was often rejected as a vulgar error. And while the defenders of the ancient iron right of the father thus refused to give up their position, the feminists often quoted the new theory to support their demands.

Today the anthropologists agree that there are two types of human families—the patrilineal, such as found its expression in the *patria potestas* of Roman law, and prevails in modern society, and the matrilineal, in which kinship is derived through the mother only and succession and inheritance follow the female line. The latter form of society has often been directly observed by modern anthropologists, as for instance by Malinowski among the Trobriand Islanders of northeastern New Guinea or northwestern Melanesia.[1]

Briffault, an enthusiastic partisan of the matriarchal theory, criticizes the patriarchal theory of social origins in his book *The Mothers*.[2] His argument is based on biologic factors. According to his view, the social relations occurring in the animal kingdom outside humanity are grounded upon reproductive functions and not upon social instincts, and paternity plays only a small part in the animal world. The family group consists of the mother and her offspring; the male may join this group, but his role is insignificant and without functional importance.

The parental relation is confined to that between mother and brood. Paternity does not exist. The family among animals is not, as the human family is supposed to be, the result of the association of male and female, but is the product of the maternal functions. The mother is the sole center and bond of it. There is no division of labor between the sexes in procuring the means of subsistence. The protective functions are exercised by the female, not by the male. The abode, movements, and conduct of the group are determined by the female alone. The animal family is a group produced not by the sexual but by the maternal impulses, not by the father, but by the mother.[3]

Briffault deduces all the social feelings in human society from the mother-child relationship and transfers their origin to the period of the prolonged dependence of the offspring upon motherly protection.

[1] MALINOWSKI, B.: Sex and repression in savage society. New York: Harcourt, 1927.
[2] BRIFFAULT, R.: The mothers. New York: Macmillan, 1931, p. 23.
[3] Op. cit., p. 66.

Those determining factors in the origin of the human race and of society are dependent upon the operation of the maternal impulses. They are the outcome of their favorable activity in the maternally constituted animal family.

According to Briffault, the matriarchal theory of social origins is a consequence of this development.

It must be noted that in his conclusion Briffault emphasizes his reservations against feminist views.

The conditions in the former phases being entirely different from those obtaining in the more advanced stages of culture, the matriarchal theory of social origins bears only indirectly upon the doctrines of feminism. There can be no doubt that a large proportion of the secondary sexual characters, both psychical and physical, which have been set down as biological, are in reality the effects of the operation of the social circumstances obtaining in a patriarchal order. At the same time it cannot be assumed that sexual differentiation is devoid of biological foundation ... The matriarchal theory of social origins bears undoubtedly upon the claim of women to share in social and intellectual activities in a manner which has been denied to them by the organisation of patriarchal society, but it cannot be adduced as a proof of any biological aptitude. The questions raised by the claims of feminism rest upon entirely different grounds.[4]

The reasons why intellectual women are so fond of the matriarchal theory are obvious. It is a form of protest against woman's alleged social inferiority and against cultural injustice.

It is difficult to find one's way through the labyrinth of conflicting anthropologic theories, and our study of the past has yielded much contradictory evidence. Nor is psychology always a reliable auxiliary in historical reconstructions. Everything that the explorer imagines he sees in the remote past is for the most part colored by his own subjective experiences, by a kind of rediscovery of his own self and psychic world that he projects into an outside world that has long since vanished.

Sometimes his frantic attempt to obtain an objective view of the world through "science" is only an intensified attempt to escape from himself—as a rule an only partly successful effort. As a scientist he tries to find the truth by organizing the facts he has discovered, but his interpretations are always subjective.

[4]Op. cit., p. 313.

Malinowski, himself an anthropologist, speaks skeptically of anthropologic constructions that, he says, "combine some fact with much hypothesis." He failed, however, to take into account the psychologic motives that are often responsible for such hypotheses.

The subjectivity of scientific theories can be experimentally demonstrated when the psychic life of a scientist honestly trying to achieve objectivity is subjected to psychoanalytic observation. Fortunately several members of a small scientific circle that was studying the problems mentioned above became accessible to such observation. I shall mention only a few of the results obtained. It was revealed that the enthusiastic partisans of the matriarchal theory, men as well as women, were influenced in their scientific views by deeply unconscious motives. However, they did not all belong to the same psychologic type, and identical views in different individuals often derived from diametrically opposed psychic tendencies. Thus, one anthropologist believed in the matriarchal theory because in his neurotically inhibited hatred he was fighting in vain against the patriarchal power of his own father. Another wanted to replace his strong, domineering mother, whom he had worshiped as a child but later devaluated because she was unequal to his ideal demands, with the "great mother" of the primitive past. He did not realize that actually he hoped that this mythical figure would help him to rediscover his own once powerful mother, whom he had long since lost emotionally. Another young anthropologist's numerous "objective" arguments in favor of masculine superiority and the patriarchal theory proved to be based upon his narcissistic pride, while another partisan of the same views gratified his passive attitude toward his own father by transferring it to the fathers of the past, to whose rule he wanted to submit as to an ever recurring principle. My aim in pointing out such subjective influences in objective science is not to diminish the value of the latter, but rather to emphasize the caution imposed by such direct psychologic observations.

There is much evidence in support of the theory that the

causes of the first human social organizations are to be found in organic-biologic processes. More particularly, a certain stage in the development of the mother-offspring relation seems to be the prototype of the first social organization.

Concerning the second type of sociologic approach to the problem of motherhood, we shall quote an expert[5]:

Let us briefly summarize and characterize these social codeterminants of motherhood in our own society. Maternity is a moral, religious, and even artistic ideal of civilization; a pregnant woman is protected by law and custom and should be regarded as a sacred object, while she herself ought to feel proud and happy in her condition. That this is an ideal which can be realized is vouched for by historical and ethnographical data. Even in modern Europe, the orthodox Jewish communities of Poland keep it up in practice, and amongst them a pregnant woman is an object of real veneration, and feels proud of her condition. In the Christian Aryan societies, however, pregnancy among the lower classes is made a burden, and regarded as a nuisance; among the well-to-do people it is a source of embarrassment, discomfort, and temporary ostracism from ordinary social life. Since we thus have to recognize the importance of the mother's prenatal attitude for her future sentiment towards her offspring, and since this attitude varies greatly with the milieu and depends on social values, it is important that this sociological problem should be studied more closely.

At birth, the biological patterns and the instinctive impulses of the mother are endorsed and strengthened by society, which, in many of its customs, moral rules, and ideals makes the mother the nurse of the child, and this, broadly speaking, in the low as in the high strata of almost all the nations of Europe. Yet even here in a relation so fundamental, so biologically secured, there are certain societies where custom and laxity of innate impulses allow of notable aberrations. Thus we have the system of sending the child away for the first year or so of its life to a hired foster mother, a custom once highly prevalent in the middle classes of France; or the almost equally harmful system of protecting the woman's breasts by hiring a foster mother, or by feeding the child on artificial food, a custom once prevalent among the wealthy classes, though today generally stigmatized as unnatural. Here again the sociologist has to add his share in order to give the true picture of motherhood, as it varies according to national, economic, and moral differences.

Let us now turn to consider the same relation in a matrilineal society on the shores of the Pacific. The Melanesian woman shows invariably a passionate craving for her child, and the surrounding society seconds her feelings, fosters her inclinations, and idealizes them by custom and usage. From the first

[5]MALINOWSKI, B.: Op. cit., pp. 19–22.

moment of pregnancy, the expectant mother is made to watch over the welfare of her future offspring by keeping a number of food taboos and other observances. The pregnant woman is regarded by custom as an object of reverence, an ideal which is fully realized by the actual behavior and feelings of these natives. There exists an elaborate ceremony performed at the first pregnancy, with an intricate and somewhat obscure aim, but emphasizing the importance of the event and conferring on the pregnant woman distinction and honor.

After the birth, mother and child are secluded for about a month, the mother constantly tending her child and nursing it, while certain female relatives only are admitted into the hut. Adoption under normal circumstances is very rare, and even then the child is usually given over only after it has been weaned, nor is it ever adopted by strangers, but by nearest relatives exclusively. A number of observances, such as ritual washing of mother and child, special taboos to be kept by the mother, and visits of presentation, bind mother and child by links of custom superimposed upon the natural ones.

Thus in both societies, to the biological adjustment of instinct there are added the social forces of custom, morals, and manners, all working in the same direction of binding mother and child to each other, of giving them full scope for the passionate intimacy of motherhood. This harmony between social and biological forces ensures full satisfaction and the highest bliss.

At this point the psychoanalyst cannot help asking: What is the psychology of a mother living in a social order in which this harmony between social custom and biologic factors does not exist? The sociologist calls our attention to sociologic differences; he can observe the behavior of women who must adjust themselves to existing social relations, but he cannot describe their emotional reactions, conscious or unconscious, for this is the domain of the psychologist.

Let us first concentrate on the biologic aspect of the problem. In the lower forms of life the mother organism throws off unfecundated reproductive cells and is no longer interested in their future fate. With internal fecundation, the sexual cell obtains the most favorable conditions for its development: it remains at rest and is supplied with food, warmth, and shelter. Thus protected from outer dangers, the fecundated ovum can use all its vital energy for its own maturation. With the prolongation of the period of gestation, the female sex undertook a greater share of the work involved in reproduction, and this share gradually increased in the higher animal species. By the transfer of a part of the reproductive task to the interior of the body, the preservation of the species was further insured; physiologic relations were created between mother and offspring from the very beginning, and as a result of this physical union, instincts awakened in the mother animal that persisted beyond the birth of the young. The alliance between mother and offspring continued tor the length of time in which the offspring was not mature enough to take over the task of self-preservation and adjustment to the environment.

In the course of phylogenetic development, increasingly complex relationships arose between mother and offspring during this period of protective care, and have gradually led to the highly organized manifestations of the mother instinct. These manifestations developed in all the animal species into certain stereotyped, hereditary forms, which are always, in every generation, determined by physiologic processes in the mother's body. They are often so strong that they seem to have a superior intelligence and all the power of the emotions at their disposal. The animal's individual self-preservation, her avoidance of personal dangers by means of fear signals, the procurement of her food, and her self-protection against the hostile environment are often served by excellent auxiliary instruments.

But all these considerations pale when the mother animal is studied as the representative of the species. Among animals the rule of the instinct is confined to their organic relationship with their young and ends with the close of the period of the offspring's helplessness. Our anthropomorphic attitude toward the outside world makes us assume that the instinctual manifestations of animals are accompanied by emotions that we ourselves would experience in similar situations. But an examination of the facts destroys this illusion. The operation of the animal's mother instinct springs from physiologic necessity; it functions and continues only on the basis of definite somatic sensations; it decreases as the young grow independent and sometimes breaks off abruptly without leaving the slightest trace of an emotional relationship. A cow or a ewe (this is my personal observation) when separated from her newborn off-spring displays all the signs of emotional agitation that, in our identification with the animal, we might be inclined to call "longing and despair." But the cow's or ewe's interest in her calf or lamb vanishes as soon as the purely physical need of proximity is gratified. Thus we can reduce this seemingly emotional attitude to a simple physiologic reaction to separation. And, as we have said, the manifestations of the instinct vary in different species. The maternal instinct of the ewe, for instance, is strongly connected with the nature of the lamb's skin. She brutally refuses her teats to a lamb that is not her own, even if it is of the same age and appearance as her own. But it is sufficient to attach a piece of the skin of her own lamb to the substitute to make the ewe behave like a mother Unlike the ewe, the sow allows every little piglet that is placed at her teats to suckle, regardless of its origin, and displays great patience and motherliness toward it. But it is well known that if she herself lacks food and reaches a certain stage of hunger, she will devour her own young.

The difference between the instinctual manifestations of maternity in animals and the maternal emotion in human beings seems surprising, until we realize that we have been trying to treat two completely different phenomena as identical. One, the animal instinctual manifestation, is a physiologically determined process; the other relates to a human psychologic process. What the two have in common is that they serve the reproductive function.

However, the transformation of the maternal instinct into "maternal love" takes place not only in the human species. Among the primates it is possible to observe a certain behavior suggesting that the inherited instincts are here accompanied by certain elements closely related to human emotions.

At what point and to what extent the instinctive actions of the higher animals are endowed with an emotional character, is an interesting problem. At any rate, the dependence of maternal behavior upon hormonal processes has been experimentally established with regard to animals. Attempts are being made to establish this dependence with regard to the human female as well.[6]

At present it is difficult to decide to what extent the complex emotional attribute that we call "motherliness" expresses a biologic condition. Without doubt, it started directly from a primal biologic situation, but in the course of time the non-hereditary, plastic, variable elements gradually gained the upper hand, and under the influence of cultural developments and individual experiences, crystallized as maternal love, which is a powerful and complex emotion.

It is clear that the unique intimacy between these two living beings, mother and child, tends to support the theory that finds the origin of the human family in this biologic "group." In our society, further, the social emotions and the social capacity for adjustment are based upon the first relation of the little human being to its mother.

Even if experiments should some day prove that the complicated phenomenon of motherhood depends upon the existence of a hormonal, physiologic, instinctive condition, our psychologic point of view will not be greatly affected. In the first place, even within the sphere of the hormonal functions we shall be confronted not by a simple process, but by a complicated interaction that probably inaccessible to our present methods of investigation. In the second place, the extraordinarily rich determinants of emotional motherhood, which derive from multiple sources, place it beyond the domain of direct physiologic causation. Only a fraction of the difficulties that confront us in the psychic manifestations of motherhood can be explained physiologically.

The instinctual components of motherhood have become sublimated, and the evolution from "wisdom of instinct" to spiritualization has been a very complicated one. Possibly part of the deeply feminine quality of intuition is a remnant of that

[6] BENEDEK, T., AND RUBENSTEIN, B. B.: Ovarian activity and psychodynamic processes. Psychosom. Med., vol. 1, 1939.

strong instinct, to which, we are told, woman once owed her dominant position in primitive society. If woman moves too far away from the instinctual, she loses her specificity. Since human society in later periods, unlike primitive society, was not built upon the instinctual elements, woman had to surrender her dominant role. She is now trying to reconquer a better social position by the detour of intelligence and by practical achievements that make her more similar to man, and this necessarily involves the danger that she will increasingly lose her specific feminine characteristics. However, a great part of the deeply rooted hereditary acquisitions, although modified from the outside by cultural and educational influences strongly varying from individual to individual, and although reshaped by the tremendous differentiation of psychic life, has been preserved in woman's reproductive functions. In so far as this fact involves biologic problems, we shall leave its investigation to the biologists, just as we have left questions of cultural development to the anthropologists. But occasionally we shall have to resort to biology and anthropology in order to draw parallels and make comparisons.

All the expressions of life seem to move within the narrow limits of repetition. Thus, much in the behavior of the human mother is reminiscent of long forgotten modes of behavior of various animal species, from the lowest to the highest. Ontogeny recapitulates phylogeny; highly civilized reactions often remind us of deeply primitive ones, especially when their motives are differentiated and complex. We have seen, for instance, that in primitive modes of reproduction, including external fecundation, the mother has no interest in the further existence of the detached reproductive cells. On the other hand, rejection of the offspring, and the mother's denial of every emotional bond with it, occurs in the human female relatively more often than in mothers of other higher animal species. This behavior seems to be a regression to a phase of development in which the maternal instinct did not exist. It occurs in cases of severe mental defect, for example among idiots, but occasionally also in psychotic conditions. It is curious how completely the maternal instinct can fail here. The same behavior can be observed in certain emotional disturbances that seem so absolutely to deny the most elementary maternal feelings that one has the impression of a primitive condition characterized by a total absence of motherliness. Closer examination shows that in these cases there is not a regression to a real absence of motherliness, but rather a complicated psychologic process in which the maternal feelings are repressed.

Another example may be added. An analogy to the biologic phenomenon of parthenogenesis emerges in primitive man's naïve idea of the process of reproduction. The causal connection between sexual intercourse and fertilization and pregnancy probably was not grasped by primitive intelligence for a very long time. During highly civilized periods the idea of parthenogenesis has been recalled in myths and religions. Many mythical individuals were thought to be sons of virgins; among the deeply emotional elements of Christianity, the precept of Mary's immaculate conception represents another recurrence of the idea of parthenogenesis. In modern women we often find the fantasy of the parthenogenetic child, born of the masculine wish in woman for power of her own and complete independence of man, or of an even deeper and more complex psychologic process. Innumerable other examples and parallels could be cited.

Thus, the natural and primitive phenomenon of motherhood conceals a world of events within itself—i.e., physiologic processes accessible to direct observation, the operation of biologic laws of heredity and adjustment, rational processes and seemingly absurd processes, historical and individual psychic elements, etc. All this combines into a great complex whole in which there is much still to be explained. But a good deal of it can be clarified by means of psychoanalysis.

CHAPTER TWO

Motherhood, Motherliness, and Sexuality

I N this book the terms "motherhood" and "motherliness" are used to denote two sharply distinguished concepts. *Motherhood* refers to the relationship of the mother to her child as a sociologic, physiologic, and emotional whole. This relationship begins with the conception of the child and extends throughout the further physiologic processes of pregnancy, birth, feeding, and care. All these functions are accompanied by emotional reactions that are to some extent typical of or common to the species but for the most part vary individually, for they are inseparably connected, in each woman, with the total personality. The intensity of these reactions, and the new obligations and emotional relationships, mobilize fears and displace the existing boundaries both in the individual psyche and in its relations to the environment.

When I speak of *motherliness* I have in mind two ideas: (1) a definite quality of character that stamps the woman's whole personality; (2) emotional phenomena that seem to be related to the child's helplessness and need for care. What I have said in volume 1 about the feminine woman applies, with some reservations and additions, to the motherly woman. But while trying to establish this identity we must also remember the differences. These arise from the quantitative displacement of individual components and from the differences in purpose. I have defined as characteristic of the feminine woman a harmonious interplay between narcissistic tendencies and masochistic readiness for painful giving and loving. In the motherly woman, the narcissistic wish to be loved, so typical of the feminine woman, is metamorphosed; it is transferred from the ego to the child or his substitute. However, it can be clearly observed that despite this altruistic transformation the narcissistic elements are preserved. For instance, the mother's love for the child is often associated with the fact that she considers herself absolutely and exclusively indispensable to him. In the strongly narcissistic woman, the intensity of maternal love decreases when her children outgrow their need of her. Another effect of the narcissistic component of maternal love is the mother's frequent intolerance of the environment when the child is in question. The narcissistic mother demands of fate particular kindness toward *her* child and cannot accept the normal human frustrations in his case.

The masochistic components of motherliness manifest themselves in the mother's readiness for self-sacrifice, but—in contrast to the attitude of the feminine woman—without demand for any obvious return on the part of the object, i.e., the child, and also in her willingness to undergo pain for the sake of her child as well as to renounce the child's dependence upon her when his hour of liberation comes.[1]

This readiness to accept pain could become dangerous for the woman's ego if protective psychic counterforces were not also operative. The joys of motherhood, as the experiences of motherliness are popularly called, are a powerful reward and a force counteracting masochism. Moreover, motherliness is accompanied by specific active ingredients. Freud has already called attention to the mother's activity. In volume I I tried to cast some light on the nature of this activity and recently D. Levy[1a] has particularly emphasized this aspect of the maternal function. This activity is not of an aggressive, masculine character. On the contrary, I believe that it represents that component of motherliness which is closest to the phylogenetic and the instinctual. Much of it reminds us of the great achievements of the female animal that tries to find a safe shelter and food for her young and defends them against the dangers of the environment. If this protective, defensive,

---

[1] Sachs classifies these women, who in my opinion represent the motherly type par excellence, as "Marthas and Marys"—i.e., "their self-mortification consists simply in renunciation." Cf. SACHS, H.: One of the motive features in the formation of the superego in women. Internat. J. Psycho-Analysis, 10: 50, 1929.

[1a] LEVY, D. M.: Maternal overprotection. New York: Columbia Univ. Press, 1943.

and nurturing activity is accompanied by aggressive-masculine components, these do not draw upon the sources of feminine motherliness, but upon adjoining psychic spheres hostile to it. There are women whose motherliness has this aggressive character, and we shall meet them again when discussing the different types of mothers.

"Maternal instinct" and "maternal love" are differentiated ingredients of motherliness as a whole. The instinct has a biologic-chemical source and lies beyond the psychologic sphere. Its primitive forms are hardly accessible to us in our civilization; they are buried under individual personalities and environmental influences—in brief, under the totality of the psychologic contents. Maternal love is the direct affective expression of the positive relationship to the child (or his substitute). Its chief characteristic is *tenderness*. All the aggression and sexual sensuality in the woman's personality are suppressed and diverted by this central emotional expression of motherliness. It is true that the influences of aggressiveness and sensuality are discernible in maternal love; but in the motherly woman the surplus of the existing aggressive ingredients is diverted from the child to the environment, often in defense of the child and in his favor. As for the sexual ingredient, there is sufficient room for it in the physical contact with the child, in caresses, and in many actions connected with care of him.

To a varying degree in each woman, the physiologic functions of the mother and the needs of the child mobilize impulses that were present before, but in a state of relative quiescence. However, we find that such impulses in the motherly woman also manifest themselves independently of the direct influence of the reproductive functions. The character and intensity of these impulses vary individually according to the structure of the personality as a whole. For example, let us take a certain tendency that is always contained in motherliness—the typical tendency of woman to give food to every object of her solicitude, not only to her child. Expressed in terms of the so-called "partial drives," this is the "oral" component of motherliness. In order to satisfy it the woman develops a special interest in the nutritional processes of the objects of her love and shows much solicitude about their food. Certain women direct this interest exclusively or chiefly to their own children, and sometimes extend it to the nearest members of their families. This overemphasis on eating is especially typical of Jewish women. Another example is the hostess, who directs her oral-motherly giving to more distant objects. This type is more frequent among French and Slavic women. The ascetic New England woman often denies herself this kind of motherly satisfaction with regard to her own children, preferring to feed the hungry and needy.

The development of motherliness, the paths it takes, the manner of its application, and the relation of the mother to the child are determined by many factors. The child, even when it is of central importance to the mother, remains only a link in the chain of all the vital factors that surround the mother and on which she is dependent. Later we shall illustrate this by numerous examples.

Although we assume the existence of numerous factors in the psychologic concomitants of motherhood, we do not exclude a deep-rooted instinctual background. Perhaps much in woman's psychic life is still under the dominance of an all-powerful instinct that we do not understand, but that influences woman's psychologic processes even beyond the domain of the direct reproductive functions. In making such a hypothesis we must ask: How far does the analogy go, and what are the differences between the instinctual manifestations of human and of animal females? After all, in the animal world too there are great differences of instinctual behavior in various species, and its strength or weakness is not always parallel to the degree of development of the species.

First of all, as we have said above, the emotional relations of the human mother to her child depend upon a number of indirect psychologic influences, by which they are complicated and removed from the primitiveness of the instincts.

Motherliness may harmonize with the other psychic tendencies or oppose and disturb them, inhibit them, or direct them into false channels.   One well known example is its frequent inhibiting influence on eroticism.   Similarly, an excess of motherliness can have a disturbing or furthering influence in the practice of several motherly professions (teaching, nursing, etc.).   Conversely, other interests and emotional relations—especially erotic ones—may lead to impoverishment of the motherly feelings.

As "aberrant" motherliness, excessive motherly feelings can empty real motherliness of its emotional components and direct these latter to quite different purposes that have nothing in common with the child.   As an unsatisfactory result of this process, a motherly woman may remain childless or be completely frustrated as a real mother.   In contrast to what occurs among animals, the maternal emotions of the human female outlast the period of the child's helplessness and his need for his mother's care; they often accompany the child into his adulthood or continue throughout the mother's lifetime without losing their intensity.   One of the masochistic experiences of motherhood arises from the fact that the child's emotions develop centrifugally, away from the mother, while the mother remains tied to him and must renounce him.

During the various phases of the reproductive function, the maternal feelings are reinforced by *specific* emotional reactions that represent the psychology of the phases involved (conception, pregnancy, lactation, etc.)

In the human soul no one component is independent of the others; seemingly opposed elements are related to each other and manifest themselves simultaneously or alternately, while various tendencies support or inhibit one another.   This is what makes every human being so complicated and interesting. Woman's psyche contains a factor that is lacking in that of the masculine sex—the psychologic world of motherhood.   As a result, she displays more varied behavior and greater complications with regard to the polarity mentioned at the beginning of this volume—that between life and death, between the instinct of self-preservation and the reproductive function; in addition there is the interaction of sexuality and motherliness. This joins the other polarities—activity-passivity, aggression-masochism, femininity-masculinity. The frequent conflicts between these forces, constantly influencing one another, lend depth and richness to the psychology of motherhood.

The distinction between the sexual instinct and the reproductive instinct, as well as that between the instinct of self-preservation and the instinct to preserve the species, regarded as the basis of the human personality, is part of a conception that is still very debatable.

The satisfaction of sexual desire and the release of its tension are the direct goal of the sexual urge. Only gradually was impregnation recognized as a more or less regular result of the sexual act. This result of the sexual urge in the service of the preservation of the species can be deliberately wished for; more than that, the desire for sexual satisfaction can even be diverted from its true goal and be rationalized by its service to the end of reproduction. Catholic asceticism demands this rationalization as an atonement for the sinfulness of the sexual urge.

Biology supplies evidence that the sexual urge in animals has been molded and directed by the reproductive instinct. For instance, the time and place of cohabitation are determined by the conditions most favorable for the birth and life of the offspring. After conception the female's sexual desire subsides and she no longer emits the odor of heat, and thus the male too loses his incentive to copulation. And in many mammals the sexual urge is stilled as long as the offspring has to be fed by the mother.

Recent experiments with animals show that there is no absolute correspondence between maternal and sexual behavior.

The cleavage between sexual and maternal behavior is sharply demarcated in animals. Previous to more recent endocrinologic studies of maternal behavior, many investigators regarded nursing and mother-love to be derived from the sexual instinct. Ceni, writing in 1927, showed in various ways that the maternal impulse has no relation to female sex processes. Using hens in his experiments, he found that the maternal impulse survived castration; implanting an ovulating ovary in a mothering hen stopped the maternal impulse; during pregnancy there was a hypo-activity and involution of the ovaries, during the period of heat the highest degree of ovarian activity; also that when through glandular implants he obtained maternal behavior in roosters, they stopped all sexual activity. Wiesner and Sheard, working with rats, found also that experimental removal of the ovaries during pregnancy or post partum had no effect on maternal behavior. Yerkes quotes Madame Abreu and gives his own observations of three female chimpanzees who stopped sex relations from the time they gave birth until they weaned the baby.[2]

It is true that this last observation could be used as an argument in favor of the theory that the maternal urge is contained in the sexual urge, and that after the first has achieved its goal, the second remains dormant.

The human desire for offspring has gone through several cultural adaptations. In religious commandments to multiply, it is closely connected with the belief in immortality. These commandments derive from purely psychic sources, from primitive ideas of man and nature, life and death. In them the reproductive instinct is reflected in a spiritualized form and is connected with the deep longing to negate death and preserve life. According to ancient Indian beliefs, for instance, the fate of every man in his future existence depends upon whether or not he has succeeded in reproducing his stock on earth. Only through having a son can a man get to heaven and remain there forever. Only through his offspring does he achieve immortality. Woman is regarded as the renewer of the race, the field in which man sows his seed.

Social and economic motives have always played an important part in reproduction and have influenced it in different ways in different civilizations. Under certain social conditions, it is useful economically to have many children. Here the motive for reproduction becomes purely practical. Sometimes social and economic reasons act inversely and restrict the will to reproduction: poverty, shortage of housing, etc., have an inhibiting effect on fertility.

It is difficult to judge to what extent woman's will to motherhood, her desire for a child, is influenced by external circum-

[2] LEVY, D. M.: Op. cit., p. 139 ff.

stances, to what extent it has passively and plastically adjusted to the wishes and ideas of men during various periods of civilization, and to what extent it corresponds to a primary tendency composed of motives both conscious and unconscious.

The relations between sexuality and motherliness are of a complicated psychologic nature, and this complexity seems to point to a determination beyond the purely hormonal. Sexuality and motherliness are sometimes in close harmony, yet at other times they appear completely separate, as in the above mentioned experiments with animals. In many cases the presence of one permits us to infer the presence of the other, and variations in one produce variations in the other. There are women who are both unerotic and unmotherly, and others who combine extraordinary erotic intensity with the warmest motherliness. The split between sexuality and motherliness can assume innumerable forms. For instance, each of these components can relate to different love objects. A given woman sexually desires one man or has the exciting wish to be desired sexually by him, but chooses another man as the father of her children and tenderly and faithfully loves him in this capacity. A psychically integrated woman can gratify both sexuality and motherhood through the mediation of one man.

Either component may completely dominate the conscious life while the other remains hidden in the unconscious until brought to consciousness by analysis. The genius of Balzac perceived intuitively what the painstaking efforts of analysis have empirically disclosed. In his *Two Women* he gives a masterful description of these two opposing tendencies in the female psyche.[3] Two friends relate their experiences in letters to each other. They represent opposite types, but each discovers deep within herself a hidden longing for something else, for experiencing the opposite. The longing is in itself evidence of the fact that something else is present, even though in a rudimentary form, and repressed. It would seem indeed that in this case Balzac made use of a favorite literary device—the separate personification of two opposing psychic reactions.

[3]DEUTSCH, H.: Motherhood and sexuality. Psychoanalyt. Quart., vol. 2, 1933.

Actually the two women represent the contradictory tendencies of one woman. The coexistence of such opposing tendencies is normal, and only a marked preponderance of the one or the other leads to complications and neurotic difficulties.

Baroness Louise de Macumère is the courtesan type, the devotee of love, whose only aim in life is the pursuit of passion, the enjoyment of intense erotic experiences. Her friend, Renée de l'Estorade, on the other hand, is completely a mother even in her relations with her husband. Louise writes:

> We are both women, I a most blissful goddess of love, you the happiest of mothers. . . . Nothing can be compared to the delights of love . . . .You, my dear friend, must describe for me the joys of motherhood, so that I may enjoy it through you.

And yet, even in the midst of her ecstasies in her love relationships, a voice within Louise cries out:

> A childless woman is a monstrosity; we are born to be mothers. I too want to sacrifice myself, and I am often absorbed in gloomy thoughts these days: will there never be a little one to call me mother?

However, this flicker of the urge to motherhood is extinguished by the flame of passionate love, and Louise is consumed in that fire without ever fulfilling her womanhood in the sense of becoming a mother.

The motherly Madame de l'Estorade writes on the other hand:

> My one real happiness (and how precious that was!) lay in my certainty that I had given renewed life to this poor man, even before I had borne him a child!

Thus motherhood was the essence even of her love relations with her husband.

Desire for children and motherhood completely fill this woman's emotional life. In her repudiation of sexuality she admits no feeling beyond motherhood. And yet she writes to her erotic friend:

> I have had to renounce the pleasures of love and the sensual joys for which I long and which I can only experience through you, the nocturnal meeting

on the starlit balcony, the passionate yearnings and unbridled effusions of love.

Thus the longing for the pleasures of love lurks deep within the virtuous Renée, just as the longing for motherhood lurks within the erotic Louise. She even betrays the fact that a child, in spite of the most self-sacrificing commitment to motherhood, can arouse a hate the origin of which lies in the renunciation of erotic satisfaction, in a curtailment of the ego's expectation of erotic fulfillment. The motherly Madame de l'Estorade holds her child on her lap and writes to her frivolous friend: "Marriage has brought me motherhood, and so I am happy too." But a little later she says:

> Everyone talks about the joy of being a mother! I alone cannot feel it; I am almost ashamed to confess to you my total lack of feeling. . . . I should like to know at just what point this joy of motherhood appears. Good-by, my happy friend, through whom I relive and enjoy those rapturous delights of love, feelings of jealousy at a wayward glance, the secret whisper in the ear.

No clinical example could describe the phenomenon of cleavage between motherhood and eroticism in a more lucid or gripping way than does Balzac's portrayal of these two opposite and complementary types.

Madame de l'Estorade concentrates all her feminine emotions on motherliness, not only in relation to her children, but also in relation to her husband and probably in all her human relationships. Eroticism, the other aspect of femininity, is for her only a yearning that she reveals to her friend, but it is entirely repressed as regards any real functioning. She has given birth to children and gratified her maternal emotions through them, her own flesh and blood. In her case motherliness and motherhood are merged. But there are women whose motherliness is directed to objects other than their own children —i.e., to other women's children or to adults to whom they extend their motherly protection. Many such women choose professions that serve as outlets for their maternal feelings.

One of my patients was a young midwife. She had chosen this work (which was very unusual for one of her social class)

in order to keep on having children—many, many children—
and the weaker they were and the more in need of protection,
the better she liked them.   Her own fear of childbirth played
an important role in this choice; she had to leave the situation
of danger to another woman before she could identify herself
with the mother in possession of a child.   She was a highly
qualified and well trained midwife, capable of unlimited self-
sacrifice in her work.   She came to be analyzed because of
certain strange difficulties she experienced in the course of her
duties.   "A patient is in labor" was for her a battle cry, to
which she responded with great enthusiasm (at least inwardly).
The agonies of childbirth seen in other women aroused in her
a curious mixture of anxiety and pleasure.   The moment of
the child's birth, when she took it over and gave it the first care,
was an ecstatic experience for her.   No work was ever too hard
for her; she could endure sleepless nights without fatigue.   But
what she could not endure was the knowledge that a labor was
going on at which she could not be present; it was intolerable to
her to have to miss a delivery.   Since she worked in a maternity
hospital, she developed a state of excitement and exhaustion
that finally brought her to analysis.

The symptoms were self-explanatory.   Her professional
activity was intended to free her from an oppressive sense of
guilt in relation to her mother; out of her original fantasies
about killing her mother and the latter's newborn child arose
her urge to save lives.   Death and birth were closely associated
in her childhood fantasies.   As a child she had certainly heard
about pain and danger on the occasions of her mother's numerous deliveries.   This was responsible also for her extremely
masochistic conception of the female role in the sexual act.
Her own masochistic wishes had manifested themselves during
puberty in very sanguinary fantasies of violation.   So great
a danger for her ego lay in the fulfillment of these fantasies that
she completely renounced her sexuality, and she could give
expression to her maternal feelings only in the manner
described.   In her choice of work, then, she served two masters
—gratification of her sense of guilt and her masochistic tenden-

cies; the latter she satisfied by means of identification. I have in my possession a photograph of her with eight newborn babies in her arms—an ideal representation of motherhood.

A similar yet different case is described in Miguel de Unamuno's *Aunt Tula*.

Aunt Tula is obsessed with motherhood. Her whole relation to the world is maternal, and only maternal. She regards anything that approaches sensuality or eroticism as despicable or ugly; but to the act of reproduction in another woman she gives the kind of attentive care that a farmer bestows on his crops, or a gardener on his flowers. Yet it is only the product, the fruit that has ripened under her watchful care, that she appropriates as her own, and to which she devotes herself completely; in this way she gains spiritual possession of a life that someone else has brought forth in physical pain. Aunt Tula is the psychologic twin sister of our midwife—only she is even more ruthless in the asexuality of her motherhood. She retains a lifelong hold on the children another woman has borne for her, and—again more thoroughly consistent than the midwife—she cruelly lets that woman die, once her childbearing function is exhausted. She even makes a child of the man who begets the children: she kills his erotic attachment to herself, and with iron determination steers him to another woman.

Aunt Tula lets her sister marry the man whom she herself loves and by whom she is loved. She arranges the marriage, urges the couple to have a child, and then takes complete charge of it. She drives her weak sister on from one childbirth to another until the sister dies of exhaustion, leaving all her children to the care of Aunt Tula, their spiritual mother. Aunt Tula lives in her brother-in-law's house as the mother of his children and directs his sexual passion to the servant, the "debased sexual object," who in turn is allowed slowly to die after she has repeatedly borne children for Aunt Tula. Aunt Tula lays stress on her role as spiritual mother and never lets the children imagine for a moment that she conceived them in her body and gave them birth. A consciousness of the corporeal mother must always be present in the home, lest the pure, true motherhood of Aunt Tula be stained with a suspicion of physical participation. Occasionally the repressed longing breaks through and Aunt Tula leaves the village where she lives with her widowed brother-in-law and goes to the noisy city. She expresses her attitude as follows:

"There is no real purity in the country. Purity develops only when people herd together in a dirty jumble of houses, where they can isolate themselves better. The city is a cloister of lonely people. But in the country the land brings everybody together—the earth on which nearly everyone lies down to sleep. And as for the animals—they are the ancient serpents of Paradise. Back to the city!"

But of the man who desires her she says: "He is still very childish in many ways. How may I turn him into one of my children?"

Once again the unspiritual longing breaks the bonds of her spiritual motherhood.

She took her little nephew, who was whining with hunger, and shut herself in a room with him. Then she drew out one of her shriveled, virginal breasts —it was flushed and trembling as in a fever, shaken as it was by the heavy pounding of her heart—and she pushed the nipple into the baby's soft pink mouth. But his whining only grew worse as his pale lips sucked on the tremulous, desiccated nipple.

Aunt Tula's refusal to admit that she ever had a father who was coresponsible for her conception is masterfully shown. It fits in closely with our analytic knowledge. In her mind the really great and beloved father is Don Primitivo, her mother's brother and foster father. Unamuno clearly brings out how Aunt Tula in her fantasy life wants to keep her mother's purity intact, just as she preserves her own, and that her relationship to her foster children is a repetition of her reaction in her relationship to her own mother.

Thus it is easy for us to understand the following comment made by Aunt Tula to her sister about Don Primitivo:

"Always still and quiet, with hardly a spoken word for us, he consecrated our life to the cult of our own mother and grandmother, his sister and mother respectively. He gave us a mother with a rosary, and he taught you how to be a mother."

The fantasy of her mother's immaculate conception, of motherhood without a father, can be clearly recognized here. Further, the book describes Aunt Tula's memories of her childhood games with dolls, which already contained the essence of her subsequent development in this direction.

There are innumerable women who because of their *fear of sexuality* can gratify their motherliness only by detours. Many of them, not unlike our midwife, take up professions that give them opportunity to gratify their need for motherliness and leave to other women the sexual prerequisites for it and the experience of reproduction. The motives for this may be extremely varied: the woman ripe for motherhood may have only consciously given up her childish conceptions and fears connected with the nature, meaning, and dangers of childbirth; her unconscious may still be full of childhood residues that oppose the realization of her womanly wishes.

The ego ideal by which the young girl sets her own values accepts femininity in the mother role. In her desire to perfect herself she follows the ideal image that as a little girl she once vested in her mother. She wants now to fulfill the demand in which her mother disappointed her: she wants to be a mother without incurring sexual guilt and devaluating her ego. Such women are often well adjusted to reality, they direct their desire for motherliness toward the real world, and gratify it through valuable social achievements, especially in certain professions.

When the grounds of such a professional choice are examined, the affective motivation is easily recognizable. Sometimes these women actively fulfill for the children entrusted to them the emotional demand that they themselves made on their own mothers. They care for them with great zeal and try by their behavior to prove that the children's own mothers are incapable of giving them the tenderness and education they need, and that they, the substitute mothers, are much more suitable for this task. When they are tactful and not too neurotic they succeed in finding gratification in their work. But very frequently we see efficient women and girls who constantly fall into conflicts because of their inability to master their hostile feelings toward the mothers of their charges.

Numbers of women choose such professions and renounce marriage and children in order to atone for old repressed aggressions against their own mothers and younger brothers or sisters. They want to help the other mothers, sacrifice themselves, and devote themselves to little children, subordinating all selfish feelings to this task. The danger of this professional choice consists in the fact that excessive readiness for sacrifice does not always produce good pedagogic results. The teacher who becomes the target of her pupils' aggressions in the classroom or on the playground, although she is kind and self-sacrificing, belongs to this type. This unfortunate woman is also a *mater dolorosa* who tries to gratify her motherliness in the wrong way. One highly qualified kindergarten teacher whom I knew was able to conduct classes only if they contained many Chinese or Japanese children, because, being small and dainty herself, she felt that she could exert the necessary authority only over very small pupils. The youngest child of her own parents, she had remained a baby longing for adulthood and motherliness. But she could gratify her longing only through this peculiar compromise.

Another form of compromise is illustrated in the case of women who can devote themselves to a profession involving the care of children only if they have children of their own. Otherwise they fail, because of various inhibitions, neurotic incapacity, etc. There is also the opposite type of woman, who can enjoy her own child only if she can spend her motherliness on other children too. This type strongly reminds us of the woman whose marriage is happy only if she can have a man or woman friend as a love object in addition to her husband, or who, inversely, can develop an ardent passion for another man only if she finds a partial outlet for her feeling in marriage. All these are methods for favorably adapting the emotional ambivalence or distributing the split feelings that are present in all human relationships. In all such minor aberrations, psycho-analysis discovers fixed childhood situations and the tendency to continuation or repetition of these in later life.

The yearning for motherliness and at the same time for re-venge upon and triumph over the real mother are gratified in a striking and tragic manner by the woman kidnaper who acts not for financial reasons or to serve a gang or a man. Fortu-nately, such cases are fairly rare. The few that I have had occasion to observe directly were so surprisingly identical that one must assume that the same psychologic process motivated them all. Such a woman usually kidnaps a very small, helpless child about whom it is easy to construct a fantasy that he was exposed by an evil mother to the unknown dangers of the out-side world. He is unprotected and abandoned and therefore the kidnaper feels inclined or obliged to protect and help him. Usually the kidnaped child is a baby left in a perambulator in front of a store while the mother is making purchases, or near the door of an apartment house, from the window of which the mother can see the child.

The kidnaper describes her feelings exactly as does a klepto-maniac—terrific tension upon perception of the object (which in her case is a child) and an irresistible desire to possess it. She lies in wait for an opportunity and is deeply depressed and disappointed if she does not find one. But most of the time—exactly as in the case of the kleptomaniac—the desire arises from the situation; there is rarely a deliberate intention present or a particular baby in mind. Since usually the baby in ques-tion is the child of poor parents, the material factor, just as in kleptomania, is absent.

Despite the anxiety accompanying the act, the feeling on taking possession is characterized by great delight in and tender-ness for the child. The kidnaper experiences the sensation of saving the child from danger, of giving it life, so to speak. Sooner or later after her deed, she is confronted with reality and must get rid of the child as fast as possible. She wraps it in a blanket, a piece of paper, or something of the kind, deposits it in a spot where it will certainly be discovered, although not

immediately, and runs away.   She is no longer interested in the
fate of the child she wanted so much only a short time ago; she
feels no remorse and is unconscious of any guilt.   This too
reminds us of the behavior of the kleptomaniac.

Unfortunately I have never had occasion to analyze such
cases.   But I was able to subject two such women to detailed
psychiatric observation, and in addition I have followed newspaper reports of this type of kidnaping for many years.   The
2 cases that I studied personally were those of girls who could
easily have had husbands and children.   Yet their motherliness
assumed a pathologic form.   They wanted to experience birth
only as a symbolic act of rescue, while also realizing the fantasy
of an evil mother.   Their identification with the mother who
leaves the child alone, exposing it to unknown dangers, is acted
out in the kidnaper's final deed, when she behaves exactly like
such an evil mother.

Of great importance here is the acted-out punishment of the
child's real mother, who is made to feel the consequences of her
carelessness through her loss.   In each case it was clear that
the mother's despair and anxiety contributed a great deal to the
kidnaper's pleasure in committing her crime.   But at the center
of the kidnaper's emotional process was the compulsive act of
taking possession of a valuable thing that belonged not to her
but to another woman.   Because at the moment of action the
situation is dominated by the theme of rescue, the tendency to
inflict damage remains unconscious and as a result there is no
consciousness of guilt.

The two women kidnapers whom I observed came of poor families with numerous children.   Each had several younger brothers or sisters; from their earliest years they had been obliged
to help their mothers take care of these.   They certainly wished
to have these children themselves, to take them away from their
mothers, just as other little girls do in this situation.   The wish
to throw a child away, to get rid of it, is aroused in every little
girl whenever she must say to her friend: "I can't play with you
now, because I must watch my little sister."   But why such a
situation should be psychologically preserved for so long and

drive the given woman to repeat it compulsively, we cannot explain, except by speculation, for we have no psychoanalytic insight into these cases.

Similar to the teachers, nurses, etc., discussed above are women who for psychologic reasons are unable to conceive and give birth to children of their own and who try to gratify their motherliness by adopting other women's children. But the problem of adoption is so complex that we shall take it up in greater detail later.

Another form of motherliness achieved without sexuality, childbirth dangers, and men, seems to be more frequent in America than in other countries. It may be seen when two women active in some profession, and living together in a more or less sublimated friendship, adopt a child. Usually one of the women assumes the role of mother and the other that of family provider. This division of interest is only relative, for usually both women wish to gratify their motherliness. The fact that the masculine component predominates in one and the feminine in the other seems to be referable to the mechanism that is illustrated in Balzac's *Two Women:* each of the women represents an opposite tendency, and the two complement each other to form a whole of active motherliness in relation to the child. The masculine behavior is often misleading and does not always correspond to a masculinity complex. A similar situation in which the man is dispensed with can also arise between two women friends of whom one has given birth to a child in an unsuccessful marriage or out of wedlock. The more active of the two saves the other from her heterosexual misfortune and takes over the role of the excluded male. She works for the mother and child and in this pseudomasculine manner gratifies her own yearning for motherhood.

Such compromise situations can be instanced ad infinitum. We encounter them in psychiatric consultations and especially in social agencies, where mothers looking for financial or other assistance often reveal their psychologic problems. The separation between sexuality and motherliness does not always favor the latter, as it does in the case of Madame de l'Estorade.

Louise de Macumère likewise has her counterparts in real life, even though they are not always of her social class or on her cultural level. In many women we find, as we did in Madame de Macumère, deep maternal emotions hidden under a mask. One such woman was treated psychoanalytically for nymphomania. I shall refer to her as Julia.

From her fifteenth year Julia had given herself to every boy she met. She was always unsatisfied and unhappy, but, strangely enough, completely without remorse, despite her puritanical upbringing. I shall quote only a few facts from her case history. Julia's friends, who wanted to save her from a life of prostitution, twice induced her to enter into respectable marriage, which naturally ended in failure. She never had children, was unable to conceive, and did not want children. The words motherhood and motherliness aroused in her a revulsion that was extended to all words ending in "-hood" or "-ness" —in short, she was as unmotherly as possible. Yet, to give the key finding of her long analysis, in her instinctual life she was completely a mother.

It is possible to explain Julia's neurotic behavior on the basis of early childhood events and her excessive mother tie. For six years she had been an only child, extremely pampered by her mother. Then her mother had three pregnancies in rapid succession and Julia experienced the loss of her mother's love to each new child. In this connection she often heard the story of the "child under the heart," and her soul was filled with bitterness and disappointment.

She was very jealous of her intimacy with the expected babies during her mother's pregnancies, and even more so during the suckling periods. In a manner typical of girls of her age, she wanted to play both the part of her mother and that of her little brothers; the wish for bodily union between mother and child gradually replaced the sexual yearning in her fantasies. She was incapable of any other, more adult experience, and in her sexual relations she gratified the desire for the mother-child union. The young boys to whom she compulsively gave herself always symbolized her three brothers. She was frigid because the content of her fantasies excluded sexuality, and her sense of guilt apparently remained unaffected because, through her motherly gift of herself, she negated her hostile rivalry with the little boys, thus unburdening her conscience.

Julia reminded me extraordinarily, in her appearance and behavior, of Anna, the prostitute whose history was discussed in volume 1. Both were of the tender, blonde, blue-eyed type. Julia was always sweet-tempered, but in Anna kindliness yielded to rather vulgar outbursts of rage under certain conditions. She was tender, sweet, and helpful only toward men who, she felt, were in need of help. She regarded the others as wicked beasts who deserved harsh treatment. Whether the same form of motherliness toward men asserted itself in Anna and in Julia we do not know. At any rate, the causes of promiscuousness in Anna were different from those in Julia. Julia always acted out her motherly fantasy in sexual intercourse. As far as we could learn, Anna left the fulfillment of hers to her fantasy life. She did not reveal her fantasies to anyone, not even to me, although I enjoyed her confidence. She gave all the details about a child she pretended to have and to worship only to the head nurse of the psychiatric department of the hospital where she was interned from time to time because of her pathologic condition. She asked the head nurse to adopt her child after her death. But after Anna's death the child could not be found; it had existed only in her fantasy.

In this behavior Anna was still entirely the little girl who wants to have a child with her beloved mother, the father being completely excluded. The head nurse, as participant in her fantasy, was obviously a representative of her mother. In contrast to Julia, Anna had coarsely realistic motives for her behavior: her father was a brutal drunkard, and the children he had given her mother meant for her—so Anna felt—only a burden imposed by sexual maltreatment. For definite reasons Anna's motherliness could not unfold but, concealed under the realistic behavior of an aggressive prostitute, and deeply repressed, there was, just as in Madame de Macumère, a deep yearning for motherhood.

Julia's psychic development led to difficulties because two

opposite tendencies (sexuality and motherliness) became associated in her in such a way that neither of the two could achieve
happy fulfillment. In the case of Anna, brutal realities prevented the achieving of normal motherhood. While Julia
belonged to a class that had given her a good education and
social protection, Anna was driven into the streets by material
conditions of her milieu; yet she preserved and asserted her
motherly feelings, although in a masked form.

If the various components of woman's psyche were measur-
able like chemical elements, what would analysis of them in
Julia and Anna show? Would the amount of motherliness in
these girls be different from that in a mother who experiences
her emotion directly in relations with her own children?
Should we judge the degree of motherliness from the way in
which it is applied, or disregard this and merely compare the
intensity of its manifestations?

In some women motherliness so completely fills the emotional
life that the boundary between the maternal and all other emotions disappears. In such cases sexuality is not differentiated
from motherliness, for the sexuality of these women, monogamous or promiscuous, is included in their motherliness. Madame de l'Estorade was nothing but a mother, even in her
strictly monogamous sexual life, and was compelled to renounce
the sexual experience. Julia and Anna were both promiscuous
and deeply maternal, but without either sexual gratification or
motherly joys (cf. vol. 1, pp. 264 ff.).

In *A Tree Grows in Brooklyn*,[4] Sissy, a character seemingly
taken directly from life, experiences both in one. An illiterate
slum harlot, Sissy is a passionate mistress of many men; endowed with a subtle feminine-motherly intuition she makes all
of them happy, because she is a genuine mother. Deprived of
direct motherhood for many years, she transforms into a child
every man whom she embraces, without, however, making him
less masculine, because she also desires him sexually as a man.

> Sissy had two great failings. She was a great lover and a great mother.
> She had so much of tenderness in her, so much of wanting to give herself to
> whoever needed what she had, whether it was her money, her time, the clothes

4 SMITH, B.: A tree grows in Brooklyn. New York: Harper, 1943.

off her back, her pity, her understanding, her friendship, or her companionship and love. She was mother to everything that came her way. She
loved men, yes. She loved women, too, and old people and especially children. How she loved children! She loved the down-and-outers. She
wanted to make everybody happy. She had tried to seduce the good priest
who heard her infrequent confessions, because she felt sorry for him. She
thought he was missing the greatest joy on earth by being committed to a
life of celibacy.

Sissy became pregnant when she was 14 years old.

At twenty-four Sissy had borne eight children, none of whom had lived. . . .
After each futile birth her love for children grew stronger. She had dark
moods in which she thought she would go crazy if she didn't have a child
to love. She poured out her frustrated maternity on the men she slept with,
on her two sisters, and on their children.

Our next question is: Are there women whose motherliness
vanishes completely in favor of their sexuality?

Anna, the prostitute, who made sexuality her profession,
clearly showed us her longing for motherliness. Although I
have studied numerous professional prostitutes, I have never
met the aggressive type of prostitute who is without a trace of
tenderness, a prostitute who is not only unmaternal but amater-
nal. This completely unmotherly type is possibly a fantasy
product in a certain type of men who have in their own imagi-
nations established a sharp division between sexuality (prostitutes) and motherliness (unsexual mothers). We must be all
the more impressed by an ethnologist's report of a civilization
in which the women seem to have lost every trace of motherliness. This report is given us by Carl Linton in Kardiner's book
on Marquesas culture, *The Individual and Society*.[5]

Kardiner adds an excellent analytic study to this report. We
shall not engage here in a discussion of his views; we are interested only in definite questions concerning one component of the
psychology of the Marquesas women, i.e., their motherliness.
Before taking up this problem we shall quote some of the relevant passages from Linton's report.

[5] KARDINER, A.: The individual and his society. New York: Columbia Univ. Press,
1939, pp. 154 ff.

The eldest child of *either sex*, or the child who was adopted to take the position of the eldest, became the official head of the household from the moment of birth or arrival.   One is struck by the fact that in the Marquesan myths *the story of a man always ends when his first child is born*; after this event he drops out of the picture and the saga continues with the adventures of the child. . . .

The men in a household far outnumbered the women.   The numerical disparity of the sexes on these islands was puzzling.   The Marquesans swore that they did not practice infanticide, yet the ratio of males to females was about two and a half males to one female.   It is probable that they did away with the younger girls but kept the practice from cultural notice.   The motive for this is hard to ascertain, but it is reasonable to suppose that the group were merely breeding up to their food resources . . . for in bad seasons, when food was scarce, it was necessary to limit the number of child-bearing women. . . .

The handsomest and most sexually skillful girls were sought in marriage by eldest sons, for the sexual attraction of the women promoted the prestige and power of the household. . . . The effective power lay in the hands of the woman, since by the distribution of sexual favors she controlled the men. . . .

There were few formal claims on the child for loyalty or assistance. . . . There did not appear to be any very close emotional attachment between the child and the adults of the household.   Children were respectful but indifferent toward their mothers; they seemed much more interested in the males of the household. . . .

Deaths during pregnancy and labor were frequent, which occasioned much anxiety and speculation among the natives.   They believed that the deaths were caused by malevolent magic or possession by evil spirits.   There was also not infrequent occurrence of feigned pregnancy, which was undoubtedly of neurotic origin and may have been motivated by the desire on the part of the woman to exercise the privilege of control over chief and secondary husbands that went with the state of pregnancy.   When the feigned pregnancy failed to materialize it was believed that the child had been carried away by the vehini-hai (female ogres) or that a fanaua was responsible. . . .

The father assisted at the birth if necessary.   There were no midwives, for it was believed that malevolent spirits were present at this time and women were afraid to go near. . . . Immediately after delivery the mother severed the umbilical cord, biting it off or working it off with her fingernails. . . .

The Marquesans believe that nursing makes a child hard to raise and not properly submissive.   There was probably a certain amount of nursing, dependent upon the will of the mother, but in any event the nursing period was very short.   Women took great pride in the firmness and beautiful shape of their breasts, which were important in sexual play.   They believed that prolonged nursing spoiled the breasts and consequently were reluctant to do it.

The feeding process was brutal. The child was laid flat on its back on the house platform while the mother stood alongside with a mixture of cocoanut milk and baked breadfruit which had been made into a thin, pasty gruel. She would take a handful of this stuff, and, holding her hand over the infant's face, pour the food in its mouth. The child would gasp and sputter, and gulp down as much as possible. Then the mother would wipe off the child's face with a sweep of her hand and pour down another handful of the mixture. . . .

From birth on, the child was never alone. The small child was under constant threat from the female ogre spirits, vehini-hai, who are supposed to steal small children and eat them. . . .

They [the vehini-hai] were also dangerous to young men. Appearing as beautiful women, the vehini-hai would present themselves to some charming young man in a lonely place and invite him to go along with them. If he complied, they would lead him to their caves, where they would turn back into ogresses and devour him. Occasionally, however, the vehini-hai, instead of eating her victim, would try to establish him in an affectionate relationship, which was, needless to say, a very comfortable and dangerous position for the young man. The men who had encountered these vehini-hai said that they usually appeared as beautiful young girls, but that they were always hungry, and if one could steal glances at them when they were off guard, one could see their eyes shoot out and their long, hungry tongues pop out and lick the ground. . . .

Still another series of supernatural beings were the fanaua. They were the spirits of the dead men, who became the familiars of women, helping them and injuring other women at their bidding. . . .

The techniques of fanaua attack were primarily connected with pregnancy. The fanaua might destroy the child in the womb (cases of neurotic symptoms of imaginary pregnancy were . . . a fairly common phenomenon here) or cause the woman to die, during either pregnancy or childbirth. Practically all such deaths were explained on this basis.

Linton's report and Kardiner's interpretations give us considerable insight into the cultural status of the Marquesans. To this I should like to add a conjecture. It is clear that the Marquesas women are not only unmotherly but wicked. They do not feed their children or they do it in the most brutal fashion, they leave them to the care of men so far as there is a question of external dangers, and their whole relationship to the environment has a purely sexual character. These women are the quintessence of sexuality. They owe their social position only to their sexual value, their central experiences are sexual, their ambitions are directed solely toward sexual efficiency. They do not seem capable of developing tender feelings toward either their children or their men.

From all we are told about them, it seems that they are also aggressive figures hated by the men. In the myths they appear as vehini-hai, legendary wild, young, and dazzlingly beautiful women who devour children and seduce men only to devour them too. The myth of the vehini-hai was born in the fantasy of a people for whom food and everything connected with eating is of the greatest importance. All the affective life of the Marquesans, their fantasy, their religious customs, etc., are full of oral elements. They are cannibals, but they devour their children and relatives only in exceptional cases. The sexes are equal and the women actively participate in cannibalism.

The vehini-hai, fantasy product of a culture so alien to us, is a familiar figure that we find in other cultures too, including our own. It has been known for a long time that

The witch in fairy tales as a counterpart of the good fairy represents the "wicked mother" for all of us and serves to embody our own wicked attitude in the primordial ambivalence of our conflicts with the mother.[6]

The story of Hänsel and Gretel is particularly impressive in this respect. Kardiner uses it as an illustration:

In this story the cruel mother starves the children and throws them out into the forest. In the forest they dream of a fairy godmother who promises to look after them. The next day they come upon the witch, who tries to lure the children to the door of the oven, to push them in and make gingerbread out of them.[7]

In other versions the witch brews poison and magic love potions—the poison to be used upon her rivals and the potions to seduce men. Not so long ago in our own civilization there were witch trials, in which women were accused of brewing poison for criminal purposes. In her cannibalistic desire for children our own native witch comes very close to the vehini-hai. The conflict with the mother, to which the witch of our fantasy owes

[6] DEUTSCH, H.: Psychoanalysis of the neuroses. London: Hogarth, 1932, p. 124.
[7] Op. cit. p. 224.

her existence, derives from an unconscious hateful reproach of the mother. It is difficult to judge to what extent the feeling that the mother has been inadequate is based upon reality and to what extent it derives from unfulfillable childish demands. Among the Marquesans, the hatred for the mother who emotionally deserts her child has a real basis. Since food is at the center of all interests, the oral frustration brought about by the mother can never be made good again. The mothers themselves, who live in the same oral atmosphere of cannibalistic culture, undermine their own motherliness and capacity for tender emotions by their refusal to feed their children. Kardiner says: "These women are devoid of maternal instinct." All the evidence tends to support his view. But how does such a situation arise? Are the Marquesas women deprived of maternal tendencies from their very birth? It goes counter to our biologic ideas to accept the existence of a society in which a definite cultural pattern violates the most elementary forces of nature and psychic life as completely as does Marquesas culture.[8] In the animal world, the maternal instinct predominates, and among many animals we can observe phenomena suggesting motherly tenderness. Can the sexual customs—not sexual passion, of which we see hardly any trace in the Marquesas culture—so radically eliminate the biologic tendencies and the capacity for tender emotions? And if such extermination of biologic processes does take place, what forces bring it about?

In our own civilization, women who have not received maternal love in their childhood—from their mothers or substitute persons—develop less motherliness than others. Often their own rejection of the mother inhibits their maternal feelings. However, we are also acquainted with the type of overindulgent mother who, in contrast to the withholding type, wants to give her own child an excess of what she was deprived of in her own childhood.

Failure on the part of the mother, as a socially determined,

---

[8] The observations of Margaret Mead concerning various emotional reactions of primitive mothers and children are very instructive. Cf. MEAD, M.: Sex and temperament, New York: Morrow, 1935.

almost hereditary, and really experienced evil, is certainly present in Marquesas culture. The absence of maternal instinct is perpetuated from generation to generation; and yet we feel that an individual element must be present in addition to the inherited disposition, operating to strengthen the latter.

My own conjecture is that the atrophy of maternal feelings begins immediately after the event of birth. The first manifestation of the oral drive of the newborn baby probably produces in the Marquesas woman a panic fear, cannibalistic in origin, that she will be devoured by her child. This fear has a real basis, for the suckling child actually does eat a part of the mother's body.

In our culture also, direct observations of mothers show that the problem of feeding is in the foreground of the mother-child relation; the feeding of the child is the first interaction between the child's demands and the mother's willingness to satisfy them, between taking and giving. Many women, even though free of cannibalistic wishes and taboos, react to the suckling demands with a fear that is largely unconscious. This fear exerts a powerful influence in the many difficulties involved in feeding children. In the mother, it often becomes an unconscious motive for refusing to nurse her children and can influence the hormonal process of lactation, the unconscious refusal thus proving stronger than the mother's conscious wish to nurse her child.[9] In narcissistic women who are physically vain and belong to the courtesan type (as Kardiner calls the Marquesas type), the concern with beauty and sexual attraction becomes, just as in the Marquesas women, a motive for rejection of the maternal function. In our own civilization, just as among the Marquesans, such motives are only a superficial rationalization of the woman's deep-lying fear that her ego will be destroyed. Among the Marquesans this fear of destruction originates in cannibalistic desires; in our culture, it inheres in the more spiritualized danger of loss of the ego in favor of the child. In

[9] For those interested in biologic processes, the question arises: What form does the hormonal activity of lactation take in the Marquesas women: do they produce milk at all?

both cases the fear must prove stronger than the positive forces operating in the mother-child relationship if it is to achieve far reaching consequences.   In our civilization, the conflicts of the nursing period can have effects that continue to operate for a long time afterward, but the mother has an opportunity to repair her relationship with the child on another plane.   Not so in the Marquesas culture, where the conflict determined by cannibalism remains irreparable.

We can pursue the identity of the fantasies in our own and the Marquesas culture a little farther.   "The Mother," a painting by a German artist, Max Klinger, shows a plump baby, glowing with vitality, sitting on its mother's breast; the woman's body is emaciated, lifeless.   This painting realistically expresses the idea that the new life flourishes on the ruin of the mother's at the cost of her life.

In the report on the Marquesas myths we read: "The story of a man always ends when his first child is born."   Socially the man gives up his existence in favor of his child's.   It is natural to assume that the idea of a similar relinquishment haunts the mother when she gives birth to a child, especially a daughter, and fills her with fear.   This fear may have a deeper biologic source in women than in men.   In addition, social position among the Marquesans is determined by primogeniture, regardless of sex.   We are told that the Marquesas women are extremely jealous of other women, particularly on the score of sexual attraction, which gives women access to social position.

This jealousy is perhaps also directed against the newborn daughter and contributes to intensifying the cannibalistic fear of the mother.   And we are told that the Oedipus complex is known among the Marquesans only in its Electra counterpart, and incest between father and daughter is assumed in advance. On this score too, many of our experiences with the mother-daughter relationship in our own civilization provide parallels.

The Marquesas woman is a wicked woman.   Her fantasy has created the fanaua, a male spirit, who, in return for the sexual pleasure she gives him, helps her to carry out her murderous wishes in relation to other women.   By order of his patroness the fanaua kills mothers and babies during delivery and destroys the fetus in the mother's body.   In brief, he realizes for the Marquesas women all those evil wishes that analysis discovers in our civilized female patients and that heavily contribute to their sense of guilt.   The fears and the defense reactions accompanying the events of reproduction are very close to the belief in fanauas.   It is difficult to judge whether the fanaua is created by fantasy of the men, who recognize the wishes of the wicked woman and express their disdain in the fanaua, or whether the Marquesas women project their own perceptions in this myth.   But the vehini-hai is the Marquesas woman herself, the wicked mother, who in her cannibalistic fear of being devoured by the child, deprives it of her milk-giving breasts, and wards off her fear by converting the passive being-devoured by the child into the active devouring of it.   It is quite possible that the woman in labor, in panic lest she lose her feminine value as a sexual object, restores her youthful charm by eating the new-born girl: in other words, she herself becomes a vehini-hai.

The delivery place among the Marquesans is a dangerous spot, teeming with evil spirits; everyone avoids it and only the husband is present at the birth.   The place itself is under a taboo; this is very reminiscent of food taboos.   Under the prevailing hygienic conditions naturally many mothers and children die, which sufficiently explains the belief in evil spirits.

It is very striking that the ethnologist was unable to answer the important sociologic question: Why is the ratio of males to females among these people 2.5:1.0?

Since it is impossible to assume that fewer girls than boys are born, the mortality among female infants must be higher.   Our ethnologist does not quite give credence to the information he received that the Marquesans do not practice infanticide.   He suspects that the birthrate is in part deliberately regulated according to the scarcity of food.   My own conjecture is that this regulation is accomplished with the help of the vehini-hai—the bad Marquesas women themselves.

We know that in our culture, after a very painful and exhausting delivery, the young mother's anxiety and aggression are intensified. When the primitive woman is in this state, it is quite possible that the vehini-hai enters her soul and makes her perform a cannibalistic act against the newborn. We are told that the mother severs the umbilical cord by biting it off; I cannot help suspecting that the mother bites off more than the cord, and thus regulates the proportion of girls to boys.

It is permissible to indulge in such a speculation if one does not use it as proof. For the psychologist, the discovery of psychologic identities under very different social conditions is particularly fascinating. In my own observations of woman's reproductive functions, I have long been struck by the frequency with which ideas of wild animals that devour the mother or the child, or both, haunt the delirious minds of women suffering from puerperal fever. This is particularly the case in so-called lacteal fever; the painful tension accompanying the flow of milk in the breasts, together with exhaustion, transforms the powerful biologically rooted impulse to give suck into a feverish delirium about devouring and being devoured. Some animals devour their own offspring immediately after the birth; this act seems to result from fear and is perhaps intended to protect the offspring by incorporation. In the animal world, the instinctual actions are very powerful, and in exceptional cases their purposes may become confused.

These delirious ideas of women after parturition reveal the conflict connected with the nursing of the child. In cultures other than the Marquesan, the vehini-hai is mastered when the normal bodily condition is restored and the child is given the breast.

In the history of civilization we often find birth customs that require the presence of women en masse at deliveries. The woman in labor needs the presence of a helpful and loving circle of women in order to overcome her fear of death. Up until the last generation, mothers were asked to be present at their daughters' deliveries. They shared their daughters' anxious expectations and initiated them into the first activities of motherhood. This custom concealed woman's deep psychologic need of complete reconciliation with her mother in order to become a motherly woman herself. Whenever even traces of vehini-hai are present at delivery, difficulties affecting various reproductive functions appear sooner or later.

The Marquesas woman is a wicked woman because she is deprived of maternal love in her childhood and because she is cheated of her motherliness, which is stifled from the beginning by her cannibalistic fear and her efforts to ward it off.

A woman need not have given birth to a child in order to be motherly, because, as we have seen, motherliness can also be turned toward indirect goals. The psychologic difficulty that stands in the way of direct realization of motherhood can have various causes; their most frequent common denominator is woman's fear of losing her personality in favor of the child. This fear may manifest itself as primitive fear of death or as concern over the threatened erotic values and physical beauty; it may derive from the fear of real obligations and restrictions through pregnancy, etc.; it is often an oppressive fear of the loss of professional and intellectual values or a feeling of insufficiency with regard to the great emotional demands of motherhood. All these and many other fears, often justified, are based upon the natural law that the old must yield to the new. The Marquesas culture is a perfect expression of these fears.

The wisdom of nature has provided means for conquering them. Woman's love for her child is normally greater than her self-love, and the idea of eternity inherent in reproduction overcomes her fear of being destroyed. The future triumphs over the present, but only if the past is favorably disposed of.

In our civilization too, sexuality or woman's eroticism can overshadow the maternal feelings. The capacity of the psychic energies for mutually exchanging their goals, for replacing one another, is well known. We have given examples that show how the one component of woman's psychic life drives out the other, and how the other nevertheless remains present in a repressed form. We have also seen some of the masks under which this other component is concealed.

The distinguishing characteristic of every great passion is that it represses all other feelings and life contents. A woman passionately in love may for a time become estranged from her children and regard them as a nuisance. A mother trembling for the life of her child negates all her feelings for her lover. Social fears often prevent a woman from experiencing the fulfillment of her greatest longing as a real joy, and the most motherly young women are often ready to renounce their illegitimate children, without the slightest painful reaction, under pressure of the instinct of self-preservation.

An erotic woman may invest so much passion and tenderness in her love for her man that she easily diverts her motherliness from its direct goal. A productive woman may regard her intellectual product as her child and thus renounce motherliness. Masculine women endow their motherliness with definite qualities. According to inner and outer conditions, a woman can manifest now more, now less of the quality of motherhood, and show herself alternately as erotic or as maternal.

If again we turn to literature for illustrations, we find in Tolstoy's *Anna Karenina* a rich harvest of psychologic insight into the conflicts between motherliness and eroticism.

Anna Arkadievna is introduced as a mother before her passionate eroticism is revealed to us. At the very beginning we learn that she has an 8-year-old son; "she has never been separated from him before, and it troubles her to leave him." During this first separation, amidst the bustle of social activities and in the first excitement of her nascent passion, she is seized with longing for her child:

> It was usually about ten o'clock when she bade her son good-night. Often she herself put him to bed before she went out to parties, and now she felt a sensation of sadness to be so far from him. No matter what people were speaking about, her thoughts reverted always to her little curly-haired Serozha, and the desire seized her to go and look at his picture, and to talk about him.

We shall understand Anna's excessive love for her Serozha if we recall that she loves him not only because she is motherly, but because her love for him compensates her for the erotic frustration she suffers at the hands of her unloved husband.

We are here confronted with the familiar fact that the mother's love for her child is determined by many factors, and that the simplified psychologic formula according to which the child of a beloved husband (or lover) is more cherished than the child born of a conventional marriage, does not always hold true. The expectation of compensation through the child gradually assumes the genuine character of maternal love in the motherly woman. In Anna Karenina's life the child also plays the part of protector of her social position and symbol of her attachment to her home. This must not be neglected as a factor in Anna's tragic conflict between maternal love and eroticism. No matter what the social conditions and political ideology under which a woman lives, her attachment to her home is part of her motherliness, and we must not consider Anna's inability to renounce her home as merely the result of her reactionary ideas.

Liberated for the first time from the protection of her little son, who is the guardian of her marital fidelity, Anna falls in love at the first assault, so to speak, and at once her maternal love begins to waver. When she returns home full of suppressed passion for her future lover, and her longed-for little boy embraces her,

The son, no less than the husband, awakened in Anna a feeling like disillusion. She imagined him better than he was in reality. She was obliged to descend to reality in order to look on him as he was.

She repeatedly takes flight from her love in her son—either in reality or in her maternal fantasies. Everything that Anna experiences in her struggle between erotic love and maternal love is typical. She is unable to enjoy either of these two gratifying emotions, because one is disturbed by the other. The more completely she turns toward her son and the more willing she feels to sacrifice her love for his sake, the more ardent is her longing for the man she loves. Serozha, her son, could protect her from eroticism only as long as his opponent was a longing, not an active reality. But Serozha now has an ally more powerful than his mother's conservative fear of erotic dangers: this ally is Anna's heavy sense of guilt, the most potent factor

in the whole psychologic picture of motherliness.   The maternal
heart can bear the child's aggession and his hatred, his unhappiness and his misdeeds, even his death—it can bear anything
more easily than his childish longing for his mother and his
yearning for love.   The responsiveness of the maternal sense of
guilt as it is expressed in Anna is one of the characteristics of
motherliness.

This sense of guilt is cruel, merciless, and appeasable only by
absolute readiness for sacrifice.   Wherever feminine masochism
with its active-maternal readiness for sacrifice does not operate,
the woman's psyche can become the victim of a much crueler
aggressive masochism, i.e., that stemming from the sense of
guilt.   For this reason Anna could find only one solution for her
conflict—suicide.   In the end, what determines her destiny is
not the triumph of her eroticism over her motherliness, but her
feminine passivity:

> Since the arrival of her husband's letter, she had felt in the bottom of her
> heart that all would remain as before; that she would not have the strength
> to sacrifice her position in the world, to abandon her son and join her lover.
> . . . If, on hearing this news, he [Vronsky] had said decidedly, passionately,
> without a moment's hesitation, "Leave all, and come with me," she would
> have even abandoned her son, and gone with him.

More and more Anna mobilizes her hatred against her husband in order to conquer her son.   But this hatred is not a good
ally, for it adds to her sense of guilt and eventually becomes
fatal to her because at a given moment it turns against her own
ego.

Anna Karenina's death sentence upon herself manifests itself
in a typical way during her pregnancy.   The executioner of the
death sentence imposed for conscious and unconscious sins approaches all women at the very instant when they begin to bear
a new life.   Anna's dream of the little old man who says, "You
are going to die, you are going to die in childbed, *matushka*,"
is a typical anxiety dream of pregnancy that appears in many
variations.   And all women desist from their horror for the
same reason as Anna:

Horror and emotion disappeared from her face, which assumed an expression of gentle, serious, and affectionate solicitude . . . . She had felt within her the motion of a new life.

A motherly woman can replace one child by another only when she has resolved the loss of the first by an adequate period of mourning. For all her children are one child, *the* child; they are unified by the feeling of motherliness.

An unresolved mourning, unresolved because of the strength of the sense of guilt, prevents the growth of motherly feelings for a new child. Anna Karenina wants to suckle her child, but she cannot; she wants to love it, but she can only perform the duties of child care. For a short time the baby succeeds in winning her heart and then she only rarely thinks of her boy. But later her guilty yearning for him rages even more cruelly than before:

The sight of this child made her feel clearly that the affection she felt for it was not the same kind of love that she had for Serozha. Everything about this girl was lovely; but somehow she did not fill the needs of her heart. . . . In her first-born, although he was the child of a man she did not love, was concentrated all the strength of a love which had not been satisfied. Her daughter, born in the most trying circumstances, had never received the one-hundreth part of the care which she had spent on Serozha. Moreover, the little girl as yet only represented hopes, while Serozha was almost a man, and a lovely man!

When the little girl falls sick, Anna Karenina takes care of her, but

Do the best she could, she could not love this child, and she could not pretend to feelings which had no existence.

This little girl was her child by the man she loved. Yet she was unable to make this daughter her child and her lover a father.

In brief, Anna conceives her fate as the struggle between two modes of love that she cannot unite:

"Just think, I love these two almost equally, both more than myself; these two, Serozha and Alexei . . . These two only I love, and the one ex-

cludes the other.   I cannot bring them together, and yet this is the one thing
I want."

The tragic struggle between eroticism and motherliness in
Anna is represented in a portrayal that goes beyond the individual destiny of this character and reflects a universal element
in woman's fate.   Why are both of Anna's men called Alexei?
Anna herself asks this question during her fever.   Has not the
great Russian writer here resorted to the same psychologic
mechanism as Balzac in his *Two Women?*   Perhaps the two
Alexeis are only one man, divided into the figure of the dutiful
but erotically rejected father and that of the erotically desired
lover who is rejected as father.   The father role of Alexei the
husband is clearly shown during Anna's delivery.   If our hypothesis is correct, the two writers, so different from each other,
have represented the eternal feminine conflict between motherliness and eroticism in a similar way.   In Balzac it is personified
in two women, in Tolstoy in a projection in two men.   The
French writer lets life triumph, the Russian writer leaves the
decision to the cruel superego.

Another type of woman, who as a young girl was charming
and full of feminine longing for love and being loved, can renounce all her feminine charm, in its conscious and unconscious
expression, in favor of motherliness.   Natasha in *War and
Peace* is a wonderful example of this type.   Let us again quote
Tolstoy, who, as we have seen, has a profound knowledge of the
feminine psyche:

Natasha had married in the early spring of 1813, and in 1820 already had
three daughters, besides a son for whom she had longed and whom she was
now nursing.   She had grown stouter and broader, so that it was difficult to
recognize in this robust, motherly woman the slim, lively Natasha of former
days.   Her features were more defined and had a calm, soft, and serene
expression.   In her face there was none of the ever-glowing animation that
had formerly burned there and constituted its charm.   Now her face and
body were often all that one saw, and her soul was not visible at all.   All
that struck the eye was a strong, handsome, and fertile woman.   The old
fire very rarely kindled in her face now . . . .
The young Countess Bezukhova [Natasha] was not often seen in society,
and those who met her there were not pleased with her and found her neither

attractive nor amiable. Not that Natasha liked solitude—she did not know whether she liked it or not, she even thought that she did not—but with her pregnancies, her confinements, the nursing of her children, and sharing every moment of her husband's life, she had demands on her time which could be satisfied only by renouncing society. All who had known Natasha before her marriage wondered at the change in her as at something extraordinary. Only the old countess with her maternal instinct had realized that all Natasha's outbursts had been due to her need of children and a husband . . . and she kept saying that she had always known that Natasha would make an exemplary wife and mother. . . .

Natasha did not follow the golden rule advocated by clever folk, especially by the French, which says that a girl should not let herself go when she marries, should not neglect her accomplishments, should be even more careful of her appearance than when she was unmarried, and should fascinate her husband as much as she did before he became her husband. Natasha, on the contrary, had at once abandoned all her witchery, of which her singing had been an unusually powerful part. *She gave it up just because it was so powerfully seductive.* She took no pains with her manners or with delicacy of speech, or with her toilet, or to show herself to her husband in her most becoming attitudes, or to avoid inconveniencing him by being too exacting. She acted in contradiction to all those rules. She felt that the allurements instinct had formerly taught her to use would now be merely ridiculous in the eyes of her husband, to whom she had from the first moment given herself entirely—that is, with her whole soul, leaving no corner of it hidden from him. She felt that her unity with her husband was not maintained by the poetic feelings that had attracted him to her, but by something else—indefinite but firm as the bond between her own body and soul. . . .

We know that man has the faculty of becoming completely absorbed in a subject, however trivial it may be, and that there is no subject so trivial that it will not grow to infinite proportions if one's entire attention is devoted to it. . . .

The subject which wholly engrossed Natasha's attention was her family— that is, her husband whom she had to keep so that he should belong entirely to her and to the home, and the children whom she had to bear, bring into the world, nurse, and bring up. . . .

And the deeper she penetrated, not with her mind only but with her whole soul, her whole being, into the subject that absorbed her, the larger did that subject grow and the weaker and more inadequate did her own powers appear, so that she concentrated them wholly on that one thing and yet was unable to accomplish all that she considered necessary.

This replacement of one form of feminine affectivity with another, of eroticism with motherliness, usually is more complicated than it may seem. We recall how much mischief Natasha's feminine charm had caused, how heavy her sense of guilt had been, and we understand how tremendous was the renunciation of everything that in her eyes was "so powerfully seductive."

In this process of achieving absolute motherliness, Natasha preserves the qualities that we have described as typically feminine (vol. 1):

> The general opinion was that Pierre was under his wife's thumb, which was really true. From the very first days of their married life Natasha had announced her demands. Pierre was greatly surprised by his wife's view, to him a perfectly novel one, that every moment of his life belonged to her and to the family. His wife's demands astonished him, but they also flattered. him, and he submitted to them. . . . It very often happened that in a moment of irritation husband and wife would have a dispute, but long afterward Pierre to his surprise and delight would find in his wife's ideas and actions the very thought against which she had argued. . . . After seven years of marriage Pierre had the joyous and firm consciousness that he was not a bad man and he felt this because he saw himself reflected in his wife. He felt the good and bad within himself inextricably mingled and overlapping. But only what was really good in him was reflected in his wife, all that was not quite good was rejected. And this was not the result of logical reasoning but was a direct and mysterious reflection.

Here we have Natasha the feminine woman: giving motherliness becomes her world, to which she devotes herself completely. Yet she presents her feminine-narcissistic demands—to an intensified extent—to her husband, in order later to identify herself with him and to be both the giver and the taker. And because Natasha is motherly, she is good, and makes Pierre good too, and this clarifies the "mysterious reflection."

When all the elementary emotions of jealousy, competition, and desire for pleasure, in whatever form they may manifest themselves, are ready to yield in favor of another being, when even the instinct of self-preservation loses its predominance and the fears connected with it are overcome, we can speak of "pure motherliness." The judgment of Solomon is one of the most beautiful illustrations of this.

Even psychically healthy women do not all experience motherliness in the same manner. But in the innumerable individual variations two types can be discerned: one type is the woman who awakens to a new life through her child without having the feeling of a loss.   Such a woman develops her charm and beauty fully only after her first child is born.   The other type is the woman who from the first feels a kind of depersonalization in her relation to her child.   Usually such a woman has spent her affectivity on other values (eroticism, art, or masculine aspirations) or this affectivity was too poor or ambivalent originally and cannot stand a new emotional burden.   The first type expands her ego through the child, the second feels restricted and impoverished.

The material conditions of life, the social milieu, and old and new experiences endow the different types with individual variations.   The woman's relation to her husband and family, her economic situation, and the position of the child in her existence, give a personal color to each woman's motherliness.

CHAPTER THREE
The Preliminary Phases

THE great experiences of our lives are not isolated but linked together in a long chain. In studying woman's reproductive function, we are constantly confronted with the re-emergence of past situations, frequently traumatic in character. Successful mastering of the past is a prerequisite for woman's psychic health; otherwise, new situations provoke new traumas. If the woman endures well the strong emotional tensions accompanying the reproductive process, they constitute a kind of psychic catharsis for her. The capacity of the psychic organism to resolve the old together with the new can be intensified in this catharsis, and then the woman's ego expands in motherhood. The new emotions of motherhood enable the ego to solve problems that it could not successfully solve before. And since everything that has remained unsolved and inhibited in psychic life creates a disposition to develop anxiety, what we have said above can be briefly summarized as follows: The reproductive experience gives woman the opportunity to master old anxieties by mastering new ones.

When entering upon her service to the species, every woman brings with her a certain amount of helpless dependence, of aggressive tendency to revenge for frustrations, of guilt feeling, and of desire for masochistic self-punishment; these constitute her old dispositional equipment. We know that elements that have followed one another in time are juxtaposed in the unconscious. This juxtaposition creates the chaotic richness of the human soul. Psychoanalysis is able to give an orderly pattern to this chaos by reconstructing the temporal order of psychic development.

Each single act of the reproductive function requires careful study. Each is associated with a definite phase of the past and subject to general physiologic and psychologic laws. But the psychic material that confronts us is at the same time completely individual; every woman draws her own experience, different from that of any other woman, from the same process.

The reproductive processes have a prehistory that can be divided into two periods—for motherhood, like instinctual life as a whole, goes through an infantile and a puberal phase.

The ontogeny of the female sexual functions teaches us that the adult woman solves her biologic tasks partly by the same means that the child uses for the satisfaction and mastering of the elementary bodily impulses.

We know that in certain life phases the interest of the little child is entirely directed to definite biologic processes of the organism that serve not only for its nourishment, preservation, and growth, but also as a source of pleasure toward which it passionately strives. Thus from the very start there are established psychophysical correlations that have a different goal at every stage of development but only limited possibilities of expression. They constantly reappear in three tendencies: the tendencies to incorporate, to eliminate, and to retain[1]. At each stage, their operation produces a different behavior according to the current level of development.

Because of the presence of the above mentioned tendencies, analogies during different phases can be noted. As a result of these analogies, an earlier phase of development may include progressive elements and a higher phase may include regressive elements.

Let us clarify this by examples. The elimination of undigested remnants of food that have become unnecessary or harmful for the organism—defecation—is associated with complicated emotional reactions. These arise from the struggle between the tendency to retention and that to elimination as well as from the problem of intake of food. The psychoanalytic theory of instincts has taught us what instinctual drives, pleasure sensations, renunciations, etc., are involved in this process. The restrictive influences of training, the environment's evaluation of the "product," the formation of the "sphincter

[1]Alexander calls these tendencies "vector mechanisms." Cf. ALEXANDER, F.: The medical value of psychoanalysis. New York: Norton, 1936.

morality," the fantasies associated with excrements staying inside the body, etc., all lend the greatest psychologic significance to this biologic process.

Certain elements in this process are progressive, because much later they become the pattern for childbirth. In childbirth too the innervations are alternatively eliminative and retentive, just as in defecation. But the analogy goes even further. The preliminary act in the digestive process, the intake of food, begins ontogenetically with sucking. We know that this primitive function of self-preservation is accompanied by instinctual drives and it too can become the prototype of many future psychologic processes. The first preparatory act in motherhood, the coitus, has a complete functional analogy with the sucking activity of the nursing child; the sucking motions of the vagina, the receptive readiness of the vagina, are analogous to the receptive function of the mouth. The cannibalistic impulses connected with intake of food that lead to painful biting of the mother's breasts also have their genital counterpart in the well known neurotic fantasy that the vagina is a snapping, biting organ. In men such fantasies sometimes cause impotence.

In brief, the prototype for the final aspect of reproduction is supplied long before the event, in earlier psychophysiologic functions. From this point of view reproduction is a highly differentiated activity shot through with regressive elements.

We have pointed out that these organic prototypes of childhood are connected with various instinctual drives that supply a stimulus for fantasies, wishes, and fears. By combining internal experiences and external impressions, the fantasy life of children of both sexes regularly identifies the fetus with the intestinal content. Thus patterns for the girl's future motherhood are created and these can influence the real processes.

In this manner an interaction arises: the events of the reproductive process have their prelude in infantile fantasies, and the events of childhood more or less influence the later reproductive function. The functions of incorporation, elimination, and retention constitute the connecting bridges.

We shall now consider these infantile processes in somewhat greater detail. Above all, we must take into account the fact that in the little girl's whole development, her female organs, the vagina and uterus, occupy a peculiar position: although they are destined to perform great tasks, they remain unknown to their possessor until the day they enter into the service of the reproductive function. Experience teaches us that the little girl's fantasies and fears relating to the reproductive functions are connected with the inside of the body, conceived as identical with the digestive organs and excluding awareness of the female sexual organs.

The predominance of one or another component in the preoccupation with the "insides" can have serious consequences later. The child's ideas about these insides may be connected with tender impulses, pride, and positive evaluation; in other cases, a wicked, dangerous enemy equipped with explosives is thought to dwell inside, and the child frees herself from him by fits of vomiting or diarrhea. The difficult struggle to bring forth this evil or desired being is often expressed in painful constipation.

The fantasy of little girls (or boys) manufactures innumerable theories about birth: in their ideas conception usually takes place by way of the mouth, and birth via the anus, navel, or breast. The size of the penis penetrating the body, and that of the "child" that is to be brought forth, are compared with the smallness of the child's own body apertures, and the unconscious of the adult sometimes preserves horrible ideas from the fantasies of the child.

All the body apertures may be involved in these fantasies.[2] A 3-year-old girl whose mother had told her about the imminent arrival of a little brother or sister was found at night in her bed trying to stop up all the orifices in her body—her ears so that she would not be able to hear her mother's cries, her nose because the baby would have a bad odor, and her lower openings because the stork might stick the baby up her rectum by mistake. The little girl had been completely informed about

[2] DEUTSCH, F.: Studies in pathogenesis. Psychoanalyt. Quart., vol. 2, 1933.

the process of birth by her mother, but could not help giving free rein to her numerous and transparent fantasies. Probably her ideas about the cries of the mother and the bad odor of the baby were realizations of her fear that no opening of the body was safe from dangers.[3]

At this point one may ask why the little boy, whose development has taken its course through the same bodily functions and the same instinctual satisfactions connected with them, diverts his interests more rapidly and more permanently from the inside of the body to the outside world, and only in exceptional cases of development of a feminine attitude clings to his own fantasies connecting pregnancy and birth with the process of digestion.

We think that the anatomic difference between the sexes is responsible for this fact. The boy's interest turns to the activity of his genital organ, which now becomes the outlet of his sexual energies, his strivings for pleasure, and the fears connected with these. In contrast to the boy, the girl is compelled—after vain attempts and hopes—to internalize her interest, and this time in a grossly somatic sense, as distinct from the psychologic turn inward (vol. 1, p. 130). Step by step she gives up her emotional reactions to the lack of an organ, and her fantasy life becomes, so to speak, feminized, i.e., her interests turn gradually to the idea of the child, and she reaches an infantile stage that we might call the outpost phase of future motherhood.

From this point on, the sexual development of the two sexes is definitely different: the boy preserves his anxious interest in his external genitals into his maturity; the girl continues elaborating the problem of the child. Since for a long time she is not aware of her reproductive apparatus, her idea of reproduction and of the child remains tied to the digestive act. This idea is one of the most tenacious in the inventory of the mature woman's infantilisms and often exerts a disturbing influence in the prime of her maturity. Gradually many other problems are added, both general and individual.

[3] For an interesting reaction of a 4-year-old girl to her mother's pregnancy, cf. BARRETT, W. G.: Penis envy and urinary control, pregnancy fantasies and constipation: Episodes in the life of a little girl. Psychoanalyt. Quart., vol. 8, 1939.

Woman overcomes the genital trauma and the penis wish and begins to want a child in the course of a complicated process that has often been misunderstood.   Above all there seems to be a great deal of confusion about the identification of the penis and the child.   The transformation of the penis wish into the wish for a child is often considered a substitute formation instead of a biologically determined dynamic process.   The fact is that in the girl's fantasy life there arise analogies that have various motives.   In the process of transferring her interest from the outside to the inside of the body, the little girl may include the penis conceived as an internal organ and for some time hold to this concept; thus the penis and the child may be identified with each other in that both are considered parts of the girl's body.   We often find this identity still preserved in puberal anxieties and in the growing girl's urge to be operated upon.   In many women, even real pregnancy mobilizes the old idea of an internal bodily possession still largely identified with the boy's sexual organ.   I do not think, however, that all girls consider the child a compensation for the anatomic inferiority, because during childhood and puberty something nonexistent cannot be a compensation, and during the reproductive phase the child acquires a new significance that springs from other sources.

We have now briefly surveyed the childhood stages of the reproductive function in so far as they relate to the preliminary physiologic stages and the instinctual impulses connected with them.   In these stages the child does not yet figure as a desired object in the outside world.   It is a fantasied possession still incorporated in a number of earlier developments, in which existing or desired parts of the girl's body—excrements, the penis, the child—are not sharply distinguished in the unconscious.   This wish for a child still has little in common with the later emotional experience of motherhood; it expresses an instinctual striving for a possession.   The reactions of envy and frustration make this wish akin to the penis wish, for the very reason that this wish cannot be fulfilled.

This part of the infantile prehistory of motherhood is closer to the sphere of biology than to that of psychology. · But there are other manifestations in the little girl that can be considered as preparatory for motherhood.

I have previously often referred to the girl's identification with the active mother as one of the sources of feminine activity (vol. 1). Even though the mother's activity with regard to her child is biologically determined, an infantile pattern underlies active motherliness, a pattern that normally is preserved throughout all the phases of development and that is a prerequisite for later successful achievement of a motherly role.

Even before the little girl has assumed an active attitude toward her father as representative of external reality, she is stirred by active ego strivings through which she spontaneously and gradually frees herself trom her passive, helpless dependence upon her mother. Moved by this urge, she first of all imitates her mother in everything; increasingly successful in this endeavor, she begins gradually to reverse the roles.[4] She tries energetically to endow all the situations of everyday life accessible to her with this reversed character, preferably in games with the mother herself, and, next to the mother, with smaller children, dolls, etc. After all, dolls were invented by adults who recognized this tendency in little girls to imitate their mothers and wisely encouraged it. The little girl would gladly do to her mother everything her mother does to her, and even more; if she could, she would certainly, through her own infantile aggressions, bring her mother to a condition that she violently rejects for herself. She often succeeds in gratifying these aggressive "maternal" tendencies by means of her doll: tormenting the doll, tearing out or breaking its limbs, etc., certainly exceeds identification with a mother who is often gentle and kindly.

What the little girl cannot achieve in actual fact, she betrays in her fantasies (vol. 1, p. 86). Often these begin: "When you are little and I am big." If one investigates what she thinks will happen then, one discovers that the little girl does not conceive her motherly role as a mere reversal from passivity to activity, but uses this role in order fully to gratify her aggressive

[4] Freud, S.: Concerning the sexuality of woman. Psychoanalyt. Quart., vol. 1, 1932.

impulses. For instance, in her fantasies, the mother begins to grow smaller as the child grows bigger and continues to grow smaller until she disappears entirely. Childish fantasy is vast and reaches beyond the frontiers of life. Later when the little girl has achieved real motherhood, these primitive aggressions may reappear in relation to her own child.

The tendency to develop from passivity to activity is rooted in the ego, but it certainly receives instinctual reinforcements. For instance, the influence of digestive ideas on activity expresses itself in the child's eagerly giving enemas to a doll or to a smaller child while playing mother or doctor.

The little girl's motherliness can also assume a more complicated character and actively reproduce the family situation without including the father or even eliminating him altogether. The girl produces the child in partnership with the mother and plays parents with her. According to the richness of her imagination, the child is received from the mother, or is created by the girl herself, while the mother is reduced to a completely passive role. Intelligent mothers encourage all such activities on the part of their little daughters; they know that their daughters' femininity is furthered in this way, much more than by the naïve and to them completely worthless assurances: "It's true you have no penis, but when you grow up, you'll have a child." As is well known, such a promise of postponed fulfillment often has the effect of a frustration.

All these motherhood games may be repeated in later life in the wish for a parthenogenetic, fatherless child, or by means of adoption of a child in common with a woman friend, etc. In other cases, the mother-child game is later transformed into a sexual situation in which all the forms of childish instinctual gratification are repeated within the framework of a homosexual relation. However, such a revival of the original mother-child relation does not proceed along a straight line, but by detours that involve repression of later processes (vol. I, chap. IX).

The subsequent prehistory of motherhood evolves within the framework of the Oedipus complex; in the little girl's fantasy life the father is obscurely connected with the idea of her child.

At this period the little girl is still entirely ignorant of the origin of this child, even when she is sexually enlightened. Her fantasies still cling to the digestive processes; usually the father's role is in accord with masochistic ideas, the mother becomes a rival, etc. It goes without saying that all these fantasies, theories, and fears are intensified by the births of siblings or neighbors' babies.

Thus the early infantile period of motherhood includes two phases that influence later motherhood. The first phase, that in which the girl has the child with her mother, supplies the prototype of active motherliness. The second phase is the Oedipus phase with all its complications, and is characterized by the wish to receive the child passively. As we have seen, the physiologic processes of childhood and their psychic accompaniments supply the pattern for the psychophysical aspects of reproduction.

We can easily understand that the little girl's interest in the problems of reproduction is aroused by the birth of a little brother or sister, and the fact that she immediately places herself in the center of this problem can be explained by her narcissistic interest in herself. But when there is no such birth, we are confronted with a riddle: How does the little girl make up all these complicated ideas and theories? More than that: Even if she is the only or last child, psychoanalysis reveals that her unconscious behaves as though she had actually experienced all the impressions connected with her mother's having a pregnancy and all the feelings of protest against a child born after her. Or, if she is the oldest child, we find that her fantasy creates a predecessor (usually of the masculine sex) who must disappear before she can be born. If she is helped in these fantasies by actual happenings—for instance, if she knows that a child was born before her and was lost—she takes upon herself the guilt for his loss and imposes upon herself obligations to compensate for him. Every death of a brother or sister that takes place later, every actual or even merely suspected miscarriage of her mother's, becomes in her mind a criminal action perpetrated by herself that may later be atoned for in her own reproductive function.

Thus, the little girl's fantasies are frequently so absorbed in the problems of pregnancy and birth, she experiences her fears, wishes, and guilt feelings with such intensity, that they acquire total reality value. Normal and healthy children seem free of all these problems, but closer examination of their psychic life shows that they are greatly preoccupied by two important problems, birth and death, and that these polarities are associated because the nature of both is unexplained, mysterious, forbidden. Even psychically healthy women carry all these problems into their motherhood.

The prehistory of motherhood has its second act in puberty and at that period is already an expression of the biologic assault that urges the girl in the direction of realization. The puberal processes relating to motherhood have previously been discussed (vol. 1, pp. 140 ff.). We have seen that the pubescent girl's relation to the reproductive function repeats the events of childhood.

The sexual fantasies remain unconscious; the other fantasies, those of identification with the active mother, being less dangerous, may lead to direct, conscious acting out. The component that remains in the unconscious fantasy life is mobilized by the appearance of menstruation. We find it in pathologic reactions, usually in somatic conversion symptoms that conceal pregnancy fantasies and fears, or in diffuse anxiety states and phobias. We have mentioned the young girl's wish to be operated upon (cf. vol. 1, case history of Nancy), in which the appendix usually plays the part of a body in one's insides, both desired and feared. We do not doubt that in such cases the young girl's fantasies are not ripe for realization, even if the biologic equipment has achieved maturity. The girl still needs time not only to liberate herself from the dross of the Oedipus complex and from the burden of her fantasies, but also to develop her ego by further inner growth and thus make it ripe for motherhood.

We know a type of puberty in which motherliness does not remain moored in fantasy life but is translated into action. We have in mind the type of young girl who does not miss a single opportunity to be active in a motherly way: she self-sacrificingly takes care of her younger sisters or brothers, offers herself as a substitute to mothers in the neighborhood; in brief, she is a typical figure, often dubbed a "neighborhood mother." Closer acquaintance with such girls will reveal that their motherliness is not very different from that displayed by little girls when they play with dolls and assume the role of the active mother in their identification with her. Such young girls likewise need a period of maturation in order to develop into real mothers. In some cases they really have a predisposition to motherhood, in others this activity expresses an inhibition in development and the girl's incapacity for further sublimation.

Between this type of girl and mature motherliness there is a long path to travel before she can become an independent mother of her own children. Until that time she can act as a mother only if she is free of responsibility or shares responsibility with another mother figure. The following two examples will illustrate this point.

Lydia was a 16-year-old girl who, after graduating from high school, took the position of mother's helper in a family with three children between 1 and 5 years of age. The father was in military service.

Lydia was an ideal mother's helper. After a few weeks she became so familiar with her duties that the mother could rely on her to an ever increasing extent. The children worshiped Lydia, who was so happy in their love that she did not make any other demands on life, and Mrs. K., her employer, complained only of the fact that the young girl lived too ascetically and devoted herself too exclusively to the children. Soon Mrs. K. felt secure enough to return to her previous occupation and to leave Lydia alone with the children for almost the entire day.

After a time Mrs. K. fell ill and had to be operated upon, and Lydia assumed full responsibility for the children. She showed great energy in carrying out her tasks and her reliability seemed unquestionable. She reported regularly to Mrs. K. about the children and asked for directives, although she did not really need them.

But after a short time Lydia's energy began to ebb; she neglected the children, left them at night to go to the movies, telephoned her former schoolmates—in brief, behaved exactly like most girls of her age.

An attempt was made to help Lydia in her task by inviting the children's grandmother to enter the home. On the day of her arrival, Lydia became completely unmanageable. She lost her interest in the children, and finally left her position to take a job in a factory. Here she worked well, although without enthusiasm.

At Mrs. K.'s request and out of personal interest I met Lydia. She impressed me at once as a normal girl, without any obvious neurotic difficulties. I learned from her that she was an only child, that her father had been tubercular, that she had a tender attachment to her mother. Her father spent many years in a hospital and died when Lydia was 10 years old. She and her mother always discussed babies a great deal and planned to have some. Obviously, her mother was a very motherly person, who devoted herself a great deal to her little daughter. They had common daydreams concerning babies. On the basis of these games and daydreams Lydia obviously identified herself with her active-motherly mother. Lydia also disclosed to me a dream of her puberty: after saving enough money she wanted to continue her studies and take her mother into her home. She would marry, have many children, and her mother would help her to bring them up.

The husband played a rather pale role in her fantasies. Accidentally, her daydreams were largely realized: she transferred her positive mother relationship to Mrs. K. and actively continued her identification with her mother in her solicitude for Mrs. K.'s children. When Mrs. K. fell ill and Lydia had to assume all the responsibility, her motherly activity collapsed because it was tied to the condition of a constant identification with a real, external mother. Lydia told me that a short time after Mrs. K. left her home, she began to be consciously afraid of her responsibility, became oversolicitous, feared that the children might fall ill, etc. She became short-tempered and impatient and could not bear staying at home. The children bored and fatigued her, although she still loved them and now kept away from them only because it was easier for her to bear being separated from them that way. She was satisfied with her new job and expressed a wish later to attend a school for secretaries. She still clung to her plan of marrying, having children, and taking her mother into her home.

I do not know whether Lydia will some day develop into an independent, adult mother. When I stopped treating her she was still caught in her primitive identification with the active mother: that is to say, if she was successfully to take care of children, the mother or her substitute had to be present, because Lydia had not yet attained the adult stage of motherliness. She lacked the aggressiveness necessary to become a kidnaper who takes possession of children against the mother's will, although psychologically she was perhaps closer to the kid-naper type than is apparent at first glance.

My second observation concerns a mother whom I met through a social agency. Mrs. Baron was a young woman of Swedish origin who came to this country as a little child. She came to the agency in order to obtain help for her 4½-year-old son, who was afflicted with enuresis, nightmares, and fits of screaming and sobbing in his sleep. In the daytime the little boy was very active and showed marked readiness to fight with other children in the neighborhood. In relation to his mother he was obviously anxious and watchful, and from time to time he expressed a longing for his father, to whom, according to Mrs. Baron, he was greatly attached. Mr. Baron had been in the Marine Corps for some months and was expecting to be sent overseas soon. Mrs. Baron had another boy 3 years old and discovered a few days after her husband's enlistment that she was pregnant again. What worried her was not the financial burden nor the additional work involved in having another child, but something else that she was unable to define clearly. It was the ingredient of anxiety in her entire relationship with her children, the emotional obligation that she so badly needed to share with her husband. She became more and more depressed and anxious and was afraid to be at home alone.

Loss of weight had resulted from loss of appetite and sleepless nights. She often had nightmares and woke up screaming.

She had little patience with her children's difficulties, even when these were within a normal range, although she tried not to betray her nervousness to them. The nocturnal anxieties of her older boy, which in the beginning were perhaps more or less normal, immediately created in her a feeling of helplessness, especially when he began to wet his bed. His jealousy of his younger brother worried her a great deal, and the little sibling hostilities between the children put her into a sort of panic. She complained about the older boy's extreme jealousy of the baby and about how "meanly" he treated the child, pinching and slapping it whenever her back was turned. People who knew her commented that both children were unusually active and that Mrs. Baron was cranky and too strict with them when she was not feeling well. On the other hand, she would not consider temporarily placing them. She felt that under the circumstances she would be even more lonely as well as more anxious about her children. It was evident that she felt much calmer when she knew that her children were in the charge of a person whom she trusted completely, for instance her youthful sister-in-law. She could not ask her mother to help her actively, because the latter was completely absorbed in caring for her own mother.

Mrs. Baron gave me the following life story. At the age of 15 she was impregnated by a playmate of the same age and married him a short time before giving birth to her child. The young couple were happy and awaited the birth of the child with great joy. After the little boy was born they took care of him together. Her vivid descriptions gave the impression that the child was cared for not by a mother and a father, but by two mothers, so that Mrs. Baron, who had always felt insecure and weak with children, was aided in carrying the emotional burdens of motherhood by the active participation of her husband in all her child care duties. Particularly striking was her insistence that her greatest difficulty was not the work connected with caring for the child, but the anxiety she had felt ever since his birth.　Her anxious dependence upon her husband was further intensified after the birth of her second boy, which took place a year and a half later.　Her second delivery and confinement were followed by hemorrhages after which she required blood transfusions.

Mrs. Baron told happily how her husband had supplied the blood she needed, whereby she wanted to suggest that in fact he had actively shared the dangers of the delivery.　The first problems arose when Mr. Baron's work took him away from home for long hours, so that his wife was alone much of the day and night and had most of the responsibility for the home and children.　By and by she found herself becoming more and more nervous at night; she was so frightened at being alone that her husband was urged to take more responsibility for the family and to find work with shorter hours during the day.　He finally did this, after which his wife's health improved.

She described her state during her husband's absence as a feeling of loss and helplessness, especially with regard to her children.　During the day she found it easier to bear his absence, especially when the children were well and her care for them did not exceed the normal limits.　She insisted that she could be free of her anxiety only when she knew that her husband was close at hand and ready to care lovingly for the children.　The husband, according to her entirely credible account, was very happy to do this: he gladly cooked for the little boys, took care of their physical needs, and was always full of tenderness toward them.　Mrs. Baron never had the impression that the children were a burden to him or that he felt disturbed in his outside activities by his family duties.　He was a good worker, glad to take the most arduous job if it enabled him to provide properly for his wife and children. So long as her husband was with her, Mrs. Baron was free of anxiety and nervousness.　During the months just preceding, after Mr. Baron entered the service, the symptoms she had formerly had during his night-time absences reappeared.

Mr. Baron had taken great satisfaction in his work, he was capable and efficient, and was enthusiastic about joining the

Marines. Now he was evidently worried about his wife's being pregnant again and alone. He wrote anxious letters to her relatives and to friends and was dissatisfied with his training. We may conjecture that a sense of guilt and a sort of motherly solicitude for his family burdened and inhibited his masculine activity. Even though I considered Mrs. Baron a victim of the war, one of the many women who find it hard to live separated from their husbands, it was evident that her difficulties were intensified by her special psychologic situation.

Mrs. Baron informed me that motherliness had been her outstanding personality trait from early childhood. She had older sisters and brothers and a little brother two years younger than herself. So far as she could remember she had always helped her mother in caring for this child and had also taken care of neighbors' children. She was very young when she became pregnant and from the beginning was so overjoyed at the idea of having a child that she was hardly aware of the social and financial aspects of her position. Although her husband was only 16 years old when they married (it is to be recalled that she was then in her sixth month of pregnancy) he accepted his fatherly duties with joy; yet his relation to the children did not seem to reveal a strong masculine-fatherly personality.

My general impression was that Mrs. Baron, despite her extraordinary motherliness, lacked an element that she found in her husband's contribution to the family life. In the so-called patriarchal society it is normal for woman to need man not only as a love object but also as a provider and protector against the outer world. Moreover, the family relationships of her own childhood, and her emotional experiences with her father and mother, create in every woman a psychologic predisposition to carry the prototype triangle into her own motherhood situation (cf. vol. 1). But in Mrs. Baron's case something else was involved. It was as though a dependable active ingredient were lacking in her motherliness. Women of this kind become helpless when they are left alone with their children. Their nervous anxiety is communicated to their children and arouses an anxious reaction in them; thus a vicious circle of mutual excitation is created. The children's normal emotional difficulties, such as their jealousy of younger brothers or sisters, are overestimated and put the mother in such a state that she feels that she must "do something" to rectify her children's bad character traits, which she exaggerates. In the usual children's quarrels she feels that she must take the side of the weaker; then she becomes afraid of her own possible unfairness, and her conflicts and helplessness are intensified. Under certain conditions she calls upon her own mother for help, but then there arises an aggressive protest against her parent, born of the feeling that the mother is trying to inhibit the daughter's motherly activity.

Many women solve these difficulties as Mrs. Baron did—by drawing their husbands into the field of their motherly activities. Naturally, the husband must have a large amount of feminine readiness in order to agree to this emotional proposal of his wife's. Many marital conflicts, brutality in the husband toward the wife, excessive drinking and extramarital love affairs on his part, originate in the fact that the husband feels threatened in his masculinity by his wife's demands and begins to avoid his home. This did not seem to be the case with Mr. Baron. Yet one had the impression that here too a conflict would result in the course of time, that the young man would be unable to carry on his masculine activities because of his feeling that he was urgently needed at home to do his share of mother's work. It seemed clear that Mrs. Baron's motherliness lacked an active-motherly component that normally is intensified with greater needs and on which the mother's care of her children is solidly built.

As a rule the prerequisite for harmonious development of this component is that the various duties that in our society are transferred to the husband be actually performed by him. If this is not the case, and if the demands made upon the woman's activity overburden her active motherliness, she will fail with regard to her children. For instance, one of the unfortunate consequences of the war is that women must contribute to the economic support of their families to a greater extent than before. Many women achieve this by the strength of their motherliness without being disturbed in their relationship with their children. But the majority fail under the impact of their double activity and there arises a vicious circle of anxiety and nervousness, such as we have seen in the case of Mrs. Baron. Only outside help, expert care of the children, and real understanding of the mothers can cope with this war evil.

Another situation arises when the woman's activity is overtaxed by the man's passive disposition, for instance as a result of his unreliability, or of the excessive demands he makes upon his wife, etc. Erotic preoccupations (a love relationship) also can divert motherly activity and produce difficulties in its direct applications.

No such possibilities were involved in Mrs. Baron's case. A careful analysis of her personality would probably have explained why she was so helpless as a mother when she was deprived of her husband's help. This is how I imagine the situation: Mrs. Baron became a mother at a time when psychologically she was still an "assistant mother" (if I may use this term for the sake of clarity); that is to say, she could love and take care of children only if the chief responsibility was left to an adult mother. She had remained an assistant mother in relation to her own children, not with the responsible assistance of another mother, as was the case with Lydia, but by sharing her maternal duties with her husband. We may even conjecture that she would have been unwilling to entrust to another woman the role assumed by her husband. For she had certainly preserved the normal wish of the little girl that not her mother, but she herself, should be in full possession of the child. It is significant that Mrs. Baron felt at ease when her children were entrusted to her youthful sister-in-law, who helped her without presenting the dangers of a real mother figure. One reason why she so energetically resisted placing her children was perhaps her feeling that if she did, another woman would take possession of them.

Mrs. Baron's difficulties were similar to Lydia's, although the *mise en scène* was different. Her maternal love was disturbed by an unmastered developmental inhibition, just as in the case of Lydia. Like Lydia, she was close to the little girl who plays at motherliness, who acts out tenderness, but whose actions are still very much under the sign of her identification with her mother, and who has not acquired the qualities of actual experience and independent activity. If we observe the games and occupations of young girls, we notice that those who for long periods, or repeatedly, are interested in smaller children, are also the ones who are more attached to their homes and more passive. The active girl likewise often plunges into motherly activity and identifies herself with her mother, but she soon gets tired of this role, as did Lydia, and turns to other occupations. This is true of early childhood and even more often of prepuberty and early puberty. The birth of a younger child usually mobilizes this kind of motherliness. In this period of life passive girls assume a motherly attitude toward the newborn brother or sister and often self-sacrificingly take over a share of the burdens created by the new child. The reason for this is not always and not only the intensification of the young girl's motherly feelings. A strong resentment against the mother who achieves a situation to which her daughter will in the very near future lay claim herself, and a protest against the mother's anachronistic action, arise in the maturing young girl. If this resentment were conscious the girl would say: "You should be the grandmother of *my* child, not the mother of your own." In certain passive girls who have a strong predisposition to guilt feelings, this resentment is expressed by excessive devotion to the mother's new child, which often inhibits their own further development.

The girl who is later to become a real mother, endowed with all the mother's active qualities, does not develop along a straight line. Other interests and activities free her from the danger of excessive identification with her mother, which should be only a preliminary phase of motherliness. If the girl remains in this phase she acquires an increasingly passive character and continues all the emotional conflicts of puberty in later years.

During early childhood the girl's resentment against the child for whose possession she may be competing with her mother, is much more primitive and intense. In fact, what she would prefer is to remove, to throw out the little peace disturber, to kill him in a psychologic sense. This is especially the case when the girl competes with the newborn brother or sister for her mother's or father's love, when she feels neglected because of the baby, or when she happens to be passing through the phase in which her aggressive envy may be aggravated by the masculine sex of the newborn. Her wish to have this child herself may be strong in her fantasy, and her playing mother may simulate motherliness, but this must not be interpreted as a particular indication of the presence of a maternal instinct or as its harbinger. It can be observed that whenever this identification with her mother causes her any discomfort, she renounces it very soon, and then her aggression against the younger child comes to the fore all the more intensely.

I have called Mrs. Baron an assistant mother and explained her immaturity by the fact that she realized motherhood prematurely in a life phase in which it still belongs in largest part to fantasy and should remain there. Mrs. Baron had always had a somewhat passive personality and it could be expected that she would only gradually be able to assume the role of a real mother. Her premature pregnancy, extraordinarily unfavorable conditions of existence, financial worries, physical exhaustion, and separation from her husband interrupted her psychic growth. Her fear of responsibility got the better of her and assumed a neurotic character. We conjecture that the regressive tendency brought her back to a period in her life when she took motherly care of her brother. During our interviews, Mrs. Baron recalled this little boy with striking frequency, and we are justified in suspecting that her impatience with and intolerance of her own boys derived from her old aggressions against him. She seemed to disavow these aggressions by her absolute refusal to be separated from her children; and she had no word of complaint about her new pregnancy, which came so soon after her last one. On the contrary, she accepted it willingly, and when birth control was mentioned as a suggestion for the future, she emphatically rejected it.

Both Lydia and Mrs. Baron prematurely assumed an active and independent mother role. Real motherliness requires a strength of ego that pubescent girls have not yet reached. Both belonged to the type for which I suggest the name of assistant mother.

Many women remain such assistant mothers for life because in them the process of maturation has been inhibited for some reason, just as there are innumerable mothers who have long ago passed the puberty phase but whose motherhood still remains in this phase. Usually we meet them when this situation results in neurotic difficulties. Adolescent girls often discuss the wish to have many children, draw up plans for their upbringing, etc. This motherliness should not be trusted. Usually it still has the character of a fantasy, not that of a warm emotional need, or the real need is still separated from possible fulfillment by the girl's incapacity for full motherly responsibility. The young girl's behavior during her adolescence enables us to formulate a prognosis of her future motherliness. The "modern" young girl's sober, purposeful intellectualism and her excessive valuation of efficiency can make her an excellent mother, who dutifully applies all the precepts of modern pedagogy; but real motherliness will probably remain alien to her forever. Whenever the young girl exchanges a rich emotional life for scientific thinking, it is to be expected that later in her life sterility will take the place of motherliness even if she has given birth to many children.

A favorable forecast as regards motherliness does not necessarily depend upon the girl's beginning to manifest love and understanding for children in her adolescence. Readiness for motherhood is rather expressed indirectly. To the real motherly type belong those girls who, without being neurotic and masochistic, show an emotional disposition to subordinate the instinct of self-preservation to altruistic feelings.

CHAPTER FOUR

The Psychology of the Sexual Act

THE sexual act, in both men and women, serves two related ends—individual sexual satisfaction and reproduction. In the individual consciousness, reproduction is often a desired accompaniment of sexual satisfaction; at other times, however, the individual tries successfully or unsuccessfully to avoid it. Normally, in the fire of sexual excitement, reproduction is completely neglected in the emotions of both partners. In analyzing the psychologic processes, we must keep in mind a fundamental difference between the two sexes—namely, that the two components, sexual satisfaction and service to the species, are not present in the same quantitative relation in man and in woman. In man, the reproductive function is appended to the sexual satisfaction; in woman, the sexual act is a pleasure prize that is appended to her service to the species. Freud's observation[1] that "the individual himself regards sexuality as one of his own ends, while from another point of view he is only an appendage to his germ plasm, to which he lends his energies, taking in return his toll of pleasure—the mortal vehicle of a (possibly) immortal substance," applies especially to woman.

This fundamental difference results from two circumstances:

1. In man, somatic satisfaction through the pleasurable discharge of the germ plasm and disposition of this plasm in a safe and fostering body are integral parts of a *single* act. The service to the species takes place at the same time as the sexual satisfaction and can subsequently be completely disregarded by him.

In woman, the goal of her germ plasm, that is to say, her service to the species, is realized only much later, after a certain

[1] FREUD, S.: On narcissism: An introduction. Collected Papers, vol. 4, p. 35.

fixed interval of time. Even the internal processes in the woman's body are subject to separation in time, for the maturation of the ovum and its fecundation are two temporally separated functions.

The long delay between fecundation and childbirth in the human female, just like the long period of the child's dependence upon its mother, represents a phylogenetic advance that involved the separation of the two functions, the sexual act and childbirth. In lower animals, the two functions are closer to each other, and in certain species the extrusion of the fecundated ovum seems to be connected with pleasure sensations; the animal's rhythmic motions in performing this function are reminiscent of coitus motions and may be their prototype.

Human ability to force modifications of biologic processes has arbitrarily regulated the spontaneous, natural course of the sexual function and thereby contributed to making the facts more obscure. Cultural developments, especially economic conditions, woman's attempt to subordinate the reproductive function to other life interests, etc., have led to a new adjustment to reality that often contradicts the biologic tendencies. In this violation of natural processes, which in the human species include the psychophysical elements, woman's unconscious seems to have preserved the psychologic unity of coitus and reproduction. In woman, psychologic associative bridges lead from coitus to childbirth and vice versa from childbirth to coitus, and the two processes are to a large extent identified. Later I shall discuss these processes in greater detail.

2. Man can entrust the whole function to a *single* organ, while woman suffers from an overendowment, so to speak, which leads to complications. Freud assumed that the clitoris, which has become unnecessary for the mature sexual organization, transfers its pleasure sensations to the vagina and "resigns" in the latter's favor. But deeper analysis and longer experience seem to indicate that this transfer is never completely successful and that from the moment of her sexual maturity woman possesses two sexual organs, with the result

that she often fares like the donkey in Aesop's fable, which starved to death between two full mangers because of its indecision; having two organs, woman often remains sexually ungratified.

The question whether the vagina receives a hormonal erotization in the period of sexual maturity, is absolutely undecided. It seems that the tendency to sexual discharge partly remains uncentered, and partly remains tied to the clitoris. If it were true that the vagina becomes more sensitive as a result of physiochemical stimulation, its sexual excitability would spontaneously increase with time. However, the majority of adult women, especially as long as they lack direct sexual experience, do not differ much in this respect from little girls, in that they too usually masturbate by means of the clitoris, from which the excitation extends to the vaginal orifice. Possibly cultural and educational influences have led to suppression of the phylogenetically acquired hormonal excitability of the vagina; woman, as a result of her adjustment to man, has largely given up the cyclic rhythm and with it perhaps the sexual spontaneity of the vagina. Our knowledge of the sexual processes in higher mammals is insufficient to permit of any inferences.

Although vaginal contractions are clearly perceived even as early as in puberty, the clitoris remains the central organ in that life period. The vagina becomes the center of spontaneous excitation only in women who have had direct sexual experience. Some women who have had no such experience report that in the course of time their excitability has been spontaneously transferred from the clitoris to the vagina, which reacts to fantasied situations. But such cases are not the rule; usually spontaneous vaginal excitations are not a part of female experience as erections are part of the male's experience (cf. vol. i). The "undiscovered" vagina is—in normal, favorable instances —eroticized by an act of rape. By "rape" I do not refer here to that puberal fantasy in which the young girl realistically desires and fears the sexual act as a rape. That fantasy is only a psychologic preparation for a real, milder, but dynamically identical process. This process manifests itself in man's aggressive penetration on the one hand and in the "overpowering" of the vagina and its transformation into an erogenous sexual zone on the other. The original destiny of the vagina seems rather to find its expression in the acts of retaining, bearing, and giving—which are attributes of the reproductive function rather than of the sexual experience. Nature was wise in committing to man the task of furthering reproduction by creating in the vagina pleasure sensations that make the sexual act desirable to woman too, thus seemingly shifting her interest in the species to second place. However, all this must not be interpreted as denying that the vagina has physiologically determined pleasure sensations: most probably the rape is only a mobilization of a latent readiness.

Now we can better understand the purpose of that seemingly senseless inhibition in the infantile period which we called the genital trauma (cf. vol. 1). At that time the little girl is confronted by the fact of organlessness, because the clitoris has terminated its infantile role without yielding its place to the vagina. The vagina is still unable to assume its part because the reproductive function is conceived as its primary duty. It is as though the biologic architect had planned two different organs for the two functions—the clitoris for sexuality, the vagina for reproduction—but later found it safer to attach the vagina also to the more selfish aim of sexual pleasure. Thus, in the new plan, the clitoris with its infantile sexuality, useless for reproduction, was to resign, and the vagina was to take up its services only when sexual maturity and readiness for reproduction were attained. But this plan is not completely carried out: the clitoris preserves its excitability during the latency period and is unwilling to cede its function smoothly, while the vagina for its part does not prove completely willing to take over both functions, reproduction and sexual pleasure.

Because of the anatomic duality of the sexual organs, and the dual function of the vagina, constant regulation naturally is necessary, and the biologic forces are charged with the task. The dual goals are often mixed in woman, and this produces a confusion that can become the source of various disturbances.

Any psychic experience can provoke these disturbances, which can in various ways impair the sexual process (by creating frigidity) or the performance of the reproductive functions.

Woman's reproductive functions are becoming increasingly clearer to us, thanks to the development of the science of hormones. But biology fails to give us adequate information about the sexual function, especially woman's experience of the orgasm. Here we must turn to our own field, psychology, though it does not give us complete insight into the problem. Psychology has not as effective means of gaining objective knowledge as biology; on the other hand, it can go farther.

In order to approach an understanding of the nature, course, and significance of woman's orgasm, we must follow several lines of investigation. A painful bodily injury—the breaking of the hymen and the forcible stretching and enlargement of the vagina by the penis—are the prelude to woman's first complete sexual enjoyment. This injury as such is not identical with sexual pleasure in any normal woman; it produces a pain only secondarily connected with pleasure sensations, and this connection endows the sexual experience with a masochistic character. The whole psychology of woman suggests that this juncture between pleasure and pain was organized in the course of phylogenesis and that it created some measure of constitutional readiness in every woman, something we might call a masochistic reflex mechanism. As we shall see later, this readiness accompanies woman's reproductive functions and endows the psychologic component of childbirth with a definite character.[2]

Wherever the masochistic anticipation has produced an anxious defense attitude, the orgastic function will be considerably delayed or fail altogether. If this anticipation has been abnormally reinforced from other masochistic sources, perverse masochistic wishes may be aroused, either mobilizing an even stronger defense or remaining unfulfilled.

[2] It is the task of psychosomatic research to discover whether this mechanism, feminine par excellence, in which pleasure and pain are blended, does not play an important role in the diseases of the organ. What the normal constitution of the organ has imposed upon woman may in diseased conditions result from individual motives.

Freud, in his essay "The Taboo of Virginity," analyzes the psychologic and cultural aspects of defloration, its relationship to the female castration complex, etc. He draws our attention to certain taboos that forbid the husband to deflower his wife. In some tribes old women, in other tribes a specially selected group of men (often priests), were entrusted with the task of deflowering young brides. In conclusion, Freud writes:

> We may say that the act of defloration has not merely the socially useful result of binding the woman closely to the man; it also liberates an archaic reaction towards the man, which may assume pathological forms, and often enough expresses itself by inhibitions in the erotic life of the pair, and to which one may ascribe the fact that second marriages so often turn out better than first. The strange taboo of virginity—the fear which among primitive peoples induces the husband to avoid the performance of defloration—finds its full justification in this hostile turn of feeling.[3]

In psychoanalytic practice we often meet with husbands who develop a similar fear regarding defloration. Apparently out of fear of their own aggression or of the woman's possible hatred for the first overcomer of her inhibition, these husbands prefer to allow a physician to deflower their brides by surgical methods. They rationalize their action by claiming, for instance, that the partner's virginal membrane is unusually "hard" or "unbreakable." Usually this reluctance expresses a sexual inhibition in the man, who does not feel equal to his task of overcoming the woman's resistance. Whenever I have had opportunity of studying the woman's subsequent (conscious or unconscious) reactions to artificial defloration, I have found that she felt a contempt, hard to overcome, for the man who lacked the strength and courage to violate the taboo. This contempt seemed to me more dangerous for the marriage and love relations than the possible reaction of anger and revenge to the conjugal rape. The husband, while possibly achieving protection against his wife's aggressive reactions, failed to gratify her deeply feminine need to be overpowered.

Our interest must next turn to the physiologic process and

---

[3] FREUD, S. The taboo of virginity: Contribution to the psychology of love. Collected Papers, vol. 4, p. 234.

the typical emotional reactions directly connected with it. The vaginal orgastic function is manifold. Normally there are localized contractions that have the character of sucking in and relaxing. These contractions follow a rhythm completely adjusted to the male's rhythm. The physically expressed readiness for this adjustment is one of the most important elements of the female orgasm.

The normal process is, in its type of innervation, reminiscent of the sucking function of the mouth, and thus assumes the oral character of intake that is accompanied by elements of expulsion; these in turn are reminiscent of sphincter innervations.

Because of this functional analogy the oral significance of the vagina may assert itself in some form in pathologic states. An interesting illustration of this is supplied by Zilboorg.[3a] One of his patients reported that in her masturbatory fantasies, "the orgasm occurred at the instant she imagined the moment of ejaculation. She herself stressed the significance of the moment of ejaculation, since the rush of seminal fluid was in her case a prerequisite for a satisfactory orgasm." Zilboorg was able to gain psychoanalytic insight into the unconscious processes of his patient. He learned that his patient's masturbatory fantasies "usually dealt with a breast in her mouth and resulted in a vaginal orgasm in no way different from the orgasm experienced when she fantasied that she was putting something, probably a penis, into a woman's vagina." Thanks to this and other memories of the patient, it was clear that "it was the mother's breast which had become a point of concentration for our patient's sexuality." The simultaneous functioning of mouth and vagina apparently resulted from the functional analogy.

Sometimes the vagina functions abnormally in a sphincter-like manner, receiving the penetrating penis by jolts and expelling it similarly. In other cases the contractions assume the character of steady compression with accompanying painful paresthesia (vaginismus). In rare instances the contractions become so strong that the condition of penis captivus is brought

[3a] Zilboorg, G.: Some observations on the transformation of instincts. Psychoanalyst. Quart., vol. 7, 1938.

about. This change to direct sphincter-like functioning is strongly reminiscent of intestinal action (intake, expulsion, retention). In these analogies we again find the earlier physiologic mechanisms. However, in normal individuals, these mechanisms are not always regressive; rather, we have here an independent physiologic function that achieves its goals by organic means similar to those at the disposal of other functions.

It is clear that in the intrapsychic communication system the old psychic contents can exploit these analogies for their own purposes by supplying old material to the new process. For instance, when an infantile woman, primitively attached to her mother, is induced by this analogy between the vagina and the mouth to experience coitus in fantasy as though the penis were the mother's breast and the vagina the mouth, as in Zilboorg's case, we must not infer that the physiologic process suitable for this fantasy, by reason of its innervation, always serves to repeat this mother-child situation.

The orgastic function is strongly conditioned psychologically; its anomalies are almost always accessible to psychology alone. Many phenomena that psychology is for the time being unable to explain may some day be clarified by biology and more particularly by the science dealing with the physiologic-chemical aspects of our problems.

We have mentioned two difficulties that must be overcome to make the female orgasm possible. First of all, there is the constitutionally determined inhibition, i.e., the vagina comes into play only with the active reproductive function and it is closely, and not as simply as the penis, related to the reproductive function. The second difficulty consists in the proper management of feminine masochism. These two difficulties are normal components of the female sexual economy. All the other types of difficulties belong to the domain of pathology, which we take into account here only in so far as it can help us to explain normal processes.

It is of decisive importance in the understanding of this problem to give up the illusion of the equivalence of the sexual act for the two sexes. The error that stems from this can be corrected only if the processes are objectively studied and the tendency to reduce them to a common denominator is eliminated.

From the outset the motives that drive man and woman to the sexual act are tremendously different. For the male, ejaculation means release of burdensome secretions; the preceding physiologic processes are unambiguous and intelligible, and the increasing discomfort that is communicated by the sexual organ to the rest of the body creates an intense urge to discharge. This discharge is accompanied by extreme gratification in the act of copulation.

Woman's somatic urge is not comparable to man's. She forms no secretions that must be eliminated. The secretions and discharge of the accessory sexual glands in woman are often compared with man's ejaculation. But the discharge value of the female secretions is very small; the elimination does not apply to cells that have become a burden to the organism. For man, ejaculation is the actual goal; but there is no such goal for woman. Her secretions in the sexual function play a modest and subordinate role, i.e., they lubricate the vagina and thus facilitate the penetration of the penis.

In woman, the somatic tendency to discharge is replaced by the yearning for the erotic pleasure experience that is communicated to the genitals. In man, we have *primarily* an imperious physiologic urge that is accompanied by psychic elements; in woman, we have a psychologic process supported by biologic factors. In women who live in sexual abstinence, depressions usually have little in common with organic sexual tension. They are manifestations not of a physical urge but of erotic yearning, of the narcissistic need to be loved, and of the masochistic striving to give. Even in wives of impotent husbands, the typical irritability and aggressive mood express disappointment, injury, vexation, and contempt rather than a state of somatic excitability. Once the pleasure has been enjoyed, the wish for repetition is naturally intensified (this is true of all pleasure experiences), even when urgent biologic necessity is absent.

The profound difference between man's urgent, basic needs and those of woman is often expressed in legend. For instance, Adam, in the biblical story, is made to sacrifice a part of his body, probably to satisfy his urgent need for a sexual object. In many legends woman's body is endowed with the capacity to give birth to a *son* by itself, probably under pressure of a profound psychic need.[4]

Even when there is complete psychologic readiness, when the man's wooing has produced the necessary degree of excitability in the woman, physical resistance at the beginning of her sexual activity takes the form of a tension that leads to contraction of the vagina and induces the man to make an aggressive assault. This contraction often gives inexperienced persons the idea that the vagina is too small and that medical intervention is necessary. Only gradually, as an affirmative answer to the aggression, is the masochistic consent granted and the pain accepted, as prerequisite to the promised pleasure; the vagina is enlarged, it receives the penis, and the culminating act of adjustment, which manifests itself in the above mentioned manner of innervation, takes place.

To avoid misunderstandings, we repeat that in woman too the orgasm is a biologically determined, inherited function. Yet its full scope and meaning become clear only if we grasp its course psychologically. The following observation, which is far removed from biology, will serve as an illustration.

One of the most original and creative dancers of the last decades, whose genius was recognized by everyone interested in her art, sought psychoanalytic help because of numerous difficulties.

[4] A recently published translation of an ancient Sumerian story (KRAMER, S. N.: Bull. Am. Schools Oriental Research) casts new light on the biblical account of woman and her relation to Adam's rib. In the Sumerian language the word *ti* had two meanings—"rib" and "to make live." A relevant passage in the Sumerian story runs as follows:

"My brother, what hurts thee?"

"My rib hurts me."

"The goddess Ninti I have caused to be born for thee."

The authors of the Hebrew version of the myth were no doubt influenced by an unconscious motive when they interpreted the word *Ninti* to mean "lady of the rib" instead of "lady who gives life," thus not only giving man a sexual companion but also making him the first birth giver, independent of woman.

She suffered from various morbid disturbances, such as an urge to frequent change of her love objects against her will, frigidity, homosexuality, proneness to various perversions, and frequent depressions that sometimes involved the impulse to suicide. She was regarded as a highly original personality; although she was not psychotic, she betrayed so-called schizoid features. Only in the fields of music and dancing was she completely free of morbidity.   There she was great, uninhibited, productive, inspired, and an inspiration to others.

A great admirer of her art, I was fascinated by the idea of gaining insight into the nature of her artistic gifts.   Music— not all music, but music of a strictly defined type, classical and monumental—was for her a powerful assault to which she must abandon herself in complete passivity and submission.   The rhythm of such music pervaded her like a power that she was forced to follow with her own rhythm, her whole body.   Her dancing was an almost compulsive expression of this rhythmic abandon to the outside rhythm of the music she chose.   At the end of what she herself called her "rhythmic ecstasy," she was completely exhausted.   Her preparations for the ecstatic experience were absolutely reality-adjusted studies, in which, however, to the surprise of her entourage, she behaved very "originally."   She let the music pass over her and "studied" and "practiced" it with symbolic rhythmic motions of her fingers, her hands, or her feet.   The dramatic experience of the dance, the artistic ecstasy, came only at the end, as a kind of epilogue.   She was not interested in the composer, she gave herself only to the music, the rhythm.   She herself composed rather unimportant pieces of music and her creative efforts seemed to have a schizoid character: she had to experience herself in a split.   One half of herself created the musical rhythm, the other half followed it in a kind of automatism.

My impression was not that the artistic achievements of this great dancer were a mere coitus substitute, nor that they represented a sublimation of her sexuality.   I did not learn much about the nature of her genius.   Yet, thanks to her, I gained for the first time a deep and objective understanding of the function of the female orgasm.

Another observation is so closely related to the foregoing that I wish to cite it here, although it may at first appear rather far-fetched. Many years ago a young girl suspected of being in the early stages of a psychosis was sent for observation to the psychiatric department of a hospital. She behaved normally and gave me, as her physician, completely coherent information, until, after overcoming an inhibition, she declared to me mysteriously that all her troubles resulted from the fact that her "clock" could not be adjusted to his clock—that "it ticks quite differently." Under the influence of the symbols that then had just been introduced by Freud, I took up her symbolic language with youthful zeal and suggested to her that perhaps he could adjust his clock to hers. The night after I made this proposal, the patient had a hallucination in which I was treating her with electrical apparatus in order to transform her into a man. This idea became the center of her paranoic delirium, and for many years she referred to my suggestion as a proof that the hospital (or I) wanted to change her into a man. The psychotic insight of our patients often discovers more than is possible for our logical minds. This young, still completely inexperienced, sick girl understood that the adjustment of the symbolic clock was a woman's task, and that renunciation of this task involved the loss of her femininity, which had obviously been threatened from within by the psychotic process.

Like everything else connected with woman's instinctual life, this adjustment is essentially passive, even when it accompanies intense sexual activity. Moreover, we must not forget that "an individual woman may be a human being apart from this" and that she must not experience her readiness for passive abandon as servitude. In many women, bourgeois morality or their mothers' malicious frigidity has created the idea that coitus is a sacrifice they must make to the dirty needs of men, and they must dutifully let it happen to them.

The woman expects that the man's tenderness and tactfulness will lead him to endow her urge to adjustment with more dignity by means of his own efforts at adjustment. The numerous "expert" and often ridiculous recommendations concerning the husband's behavior in marital intercourse generally deal with the mechanical-technical aspects of the process. But in most instances the woman's resistance is broken by the very fact of his efforts, which she interprets as an expression of his intensified desire, or these efforts soften her inner protest against her position.

I have used the term "malicious" frigidity. There is also a benevolent frigidity, that of the woman who is deeply gratified by giving the man satisfaction in a passive, tender, motherly embrace, without feeling the urge for a more personal sexual experience. Organically this type of "frigid" readiness is expressed in the enlargement of the vagina for the reception of the penis, without any further innervation processes. The feminine woman whose eroticism has been absorbed into an excessively strong motherliness often behaves in this manner.

There is also a malicious orgasm, however paradoxic and absurd this may sound. In this, the rhythmic contractions follow their course in complete disregard of the man's rhythm. They have the character of reception and rapid expulsion and give the impression that a kind of duel is taking place. In such cases the sexual act often becomes a competition: who will be through first (or inversely, who can keep it up longest) and who has achieved the most? As might be expected, this type of orgasm will be found in masculine-aggressive women, who thus fight for the equality of the sexes even in the most intimate part of their lives. In modern marriage, the partners often strive to achieve the moment of discharge simultaneously. This looks like a perfect regulation of the sexual situation, but numerous observations have taught me that this is not necessarily so. Very often, the woman's orgasm takes place later than the man's and subsides later and gradually. These two circumstances make room for the demands in which the vagina indirectly asserts its role as a reproductive organ. The one makes for receiving tenderly, the other prepares for retaining and is psychologically the beginning of motherhood, whether fecundation takes place or not. Many women consider this last phase most gratifying.

A woman who was psychoanalytically treated for neurotic symptoms gave the following account of her erotic difficulties. She had had a certain amount of sexual experience, had never been frigid, and had absolutely satisfying orgasms, but they were usually followed by depressive moods. The same thing took place when she married a man she dearly loved. She also was unhappy because for many years she had vainly tried to become pregnant.

When I met this patient again several years later, she had a little girl and was free of her neurotic ailments. Her sexual life had undergone a change. Formerly she had felt energetic contractions accompanied by violent orgastic excitation;[5] now she enjoyed relaxing gratification in the slow course of the excitation curve. Instead of subsequent resentment against her husband, she now felt gratitude and warmth. She ascribed her conception of the child to the change in her sexual behavior. I think she was right. In some cases the vigorous "anti-motherly" orgasm—as it may be termed—successfully realizes the woman's unconscious intention: by expelling the inflowing semen the woman can keep both the man and the undesired child away from her body. It is possible that the psychogenic sterility of many women has its origin in the emotionally disturbed course of the sexual act. However, I have been unable to discover a convincing causal connection between frigidity, that is to say, lack of orgasm, and sterility.

In man the double direction of the innervation expresses itself in active penetration and withdrawal. The innervation is subordinated to a momentary tendency to retain, which in the end is overcome by a tendency to discharge. In woman, there can hardly be any question of a tendency to discharge in the sexual act; retention predominates, while discharge is postponed to the future act of birth. Thus for woman coitus is above all an act

[5] LORAND, S.: Contribution to the problem of vaginal orgasm. Internat. J. Psycho-Analysis 20: 432, 1929. The case cited in this paper exemplifies similar behavior: "When later she was able to achieve orgasm, it was accompanied by angry shrieking and grasping sensations, as if her vagina were reaching out like an octopus."

of fecundation, the beginning of the reproductive function, which ends with the birth of the child.

It would be unintelligible if in this dual function, one factor, the sexual, yielded completely to the other. For that reason we must expect to find the sexual component again in the later reproductive activities. This division is best adapted to the interests of the species, even though it imposes a difficult, complicated, and strenuous task upon woman.

Often difficulties are encountered on the path toward the final goal. In the first place, there may be conscious rejection of the child as a result of environmental influences, or from internal, emotional motives. Psychogenic difficulties of conception, overhasty discharge tendencies, beginning with the spasmodic expulsion of the sperm from the vagina and ending with abortion (often habitual), premature delivery, or precipitate labor, etc., are the most frequent manifestations of this rejection. The psychic impulses have at their disposal numerous and complicated physiologic processes that must be set in motion in order to enable the psychic tendencies to be realized.

We are familiar with the overdetermination of one process by another. In the interrelation between coitus and birth, what is in question is not merely a juxtaposition of the two, nor the temporary suppression of one component in favor of the other, but the simultaneous realization of both elements by appropriate means. In coitus, the motherly component is gratified in the tender relationship with the love partner. The penis received in the interior of the body assumes the significance of a child because of its position and the play of the appropriate emotions. This is beautifully illustrated in the Brahmin religious myth, according to which man introjects himself into woman's body in coitus, in order to be reborn as a child and thus gain immortality. In normal dreams and in the ravings of schizophrenics this idea often asserts itself consciously. We recall that it has its prototype in childhood in the identification of the child with the penis.

In the ecstasy of the orgasm the woman experiences herself as a helpless child abandoned to her love partner—a deep experience in which her ego becomes the child that she conceives in her fantasy and with which she will continue to identify herself when her fantasy comes true. Colette,[6] the great French writer, beautifully expresses this idea:

"You will give me love, eyes filled with a maternal anxiety, you who seek, beyond the woman in your arms, the child that is yet to be yours."

Colette expresses these ideas realistically: as a poet she understands things intuitively that we learn from practical experience and that to the skeptical reader may appear farfetched.

The two components may also conflict with each other. In discussing coitus we shall first consider those conflicts which result from an anachronistic, excessive presence of birth elements in the sexual process. In the course of analytic work we often see the operation of regressive forces in disturbances; here disturbances are provoked by the premature invasion of progressive forces. A kind of separation of the components, which otherwise are joined together in a synthesis, takes place. However, in these progressive elements we shall always recognize the return of old regressive forces, which by a kind of attraction prematurely summon the progressive forces to a present situation.

Woman's frequent fear of coitus originates in the fact that it implies an injury to her physical integrity; it can be compared to man's fear of castration. Under special circumstances, the pain and masochistic character of the experience also mobilize destructive tendencies that lend this fear the character of the fear of death. In this connection, the following observation of an obsessive neurotic proved enlightening. This young woman constantly tormented herself with feelings of guilt; she accused herself of having caused the deaths of various relatives by acts of negligence. After she married and overcame the first difficulties of coitus, she achieved full orgastic gratification. But after achieving the orgastic eclipse of consciousness, she was

[6] COLETTE [pseud.]: Nuit blanche. In ASWELL, M. L. (ed): It's a woman's world New York: Whittlesey, 1944.

seized by the fear of never being able to awaken from this state. During each following coitus she convulsively watched herself in order "not to go too far," and as a result became frigid.   The destructive elements intensified her masochistic readiness and transformed her pleasure into fear of death.   Usually such a fear of death is mobilized only during childbirth or during the expectation of childbirth.   However, there are many women who cannot experience and enjoy the sexual act without conscious or unconscious ideas about childbirth, and in such cases the associative connection between the two acts has a disturbing effect.

Naturally, the justified fear of undesired pregnancy must not be termed pathologic, but it can produce the effect of a direct inhibition, particularly if it is obsessively exaggerated, as is often the case.   The other form of the conscious association with the reproductive function, the wish for a child, particularly if its fulfillment is beset with difficulties, can also exert an inhibiting effect on the orgasm and perhaps even make conception difficult.

The pathologic distortions of the normally unconscious association between coitus and birth usually escape direct observation, but psychoanalysis is familiar with them.   Let us study a case in which the influence of the two functions on each other was so manifest that it could be observed clinically.   The following history is an abstract from the hospital records in the case.

When admitted to the hospital, Mrs. Andrews was a 29-year-old married woman, the mother of six children.   Her chief complaints were of attacks of tachycardia, sweating, and palpitations.   In addition she had numerous other symptoms of an unmistakably neurotic character.   She had fits of anger toward her husband and children.

Overshadowing all her other life interests and emotions she had a constant anxiety regarding pregnancy, which tormented her night and day.   Even during intercourse she was obsessed by this idea, and she forced her husband to use several contraceptive methods simultaneously, although she refused to take

any preventive measures for her own part.   At the very first
interview she stated that she had been tormented by the fear of
pregnancy from her puberty on; nevertheless she had become
pregnant immediately after her marriage.

Her fears and the numerous pregnancies she had gone through
against her conscious will made her marital life stormy and unhappy.   She also had panic fears about her periods, and from
the time she had married had taken something almost every
month to bring the menses on, becoming frantic if they were
late.   She had been treated twice for ergot poisoning contracted
in the course of her desperate struggle against pregnancy.

What makes this woman's attitudes peculiar and morbid is
the fact that, despite her fear of pregnancy, her wish fantasy
centered constantly on being impregnated.   She made her
husband keep track of her periods and was furious when he
failed to do it.   Her feelings toward him were decidedly mixed.
On the one hand she looked forward to his coming home, and
on the other, when she thought of pregnancy, she was furious
with him and wanted to hurt him.   As a result of her obsession
she could not even listen to other women talking about pregnancy, because she immediately identified herself with them
and became terribly anxious.   She frequently fantasied that
she was in the delivery room, with her feet in the stirrups.   She
usually worked so hard on her job (outside her home) that when
her husband approached her sexually she could honestly say
that she was too tired.

She had one pregnancy after another and brought six children
into the world.   With each one she fought for an abortion,
raved against physicians who refused to comply with her demands, and several times managed to abort.

After each pregnancy she was filled with hatred for her husband and held him responsible.   She suffered from repeated
inflammations of the genitals, underwent a number of serious
operations, and yet became pregnant again and again.   She
even left her husband for a time, only to become pregnant as
soon as she returned to him.

Mrs. Andrews never had any real interest in her children or
in physical care of them.   She never nursed them and never

wanted to.   She never took care of them in any of their illnesses or in their physical needs at night.   Instead, it was the
husband who always got up and attended to them, and they
always called for him.   When she worked at night, her husband
gave the children their supper and put them to bed.   Throughout their married life he had done a great deal of the housework
and cooking.   She did not worry much about the children while
she was in the hospital.   The oldest girl now did much of the
housework.   Mrs. Andrews was upset, however, when her
children were sick, and exaggerated their illnesses and their
suffering in somewhat the same way in which she spoke of the
great pain she herself suffered during her pregnancies and
deliveries.   When she told of the abdominal operation her
second daughter had recently undergone, she clutched her own
abdomen and behaved as though she herself were being operated
on, screamed, and told the social worker that she was all mixed
up.   She was also disturbed by the appearance of her eldest
girl's first menstruation, to which she reacted as though it were
her own.

To gain a better insight into her psychology, we must
briefly review her life history.   She was of French descent.
Her parents never got along together.   Her mother had married her father for his money and their marital life was complicated by quarrels.   Mrs. Andrews was the oldest of five children, two girls and three boys.   Her father was a quiet, well
educated, likable man.   He worked for various firms as a
traveling salesman and buyer, and during his absences from
home, his wife—according to Mrs. Andrews—was unfaithful to
him.   When Mrs. Andrews was 6 years old, her mother was
believed to be having an affair with a much younger man.
After the birth of one of Mrs. Andrews' brothers, the neighborhood gossips whispered that he was not her father's child.
When Mrs. Andrews was 16 years old, her next brother was
born; she was very much upset because her mother would allow
only "a certain young man" to be present during her delivery,
which naturally strengthened the young girl's suspicion that
he was the child's father.

This young man dominated the home and disciplined the

children in the absence of the father. On many occasions the
patient suffered a good deal of physical abuse. Her mother was
nervous and irritable and frequently became so angry at the
children that she did not know what she was doing. The young
man was the chief support of the home. The father was more
or less resigned to the situation, until the mother started a new
relationship with another young man. There followed a good
deal of rivalry between the two lovers. This time the father
left for a longer period. In speaking of the severe discipline to
which she was subjected, the patient said that she and her siblings were always cut up and bruised because the mother and
her lover used to beat them with a strap soaked in oil. Once
they beat her sister until she could not rise from the floor. If
the patient disobeyed them, they called a policeman friend, who
threatened to send her to a reformatory. Until she was 13 or
14 years of age the patient and her sister were forbidden to go
out and had to be in bed at 6 p.m.

In our interviews we learned that Mrs. Andrews felt a deep
aggressive hatred for her mother, that she held a deep grudge
against her for her extramarital relationships, that she had
strong emotional reactions to her mother's deliveries, and that
she harbored a jealous hatred of her mother's lovers and her two
younger brothers.

She was in constant conflict with her mother's second lover
and certainly provoked him to beat her. It is difficult to decide
whether she was actually maltreated or whether her childhood
experiences were partly a product of her fantasy. At any rate
she began to display neurotic traits at an early age, in the form
of violent tantrums during which she screamed and threw things.
She suffered from fainting spells, nightmares, and several times
ran away from home.

During her childhood she never liked dolls, but preferred to
play Indians and cowboys. In grammar school she captained
the baseball teams. She fought a great deal in school and on
one occasion was expelled. She said that she had never desired children, but always pictured herself as a professional
woman, for example as a schoolteacher. She was always ambi-

tious and resented having to leave school at 16, when her family found her a job. At this time her father was out of work and the girl had to contribute to the family income.

She worked steadily from then on, even after her marriage at 18. Her pregnancies represented the only interruptions in her work. First she went to work as a seamstress and had a job in a drugstore in the evenings. After her marriage she did factory work, sometimes on day shifts, sometimes on a night shift. She insisted on getting out as much work as a man, which meant accomplishing more than the other women in the factory, and was also chairman of a trade union local, which took up a great deal of her energy. She loved to give the employers a good fight and to make stump speeches.

On the ward the patient was very anxious and greatly agitated for the first few days; she walked restlessly up and down, ran her fingers through her hair, and twisted her hands during the interviews. Acute anxiety attacks occurred whenever the question of pregnancy was discussed. At other times she was pleasant, smiling, cheerful, cooperative, warm, and friendly. She said that when she was pregnant she thought of dying, insisted that she needed an operation for repairs, and also asked to be sterilized. She had two menstrual periods while on the ward; before each she was terribly agitated and depressed.

Mrs. Andrews' whole past life had a hysterical character, as evidenced by her dramatic collapses, fainting spells, slight twilight states, impulsive running away, etc. Most of the bodily sensations she produced at the time of her hospitalization, such as feeling her heart "turning over," palpitations, gastrointestinal disorders, dizziness, sweating, were also hysterical.

We were able to gain an insight into the psychic processes that caused these manifestations. In the course of time it became clear that the patient's fear of pregnancy was bound up with a fear of death based principally upon a hysterical identification. The object of identification was sometimes her grandmother, who died of heart disease (a substitute for her mother), or some other woman with whom in her fantasy she would live through the dangers of childbirth. Her tendency to identify her own person with that of another pregnant woman often created a confusing impression; this was dispelled when one realized that all these women were substitutes for one woman—her mother—who was the basis of the identification. For example, Mrs. Andrews told us that during her first pregnancy she used to wake up in a sweat, thinking that an "Indian woman" was having a baby. (The Indian woman here was the "strange" woman whom we meet so often in the dreams and fantasies of our patients. She is a mother figure represented by a contrast that expresses the thought, "It is not the most familiar woman—my mother—it is a strange woman.") Mrs. Andrews said: "I can stand any kind of sickness, but if a woman is having a baby I can't go anywhere near the place." She was always upset when talking about a woman who was going to have a baby: "I do not want to hear about it or talk about it or see it."

The compulsive identification with her mother and the repudiation of this identification were often quite conscious in her. She told us that she tried to make herself different from her mother, to do things just opposite to those her mother did, but herself acknowledged that for some reason she had to be like her mother. Of her temper tantrums she said: "That's my mother," and again, "My mother always bossed my father and what I disliked so much in my mother I've imposed on my own husband. My mother never wanted to have children either."

Yet the mother had had several children and this fact was probably the strongest reason for Mrs. Andrews' pregnancy obsession.

Closer examination showed that Mrs. Andrews' neurosis was not purely hysterical. She herself described her symptoms in a manner characteristic of obsessions when she said: "I have one side pulling one way and one another."

She would have an idea, then doubt it. She was always in a conflict about religion, etc. She did not know whether she cared for her husband or not. Sometimes she adored her children, at other times she did not care for them at all. Another obsessional symptom was her urge to "plan." She said: "I went haywire with my first pregnancy because I had not planned it.

Planning matters beforehand gave her a feeling of security, freedom from anxiety. If things were not planned, she felt terrified and did not know what would happen. Such an attitude is typical of obsessional neurotics. This patient's obsessional-neurotic conflicts, however, were activated by a certain group of emotionally charged ideas related to the problems of pregnancy. The conflict between the impulsive urge to become pregnant and the anxious repudiation of this wish was at the heart of her obsessions. The yes and no of the question of pregnancy dominated her thinking and her emotional life.

However, this battle between opposites did not have the usual character of obsessional neurosis, in which the struggle of ambivalence is played out in the mind, tormenting the patient with the question "Shall I or shall I not become pregnant?" As far as her thinking was concerned, our patient answered this question with a consistent "No." The "Yes" disappeared from her thinking and made itself felt in an indirect and much more complicated manner. It was hidden behind the conditions that the patient demanded in the sexual act. She could experience pleasure and orgasm only if she had the idea that the semen was entering her body freely. She longed for coitus and was very impulsive in demanding it. One definitely felt that this was not an expression of a real erotic need or of sexual attraction to her husband, but of an intense desire to receive the semen into her body in order to be impregnated. The compulsive character of the whole process is confirmed by the fact that her satisfaction in the sexual act was disturbed by the anxiety-producing thought "I do not want to become pregnant."

Though the material produced by the patient is used here to illustrate a specific problem, we must not forget that—as is usually the case—it had multiple determinants. Thus I conjecture that one of the conditions of her sexual enjoyment was that she herself must take the masculine role. This masculinity was manifested in all her behavior—in her childhood games, in her replacement of her father as the family bread

winner during her adolescence, in her satisfaction with her
professional activity, in her ambitions, in her tendency actively
and aggressively to represent her comrades in labor struggles,
and above all in the reversal of roles in her home, where her
husband performed the duties of housekeeper and nurse while
she herself was the family supporter.   She even wanted her husband to keep track of her periods, as though not she but he were
menstruating.   Characteristically, she used her occupation as an
escape from femininity, which she identified with being pregnant.
She also associated the process of parturition with humiliation:
"Woman's most degrading position is on the delivery table,
with her feet in the stirrups and men taking charge of her."

The intensified sensation of her husband's ejaculation, as we
have often observed in other cases, produced in her the feeling
that she possessed the male organ and that her orgasm produced the seminal fluid.

Many things that the patient spontaneously told us about her
childhood helped us to understand her neurosis.   Her mother
was twice made pregnant by her lovers.   To the first of these
pregnancies, the patient, then 8 years old, obviously reacted with
organic symptoms similar to her later ones.   She had outbursts
of rage against her mother and provoked her mother's lover to
beat her (or fantasied that he beat her).   We may surmise that
even then she had pregnancy fantasies and that her anger and
aggression against her mother at that time laid the foundations
for her later fear of pregnancy and death.   In this connection
the patient told me repeatedly that her mother wished that she
(the patient) might die in giving birth to her first child.   This
fantasied curse of the mother is well known to us, in the anxieties of women in their first pregnancies, as the converse of the
child's death wish in regard to the pregnant mother.

During the patient's puberty, her mother again had an illegitimate pregnancy, and this time the girl attempted to resolve
her severe conflict at home by becoming extremely active and
supporting her family, particularly the newborn child, by her
work.   This was obviously a flight into activity, which did not,
however, enable her to avert the fate she was trying to escape.

She very soon became pregnant by the husband whom she did not love. Later she tried quite consciously to avoid the feminine fate of her compulsive pregnancies by the same device of overactivity, but met with the same negative results, because her unconscious urges proved stronger.

Observation of her symptoms showed that we were justified in assuming that her then still active unconscious wish for pregnancy found expression in bodily symptoms, and that specified sensations, such as belching, a feeling of pressure in the rectum, sensations of swelling, etc., expressed this unconscious fantasy.

Another type of symptom formation in our patient related to her fluctuations in mood. She was at times elated, clearly manic. This was sometimes followed by depressive states that lent her behavior the character of a manic-depressive condition.

Observation of the patient indicated that the manic phase represented joy over the onset of menstruation. One was inclined to take this joy at its face value, particularly because before her menstruation the patient was observed to be anxious and tense. But the quantitative manifestation, the lack of control, the plus, went beyond the limits of a normal reaction.

Recalling that the patient felt herself to be under her mother's curse invoking death for her in childbirth, we are justified in assuming that her manic joy related to her release not only from the fear of pregnancy but also from the threat of death.

The clinical problem of the wide variety of her neurotic symptoms ceased to be a problem when we understood these various symptoms as different expressions of the same conflict. This conflict always related to pregnancy. Even when pregnancy was really experienced, really desired, and really feared, it was none the less the fantasied pregnancy of childhood, with all its impossibility of realization, its infantile theories and identification, its turning of the aggressions against the individual's own ego, its fear of death, etc.

These infantile wishes and anxieties were combated with three kinds of weapons—obsessional-neurotic, hysterical, and manic-depressive symptoms, which were, however, all directed against the same inner enemy and served the same masters. We may compare the situation to a battle in which the goal is one and the same but the weapons used are guns, ships, and airplanes.

What most interests us in Mrs. Andrew's case is her peculiar relation to coitus and childbirth. All her symptoms seemed to originate in the fact that the identity coitus-impregnation-birth assumed a morbid character in her, because she originally made it under extremely unfavorable conditions—first as a child and later as a pubescent girl, in connection with the births of her allegedly illegitimate brothers, which were disastrous for her. Her wish to become pregnant was compulsive and no preventive measures were of any avail. She yearned for orgasms but could experience them only at the moment of the man's ejaculation—that is to say, only if they were accompanied by the idea of impregnation and later delivery. As a result of her aggressive reactions against her mother, this idea was each time also associated with death.

Mrs. Andrews' case is a pathologic illustration of my theory that woman psychologically perceives coitus as the beginning of a process that culminates in delivery. The identity of the sexual act with impregnation and birth appears so often in the fantasy life of women that one feels that the psychologic phenomena are deeply rooted in biologic factors in which the sexual experience and the service to the species are united. This identity is manifested in the double function of the vagina, and in the analogies of the physiologic innervation in coitus and in birth. This identity also manifests itself in the identical symbolism of the two functions. Childhood theories about sexual matters usually prepare this connection by identifying the sexual act with impregnation. Our patient also seemed to cling to infantile theories, for she asked the doctor: "Can one become pregnant from a kiss?" Or she would say, "It's as if the impregnating germs were flying around in the air."

These remarks were meant as jokes, but they were highly significant.

The two components, coitus and birth, must be in a dynamic (and quantitative), harmonious relation to each other. In our patient the idea of birth (and death) disengaged itself obsessively from the whole and dominated the sexual situation in a pathologic manner. Later we shall see that the idea of death, which broke through here anachronistically, always lurks in the mind during birth, and under certain circumstances becomes obsessive, as it did in our patient.

"You will die in childbirth . . . you will die in childbirth," says Anna Karenina's guilt feeling in her dreams. In Mrs. Andrews the curse of her mother—"You will die in giving birth to your first child"—appeared for similar reasons not only in dreams but also at the moment of desired sexual pleasure.

In every ecstasy conflicts are temporarily resolved, disappointments forgotten, unfulfilled wishes of the past and hopes for the future fulfilled. In the most primitive form of ecstasy, the orgasm, one can learn, by analyzing the interwoven strands, which of the wishes relating to the past and future are experienced as fulfilled. In the light of psychoanalysis, the sexual act assumes an immense, dramatic, and profoundly cathartic significance for the woman—but this only under the condition that it is experienced in a feminine, dynamic way and is not transformed into an act of erotic play or sexual "equality."

The biologically determined childhood development of every human being, man or woman, is marked by a chain of difficulties that must be overcome, and that produce a number of traumas that later have more or less powerful effects. At best, they leave behind a traumatic disposition, that is to say, every new difficulty in life mobilizes the old, unresolved remnants and adds them to the new conflict, or refreshes the traumatic properties of the old difficulties.

The first trauma common to all humans, the birth trauma, is the never overcome reaction to the separation from the original union with the mother.

Anyone who has gained insight into the deepest layers of the human psyche can ascertain empirically that not only our anxieties but also all our longings and aspirations for perfection and eternity, the flight from death and the yearning for death, the torments of love and the wish for solitude, the symbols of dreams and delirious fantasies, express the idea of the original unity with the mother and the striving to restore it.

The second traumatic situation stems from the necessary loss of the gratification the child receives in the first phases of his life, the oral gratification, so named because the essential interest of this phase is feeding and because the mouth is the organ through which the child receives care, love, and contact with life. We explain the trauma of this phase on the basis of the separation of the child from the mother's breast. It seems, however, that what is involved here is not so much the breast as the intimate relationship with the mother, the preservation of the unity secured through nursing.

The necessary renunciation of this effortless and pleasurable gratification of the instinct of self-preservation is known as the weaning trauma. The two traumatic situations mentioned here are characterized by the biologically determined separation from the mother and the cruel destruction of the unity between the subject and the environment, the boundless union between the I and the you.

The third great trauma is only woman's; I have called it the genital trauma (vol. 1). It stems from a biologic inhibition and manifests itself psychologically as the penis envy.

Man's most primitive needs and highest aspirations contain energies striving for the restoration of the original unity with the mother. In the ecstasy of the sexual act, the emotional boundaries between the I and the you disappear. Through the physiologic act of penetration, the bodily unity is really achieved, and the birth trauma is symbolically healed. Under the active stimulation of the penis, the vagina, in complete analogy innervationally with the suckling's mouth, now assumes in the depth of the unconscious the passive function of sucking, thus endowing the penis with the symbolic significance of the mother's breast. The weaning trauma is offset symbolically with the help of the physiologic analogy.

The genital trauma can be healed to a great extent, for in the physical situation of the sexual act the problem of the developmental phase of woman in which she was confronted with the inferiority of having neither a penis nor a vagina, is really eliminated. Now she has both: she receives the penis and discovers the vagina as a functioning organ.

In later reproductive functions we shall see clearer and more dramatic repetitions of and compensations for the past.

The feminine woman, who is characterized by her struggle for a harmonious accord between the narcissistic forces of self-love and the masochistic forces of dangerous and painful giving, celebrates her greatest triumphs in her sexual functioning. In the sexual act her partner's elemental desire gratifies her self-love and helps her to accept masochistic pleasure without damaging her ego, while the psychologic promise of a child creates a satisfying future prospect for both tendencies.

CHAPTER FIVE

Problems of Conception: Psychologic Prerequisites of Pregnancy

THE problems of woman's reproductive function are complex and we shall achieve greater clarity if we study them in chronologic order. Thus, before taking up the psychology of pregnancy in greater detail, we shall turn our attention to its prerequisite, fecundation.

Successful fecundation presupposes fertility, which exists only during a definite period in woman's life. In our civilization this period is bounded by the ages of 16 and 50. It is associated with definite bodily processes that are determined physiologically and anatomically. The entire internal-secretory physiologic process that prepares for fecundation is probably a psychosomatic unit in all its phases and is constantly influenced by both the psychic and the organic life. The function of the hormones as "chemical messengers"—this term is often used— is in all probability constantly influenced by psychic factors. This complicated messenger service is highly organized, with a central station, branches, interactions, and separate functions; it extends to the organs situated far from the original source of the message as well as to the immediately adjacent organs. Determination of the spot in the route of the messenger service in which a psychogenic disturbance may be taking place is usually a physiologic problem.

When we refer to psychologic difficulties of conception, we mean that the given woman's inability to become a mother has psychic causes that have disturbed some part of the physiologic process. Modern medicine recognizes that various disturbances of the bodily functions, especially where no organic reason for them can be discovered, are in causal connection with psychic disturbances. Such an involvement of psychologic factors is generally assumed in the development of gynecologic functional disorders. The psychic influence here affects especially the hormonal factors.

Seen as a functional disorder, psychogenic sterility in woman is a very complicated and stubborn phenomenon; its initial cause is usually difficult to discover, even though modern methods of investigation can find the disturbances in the hormonal messenger service. Yet, strikingly enough, the symptom (sterility) frequently persists despite favorable treatment of the hormonal defect, because—in our opinion—it continues to be ted by psychic energies. Vice versa, psychologic treatment proves ineffective if it is opposed by incorrigible organic factors (even if originally these latter were psychically determined).

Although the various psychologic tendencies that under certain circumstances may lead to sterility appear with greater clarity and plasticity in the processes of pregnancy, delivery, and motherhood, it seems appropriate to survey the psychic factors that can prevent pregnancy before dealing with the later processes.

We have seen that for the normal, healthy woman coitus psychologically represents the first act of motherhood. Difficulties of conception resulting from disturbing psychic factors can appear directly in the mechanical aspects of coitus without the complicated detour of hormonal disorders. The innervation process can be influenced psychically in such a way that the woman by means of precise muscular motions succeeds in mechanically preventing the sperm from entering her body. In such cases, the woman attributes her excessive secretion of fluid to her masculine partner's clumsiness or to a peculiarity of her vaginal glands. She remains completely unconscious of the psychic influences involved. Usually, however, sterility stems from more complicated sources. Correct insight into the processes of the sexual act helps us to understand many a case of sterility caused by a psychogenic difficulty of conception. This does not mean that we hold the course of the act responsible for the failure to conceive; but the act often supplies us with a clue to the given woman's whole psychic preparation and to the structure of her psychic personality, especially to that psychic component which is directly connected with reproduction.[1]

We have analyzed woman's sexual act and studied its component parts—sexual gratification and the first act of motherhood, feminine giving and taking, energetic sucking-like intake and gentle expulsion, the will to be a child herself, motherly tenderness toward the man-child, feminine-erotic readiness for adjustment, and competing aggressive independence. We know that deep in the unconscious, associative bridges between coitus and the act of birth are hidden.   All this forms a psychologically closed circle, partly real and partly symbolic—the beginning and the end of the reproductive service.   Each of these components, when taken out of the synthetic unity of the circle, can become a peace breaker with regard to the sexual act or the reproductive function or both.   Predominance of giving, that is to say, of passivity, may restrict woman's active participation in the sexual process, and we do not know what amount of activity on the part of the woman is required for conception; excessively strong taking may be associated with simultaneous aggressive expulsion, or the motherly component may be entirely spent on the man and may divert the wish for the child and its conception.   On the other hand, a woman who is emotionally unprepared to grant her sexual partner the maternal tenderness that involves such great—perhaps the greatest—gratification for herself, begins her pregnancy in an unmaternal way, even though she may later compensate for this deficiency in her relation to her child.   We have mentioned that such a maternal attitude is probably necessary for the harmonious course of the sexual act, but that it does not always lead to orgastic gratification and sometimes even inhibits it.   The conflict between the woman's individual pleasure experience and service to the species can thus begin in the sexual act.   Her idea of the reproductive function may come too strongly into consciousness (as in the case of Mrs. Andrews)

[1] I do not discuss here the psychology of conscious birth control.   For a treatment of this problem, cf. MENNINGER, K.: Psychiatric aspects of contraception, Bull.Menninger Clin., vol. 7, 1943; IDEM: Love against hate, New York: Harcourt, 1942.

and influence sexual pleasure; or unconscious fears connected with reproduction may have an indirect inhibiting effect.

It may also happen that although the sexual act is fully gratifying, such ideas of reproduction, successfully suppressed in favor of the pleasure experience, may act all the more powerfully internally and become a psychic influence for sterility; in other cases they appear only later, during pregnancy, and lead to complications.

I recall a 28-year-old woman who suffered from depression and states of inhibition. She had been married for several years, and from the beginning her relations with her husband had taken an unfavorable form, although she had married him out of love, after a long period of friendship. Later she even felt an insurmountable aversion to him that seemed wholly unjustified by any real facts. She stayed married only because of the great gratification she obtained in her sexual relations with her husband. Her orgasms were extraordinarily gratifying; according to her description, she experienced them in full consciousness, but had the impression that she was not herself: she felt as though she were living in a different world, "as though in heaven." Her husband lost his real significance in the act, and she seemed to merge with him in a marvelous unity alien to the rest of her being. After these orgasms, she explained, there followed immediately a feeling of emptiness, solitude, and estrangement from her husband and a depression that was interrupted only by the next intercourse.

This patient's state of mind was all the more surprising because usually a woman achieves full readiness for sexual gratification only when she loves and respects her partner and feels an erotic interest in him during intervals free of sexual tension. Analytic observation revealed the mechanisms that led to her peculiar behavior. Her sexual gratification could be achieved for the very reason that she depreciated her husband in the intervals between intercourse by depriving him of his fatherly-tender role and punished herself, in her depressions, for the various forbidden and suppressed wishes that she fulfilled unconsciously during the ecstasy of intercourse. Her painful renunciation of tender love and her self-punishment through suffering were prerequisites for her achievement of pleasure. As a result of this spacing in time, she could experience the sexual act with almost supernormal pleasure. Her reaction of disappointment began immediately after the state of tension was over. But her renunciation and self-punishment were most profoundly expressed in the fact that her ardent but unconscious wish for a child remained unfulfilled. This fact was also the core of her depression. She felt that she had no right to receive a child from a tenderly loved man, and she did not want a child from a devaluated and unloved man. Thus she nad nothing left in life but sexual pleasure, which she experienced in a state of depersonalization (as though she were not herself), because her real ego was absorbed in the repressed and forbidden motherhood. In her case, an unconscious but deep sense of guilt became the cause of psychogenic sterility.

Another illustration is offered by an obsessive-neurotic patient of mine who remained childless after being married for five years. After a fairly long psychoanalytic treatment, her severe neurotic symptoms markedly regressed. Although all the psychic material clearly showed that her sterility was a partial manifestation of her illness, and was connected with the severe sense of guilt so characteristic of obsessional neurotics, no noticeable change occurred with respect to fecundation. Shortly before the end of her analysis she fell gravely ill of pneumonia, which almost caused her death. A few months after her recovery she became pregnant. Those who ascribe great importance to somatic factors might be inclined to explain this occurrence as due to physical circumstances connected with her pneumonia. But to the patient and myself it was clear that the threat of death acting as a punishment, and the expiation of her guilt feeling through her suffering, supplied a therapeutic reinforcement that made possible the final success that could not be achieved by analysis alone.

In cases psychologically less complicated, unconscious feelings of guilt also frequently cause psychogenic sterility. In every woman's psychic life the idea of the child plays an enormous part, and this is true in all the phases of her development and maturity. We have seen that woman's valuation of her own body and the fear of punishment related to it are transferred from the genitals to the inside of the body and thence to the child. Instead of man's fear of castration, we have in woman the death fears connected with childbirth and the fears for her child. But long before the wish for a child is realized, the obscure anxiety-laden idea "I will never have a child" is present, and this idea, stemming from various fears, serves chiefly to gratify punitive psychic tendencies.

In this process we see the dynamism underlying the identification of the penis and the child, which at first sight appears so absurd. In his idea of his organ, man connects already enjoyed and always expected pleasure with the obscure unconscious urge to reproduction; and the fear of loss of the organ—the fear of castration—relates to both these goals. The deepest root of this fear is, as we know, the sense of guilt. In woman, the anticipation of sexual pleasure is connected with the dynamically much stronger wish for a child, and the threat of loss and fear of punishment are transferred to the idea of the child.

The symbolic agency of this punishment, the "witch," exerts much greater influence on woman's sterility than is generally suspected by gynecologists. I know of numerous cases in which the Black Madonna of Czestochowa (Poland) asserted her supernatural power against the witch and helped barren women to conceive children. Psychotherapeutists, especially women, are often able to influence their patients before the rational effects of scientific treatment have manifested themselves. At the risk of injuring our own professional pride, we must admit that such seemingly irrational interventions are often more reliable in cases of psychogenic sterility than the long drawn out reconstruction of the patient's psychic personality by an analyst.

Many gynecologists who treat sterility by physical methods admit the part played by psychic influences, but insist that these are only secondary. In many cases, however, the opposite is true. Physical treatment actually plays the part of liberating punishment, permission, or some other psychologic factor, and it is this factor that is often of primary importance in achieving a successful result.

From my own psychoanalytic experience I can define specific types of psychogenic sterility. But I wish to emphasize that every form of psychogenic sterility is only relative, that is to say, it can be eliminated if the psychic conditions are changed (provided the organic situation permits), and that the same psychic factors may manifest themselves only in later phases of the reproductive function without disturbing its first phase, fecundation. In such cases the energy of the germ plasm proves stronger than the counteracting psychic tendencies.

In general, it can be said that the most frequent cause of sterility is unconscious fear. This fear may relate not only to the reproductive function, but to everything sexual, thus eliminating any possibility of physical motherhood by exclusion of the sexual experience.

The sources of this fear are manifold, and puberal experiences seem to play a great part in its later effects (cf. case history of Molly and its analysis, vol. 1). Its principal element is the sense of guilt, which usually derives from the deeper unconscious sources of psychic life. But we must not forget the case of Mrs. Andrews, which shows us in a very instructive manner that the same kind of fear, instead of functioning as a warning signal, can be a condition for pleasurable experience of intercourse, and thus lead to a result opposite to sterility, that is to say, to compulsive conceptions.

With these reservations, I shall now define several types of psychogenic sterility on the basis of my own observations.

1. One type is found in the physically and psychologically infantile woman, who, despite her normally functioning reproductive organs, seems to exclude the idea of motherhood even in its natural habitat.[2] She is small and dainty and always needs someone to lean upon. At first she leans upon her mother

[2] Cf. WITTKOWER, E., AND WILSON, A. T. M.: Dysmenorrhea and sterility: Personality Studies, Brit. M. J., vol. 2, 1940; WITTKOWER, E.: New developments in the investigation and treatment of sterility, Proc. Roy. Soc. Med., vol. 36, 1943.

or father (usually the former), then upon her husband. Usually she is vaginally frigid; nevertheless she enjoys sexual intercourse a great deal. Her sexual organ was and remains the clitoris, but she knows how to handle the situation in such a way that her vaginal "unawakenedness" disturbs neither herself nor her husband. She insatiably demands proofs of tenderness, and her own tenderness is that of a child, not of a mother. In many cases, such women long before marriage—usually in puberty—develop physical symptoms that we regard as typical manifestations of pregnancy fantasies. These include vomiting, tendency to swellings, painful sensations in various organs, with typical transferences from upper to lower ones (or vice versa) and from inside to outside (and vice versa), desire for operations, and, above all, eating disturbances of all kinds, including anorexia nervosa.

When confronted later with the possibility of realizing these fantasies, this type of woman proves completely incapable of it. She remains immature, tormented by fears, and often her main interest in life is the treatment of her sterility. Sometimes she conceives after many years, more under the influence of events in her life that make her more mature than of the various treatments to which she has subjected herself. Often she conceives, only to transfer her psychic difficulties to the later phases of the reproductive function.

In psychosomatic medicine there is a tendency to ascribe certain organic disturbances to definite personality types. The type of sterile woman discussed here would fit into such a scheme, were it not for the fact that this same type, with similar bodily and psychic characteristics, is found among women who conceive with particular facility and bring forth many children in quick succession; I have often had opportunity to observe this type of mother. Obscurely realizing her immaturity and lack of motherliness, such a woman tries with the help of reality to grow into the role that she consciously wishes very much to play. Often she belongs to a circle of young women who are all more or less of the same type and goad one another into competing for motherhood.

2. A diametrically opposite type is that of the woman who,

although endowed with all the qualities of motherliness, remains sterile for psychic reasons.   If we observe her sexual personality as manifested in coitus, we find that she is of the type that achieves the greatest gratification in tender giving and motherly embraces.   The physical and psychic structure of this woman is almost the exact opposite of that of our first type; what both have in common is the inability to conceive.

The type of woman we are now discussing spends her rich motherliness on her love for her husband; guided by profound feminine intuition, she feels that he does not and cannot want a child.   His love for her is based on her motherliness: he needs her for himself, for his aims, his prosperity, his achievements. If she is ripe for motherhood, he is not ripe for fatherhood; he is often an introverted artist or scholar, still (or always) restless, who needs a mother and freedom from responsibility in order to develop further or even to be what he is.   His motherly wife senses the dangers threatening him through fatherhood and renounces the child out of love for him.   Her instinct of self-preservation also warns her against the burdens she would have to assume if she made an unfatherly man the father of her children.   Moreover, she sees the erotic harmony of her marriage threatened in the event of her pregnancy, not because she opposes eroticism to motherhood in herself, nor because she fears loss of her attractiveness, but because her husband's erotic capacity would not stand up in face of real motherhood in her.

The man, although he loves a motherly woman, sets a definite limit to her motherliness; exceeding this limit involves dangers for him.   Thus there are men who choose motherly women for their love partners, but become impotent when their wives are pregnant, or later after the children are born.   In some cases that I have observed, such men fled from their homes in a panic when their wives became pregnant.   In one case, the husband vanished for several years; in two others, the beginning signs of acute alcoholism appeared in the husbands at this time.

The motherly woman is more or less consciously aware of such dangers and wards them off by unconsciously influencing her ability to conceive.   The current belief that a man matures by achieving fatherhood is usually invalid in such cases, and more often than not an intuitive grasp of the situation on the part of the wife can be relied upon. On the other hand, the woman's unconscious distrust of her husband's capacity for fatherhood sometimes proves unjustified. In two instances I observed couples who decided to adopt children; the women took this step because they did not want to remain childless any longer, the men because they lovingly respected their wives' wishes. In both cases, the husbands—to their own and their wives' surprise—reacted to the adopted children with great tenderness and pride, and grew more ambitious in their work and more attached to their wives. In both cases the women became pregnant less than a year after the adoptions. One of these two women told me: "I would never have believed that my husband could be such a good father. If I had, I might have become a mother earlier." Such changes in the psychologic situation are often decisive in removing the cause of relative sterility (cf. chap. xi).

The type of women discussed here must not be confused with the motherly woman, described in chapter ii, who avoids physical motherhood and directs her motherliness into other channels (the midwife, Aunt Tula, etc.). In the latter the protective mechanism has developed a long time before and is present in early youth, so that physical motherhood is completely avoided. This type tries to sidestep the conflict by renouncing sexuality and gratifying maternal feelings with secondhand motherhood. The sterile woman whom we classify as our second type is completely willing to be a real mother and her sterility is a kind of secondary adjustment to her husband. Modern medical practice requires that gynecologists in treating sterile women take the husbands' generative processes into account. Usually physicians content themselves with establishing the fact of the husband's potency and of normal behavior of his sperm. But in many cases it seems as important to examine the husband's psychologic make-up as it is to investigate the wife's. And usually, if we are to gain a clear psychologic picture, it is not enough to know that the couple want a child and have a satisfactory relationship with each other.

3. The third type is represented by the woman who often

is diverted from motherhood by other interests, although, like
the second type, she may possess great capacity for motherliness.   I propose to divide this type into two subtypes:

  a) The feminine-erotic woman who fears the competition of
      motherhood with her warm, rich erotic life. All her
      motherliness is consumed in the fire of erotic love. Her
      type is particularly close to the second type, without being
      identical with it.
  b) The woman who devotes her life to an ideology or another
      emotionally determined interest. Here belong those
      women who play a part in great revolutionary movements,
      the artists, scientists, etc. They are not averse to mother-
      hood, they often long for children, but they unconsciously
      avoid the conflict that might result from a split in their
      affective interests, and thus remain sterile.

   4. A very frequent type is the masculine-aggressive woman
who refuses to accept femininity. She may remain sterile, but
usually her active-aggressive striving asserts itself here too, and
she often has many children. She succeeds in finding an outlet
for her aggressiveness in pregnancy and motherhood.

   5. Finally there is the emotionally disturbed woman who
fears additional emotional burdens and remains sterile not
because she has found an outlet for her feelings elsewhere, but
because she perceives the poverty of her own emotional life.
Like our first type, she tries in many cases to overcome her
deficiency by means of frequent pregnancies and numerous
children.

   As occurs in all attempts at classification, these types are not
pure, their characteristics often merge. Moreover, as I have
said, the difficulties of conception can lead to a shift in behavior
in an opposite direction. For this reason, we shall encounter
all these women again in discussing the later phases of reproduction.

   Many other types of sterile women could be established.
Furthermore, there are cases of psychogenic sterility that have
purely individual explanations, as for instance the following.
A young woman was childless after four years of marriage. She

was the elder of two children; her brother was one year younger than she.   Brought up in an exceptionally cultured milieu, both brother and sister had had a definite ideology and definite life tasks from their childhood on.   The boy was supposed to enter the ministry, as his father had; the girl was to become an intelligent, educated, feminine mother.   Common family plans were often made, in which the girl figured as the mother of numerous children and her parents as happy grandparents. This plan seemed to promise realization, but was frustrated by the fact that the brother married before the sister and soon brought a child into his parents' home.   The girl, who until then had brilliantly compensated her competitive feelings toward her brother by her femininity, had a neurotic collapse because her brother had outstripped her in achieving the special goal of parenthood.   She married hastily to compete with her brother, but he had a head start; gradually she formed an attitude that can be defined thus: "Since you have usurped my role, I will assume yours."

She conceived intellectual ambitions, felt inferior, and, already very neurotic, tried to transfer the arena of her struggle to her own body.   In order to minimize its feminine character, she stopped eating; her menstruation was interrupted, and she developed anorexia nervosa, with fits of ravenous hunger during which she unconsciously tried to realize the typical infantile idea of pregnancy by absorbing the fecundation material through the mouth.   Because she realized her pregnancy fantasies through compulsive eating, and because she harmed herself physically by combating her femininity, she did not become pregnant, although she was obsessed by the desire for a child.   A large number of similar examples could be cited.

We justly ascribe psychic difficulties to the destructive forces in the human soul.   For instance, when we are dealing with a sterile woman's relation to her husband, it is easy to assume that her hatred, indifference, jealousy, her fear of the effect of pregnancy on the harmony of her marital relationship, etc., are the cause of her sterility.   But sometimes, although not often, one encounters a married couple, ardently in love, who experience great happiness in their love relation and feel a constant urge to make it even more perfect: they wish for a child, yet are unconsciously compelled to renounce the fulfillment of this wish.   Realization seems to be prevented by their unconscious fear that their harmony will be disturbed, that fate might be tempted to turn against them if they had an excess of good fortune; this is the old mythical fear of the revenge of the gods.

An endless number of variations, types, individual histories, etc., could be adduced to illustrate the reasons for psychogenic sterility.   In former years the task of psychiatrists and psychoanalysts was in a sense easier.   A reliable gynecologist would declare that physically everything was in order and that the therapeutic task was now entirely the psychiatrist's.   But the latter's efforts were not always crowned with success and he alone bore all of the responsibility for failure.   It is certainly better to have a companion in misfortune in this respect.   However, with the immense advance of the science of hormones, the two methods of treatment and investigation often clash and occasionally interfere with each other.   Gynecologists now are not so ready to declare that everything is in order; they attempt more and more frequently to explain sterility on the basis of defective functioning of one or more hormonal factors, and their attitude toward the psychiatrist is one of deprecation and rejection or, at best, tolerant forbearance.   They turn to the rejected psychiatrist only if their own failures leave them unsatisfied.

Even if sterility is often—and perhaps in most cases—determined psychically, there still remains to be answered the vexatious question: How does the physical result come about, where does the psychic factor intervene in order to assert itself in this form?   The science of hormones still owes us an answer to this question, and it promises to give us a certain one in the future. Neither has the priority of the organic as against the psychic cause been clearly established as yet.   Does a definite hormonal disturbance create a predisposition to certain psychic reactions, paving a way for them, or do psychic elements provoke a hormonal disturbance through the detour of the autonomic nervous system? The important practical question is: To what extent can somatic disturbances, whether psychogenically determined or not, be cured by psychotherapeutic intervention? Possibly, the therapy of the future is in the hands of somatic medicine, but we feel that the chances of success in this field will be increased if psychology can help medicine to find its way in the psychic elements. For the time being, the two sciences march separately and strike together—somewhat after the fashion of the allies in the present war.

I have discussed the problem of sterility from the aspect of inability to conceive or difficulty of conception. Several other related questions will be discussed later, such as psychogenic abortions, secondary reactions to sterility, etc. However, one problem, because it seems diametrically opposed to that of sterility, calls for immediate discussion. I refer to the numerous cases of quasicompulsive readiness for fecundation, to what might be termed "overfertility" in women. It may seem incredible or even absurd that psychologically this condition is as close to abnormality as sterility. Theoretically, the normal and ideal condition of fertility in woman is this: conception follows her first intercourse, a child is born after the regular period of gestation, and the same process is repeated just about every year until the end of the woman's sexual life. But among humans this scheme undergoes far reaching changes, even without conscious, voluntary influence. Fecundation in the first coitus is rare, and woman's reproductive powers are only exceptionally used to the fullest during her years of sexual activity. In addition to voluntary control of fertility, unconscious inhibitive psychic influence certainly plays an important part in these "phenomena of degeneration," as they would be termed from the point of view of sociology or biology.

It seems that voluntary control and "degeneration," that is to say, the processes by which fertility has moved away from the above described ideal condition, have gradually led to a readjustment and reduction of woman's service to the species. For the time being it looks as though woman's social situation will further this movement—until new changes begin to operate in a different direction. Biology and the psychology of the unconscious will play their part here.

Within the framework of the existing state of affairs, what may biologically be an ideal condition may paradoxically become a manifestation of abnormality. Thus there are women whose fertility defies every attempt to reduce it, and who are constantly taxed to the limits of their physiologic potentialities by the business of reproduction. Their entire emotional interest is devoted to their struggle against their fertility, just as that of the sterile woman is centered upon her inability to conceive. Since the fertile woman often uses every means to prevent conception, her failure seems just as inexplicable as psychogenic sterility that has no discoverable physiologic causes. But it is naturally easier to assume unconscious neglect of preventive measures in fertility than to concede unconscious influence on physiologic processes in sterility, all the more so because we regard fertility as normal and sterility as abnormal.

Women who conceive so very much against their will usually complain, like Mrs. Andrews, that a man needs only to look at them or touch them to make them pregnant. Psychoanalysis of overfertile women shows that their problem is not one of exuberant motherliness yearning unconditionally for fulfillment. On the contrary, these women are usually unmotherly, they bear their children a grudge for having been born, and are too much preoccupied with trying to prevent increase of their offspring to turn to the children already borne with joy and solicitude. Their compulsive conceptions have motives far removed from anything like an instinctual urge to motherhood.

Many of the women who passively "do nothing about it" rationalize their behavior with a curiously naïve ignorance. "I cannot help it," they say. Others adduce ideologic or religious motives that may mislead the ill-informed. Where such motives are absent, they wage a pseudostruggle against fertility with all the means at their disposal. But this struggle remains unsuccessful, because (like the struggle against sterility) it runs into unconscious opposition. They have frequent abortions and the condition of their generative organs is such that it is often incomprehensible that they are still able to conceive and bear children. They often insist upon being sterilized, and if they succeed in having this wish fulfilled, they usually react to the operation with severe depression and organic misery. If we consider psychogenic sterility as a psychosomatic syndrome, we should perhaps not reject completely the possibility that the converse phenomenon of overfertility is also connected with a hormonal condition. Possibly a particular potency of the germ plasm and an intensified activity of the hormonal energies are here put at the disposal of the psychic tendencies, and an interaction between psychic and somatic elements produces the condition described by Mrs. Andrews: "The germs fly in the air to fecundate me." We must not be misled by the pseudo-normal.

We shall later have occasion to discuss in detail some cases of such excessive fertility. It will then be seen how often sterility and excessive fertility stem from identical sources and merely represent two faces of a psychic Janus.

After this short digression into pathology, let us return to the normal reproductive functions. Although the sexual act is intertwined with these functions, the goal of the conscious experience is "pleasure, undisturbed pleasure." In the later processes, this question always emerges for the woman: To what extent does the child disturb me in the pursuit of my individual interests? The polarity of the experience, "I or the child," is thus defined from the outset. Every mother experiences this polarity to some extent, deeply or superficially. The child always represents a disturbance of her individual life, but at the same time a *promise*, an optimistic experience with regard to the future. Every pregnancy, especially the first, is for the woman the dawn of a new development, a new turn in her fate, if the imminent motherhood expresses her true personal wish. If this inner expectation of the future is absent, the experience of motherhood is less complete, and the child has only the significance of a desired, tolerated, or undesired reality, without the gratifying emotional, optimistic investiture. As a result there are mothers who from the outset bloom and mothers who fade, mothers who serve the future embodied in the child and mothers who, in a metaphorical sense, feel that their own ego is consumed by the child.

Still other conditions must be fulfilled to endow the feminine woman's pregnancy with the character of completeness. To the principal one of these I apply the term "interiorized social security." It consists in woman's need to feel in her man fatherly tenderness and secure protection. All the dangers of motherhood, the real and the fantasied ones, the inner fears related to the reproductive functions, fears that are present from the beginning to the end of the process, are assuaged if the woman senses fatherliness in the father of her children.

Each woman experiences pregnancy in an individual manner; yet there are definite forms within which the individual variations take place. Is this general framework "an attribute of the species, a manifestation of instinct," so to speak, a re-awakening or renewal of phylogenetic memory? To the psychologist the notions of biologic determination or disposition seem narrow and restrictive, but they give him the comfortable feeling of having a scientific basis and of being able to place the results of his subjective observations into an objective frame. It is advisable to cling to a recognized pattern, in order to increase the objective value of the facts observed, if in so doing one is able to avoid the danger of being inhibited in seeing, understanding, and above all in communicating to others things that cannot be explained by biologic or sociologic realities.

The organic phenomenon of pregnancy is filled with psychic material; more quantitative and qualitative psychic elements enter into the normal biologic condition then is generally assumed even by experts. What is typical, valid for all women, will be found above all in the psychologic accompanying phenomena of certain constant organic manifestations of pregnancy. For example, the very anatomic characteristics of pregnancy favor the mobilization of various tendencies that we encounter in childish psychic life and neurotic symptoms. The inside of the body, we know, is a source of the most peculiar ideas and above all of anxiety in early childhood fantasies. What panic fear seizes the little girl when she hears of an inflammation or a foreign body in someone's insides! As we have seen, many operations are performed upon young girls, especially during their puberty, because they persistently demand them. This demand stems from anxiety expressed in organic symptoms.

Another instance of interest in the anatomy of the inside of the body is the childish fear of worms coming from the stomach; this fear, as we know, is often repeated later in symbolic dreams in which the "worms" acquire the significance of small, usually newborn children.

Also in accord with the realism of childish thinking is the idea that one can find in the inside of the body only what has been put there, that is to say, food.

Still another group of ideas is connected with fear of the mother's menstrual blood, which can be associated with the processes inside the body and later endow them with a dangerous character.

Even more than the anatomy, the physiologic processes of pregnancy are apt to provoke accompanying psychic phenomena. In fact, every physiologic phase in the course of pregnancy has its specific psychologic accompaniment. The surplus of innervations, the gradual reorganization of the somatic excitation processes, the changes in the circulation of the blood, the glandular functions, and the process of nourishment of the tissues connected with pregnancy constitute an added physical strain that naturally must extend to the psychic sphere. It may be said that we have here automatic, reflex-like psychic reactions for which the normal course of the somatic process is a prerequisite. These processes are tied up with definite groups of reactions that must be termed normal and typical.

When speaking of the more individual psychic reactions to

pregnancy, we must above all consider the influence of the environment in a narrow and in a large sense. Naturally every civilization has its own forms of expression. How does the concept of a "psychology of pregnancy" relate to the mental life of a highly civilized woman in North America or western Europe, to that of a Slavic peasant woman, of an orthodox Jewess, or of a primitive North African?

The psychologic processes studied here are certainly not timeless and I do not claim universal validity for them; I do not wish to extend our horizon beyond the environment of women whom we really know, who are accessible to our direct observation. Yet many elements seem to be so deeply rooted in woman's nature that they survive for centuries and can be found at various levels of civilization. Let me cite the following example without at this time entering into detailed explanations. Periodically in every pregnant woman there arises an obscure feeling, reminiscent of old fears and superstitions, that her new happiness-giving possession will arouse the envy of supernatural forces, of the spirits and the gods. In fairy tales and myths the wicked witch wants to steal the child by means of charms; in the idea of the simple-minded peasant woman of various countries, it is the "evil eye" of the hostile neighbor that would accomplish the same purpose; in the educated woman of our own civilization, the feeling is an "irrational sensation" that perhaps corresponds to a feeling of guilt stirring in the unconscious. The threatening power is represented by the woman's own mother, who assumes the role of the witch. Fantasies of monsters and unnatural births disturb the joy of expectation and fill the pregnant woman with anxieties. These are typical and are found all over the world; women who have never been superstitious develop superstitions, fears of magic forces, etc. These examples suggest an identity of psychic reactions under completely different environmental conditions.

Naturally the woman's relation to her own pregnancy is strongly influenced by her immediate surroundings. The treatment of the pregnant woman by society depends chiefly upon the value that society ascribes to the blessing of children;

this value varies at different periods and in different countries. National political and economic interests as well as ethics and constitutional law play their part here. Social developments do not always take biologic laws and factors into account.

The psychologic experience of pregnancy to a large extent depends upon the conditions under which the woman has conceived and in which the expected child is born. That great power in human psychic life, *fear*, whatever its nature, certainly has a considerable influence on the emotional course of pregnancy. The social fear of the unmarried woman accompanies the psychologically determined normal or neurotic fears. Economic difficulties and illnesses and deaths in the family may play their part. In brief, environmental factors, direct and indirect, certainly have an effect on the course of the reproductive process.

The degree of the pregnant woman's psychic health is perhaps the most potent factor. We are rarely able to observe a process that is "normal" from the psychologic point of view. In the first place, such a normal process is unusual; in the second place, a normal woman, in life situations that hold for her the greatest positive value, is not inclined to grant another person, especially a psychoanalyst, insight into her psychic life, and rightly so. Incidentally, it is striking that the most intuitive and introspective women shy away from observing their own psychic processes during pregnancy; one might almost say they are deliberately trying not to observe them. This profoundly motivated behavior is one of the reasons why we have so little information about the psychic life of the pregnant woman.

CHAPTER SIX

Pregnancy

THE processes of pregnancy are the concern of biology, psychology, and social science. I shall deal first with the psychologic phenomena that accompany the biologic processes.

Conception is followed by a tremendous upheaval in the female organism as a whole. Many women maintain that they can perceive the occurrence of conception. However, I have heard this assertion only from women who wished to conceive and subsequently perceived their readiness for it as the process itself; this reaction is particularly frequent after a period of voluntary birth control that has deliberately been given up.

When the fecundated ovum has imbedded itself in the lining of the uterus, the womb enlarges, its blood vessels become fuller, and it increasingly adjusts itself to its task of sheltering the embryo. The genital processes enormously influence the woman's whole organism through a number of physiologic phenomena, so that it is completely mobilized to serve the reproductive task. Each cell participates more or less in this task; gradually the whole physical personality of the woman becomes the protector of the fetus; only the central executive role is assigned to the genital organs.

From these physiologic occurrences the psyche receives stimulating and depressing impulses of various kinds; it is directly implicated through the excitations experienced by the nervous apparatus ending in the genitals. The organic processes of pregnancy are readily used by the psychic apparatus to give expression to pre-existing emotional tensions; as a result, one can not only observe the influence of somatic processes on the psychic ones, but, conversely, one can also discover the relation between emotional conflicts and the physical symptoms of pregnancy. But I must again emphasize that these psychic contents must be related to the somatic process of pregnancy if this interaction is to take place.

Each woman brings into pregnancy certain emotional factors and conflict situations, which come into relation with her condition as a whole and with the organic manifestations characteristic of pregnancy. On the other hand, various typical groups of organic pregnancy processes also mobilize definite emotional attitudes that now emerge openly, exposing the entire dynamic background associated with them, even though this latter is not directly connected with pregnancy. For example, the organically determined nausea can bring to the fore all the feelings of disgust that have been preserved in the unconscious for years without manifesting themselves. Inversely, feelings of disgust that have become associated with definite ideas of pregnancy often strongly reinforce the organic provocation of nausea and may then lead to pathologic vomiting. The contrast with other psychosomatic processes is obvious here. In the latter, the organic symptoms are a complicated final result of a number of organic events, even though the change has been inaugurated by a specific psychic content. In pregnancy a normally preformed somatic phenomenon becomes the immediate expression of definite psychic contents.

We know that pregnancy fantasies fill the psychic life of children, especially girls, from their earliest childhood. These fantasies have a quite typical character and are mainly fed by that group of childish impulses which accompanies the various phases of infantile instinctual life. Oral intake and expulsion, anal retention and ejection, aggressive taking—all these primitive impulses accompany definite bodily functions. From the beginning they are connected with definite elementary psychic tendencies. They play an important role in the biologic process of pregnancy and dominate a large part of the psychic dynamism of this condition.

In discussing coitus we noted the analogy between oral intake and the receptive sucking function of the vagina. In pregnancy all the ideas and fantasies of childhood and puberty that are connected with oral intake and expulsion can be revived through the physiologically determined proneness to nausea. Here we see how definite innervation processes serve for somatic provocation of long-prepared and fixed ideas; it is a case of "organic compliance," to use a current term. But psychoanalysis has taught us that psychogenic intensification of the oral pregnancy symptom of vomiting takes place only when the oral expulsion tendencies are accompanied by unconscious and sometimes even manifest (or about to become manifest) emotions of hostility to pregnancy or to the fetus.

These emotions can be varied: they may take the form of angry protest, self-punishment for hostile feelings, fear, and similar violent affects. The more they are in the service of hostile impulses directed against the fetus, the more unconscious they are, and the more violent the use they make of the innervation process. If the unconscious tendencies are accompanied by a conscious counterwish to keep the child, there develops an inner conflict that transforms the psychosomatic process into a neurotic, usually hysterical symptom. In analysis I could often see that the psychologic content in pregnancy vomiting was exactly the same as that in the hysterical vomiting of young girls that is induced by an unconscious pregnancy fantasy and not by a real condition. The connecting bridge is usually formed by the fear contained in the symptom—in the young girl by fear of the content of the fantasy, in the pregnant woman by fear of the real, material content in her body, that is to say, of the fetus. In both cases, the old infantile idea of fecundation through the mouth is revived. But in the vomiting of the pregnant woman there is always present a strong actual affective cause that provokes the anxious negative relation to the child and thereby the symptom.

The same applies to other, frequently peculiar oral manifestations, especially during the first half of the pregnancy period. Here belong the characteristic ravenous hunger alternating with complete lack of appetite and the stomach complaints that cannot be explained on physical grounds alone, as well as eructations, heartburn, nausea, and oversensitiveness to objects that arouse disgust—in other words, normal manifestations of pregnancy that exceed the normal limits.   The various extravagant food cravings, even though seemingly in direct opposition to vomiting as manifestations of compulsiveness in intake of food, express the same conflict between destruction and preservation of the embryo; in one case the eliminatory tendencies, in the other the incorporating ones, are victorious. In vomiting, the conflicting positive wish to keep the child asserts itself in the relieved, triumphant feeling that predominates after the food has been expelled: "And yet he remained inside."   One patient always looked with panic fear for fragments of the fetus in the vomit, and always laughingly realized the absurdity of her behavior afterward.   Similarly, in connection with the wish for reincorporation expressed by cravings for certain foods, the opposite tendency manifests itself in the woman's cannibalistic, destructive attitude toward the most peculiar foodstuffs.   Madame de l'Estorade complains in letters of her lack of motherly feelings for her expected child and describes her violent cravings for certain foods.   The fact that some women suffer more from these symptoms than others results from a number of causes.   Very often these cravings express an obsession to consume foods that are familiar to psychoanalysis and folklore as symbols of fecundation (fruit, cucumbers, fish, spices, etc.).   Thus the obsessive desire is a sort of repetition of the act of fecundation, a symbolic affirmation accompanied by an opposite tendency, cannibalistic destruction.   Often the new symbolic fecundation is revealed as obsessive undoing of an unconscious tendency to destroy the child.

To be sure, the modified gastric secretions supply a provocation for the compulsion.   Whenever it is persistent, closer examination shows that the patient previously manifested compulsive tendencies, though under normal circumstances they were held in check.   Pregnancy permits woman to be free and rationalizes actions that would otherwise seem absurd.   In such cases, there is always a strongly ambivalent relation to the father of the child and to the child, as well as a strongly aggressive component intensified by pregnancy. It is as though a somatic signal from the modified secretory processes had revived a latent compulsion. In many women these cravings are confined within normal limits, in others the obsessive element is unmistakable.

Many women postpone the conflict between the eliminatory and preserving tendencies to a somewhat later phase of pregnancy and resort to other organs to express it, especially those suitable for serving such ends and associatively connected with the psychic content of the conflicting tendencies. Constipation, diarrhea, and genital expulsion tendencies express this struggle, which under certain psychosomatic conditions manifests itself in labor activity long before delivery. If the expulsion tendencies predominate, abortion may occur.

The fact that some women have these typical symptoms while others have different ones results from various factors. In the first place, the dispositions brought into pregnancy play a part. Analogies between the new condition and old ideas and memories, the need to lend psychic contents to the physical sensations of pregnancy, increased tendency to regressive revival of earlier fantasies as a result of the increased introversion characteristic of every pregnant woman—all these lead to intensified, pathologic distortion of the biologic phenomena.

What seems most important to me, however, is the fact that there is in almost every pregnant woman a constantly active tendency to interrupt the harmony of the pregnancy state.
I have found this tendency repeatedly in both healthy and neurotic individuals. But an excessively strong or abnormal reaction to the physiologic signals that are normal in pregnancy takes place only if additional motives leading to a quantitative increase of the normal response are present.

If it is true that latent hostile expulsion tendencies in relation to the fetus normally accompany pregnancy, does not this fact contradict our previous assertion of the power of motherliness? This seeming contradiction requires an explanation.

First of all, it is clear that from the biologic point of view there is no differentiation between the mother and the fetus. Mother and child are an absolute organic unity, and the same biologic process governs the needs of both. This unity is expressed with regard not only to the positive life processes but also to the destructive ones. Within the framework of the biologic process, disturbances in the organic functions of the one are also disturbances in those of the other, the well-being of the one is the well-being of the other, and the death of the one frequently involves the death of the other.

Biologically and physiologically, the mother-child identification plays a great part in the whole process of pregnancy. Psychologically this identification represents a complicated phenomenon that we shall study later. In the biologic identity the fetus lives parasitically on the mother (Ferenczi[1] calls the fetus an "endoparasite") and the mother's body is exploited. As long as there is insufficient psychologic positive willingness for masochistic loving and giving, and motherly-tender identification does not rise above the parasitic significance of the fetus, the fetus remains a trouble maker psychically and in certain circumstances physically. As we know (vol. 1), willingness for emotionally positive identification and masochistic giving are characteristic features of femininity that are also attributes of motherliness in all the phases of reproduction.

This law of femininity extends in a psychophysical parallelism: if there are psychic difficulties in the acceptance of the biologic situation, the embryo becomes psychically what it is biologically, an enemy exploiting the maternal organism. Positive counterideas lie in the realm of future wish fulfillments: they are connected with the desire to have a child. They are not rooted in a positive emotional attitude toward the fetus itself, which as yet does not at all correspond to the idea of the child. If the wish for a child is not strong enough, if it is inhibited externally or internally, or if anywhere in the pregnant woman's psyche difficulties arise in accepting the role of giver, a psychically determined protest, manifesting itself in any of the

[1] Ferenczi, S.: Thalassa: a theory of genitality. Psychoanalyt. Quart., vol. 2, 1933; vol. 3, 1934.

forms of the expulsion tendency, will oppose the biologic process.

If the pregnant woman is externally or internally deprived of love and is not sufficiently compensated for it, her own willingness to give may be weakened to such an extent that the somatic sensations that she normally tolerates only because of her willingness to give can become a signal for expulsion. Whether the expulsion takes place in the oral, anal, or genital way depends on dispositional motives. Her own still existing infantile desire to receive can be mobilized anew by the growing demands of the fetus and come to the fore as an intensification of the somatic pregnancy symptoms. It can also happen that the identification with the fetus is carried out too literally, so to speak, so that the woman regresses to a fetus-like behavior and in her pregnancy appears as a curiously passive, dependent creature absolutely intolerant of privations.

The protest against the biologic giving can assume numerous forms. If it is accompanied by strong aggressive tendencies, the expulsion tendency becomes dangerous not only for the child but also for the mother. The physical symptoms may be accompanied by a spiteful neglect of prenatal care, sometimes explainable by the woman's passive-infantile attitude and sometimes by her urge to destroy the fetus without consideration of the possible injury to herself. The form in which such a negative attitude toward pregnancy and toward the fetus manifests itself depends on the dispositional factors. The signal for its mobilization, unless we are dealing with severe psychic or physical illness, always comes from the immediate consciously or unconsciously experienced life situation.

The following case will illustrate this point. For many years Alice, a young, beautiful, and talented girl, could not make up her mind to bring her engagement to a happy conclusion by marrying her fiancé. Finally the impatient young man confronted her with an alternative that induced her to seek psychotherapeutic intervention. She declared that she loved the young man but could not make up her mind to marry him because of an idea that was unclear to herself. She feared that he would be incapable of performing his marital duties, although, as she knew, her fear was groundless, because the man in question was young, active, and successful. She had no other neurotic difficulties and considered herself absolutely healthy. Yet she granted at once that her difficulty was not real but "imaginary." Her childhood, she related, had been a happy one, except that she had suffered for many years from severe constipation, so that once she had to have her bowels cleaned out under anesthetic by a physician. Her mother used to give her enemas with the greatest patience and devotion; these were often painful but were usually followed by a feeling of relief and gratitude to her mother.

It became clear that she had transferred her old problem of defecation to her genitals, that she feared defloration, and that she did not believe that her fiancé would be able to overcome her physical difficulties and psychic resistance. She obviously reproached him for not having been aggressive enough to seduce her during their long engagement.

After a short treatment she married, and for several years her marriage was very happy. Without the slightest difficulty in either pregnancy or delivery she gave birth to two children and was in the third month of another pregnancy when her husband volunteered for military service. She consented to this patriotic action on his part but unconsciously held it against him that he had left her "in this condition."

She moved with her children to her mother's house and at once her first pregnancy difficulties began. She had contractions of the uterus and was threatened with miscarriage. Her physician prescribed absolute rest in bed; as soon as she tried to move about she felt pains similar to labor pains. At these times the presence of her mother or kind words from her or myself allayed the young woman's spasms. Simultaneously she began to suffer from very stubborn constipation and her gynecologist found it very difficult to overcome her double ailment.

With her separation from her husband and her return to her mother, the patient apparently had to solve several conflicts,

and pregnancy made it possible for her to express her psychologic problems in specific organic reactions. Neuroses have
made us quite familiar with such transfers of old and new
psychic conflicts to the body; they are characteristically frequent in pregnancy.

Our patient bore a grudge against her husband for having left
her; because he had left she did not want a child of his, a fatherless child to whom she obviously transferred her vindictive
tendencies relating to her husband. Probably her fear for
him and her increased responsibilities played a part too. Her
psychic reactions were obviously ambivalent: her genitals had
changed their receptive and retentive function into an eliminatory, expelling, hostile one, while the opposite retentive,
sparing, and preserving function was left to the intestines or the
anus. In this division she repeated something that had taken
place before. As she turned away from her husband she
resumed her old affective tie with her mother, which formerly
too had been expressed through constipation. Actually she
wanted to preserve the child; she made honest and strenuous
efforts to this end, but her impulses strayed from the genitals
to the intestines, and the more strenuous her efforts, the more
intensively did the two opposing tendencies operate in the
wrong places. We recall that such a confusion of localization
had taken place in her fantasy when she feared that her husband
would be incapable of violently penetrating her body aperture,
as her mother had done with the enemas of her childhood.

Another patient protested against her unwished-for pregnancy by continuous diarrhea; she also expressed her relation
to the fetus by mediation of the adjoining excretory organs,
although in a manner opposite to that of the patient discussed
above.

We have seen (chap. III) that the contents of the intestinal
tract and the child are generally identical in childhood fantasies.
It seems that the unconscious of the pregnant woman more
readily restores this identity than that between the fetus,
unknown as an object, and the child she is willing to love in the
future. The physiologic processes induce a revival of this

early identification and produce a psychophysical union between the child and the feces that is sometimes expressed
organically. As long as the physiologic regulatory mechanisms
of pregnancy are in a certain balance, no organic disturbances
take place. Only overdetermination—that is to say, the addition of psychologic factors to the physiologic upheaval of pregnancy—creates the organic afflictions often typical of pregnancy. This resembles the situation in childhood; here again
the psychic contents can utilize the language of the organs.

We have also seen that the physiologic signals indicating
that the mother's bodily economy is overburdened by the
fetus, and developing into *agents provocateurs* for certain prefigured somatic reactions, are often associated with various
emotional energies directed against the fetus. Sometimes the
mother's emotional relation to the fetus in her body is full
of the cruelest murderous impulses, which remain unconscious
while consciously the child is expected with love. These impulses assert themselves in the woman's general mood, in
psychic and even psychotic states, in dreams, etc., without
resort to bodily expressions. I have also often observed that
hysterical women who previously suffered from conversion
symptoms in which pregnancy fantasies were of decisive importance, remain strikingly free of bodily symptoms during
their real pregnancies, although their old neurotic conflicts
have not been solved. These conflicts are now expressed on the
psychic plane, in general states of anxiety, in phobias, etc.
The relation to the real fetus is determined by many factors
and the final effect is obtained by the combined action of all
of them.

The physiologic processes of pregnancy are self-regulatory,
unless they are disturbed by excessive quantitative or qualitative physiologic changes. If the positive relation to the child
as a future reality fills the woman's emotional life, the physiologic processes lose their abnormal psychic charge: the feces
no longer become the child, the disgust leading to vomiting is
reduced to the organically determined morning sickness of the
first months, etc. But if the infantile counterideas are too

strong, or if the expectations for the future are disturbed by the woman's negative relation to her motherhood, the physiologic process loses the proper moderation.

On the other hand, a healthy pregnancy is not always proof of motherliness. The favorable course of pregnancy or later motherhood can also be ascribed to strongly positive values deriving from secondary motives, such as desire to stabilize a shaky marriage, pride in the achievement, liberation from other burdensome obligations, etc. Or, paradoxically, pregnancy can be so completely denied that even its negative elements and physiologic burdens are not perceived. In very youthful unmarried mothers we often observe "brilliant" pregnancies that are brought about by such a denial. In other cases the emphasis the woman puts on her own efficiency, her unconcern with the disturbing phenomena, result in a brilliant pregnancy; well-being is here exhibited as superiority. This is especially often the case with masculine-aggressive women who do not allow themselves to be disturbed in their activities by pregnancy and do not develop any symptoms. From analyses of such women we know that their longing for pregnancy is often an expression of their wish for a bodily possession, a wish that conceals the old penis envy.

Whether the fetus is assigned the role of hostile parasite or receiver of the tender mother-child currents, depends upon the psychophysical situation as a whole; it expresses the end effect of that polarity which we call emotional ambivalence.

I do not intend to enter into the pathology of pregnancy. I have mentioned certain abnormal physical phenomena because they belong to the constant inventory of the normal process as well, and because they show the importance and influence of infantile instinctual development.

These influences are studied in greater detail in a publication by S. M. Payne.[2] And B. Warburg has given us an impressive insight into the instinctual processes in the case of a severely pathologic pregnant woman.[3]

[2] PAYNE, S. M.: A conception of femininity.   Brit. J. M. Psychol., 1936.
[3] WARBURG, B.: Suicide, pregnancy and rebirth.   Psychoanalyt. Quart., vol. 7, 1938.

We have just seen the influence of fantasy life on the physical symptoms and, conversely, the influence of biologic events on the psychologic. A typical and unique phenomenon of pregnancy is the interweaving of the intensified introversion with the simultaneously intensified turn toward reality. The most interesting problems of pregnancy result from this apparent opposition. The harmonious interplay of the two factors brings about a blissful pregnancy; their disharmony produces tolerant indifference or profound emotional misery.

We have mentioned the fact that pregnant women say little about their psychic experience. This is only partly the result of their unwillingness to lose the freshness of what is perhaps woman's greatest emotional experience by communicating it, or to diminish its immediacy and intensity by subjecting it to their own or others' critical observations. "Woman does not betray her secret" because she is hardly ever intellectually aware of her deepest psychic experiences. Psychoanalysts are familiar with this psychologic phenomenon. The child's strongest psychic experiences rarely reach his still immature intellect, and information received from children about their fears and fantasies rarely takes the path of conscious and formulated communication. Amnesia, the forgetting of the strongest psychic experiences of childhood, is not entirely due to the repression of conscious experiences; the greater part of the emotional reactions of childhood remain separated from the conscious ideas because the childish intellect is not mature enough to absorb these ideas and elaborate them. Even those who directly observe children rarely suspect the extent of their unconscious experiences, the childish megalomania behind their weakness and dependence, the many childish fears, unless these exceed the normal limit. Only gradually, by interpreting children's indirect utterances, have we come closer to the truth and learned to understand "the language of the childish soul" without the mediation of the intellect.

The psychic experiences of pregnancy are in this respect similar to those of childhood. But here it is no longer intellectual incapacity that keeps the psychic processes from being consciously experienced, but the intensity of the turn inward.[4]

The fact that pregnancy is accompanied by intensified introversion can easily be demonstrated. Pregnant women themselves complain that their former lively and sincere interest in various outside events seems to wane, and no particular sagacity is required to verify this statement objectively. They may continue their accustomed occupations automatically, but inner participation is lacking. The diversion of the psychic energies from the outer world means the first more or less decisive step in the process of turning inward, i.e., introversion. With this step the polarity between individual existence and service to the species changes its balance in favor of the latter. Little has as yet been accomplished thereby for the preservation of the species, but the prelude, the beginning, has taken place.

This interest diverted from the outside world now turns to that part of the mother's ego which psychically represents the biologic upheaval materialized in the fetus. This materialization gives the woman the promise of a child in the near future, but is not yet the child as the object of maternal love. The child itself still remains a fantasy product in the mother's psychic life, differing from other fantasies only in the certainty of its realization and the definite term set for this fulfillment.

Here we have the second act of the service to the species: the woman's interest turns toward a fantasy that as a preliminary stage of an imminent realization is also the preliminary stage of emotional motherliness. The fact that her emotional interest is more or less exclusively turned toward an object that will be real only at some future date, and that for the time being

[4] A sensitive writer, Nancy Hale, has aptly formulated this attitude of the pregnant woman: "When I saw her, her eyes passed me and went away to some other focus, and at the same time seemed to me to turn in upon something in her own mind. . . . They were living in a private dream, on the other side of the fence; I could not guess what they were thinking of, nor what fears they had, nor what they talked about together when they were alone. But it was all secret and all within themselves. . . . The preoccupations of pregnancy are a dream that is forgotten as entirely as the dream of birth pains." Cf. HALE, N.: The season of summer. In ASWELL, M. L., op. cit., p. 81.

does not exist, gives the real biologic process the character of a partly dreamlike experience.

Since this future reality for the time being has no independent biologic or psychologic existence, the child is psychologically what the fetus is biologically—a part of the mother's own self. The biologic process has created a unity of mother and child, in which the bodily substance of one flows into the other, and thus one larger unit is formed out of two units. The same thing takes place on the psychic level. By tender identification, by perceiving the fruit of her body as part of herself, the pregnant woman is able to transform the "parasite" into a beloved being.

Thus, mankind's eternal yearning for identity between the ego and the nonego, that deeply buried original desire to re-achieve the condition once experienced, to repeat the human dream that was once realized in the mother's womb, is fulfilled. Aspired to in coitus on the one hand and in religious ecstasy as *unio mystica* on the other, this identity becomes real in the mother-child union of pregnancy. But the feeling of unity can be achieved only if no disturbing influences assert themselves in the ego. The drives must be at rest, the ego must feel free of guilt, the ego ideal must be satisfied by the values ascribed to the still nonexistent being. These conditions are fulfilled only if fears and feelings of guilt do not burden the psychic life and hostile aggressive impulses are silenced, which is not always the case. There are women whose self-confidence is markedly disturbed during pregnancy. They see in their coming motherhood a strong obstacle to their own possible development. Instead of happiness they have feelings of bitterness, revenge, and hatred toward both the man and the still unborn child and of resigned renunciation of their own personal life.

The sense of guilt that dwells in every human soul particularly burdens the reproductive processes. Motherhood and pregnancy are laden with old guilt feelings and these lend greater power to the guilt motives acquired later. The more pregnancy is experienced as a yearned-for promise of future happiness, the more severely is the prospective mother threatened by the vengeance of fate.

In every woman, even the most mature and best balanced, imminent motherhood is a fulfillment of an old wish and a consummation of an old promise that destiny or her educators gave her at the moment when she recognized and accepted her feminine nature.

Postponement seems to every girl a disappointment and a nonfulfillment of that promise. We have had occasion to observe such disappointment reactions especially in puberty. They are often preserved in the unconscious as the idea "I cannot have a child," and thus contribute to this typical fear of pregnancy, which stems from many sources. The feeling that the promise now so real will nevertheless remain unfulfilled results from the anachronistic effects of a former bad experience. This motive often plays a large part in the sterility of the first type of sterile woman discussed above. In itself, the little girl's wish to have a child is free of guilt feelings, she never suffered prohibitions or threats of punishment as a result of it. Guilt feelings burden this wish only secondarily. One of their sources is masturbation: we recall that the most immediate expression of the sense of guilt is associated with the genital trauma and refers to the girl's fear that she has destroyed her genitals. Later, with the transference of the girl's interest to the inside of her body, the guilt reaction "I have no genitals" is transformed into the threat "I will have no child," and acts as a second powerful determinant of pregnancy fears.

The guilt feeling connected with masturbation can inhibit the reproductive functions from the outset and make conception difficult. Women who have this feeling observe all their bodily sensations during pregnancy with particular acuteness, and perceive them as threats of loss; their joy in the future child can hardly establish itself, because they doubt that their wish will be realized. Such women have a tendency to miscarry and must often bolster their tottering belief in the child by self-imposed sacrifices and renunciations of other joys and activities. These sacrifices are rationalized as "prenatal care."

It is interesting and comprehensible that normal birth and the actual achievement of motherhood do not always cause a change in this infantile attitude. Since real births do not affect the unconscious source of their doubts and thus cannot remove it, such women must prove to themselves by repeated pregnancies that their bodies are capable of producing children. These women burdened with guilt are among the many whose pregnancies serve goals other than the urge to motherhood.

A deeper and more powerful source of guilt feelings lies in the pregnant woman's relation to her mother. It can even be said that this relation is at the center of the psychologic problems of pregnancy and of the whole reproductive function. In many women the degree of their freedom from psychologic dependence upon their own mothers decides the fate of their motherhood. If the pregnant woman displays a high degree of psychic infantilism, is passively devoted to her mother, and has no active tendency to free herself, she has no guilt reactions and the course of her pregnancy is characterized by a typical lack of seriousness and dignity—she takes the whole thing as "fun." She communicates all her excitement to her mother, makes all the necessary preparations under her aegis, and in general conducts herself in a manner reminiscent of that of the little girl playing with dolls.

The psychology of the prospective grandmother plays an important part in the behavior of her daughter. The latter's pregnancy often gives the mother an occasion to realize her own frustrated wishes, and mother and daughter are involved in common daydreaming. We recall here the young girl whom I termed an assistant mother (p. 73); she constructed such motherhood fantasies with her mother even in puberty. A widowed or divorced mother, or a mother who has no other life tasks, is particularly prone to devote herself completely to her daughter's condition, to intensify her solicitude for the "poor child," and experience the responsibilities and joys of pregnancy all over again through identification with her daughter.

It is interesting to observe that the pregnancies of these infantile women are normal, smooth, without symptoms. Such a woman is not only free from the care of the future child and all practical everyday problems; the dark forces of destiny also and the fears of death are alien to her, for she has her mother or other all-powerful protectors at her side. If she is pious, God as representative of the father will see to it that she is spared all the dangers and sufferings of which other women complain. If she is an atheist, she mobilizes her old reminiscence of God in a new piety; the new God has all the features of an omnipotent father, and she entrusts her fate to him; or she gives this function, often via her mother, to her physician, who makes all the arrangements and thus reinstates the patriarchal family situation of childhood. Professionally we encounter such types fairly often when the failure of the protective powers is followed by a neurotic reaction.

In accordance with her character, many a one among these infantile mothers would neglect the prenatal care of herself and her fetus if someone else did not supervise her; she is very much inclined to treat her pregnancy in the same disorderly fashion in which she treated her room in her parents' home. Other women of this type are more conscientious; like good children, they do their maternal duty even in pregnancy with great exactitude, obediently follow all the rules, but emotionally are as unserious as the others. Their outward appearance often expresses their mental condition: they dress as before, and in their short clothes that show their knees they often seem like little girls who have stuffed out their dresses to play having a baby. They completely lack the dignity of mothers. The men they choose are often playmates or tolerant fathers who are amused by the new maternal role of the little girl. This type of woman is not necessarily youthful; psychic infantilism can outlast adolescence by many years.

In this same type the further course of motherhood often assumes a complicated character, and the conflict between the narcissistic ego and the relationship to the child usually breaks out after birth. In such cases pregnancy often acts as a guardian against all other life dangers, including those that real motherhood with its stern duties may bring to the immature and weak ego.

Dependence upon the mother is not always without friction.

The inner protest that usually accompanies such dependence often makes itself felt during pregnancy. "Now I am the mother, not you," is what the pregnant woman's attitude indicates, and this overemphasis on independence points to its opposite. The mother must know nothing of the pregnancy, she must know less of it than anyone else. These declarations of independence last only until the first weaknesses and fears manifest themselves; then the conflict between the dependence and the protest begins. The more the prospective mother feels that she will be unable to bear her new responsibility precisely because of her dependence upon her own mother, the stronger is the protest. The child was supposed to play the part of savior from the mother but instead it only intensifies the danger. "Away with him," therefore, says the unconscious in such cases. And I have observed several miscarriages provoked by the sharpening of such a mother conflict. Twice I have seen a conscious triumph when the prematurely born child died immediately after delivery. In both cases the children were much desired firstlings, and the young mothers were stunned and terrified by their unusual reaction to their loss. In the first of these cases the young woman intended, after her confinement, to join her soldier-husband in the town where he was stationed and to leave the child with her mother. She begrudged her mother the child and her unconscious preferred it to be dead. In the second case likewise, the real life situation sharpened the latent mother conflict; here too the war compelled the woman to return to her mother's home with her newborn child. The child intensified the danger of the young woman's dependence upon her mother and she unconsciously preferred its death to this dependence. It is noteworthy that the first of these women had suffered from anorexia nervosa as an adolescent and the second from agoraphobia; in both these neuroses excessive dependence upon the mother plays a great part. The psychic motive that led these two women to react abnormally to the loss of their newborn children leads others to still earlier renunciation of the child through miscarriage.

Much more difficult and complicated are those pregnancies in which an unconscious feeling of guilt with regard to the mother exceeds the normal fears and forebodings. Every woman's unconscious guilt feelings lead back to the childhood phase in which the mother's pregnancy, real or fantasied, is the greatest burden of the little girl's emotional life. The arrival of a new brother or sister naturally intensifies her interest in problems of birth and spurs her fantasy in that direction. But even without this real experience, her fantasy feeds on apprehensions, investigations, and suspicions. All her reactions to reality and the accompanying fantasies are characterized by considerable aggression. If in her fantasies she wants a child for herself, she hates her mother as a successful rival; if she clings to her mother with love demands, she takes her mother's interest in the new child very much amiss, and with childish emotional unrestraint wishes both of them dead. This wish produces reactions of guilt.

The destructive urge is particularly aggressive in relation to the pregnant mother, realistically if she is really pregnant, in fantasy if the pregnancy is only built on suspicions.

Pregnancy as the fulfillment of woman's deepest yearnings may disturb the psychic balance because it brings to the fore old conflicts that have hitherto remained relatively dormant. As long as the psychic regulatory processes had to take into account only the individual self-preservative tendencies, peace prevailed. But they no longer suffice for the emotional tasks of the reproductive function. Previously the old guilt feelings with regard to the mother and the self-punishing tendencies could find an outlet within the framework of a more or less neurotically functioning masochism. The expectation of a child may be accompanied by the strongest emotions of happiness; at the same time, the masochistic idea of the really expected pain and danger to life may grow immeasurably under the impact of guilt feelings. In women who undergo this process, the optimistic idea "I shall have a child" assumes the character of an ecstatic experience that is at once opposed by the pessimistic negation "I shall have no child, I have no right to have one, I shall lose it, I shall pay for it with my death." This split can be gradually evened out by the pregnant woman's reality adjustment to her own motherhood; otherwise the conflict continues to rage and the woman renounces the child by way of sterility or miscarriage, which act as mechanisms of defense against future dangers.

In severe cases, the destructive tendencies win the upper hand, and the more the woman wishes for a child, the more easily does she lose it or actually pay for its birth with her own life. Her own mother's threatening voice is not always as clear and unmistakable as the curse laid on Mrs. Andrews by her mother: "You will die in giving birth to your first child." Usually this voice is a more veiled and more unconscious element. Often the old guilt feeling is increased by a new burden that makes it virulent, so to speak: I have observed several instances in which motherhood was made difficult by the fact that another woman, deserted by the beloved man, accompanied the happiness of the chosen one like a shadow. The new and old shadows allied themselves into a mother's curse on the young wife's motherhood.

The fate of the identification with the mother is another factor that determines the course of pregnancy. In every instance the capacity for motherhood is related to this identification. The ego of the pregnant woman must find a harmonious compromise between her deeply unconscious identification with the child, which is directed toward the future, and her identification with her own mother, which is directed toward the past. Wherever one of these identifications is rejected, difficulties arise. In the first case the fetus becomes a hostile parasite, in the second the pregnant woman's capacity for motherhood is weakened by her unwillingness to accept her identification with her own mother.

The following case clearly illustrates this problem. The patient, whom we shall call Mrs. Smith, was the youngest in a family with many other children, one boy and several girls. After this boy had disappointed the ambitious hopes of the parents, they wanted to have another son, but instead my patient was born. Her mother never concealed her disappointment over this fact, and her attitude toward the girl was unmistakably: "It would have been better if you had not been born." The patient was saved from traumatic reactions to this attitude by two compensations—her father's deep and tender love for her, and the maternal affection of one of her sisters, twelve years older than herself. Her father's love aroused in her the wish to become a substitute for his son and she successfully turned her interests and ambitions toward this goal. She was saved from the dangers of the masculinity complex because her father's love for her emphasized and encouraged her femininity. The two tendencies frequently conflicted but did not lead to a neurotic result.

Only after she had married and conceived an ardent desire for a baby did her childhood difficulty come to the fore. As a little girl she had reacted to her mother's rejection with conscious hatred and devaluation. The idea of identification with her aggressive mother had filled her with almost conscious horror. Up to her pregnancy she had been able to be feminine by disregarding her mother problem; but this method no longer worked when she herself was about to become a mother.

Her identification with her older sister, her childhood substitute mother, was also disturbed. During her early puberty Mrs. Smith had discovered that her sister, like herself, was engaged in a hate-filled conflict with her mother, and perhaps unconsciously sensed that this sister had many children not because she was motherly but because she was sexually subjected to her husband. With whom, then, could she identify herself, in order to become a mother? Her tragic feeling that she would never achieve motherhood was intensified when she gave birth one month before term to a stillborn child.

Soon she was again pregnant; and her joy was now even more mixed with fear of loss than during her first pregnancy. By this time she had come into close relation with a former friend of hers who was also pregnant and expected her first child in joyful, undisturbed tranquillity. Thanks to this friendship,

Mrs. Smith felt relieved; only from time to time she aroused the friend's laughter by remarking, "You are the luckiest person in the world, you will have a child"—thus expressing her doubts as to the fulfillment of her own wish. In her full identification with her friend she nevertheless began to feel more hopeful. Only later, during her analysis, did she realize that the success of her identification with her friend was not due to the latter's inner harmony but to another motive. The friend had a mother who was the opposite of her own. While her own mother was tall, domineering, cold, and aggressive, her friend's mother was very small and full to the brim with maternal warmth. She spread her motherly wings both over her own loving daughter and Mrs. Smith, who was thus able to achieve motherhood by sharing in this benign mother-daughter harmony.

One danger threatened her. Her friend had conceived a whole month before her; thus during the last month of her own pregnancy she would be left to her own fate. This fact aroused great fear in her, because she had once given birth to a child one month before term. As her friend's expected date of delivery approached, she grew more and more fearful. But to the surprise of everyone concerned, her friend did not have her child at the expected time; she refused to have her delivery hastened by medical intervention, and gave birth to a boy overdue by a whole month on the very day that Mrs. Smith expected her own delivery. A few hours later, Mrs. Smith began to have labor pains and thus fulfilled her seemingly hopeless wish that both babies be born on the same day. The children were later referred to as twins of different parents.

Since I was particularly interested in the authenticity of these facts and suspected that Mrs. Smith's friend had been mistaken as to the date of her conception, I investigated the matter and ascertained beyond any doubt that her child really was born late by a whole month; and this was confirmed by her doctors, who established the fact that the child's growth during its additional stay in the uterus was more than equal to one month's normal growth of a child outside the uterus. Apparently Mrs. Smith's friend had mobilized all the energies of the "retaining" powers in order to help Mrs. Smith by waiting for her term. I think that in this case the psychologic force of simultaneous loving identification was the determining factor.

There is an epilogue to Mrs. Smith's career as a mother. The two friends now consciously adjusted themselves to each other in regard to their next pregnancies and conceived in the same month. This second time, Mrs. Smith had no fears or doubts. But during the third month of her pregnancy her friend told her that her husband had been offered a position in another town and that the family would probably move there. Mrs. Smith felt panicky and asked her friend what would happen to her own pregnancy. The friend replied laughingly that this time she would have to struggle through it alone. That very day Mrs. Smith started on a miscarriage and the physician who was summoned was unable to do anything about it. The clinical diagnosis was that of overexcitability of the uterus. This woman could not manage to have a second child. She was very motherly and greatly enjoyed her motherhood in relation to the one child she had, though with an admixture of fear. Psychoanalytic treatment did not remove her difficulties. She ironically called herself an "appendix mother" who could bring her pregnancy to a successful conclusion only by leaning on another woman. Beyond this she was not neurotic, and could solve all the other problems of her life. It was only to the heavy task of pregnancy that she was unequal, for reasons of which she herself became aware. After her friend had failed her she could no longer chase away the shadow of the mother she had rejected. We were able to study the psychologic process in Mrs. Smith; in her friend we could only conjecture it. We cannot answer the question as to what physiologic changes had taken place in both women to subject them so deeply to psychologic factors.

Upon recommendation of the attending gynecologists I have often been asked to give therapeutic assistance in cases of habitual miscarriage. Several times I have found that the first miscarriage, whatever its cause, had become an invincible trauma. The strong wish for a child was intensified by the loss, and the bad experience created or intensified the anxious tension: "Will I have a child?" There developed a compulsion to repeat the traumatic experience. After every miscarriage the wish for a new pregnancy was increased—like the desire for a drug in an addiction—and with it the tendency to miscarry. In one case the woman gave up all hope of success, adopted a child, and when she later became pregnant did not take any of the precautions against miscarriage that she had taken previously. Only then did she give birth to a normal child.

The changes that take place during pregnancy are gradual; only gradually does the pregnant woman realize that her personal real world will soon change and grow, and that this change will be her own accomplishment, already really begun with pregnancy. Later this accomplishment will reach full expression in the differentiation between the mother and child. It sounds paradoxic that we should ascribe a real meaning to such a real and present condition only by referring it to the future. However, the idea of the future sets various reactions in motion in the present: some of these share the passive character of waiting, others aim at actively preparing the environment for the future, at improving it, etc. This double attitude toward the future constitutes an important component of all the psychologic processes of pregnancy. In the passive component all the fantasies about the future find an outlet.

The tendency to fantasy, as opposed to turning toward reality, naturally characterizes those women who had it to a considerable degree before, especially those who are not satisfied with reality. Even if they are motherly and the child as a real object later gives them much satisfaction and compensates them for many privations, they enjoy pregnancy for its own sake more than for the sake of the child. It is for them a kind of refuge in which they are allowed to live their conscious and unconscious wishes, a permission to be introverted without social feelings of guilt. They assume the right to escape present responsibilities in the name of the future they bear within themselves.   In such cases delivery means the return to reality, to which these women react in typical fashion.

The fantasies of a mature, active mother naturally focus upon the future child.   However much she may be controlled by a sense of reality, every woman feels that she bears a future hero in her womb, and the content of her fantasy is the "myth" of his birth.   He not only represents her own masculinity—even when she is the most feminine of women—but he also represents all the overvaluation that once applied to her father and possesses all the virtues his own father lacks. A man likes to think that in the eyes of his wife Junior is a repetition of Senior, but this is seldom true.   Only when death or some other kind of separation glorifies the person of the husband, can he approximate in his wife's fantasy the ideal that the son is supposed to realize.   When a woman is really in love, eroticism fills her life to such an extent that her yearning for a child is not a real, elementary need.   Only when the ecstatic stage of being in love is succeeded by love does the maternal woman begin to yearn for a child from the beloved man.   But at that point her erotic overvaluation has subsided, and the ideal demand, the nonfulfillment of which has been painful, is transferred to the future child.   The model of this demand lies in the past, and a very large percentage of women want the first child to be a boy, independently of the quantitative relation of their own psychic components of masculinity and femininity.   This boy becomes for his mother the embodiment of her previously developed ego ideal and of all the perfections that were once ascribed to her own father.   Among several primitive peoples the belief prevails that the grandfather is reborn in the grandson.   T. Reik analyzed this belief.[5]

The daughter, especially the first-born girl, is supposed to fulfill these demands of the ego ideal to an even greater extent. It has been observed that pregnant women very often dream of a little child swimming.   Pregnancy is here projected into the dream with typical symbolism.   The child can always be

---

[5] REIK, T.: Probleme der Religionspsychologie: die Couvade.   Vienna: Internat. Psychoanalyt. Bibliot., vol. 5.

recognized as the dreamer herself, embodying all the qualities that make her particularly valuable and above all made her valuable in her childhood, as a kind of proof and illustration of the ideal formation for which the expected child serves. When analyzing the particularly prominent characteristics of the child in the dream, one often hears: "Oh, my father particularly liked that feature in me."

The illusion that the expected child will be blessed with all the virtues and talents is opposed by the painful idea that it will be a monster, an idiot, a cripple. This idea is sometimes obsessive and stubborn; the pregnant woman looks for supporting material in encyclopedias and medical books and her hopes are deeply shaken by such fears.

It is difficult to say which among several is the most constant motive of all these fears—feelings of guilt, masochistic disturbances of the joys of anticipation, influences of old incest wishes. Psychologic analysis discovers all these determinants. The fears are always conscious and are readily communicated to others. In contrast, the extravagant hopes are not divulged, and only in pregnancy psychoses does one hear about the "Savior within the body."

If the relations between the future child's mother and father are good, the psychologic foundations of the parent-child triangle (cf. vol. 1) are laid during pregnancy. The character of this triangle depends upon the level of the parents' maturity. A naïve form of common daydreaming arises if they are both very young and their relation is comradely, especially if they are reality-inhibited, or if the husband consents to share in the wife's playful fantasies for the sake of companionship.

Such parents speak of the child as real, assign various functions to him, anticipate his development, etc. His sex and his name assume great importance, and usually the two parents are unaware that in these preoccupations they are expressing unconscious feelings and acting out fantasies. Without realizing it, they betray what importance the child's sex has for each of them. It may be chosen narcissistically as "what I

could not be" or out of love for the partner—"a being like you."
The child may be desired as an object of care to be dominated
or as someone expected to fulfill their own unachieved ideals.
Especially the naming game expresses various long dormant
but obviously persistent tendencies.   Favorite figures of history, literature, sports, and the theatrical world with whom
the parents once identified themselves as adolescents now come
to the fore; members of the family are suggested, in order that
their names may be accepted as an expression of love or emphatically rejected as an expression of latent hostility.   In the
case of one young woman, who apparently lived in great
harmony with her mother-in-law, the suggestion that the child
be named after the latter, if it turned out to be a girl, led to
the first serious conflict with her husband.   Concealing her
hostility, the young wife herself had first suggested the name,
and it was her husband's joyful consent that aroused all her
hostile feelings against him.   Of course there are as many
different possibilities here as there are parents.

Even if the child has been accepted into the mother's ego as
an object of identification, her strong expectation, and the mobilization of her maternal feelings as a preparation for the future, also endow him with the value of an object lying outside
the ego, to which are directed many positive and negative
emotional attitudes.   The child is also the child of the sexual
partner, and much of the love and hatred that were directed
toward the latter may be transferred to the child still in the
uterus.   Thus many conflicting tendencies confront one
another: the future child is still part of the mother, surrounded
by boundless narcissistic love, the embodiment of all perfection,
the gratifying extension of her own ego.   This relation plays an
important part in the dynamism of the positive anticipations
of pregnancy.   But even this apparently most happy mother-
child union can have negative and sometimes actually dangerous effects.   If the mother's masochistic tendencies are
excessive, the child will occupy that part of her ego which she
loves because it inflicts suffering on the rest of the ego.   The

woman, turned inward, groaning under the cross of pregnancy and yet happy in this condition, exceeds the normal bounds of feminine masochism and even during pregnancy distorts her maternal function too much in the *mater dolorosa* direction.

It is important that the child as future object should be wished for, loved, expected with joy, and accompany pregnancy as a positive idea. This strengthens the optimistic energies of the genuine experience. If the child is an involuntary burden, an object of future hatred in the mother's fantasy, of hatred still unopposed by conciliatory maternal feelings, pregnancy is a curse, not a blessing.

Even in pregnancy women psychically prepare for motherhood by giving up all their emotional interests for the sake of the idea of the child and thus create the soil for instinctive altruistic devotion to the real child. Possibly the most powerful source of maternal love lies precisely in the fact that the narcissism of pregnancy erases the boundaries between the I and the you. Selfless love for the child would in that case be a continuation of this relationship, which with the birth of the child and the splitting up of the inner process is transferred to the outside world, and the child as object would thus be loved as a part of the mother's self. This curious mixture of I and non-I in the mother-child relation during pregnancy is another interesting problem of the polarity of this condition.

The harmonious course of pregnancy presupposes many factors—above all, a definite emotional maturity in the pregnant woman, a sufficient amount of psychic and physical health, and fairly favorable environmental conditions, among which rank first the marital situation, then the social and economic factors, etc. Psychic maturity and physical health are particularly important if the woman is to bear the diversion of her emotions from the outside world without affective disturbances. Excessive introversion can damage the real relation to the environment; it involves the danger of overintensified self-love.

The psychic hygiene of pregnancy must aim at making the child more and more an object, so that delivery does not have the effect of a painful separation from a part of the ego and a destructive psychic loss.   From the very beginning, the pregnant woman's psyche develops defensive mechanisms that aim at stressing the child's significance as an object.   These are manifested in her strong turn toward reality, which proceeds simultaneously with and parallel to the turn inward.   The first distinct signs of the "mother instinct" seem to appear here.   For no matter how passive and introverted, how careless and helpless, how intellectually and emotionally absorbed, how rich or poor, how proud or ashamed of her pregnancy the woman may be, she is seized at this time by a nest-building activity, a need to build, on a large or small scale, for the expected child.   A new house, a perfectly comfortable or beautiful nursery, a layette or a little sacque knitted with her own hands—all these are real even though sometimes extremely modest or symbolic products of this activity, which every pregnant woman develops in the midst of her inner absorption. The same activity is also manifested in her strict attention to prenatal care, as well as in her provisions for the immediate or remoter future, according to her temperament, degree of initiative, and possibilities.

Thus a link arises between the strongly introverted and the socially oriented ego, and even during pregnancy the maternal activity prepares the awareness of the inevitable mother-child dualism.   It depends upon the psychologic situation as a whole whether these preparations are accompanied by joyful expectation or sadness of separation, a relatively carefree spirit or the fear of death.   For the unloved woman, the "asocial" unmarried mother, the harassed working woman, the sick or tired woman, the masculine-ambitious woman who has turned her productivity to other ends, the approaching reality is full of dangers.   Worried and embittered, such women negate the inner positive energies, defiantly reject constructive solicitude, refuse help and prenatal care, and justify the skeptics' doubts as to the existence of a primary mother love.   However, the negation of it here is usually not the result of an initial lack, but the fruit of material conditions or emotional distortions—in brief, of secondary influences.

The withdrawal of large amounts of emotional energy from the outer world, and the incorporation of these into the psychic process of pregnancy, leads to various manifestations in the pregnant woman's subjective, emotional life. Many an introspective woman admits that the amount of happiness she experienced during her first wished-for pregnancy (unless it was overshadowed by negative counterideas) far exceeded the joys of real motherhood. Despite the intellectual controls, despite observations to the contrary, she had the feeling that *her* pregnancy was something extraordinary, that the child she expected would give her unprecedented bliss. But because she believes that her experience contradicts the prevalent ideas, she usually remains silent about it, since she wants above all to appear normal in the eyes of her fellow men.

There are women who, despite their "dreamlike" experience of pregnancy, subsequently have a dim memory of a "marvelous" condition, without being able to define it. All one can learn from them is that they lived in anticipation of joy. Often they also admit their strange but pleasant indifference to all the other affairs of life during pregnancy. Because of this subconscious memory, despite all rational arguments and all difficulties, they feel an ever renewed wish to re-experience the condition of pregnancy.

It goes without saying that the limits of the experience are set by various other inner and outer experiences; what is later accessible to retrospective observation is always a mixture of the original condition and newly acquired elaboration of it. The intellectual woman readily assumes a certain coolness and hardness toward the confusions of her condition. The idea of possible disappointment is always present in her as an inhibiting and protective reservation, as well as a sense of the improbability that any exaggerated anticipations will be fulfilled. Many nonintellectual women likewise are unable to experience the tremendous enrichment brought about by pregnancy and share the feelings of those to whom this condition is only a more or less burdensome biologic process. They hardly remember the more profound aspects of the experience, even less do they make use of these in their subsequent life; but they remember with particular vividness the burdensome or even morbid physical consequences of it. Women mistreated by life show no understanding or sympathy for the whole experience of pregnancy, with all its irrational fear and sensations of happiness.

Among the previously discussed overfertile women who are repeatedly pregnant without being motherly, there are those who merely want to re-experience the pleasure of pregnancy and consider the child an inevitable consequence that must be accepted. As a rule, it is impossible to find out from them what is so gratifying in this condition; most of them do not even consciously remember the pleasure they unconsciously want to re-experience. In many cases the woman feels particularly well when pregnant because this condition signifies for her a sort of vacation from her ego. The feeling of inferiority that at other times impels her to make a self-denigrating appraisal of her own abilities and inabilities, her tense desire for achievements to which she is unequal, subside during pregnancy, and she seems to be saying to herself: "Now I do not have to be anything else, after all I am pregnant." To all those who suffer from awareness of their own ego weakness, pregnancy is a welcome opportunity to enhance their own importance.

Often a kind of depersonalization takes place and the pregnant woman complains that she has no emotions. This condition is intelligible on the basis of the general situation discussed above: the outer world becomes unreal, the inner world is overcharged, the objective existence of the child to whom the emotions ordinarily turn is dubious. The forms in which this confusion of feelings manifests itself are varied. For instance, one woman declared that during her pregnancies she felt very little and had constantly to think about her child. The moment she stopped thinking about it, she was overwhelmed by the feeling that the child did not really exist. No doubt she had accepted the reality of the child intellectually but not emotionally, and instead of a sense of enlargement or shrinkage there arose a feeling of emptiness. This woman was compelled to fill her emotional vacuum by the conscious idea of the child as an object. The content of her intellectual relation to the child was very poor: "I think that I have a child and this makes me happy because I want one."

Another reported that she had to be constantly aware of the existence of the child in order to experience pregnancy as something positive, otherwise she too had a feeling of emptiness, difficult to describe. However, she was able to give us more details concerning her thoughts about the child. These had an extraordinarily gratifying but unusual character. In her "fantasies"—as she called her thoughts—she never considered the child as an object in the outside world, as something in the future; it was something that existed only as long as it was inside herself and belonged to her. For instance, she said: "It is like a stove in the winter that is always lit, that is there for you alone, entirely subject to your will. It is also like a constantly gushing cold shower in the summer, refreshing you. It is there."

For these two women the child did not exist emotionally as an object. They experienced the differentiation between themselves and their children as objects only when they thought of it. When they ceased thinking about it, this differentiation disappeared, and with it the gratifying feeling of having a child. Thus the happiness-giving mother-child union in pregnancy assumes a negative character when it weakens the mother's self-reliance and at the same time erases the independent existence of the child in the emotional experience. In both these cases, the compulsive need to give an anticipated emotional situation a concrete intellectual content, and the incapacity to experience something emotionally without objectivization, expressed a deeper emotional disturbance, which came to the fore only as a result of the new demands of pregnancy. Of course these two women were pathologic, but they present a good illustration of the normal process in a distorted form.

The objective weakness of the child's existence results from a fact I have emphasized on more than one occasion, namely, that it is only an object in the future. Hence the frequent occurrence of the curious phenomenon that precisely women with a strong emotional life—warm, loving, motherly women— declare with a kind of self-castigation that they rejoice over the future child but nevertheless do not love it. "How can I love something that does not exist?" they ask, usually later, when the child is already part of the outside world and their great self-sacrificing love for it has been stabilized. This question is asked by women who in their harmonious emotional life are particularly sensitive to the difference between the experiences of pregnancy and the object love of the mother for the child.

Many neurotic women say that they never at any other time feel as free from their neuroses as they do during pregnancy. This is understandable. Hysterical persons now have a real motive for their tendency to fantasy, and the anticipation of the future so characteristic of them achieves a worth while reality value. As for the obsessional neurotics, they can achieve a period of rest from their constant conflict between hatred and love, for the object on which they, like all other women, center their emotional interest is frequently incapable of mobilizing their ambivalence, since it does not exist independently. It is true that for many of them the absence of the conflict between love and hatred is equivalent to the absence of emotions and, like the depersonalized women, they too complain that they do not have any feeling for the child. Other obsessional-neurotic women transfer the entire conflict between hatred and love to the pale idea of the child. In them, pregnancy provokes the severest obsessional symptoms centered around the life and death of the future child. In many neurotic women, the anticipation of the painful and sometimes dangerous process of birth produces a discharge of guilt feelings that is favorable to their condition and thus results in an improvement with respect to their neurotic illness.

Seen objectively, the mother's existence develops in two opposite directions during pregnancy. First, it is enlarged physically and psychically—physically by the organic addition, psychically by the consciousness of a new being that is connected and identical with her being and creates new emotional possibilities and a new future. Second, it shrinks, also physically and psychically—physically because the woman's body is now in the service of something that is not herself, psychically because she does not receive anything but only gives, and in the next phase of her life will only give.

This duality of attitude can assume boundless proportions, so that the inner experience of the pregnant woman moves between infinite enlargement, "I am the whole world," and infinite shrinking, "I am nothing." The first attitude gives rise to life, love, motherly pride, and feelings of happiness, the second to depression, shame, hatred, destruction, death. The deeper life of the pregnant woman moves between these opposites.

In its positive, optimistic aspect, this antithesis is sometimes subjectively expressed in a feeling of gratifying harmony. During pregnancy the woman feels more and more that she bears a real life in her womb, a life that would be helpless and lost without her devotion. The fact that by her own strength she will give birth to another creature that will face her as an independent being, the approaching duality in the still existing unity, is perhaps woman's most powerful experience. But the pessimistic aspect of the antithesis arises from the same experience: severe anxieties cast a deep shadow and trouble the peace and harmony of pregnancy. They crystallize into two ideas: "I shall die in childbirth" and "I shall not have a child." Whatever individual and universally human guilt feeling, vestiges of memories, threats, and real motives feed these fears, one has the impression that something very deep and primitive lies at the bottom of them.

The realistic acceptance of the child as a future and beloved object cannot completely overcome the inner unwillingness to give up the gratifying union. The inner voice objects: "What it will be later in the outside world is not what it is now. What is now in me, with me, a part of my own self, will be lost. It will be there, but as another being, not myself—something that will breathe with other lungs, pulsate with another pulse, that will achieve independence by its own actions. Now it is still in me, but at the same time is not I.   It is another human being, soon to be a world outside me."

To make it the being that is outside her, the pregnant mother must deliver the child from the depths of herself, and thus she discharges herself not only of it, but with it, of herself. She loses not only it, but herself with it. This, I think, is at the bottom of that fear and foreboding of death that every pregnant woman has, and this turns the giving of life into the losing of life.

If the separation is not felt as the loss of one's own ego, but on a more objective plane, the fear of death is replaced by the painful feeling: "I shall not have a child, I shall lose it, for it will leave me, it will not be *here*."   This feeling corresponds to the inner perception of the later separation.

The irrational death fears of pregnant women, motivated psychologically by guilt feelings and reminiscences of older fears, had a real basis in former times.   Women used to die in childbirth, victims of their own physical constitution and unfavorable external circumstances. Today, modern science saves them from the danger of death and alleviates their pain; yet in their profound psychic life we find manifestations of the groundless lurking fear of death that has remained uninfluenced by the conquests of civilization.   Despite her fully accepted intellectual knowledge of her condition and the exact determination of the date of her delivery, despite her absorption in preparations for the expected child, every pregnant woman harbors in a corner of her soul the doubt: "Will it really come?" At first she doubts her pregnancy in proportion as she desires it, but outwardly she silences these doubts, trusting the strong argument of medical diagnosis.   Later, when the life of her child becomes increasingly manifest, she wants again and again to have its existence confirmed, she notices its movements, and is often seized by fear when she perceives a moment of rest. For behind all her intellectual knowledge there remains the painful doubt: "I shall not have a child."   Here too the old guilt feelings and experiences of childhood supply the inner rationalization.   But the unadmitted, often quite unconscious idea, "I shall not have a child," contains a deep truth. For separation is death, and only when the mother's love again receives the child in the outside world are the specters of death banished.

I have briefly surveyed the psychic processes of pregnancy. If it were possible, as in a laboratory, to isolate the phenomenon from all the influences of past and present environment, and to observe directly all the stirrings of the soul that go hand in hand with the development of the fetus, we should probably learn much more about the subtle correlations between mother and fetus. In the psychoanalytic procedure, pregnancy appears as part of the psychic whole; the condition itself, and especially the future child, appear psychologically as a product of the interaction of factors that are not directly connected with the reproductive function and not connected with it alone. The material cited above comes largely from analyses of pregnant women who wanted to be treated in order to get rid of morbid pregnancy symptoms, or to save pregnancies that they felt were threatened because of previous unfavorable experiences, e.g., miscarriages. In most cases these patients had become pregnant in the course of the analysis, sometimes even as a result of it, and it seemed wise to continue their treatment until delivery, for the sake of their psychic condition as a whole.[6]

In all these cases the individual processes of pregnancy were so interwoven with neurotic symptoms that it was almost impossible to obtain a pure picture of them. For instance, the fantasies and dreams of the patients often seemed to be influenced more by the analytic situation and the analyst's attitude than by the fact of pregnancy, and the whole experience seemed embedded in the general situation. Nevertheless, it was possible to bring out psychologic phenomena that obviously were

[6] I am opposed to psychoanalytic treatment of pregnant women unless there are indications that such treatment will have definite therapeutic results, just as I am opposed to analytic intervention in all life situations that must remain undisturbed in order to develop into real experiences, as, for instance, a happy love relationship or marriage. Only a neurotic illness that disturbs the experience justifies psychoanalytic intervention.

directly dependent upon the biologic processes of pregnancy. Sometimes I had the distinct and very curious impression that the various ontogenetic phases of the fetus affected the psychoanalytic material, especially the dream life of the pregnant woman.

The connection between successive phases in the development of infantile instinctual life and the phylogenetic forms has often been pointed out; similarly, it has been shown that phylogenesis is the formative force in the ontogenetic changes of the fetus (Haeckel's biogenetic law). Thus we have in pregnancy a triple biologically determined parallelism embracing phylogenesis, ontogenesis, and psychic excitations and sensations that provoke the return of definite infantile instinctual impulses. These impulses often supply oral material during the first stage of pregnancy: dreams centered around eating appear frequently. Somewhat later anal contents assert themselves, dirty things one would gladly get rid of. The expected child appears in typical symbols—worms, disgusting little crawling animals (which are usually destroyed)—or, fairly frequently, as a dead child. Gradually the fetus assumes a more human form; it usually appears in dreams as more mature than a newborn baby and shows traits that can be recognized as wish fulfillments in the dreamer, for instance with regard to sex, resemblance, etc. Often it appears as an ideal child, usually representing the dreamer herself endowed with her own best qualities and all those she would like to have.

We have seen pregnancy as a biologic and psychologic prelude to motherhood and have tried to make it clear that the emotional manifestations mobilized during this prelude are not identical with the emotion of motherliness. Pregnancy as an emotional complex is an independent unit from which bridges lead to motherliness and in which the relation with the child is prepared.

At this point I wish to recall what I have said before about women whose motherliness avoids pregnancy and turns to objects other than their own children. Such women wish to escape dangers that in their unconscious are in conflict with sexuality or motherhood, and voluntarily renounce the direct gratification of motherhood. Their motherliness assumes the character of a yearning that they try to gratify indirectly by means of a substitute.

I have previously pointed out the existence of psychologic inhibitions of motherhood that may manifest themselves physiologically and lead to sterility. The subsequent reactions of these women to sterility vary with the psychologic cause. For instance, if they fail to have children as a result of self-punishment, the penalty acquires full significance only if it has been imposed upon an urgent emotional need to give birth to a child. Such women become victims of self-punishment only if they narrow all their life interests, do not look for any compensations, and fall into complete dependence upon their wish for motherhood. They try one remedy after another, constantly change doctors, insist on various operations, and spend their money on quacks. This struggle for a child becomes a symbol of the woman's unique and unattainable goal in life. Sometimes, when the conscious wish succeeds in triumphing over the unconscious inhibition, the self-tormenting activity merely changes fronts. It is then expressed in fear for the child, now real, in the tyrannical role assigned to him, and in the excessive masochistic sacrifices made for him. In other cases, the struggle for motherhood is at the same time a defense against it. As patients, such women behave exactly like many organically diseased persons who want to be cured and yet do everything in their power to remain sick. It goes without saying that there are as many possible reactions to psychogenic sterility as there are motives for it.

But what happens if biology fails to supply the foundations on which motherhood can be built, if morbid incidents have interfered with physical laws, if a disturbance has taken place in the cell microcosm or in the complicated process of maturation of the ovum or spermatozoid or in the mechanism of creation resulting from their union? The energies of the corpus luteum, which builds a nest for the ovum in the mother's body, may be paralyzed for constitutional reasons or because of organic illness, or the reproductive organs may have been irreparably damaged, thus excluding the possibility of motherhood. How is a woman affected by the factual knowledge that she will never be a mother?

We can sum up the result of our observations pertaining to this question in a paradoxic formula: The more motherly the woman and the richer she is in maternal emotional qualities, the more easily will she bear the severe privation that she must suffer and the more readily will she find full even though indirect gratification of her maternal feelings. This is true of course only on condition that she does not react neurotically to her physical inferiority and that she preserves the harmony of her emotional life despite the impairment of her reproductive capacity. A woman who has never been successfully pregnant is deprived of an important experience—the joy of anticipation, the pride of achievement, the anxious tension and its mastery, the dreamlike peaceful introversion, and the joyous preparatory activity. Needless to say, this grief of deprivation presupposes the capacity for and willingness to undergo the experience, which a large number of women lack.

Recently, some interesting experiments were undertaken in the field of animal husbandry, though they seem to have stopped as a result of the war. In order to achieve speedier and more reliable breeding of a superior race of cows, ova of a fine breed of cows, fecundated by stud bulls, were transplanted into the bodies of common cows. Thus the better race was given an opportunity to produce a larger number of animals of excellent breed. In other words, the aristocratic animal was given a sort of servant cow to relieve her of the task of pregnancy so that she could be used exclusively for specialized breeding. It seems a grotesque and incredible idea to think of applying such a procedure to human beings. But if one recalls that in many countries mothers of the so-called upper classes, out of custom or a false sense of values, have had their children wet-nursed by hired servants, such a proposal seems less terrible and new.

What is repulsive in it is perhaps its social aspect—not the fact that a woman should avoid her biologic function, but that another should take it over for her. Yet there is no doubt that many women who would gladly have children, consider pregnancy an evil and would be willing to entrust it to a "fetus bearer."

Should our speculation become a reality, question would arise as to which of the two women should be recognized as the mother in case of a dispute—the one whose germ cells as representative of her whole ego, with all its hereditary factors, are alive in the new individual, or the one who has borne him, fed him with her blood, and given birth to him? In animals the inherited physiologic expressions of the mother instinct are prepared during pregnancy and begin automatically upon the birth of the young. If we consider these instinctual manifestations of the animal as analogous to the functioning of mother love, our question will be decided in favor of the birth giver; if we abide by the idea that the child is part of the woman's organic ego, the woman whose ovum has been fecundated is the mother.

However, if we take the judgment of Solomon as our precedent, we shall give the child to that one of the two women who supplies the stronger proof of altruistic maternal love. Whether this love, as woman's primal urge, is already contained in some form in the germ plasm or is stimulated by hormonal processes and further reinforced by fantasies during pregnancy, it becomes really effective only later, when the child, small, helpless, and dependent on his mother, develops into a human being through her love and tenderness. This conception of mother love is based on a late acquisition in the development of the species. The higher the animal, the more helpless its young, and the longer the time required for maturation. As a result, maternal care is more extended in time. With the increasing helplessness of the offspring in the course of the development of mankind, the function of care became increasingly intensive, the "mother instinct" underwent changes, and through the development of psychic life in man the primitive instinct was transformed into the emotional complex of maternal love. This love in turn became the source of masochistic devotion and unselfish service, at the same time providing the narcissistic compensation of maternal joy. The progressing psychic development also enabled the child to respond to the mother's tender care with his own tender emotions and gradually to replace his original primitive dependence with filial love. Mother love is thus a recent phylogenetic development, an emotional acquisition that is moving farther and farther away from the primitive instincts.

The idea that a form of motherliness is present in the female plasm, and that there are later hormonal influences in this direction, is still hypothetic. My idea of motherliness as an emotional complex is psychologic, and in my view a *woman can fully possess and enjoy motherliness even if she has not conceived, borne, and given birth to a child*. Motherliness is most immediately gratified in actual motherhood, but after that in every child who needs a mother, and in every creature that needs tenderness, care, and altruistic readiness for sacrifice in order to survive or develop. The woman must have, in all the substitute situations, as compensation for her own altruistic tendencies, a narcissistic prize analogous to the one the mother is generously given by the child as part of herself. It is erroneous to speak of sublimated motherliness, for maternal love, even if it is close to instinct, is in itself a sublimation. We are justified only in speaking of its transference, displacement, etc., to other objects. The situation is exactly the same as regards the tender love of children for their parents, which is the step from instinctual life to sublimation. The instinctual components of mother love are diverted to various physical functions. They are gratified actively, but unconsciously, in the feeding and bodily care of the child, in various physical sensations of the reproductive organs. The sensual components of mother love reveal themselves in the mother's need for and manner of physical contact with the child and in her embraces and caresses. There are mothers who exceed the normal level of sensuality, who in stormy fits of tenderness betray their voluptuousness and unconsciously seduce the child. The sterile woman is of course cut off from the direct physical pleasure sensations of motherhood, but she still has at her disposal a world of possibilities of pleasure.

The wish for a child of one's own is accompanied by tendencies that have nothing in common with motherliness as such. If we ascribe to motherliness the highest degree—perhaps a unique degree—of altruistic emotion, we must realize that all the other emotional components of motherhood are par excellence egoistic and narcissistic. The individual's will to self-preservation often falls into conflict with reproduction, but at the same time probably constitutes a powerful motive for it in both sexes. To have an heir to one's own ego, a carrier of one's own blood, a creature who springs from *me*, as fruit from a tree, and secures continuity, immortality, for *my* own transient existence—all these are psychologic motives in the desire for a child that are far removed from, indeed diametrically opposed to motherliness. The idea of immortality, as reflecting an unconscious impulse to beget children, accompanies numerous secondary narcissistic motives. The religions and customs of many peoples express the idea that the childless woman is inferior. She achieves her full status as tribe member and married woman only when she becomes a mother. Almost all nations hold woman alone responsible for sterility; to primitive peoples such a woman appears as accursed, to more developed ones as a cripple.

The history of civilization teaches us that the lot of the sterile woman has often been a tragic one. She has been despised, ridiculed, disgraced. Among Jews and Moslems sterility has been a ground for divorce; among African tribes and American Indians, the childless wife is often repudiated, although otherwise divorces are infrequent. Among many peoples, the mother is respected in proportion to the number of her children, particularly her sons. In higher civilizations, understanding and tolerance have replaced contempt, and in overcivilized circles in various nations, great fertility is sometimes regarded as degrading and "animal." But in other strata as well, births are being restricted in ever larger areas of the world. Social necessity, fear of real obligations, the limitation of personal freedom, and, last but not least, the masculinization of feminine interests and occupations, have not only contributed to the devaluation of fertility, but even threaten to weaken the normal biologic and emotional urge to reproduction.

Our greater knowledge of physiologic processes, and the now current realization that the husband too can be responsible for the lack of children, have helped to rehabilitate the sterile woman. Socially, individually, and erotically, women are today largely evaluated without regard to their capacity to bear children. And yet woman's own attitude toward childlessness seems to harbor many of the old prejudices and censures. "Your body is like a dried-up branch that does not bear fruit," she tells herself, and the feeling of physical inferiority expressed in these words can overshadow all other personal and social values. This feeling has nothing in common with the deprivation of the opportunity to express motherliness. It is a narcissistic reaction to an important organic disadvantage, and it is noteworthy that the psychologic reactions of many sterile women are extraordinarily similar to those that characterize the female castration complex. I mention only a few typical ones When the defect is perceived, the question arises: 'Why?" The explanation of the physician, the operation that has taken place, etc., all these rational elucidations are intellectually accepted. But the need to find a profounder cause ignores the rational reasons. The answer transfers this cause to the woman's own guilt feeling or to the guilt of others. All the irrational motives contained in the fertile woman's anxious question—"Will I have a child?"—come to the fore in the now rationally founded negative answer: "I myself have injured my body, I am responsible for my sterility," or, "Fate or other persons are responsible, I am an unfortunate victim." The old popular condemnation of the barren woman, and the myth of evil spirits, are revived here, deriving their contents from the infantile reactions of the little girl at the time when she first perceived her physical inferiority in her genital trauma.

Inability to find a normal solution for the psychologic difficulties resulting from sterility often leads to neurotic reactions
or a definite personality structure in the sterile woman. As a
rule, intensified narcissism and aggression characterize women
who have been unable to master the "sterility trauma." To
these women one could apply a paraphrase of the saying of a
great Polish poet: "Feminine hearts are beehives: when the
honey of maternal love does not fill them, they become vipers'
nests."

The most frequent type is the woman who transfers the
center of gravity of her existence to the organic disturbance
that is the cause of her sterility, sometimes to pursue a vain
hope, but usually—in the case of absolutely sterile women—
with a narcissistic behavior that is a caricature of motherliness.
The diseased organ is made the object of the most solicitous
care, like a beloved child. Suffering and perpetual sickliness
satisfy the masochistic wishes and, indirectly, the aggressions
against the sympathetic entourage, above all against the husband. Such women are eternal patients, frequently the torment
of their gynecologists.

Another type is the woman who denies the trauma. "As a
matter of fact, I never wanted to have a child," expresses her
narcissistic attitude, which denies any inferiority, but without
the expected favorable effect. Here the traumatic reaction is
only delayed. To replace the child, these women turn to substitutes that, they maintain, are more valuable to them than a
child. But since they have no genuine interest in or talent for
these substitute activities, they prove sterile here too and are
exposed to an additional traumatic reaction. The process of
displacement continues, and they turn to other substitutes to
prove their worth, again with the same result. In the psychic
economy, the advantage of such a displacement is that it offers
a favorable opportunity to abreact the painful frustration and
to accept one's inability. Moreover, the environment can be
accused of "not allowing me to prove my worth."

Even when these women are capable, they always turn to
fields far above their intellectual level, thus stressing their
conviction "Naturally I can do this." Narcissistic oversensi-

tiveness, pride, and self-overestimation, with a simultaneous powerful tendency to feelings of inferiority, characterize this denying type. Every disappointment experienced by such a woman is turned into an accusation against others, her depressive moods gradually intensify, and with advancing age her oversensitiveness is transformed into a paranoic change in character. Often she reproaches her mother—"She should have brought me up to be something better"—or her husband: "I cannot develop my own capacities because he overburdens me with everyday cares." The fact that these are reactions to sterility is usually denied by these women and overlooked by their entourage.

Another type is distinguished by extraordinary envy, above all envy of mothers, of pregnant women, and then in regard to everything that others possess: they feel compelled to acquire similar things in order to rid themselves of their tormenting feelings of jealousy. These things vary with the cultural milieu—they may be position, social success, absolutely or relatively valuable objects, dresses, hats, finally foodstuffs; but most of the time they are things for which someone else can be envied at a given moment. Most of the perambulator peepers are recruited from among these women—not that they want to see the babies because of their own longing for or interest in babies, but because of their gnawing envy. These women also are resentful and vindictive. As we have said, all these reactions are often identical with those deriving from the female castration complex and from penis envy. It is difficult to say whether these women are predisposed to such reactions because the castration complex or penis envy was particularly strong in them. My own impression is that the new physical trauma reopens the old wounds that to a greater or lesser extent exist in every woman, and mobilizes the old readiness for reactions. A child would probably have served normally to compensate these women and to mobilize their latent motherliness. But they have not enough of this quality to overcome the failure of direct gratification of the wish for a child. Really motherly women do not have such reactions.

There is still another sterile type that I call pseudomotherly. These women actively console themselves for the trauma by turning to occupations of a motherly character. They devote themselves to the care of the sick, preferably children, they attend courses in pedagogy, offer their services to kindergartens, nurseries, etc. Charity, often of a self-sacrificing kind, is also their domain. When they have to make a living, they try to adjust their occupations to their "maternal urge"; when they are well-to-do they also make financial efforts to the same end, and often bequeath their fortunes to this impersonal child substitute. Socially, the value of their actions is often considerable; psychologically, it is very small. They only imitate the externals of motherliness. They lack the gift of the motherly woman, the warmth that makes her the child's providence. It is striking how heartless such women often prove in personal relations; one must keep in mind their kind deeds in order not to find them repulsive. They act something that they are not, their motives are purely selfish, inspired by their desire to prove that they are motherly. Inwardly they do not mourn their lack of a child; they smart under the trauma of physical inferiority, the shock of the realization "I am a dried-up branch."[7]

It seems superfluous to give additional details regarding the difference between real motherliness and its substitutes. In the latter, as in the former, we often find an interaction of narcissistic and altruistic-masochistic forces, and a large amount of productive activity centered around objects of care. What the substitutes lack, and what distinguishes them from genuine motherliness, is motherly-loving identification with the object and the happiness deriving from this love.

So far I have limited my discussion to women who react traumatically to sterility but whose motherliness might have developed under favorable conditions.

As I have emphasized before, motherliness is a complex struc-

[7] These women should not be confused with those previously discussed who devote themselves to such substitute activities because of a real need to gratify their motherliness.

ture, not merely an emotional unit. The emotions are accompanied by a dynamic force that steers the motherly woman's activity in a definite direction. I have called this activity nest building: it has the tending, protecting character of the instinctual actions of female animals; in the human female such actions are accompanied by motherly emotions and conscious aspirations directed by will. The sense of duty toward the child that characterizes motherliness has something of the strength of an instinct and is radically different from the character trait of dependability developed under the influence of education, or from sense of duty prompted by feelings of guilt.

In the course of this study I have often referred to the type of woman in whom motherhood is at the service of masculinity. In such cases, pregnancy is explicitly experienced as bodily enlargement; the child in the womb becomes not an object of tender identification, but a possession taken hold of from the beginning of its existence, and dominated. The maternal activity here assumes a definitely aggressive character; but the boundary between masculine-aggressive and motherly-tender activity is often difficult to delineate, because both are directed toward the same goal of caring for the child.

Since pregnancy has a definite wish-fulfilling significance for women of this type, and since for them the child is a productive achievement, they react to sterility in a specific manner. They are dominated not by grief over the deprivation of motherhood, but by the tendency to self-assertion. If a woman of this type cannot master the trauma with the means at her disposal, she may become subject to a severe depression, behind which there can easily be discovered a destructive, raging aggression against the persons surrounding her, whom she holds responsible for her frustration. This is the same aggression for which she would have found a more useful outlet in motherhood. But most women of this type escape the morbid reaction and turn toward the outside world in order to gratify their urge to activity. If their creative urge finds suitable fields, if their need for productivity is matched by their capacity for achievement, they only change their life goals by accepting their sterility, and nothing essential changes for them or in them.

Here we must guard against a certain confusion in terms. Motherliness as an emotional experience cannot be further sublimated; but the productivity of child bearing can yield to another, more masculine kind of productivity, and maternal activity can serve purposes other than the most immediate, direct, and feminine purpose embodied in the child.

Feminine-motherly intuition, that quality which is woman's peculiar characteristic, can be creative in other fields, above all in artistic endeavor, provided it has a talent at its disposal. Here a conflict may arise, not the familiar and frequent opposition of masculinity and femininity, but a conflict between two manners of applying the psychic creative force inherent in motherliness, that is to say, between the direct, immediate manner and the indirect manner. I had occasion to observe the productivity of a prominent woman painter. She wanted and had several children and did not feel that they disturbed her artistic activity. During her pregnancies she even felt an increased artistic urge. But in this condition she was unable to paint anything but children. She painted them with greater artistic devotion than ever and loved her models, but what she produced was only a series of rigid photographs without a trace of soul in them. She was gradually forced to the realization that all the creative powers that at other times flowed into her artistic creation, were now concentrated on her expected child. After her confinement, she again produced notable paintings, but was unable to nurse the child or to devote herself to him in any other way. Apparently it was easier for her to turn her inner interest away from the child when he had become an outside object than during the phase of absolute identity between her ego and the fetus.

Every original production, particularly every artistic work, perhaps combines two fundamental elements—the maternal, birth-giving principle, which leads to intuitive creation, and the masculine, begetting activity. Woman usually invests her creative urge in the reproductive task and the child; man invests his in his work. But perhaps it may also be true that without a component of motherliness in his psychic condition man for his part could not bring his work into being, just as the productivity of woman cannot come about without masculine begetting.

In the case of many artists, it is possible directly to perceive these two principles in their style and work. In the statues of the French sculptress Chana Orloff, the mother-child unity, in which the child seems to be present as an individual entity and yet is still united with his mother's body, is impressively realized. Feminine empathy and experience certainly directed the tools that made such a striking projection of the pregnancy idea possible. And it is obvious that in this artist the mastery of the material and the energy of the realization have a masculine character.

Modern medical research has shown that a childless marriage is not always chargeable to the fact that the wife is sterile; it may also result from the husband's incapacity to beget children. Knowledge of how men react to sterility in their wives, and especially of how they react to this condition in themselves, would be an important contribution to the psychology of men. The urge to reproduction as a phylogenetically determined force is exhausted in man with the secretion of the sperm and the sexual discharge. As for his ontogenetic role as father—protector of the life of his offspring—he has already, in the course of phylogenesis, reallocated this to various goals outside of reproduction; he has learned to turn his urge to beget to indirect goals too. Thus, only part of the productive principle in the begetting male is reserved for care of the offspring; the rest is devoted to 'life goals other than reproductive. In contrast, woman is hardly able to separate her sexual life from motherhood; moreover, her entire psychic existence is woven by innumerable threads into the reproductive tasks and the relationship with the child. To renounce the child means far less to the man than it means to the woman, although in him likewise deeper psychic motives raise the will to fatherhood above a purely biologic level.

The Brahmanic myth of the father's rebirth in his son, the idea frequently expressed in folklore that the grandfather's spirit reappears in the grandchild, is doubtless deeply rooted in man's psychic life. Psychoanalysis casts light on this very ancient theme by the discovery that becoming a father is for a man—just as becoming a mother is for a woman—the fulfillment of old infantile longings, and that his child is not only a revival of himself but also a reconciliation with his unresolved past. Fatherhood gives him a feeling of triumph: now he can transform the old unconscious identification of the little boy with his father into a real and permanent one. The conflict between the hostile and tender impulses can now be decided in favor of tenderness. Loving care for the new generation helps the mature man to free himself from his own childhood, and the urge to this liberation is one of his motives in desiring a child. The physical proof of his masculine potency strengthens his faith in himself as a man. His unfulfilled aspirations and expectations, now charged with new hopes, can be shifted to the child's future.

Despite all this, men can much more easily renounce the direct realization of fatherhood than women can relinquish that of motherhood, provided that the personal development of these men has paved the way for sublimation of their infantile wishes and conflicts and that their other activities secure their adulthood and partial immortality.

For the woman, the failure to have a child because of her husband's incapacity constitutes a multiple trauma. First of all, she is disappointed in her husband, through whom she wants to experience the rebirth of her father in two ways—in him and in the child. Then there is the severe injury to her femininity as a result of nonfulfillment of the demands arising from her feminine passivity: she wants to have the man's virility proved by his begetting a child. The absence of the family triangle constitutes a frustration for the two partners. This situation is needed not only to help them to achieve a biologic unity, but also to enable them to create new identifications through the child, by realizing through him antagonistic and complementary elements. Thus the husband can realize a part of his motherliness through his tenderness toward the child, and the wife a part of her masculinity through common plans for the child's future; he is complemented by enriching his emotional life, she by strengthening her purposeful will in the interest of the child.

In sound, well functioning psychic organisms frustration of the desire for motherhood sets in motion protective forces that help the woman to compensate for it. But these protective forces operate only under favorable conditions. For instance, when childlessness results from the man's sexual impotence, even the most motherly and tender woman seldom succeeds in bearing her fate without being unhappy or falling victim to a neurosis. No intellectual understanding or tolerance helps her to get over her injury and her contempt for the impotent man. Women's conscious reactions to male impotence naturally vary individually. But the woman's conscious willingness to help the man is rarely successful. The intervention of the active woman only intensifies the impotent man's fear; her motherly and patient consideration increases his boyish dependency. But since even the most stubborn psychic impotence in men is often relative and can be sporadically interrupted, it does not always exclude conception. It is interesting to note how much a child, especially a son, can compensate a motherly woman for sexual frustrations. Maternal love can extend from him to the father and a harmonious triangle can come about despite the unfavorable sexual situation. But disappointment in the child, especially if it is an only child, brings to the fore the whole revenge reaction of the disappointed wife against her husband. It is easy for the mother to transfer her love for the child to the father, but it is even easier to divert her hatred from the child to the man.

A woman can accept childlessness much more easily when her husband's sexual potency seems secure, despite his inability to beget. Such a situation may be created by certain physical defects of the male genital organ. Three types of women can be distinguished, according to their reactions to the husband's deficiency.[8]

[6] To illustrate the types, I have sometimes chosen particularly gross examples; all these types, however, can be observed in numerous milder variations. It must also

1. The masculine-aggressive woman usually finds it hardest to accept the situation. She refuses to be satisfied by any substitutes, protests against proposals to adopt a child, and insists on realization of her obstinate wish for motherhood even though she knows that it is impossible. She herself must bear and give birth to the child; a child not of her own body would be worthless in her eyes. In the course of my professional activity I have seen many childless women who asserted that they loved their husbands, but demanded the latters' consent to their conceiving children by other men, under threat of dissolving their marriages. These unfeminine would-be mothers are the exact opposites of the biblical figures of Sarah and Rachel:

> Now Sarai Abram's wife bare him no children: and she had a handmaid, an Egyptian, whose name was Hagar. And Sarai said unto Abram, Behold now, the Lord hath restrained me from bearing: I pray thee, go in unto my maid; it may be that I may obtain children by her [Gen. 16:1–2]....
> And ... Rachel ... said unto Jacob ... Behold my maid Bilhah, go in unto her; and she shall bear upon my knees, that I may also have children by her [Gen. 30:1–3].

I have discussed one such case in volume 1. In the other three known to me, the marital difficulties ended in divorce, after the women were for various reasons unable to achieve their goal. This type shows us the purely narcissistic component of motherhood; here the center of gravity of the idea of "my child" lies in the "my." What is at stake here is not motherly readiness for love.

We have seen that a woman can hardly experience a real relationship with her future child even when she is pregnant, let alone when she is not pregnant. She is not confronted here with the tragic conflict between husband and child or between eroticism and motherliness. The forces of such a conflict stem from other and unconscious factors. In the type under discussion here, the revenge feelings against the husband and the narcissistic greed solve the conflict only apparently in favor of motherliness.

---

be stressed that a given mode of reaction is always based upon a pre-existing disposition.

2. The woman of the second type lives on good terms with her sterile husband; she renounces the child, but engages in a perpetual pursuit of proofs of her husband's masculinity. He must show constant successes, according to his occupation, financial, political, professional, scientific, or artistic. She has a characteristic need to be part of this achievement, to feel each success almost as a gift to herself. She records every advance in his career and is aggrieved over every failure. The substitute formation is obvious here, as well as the double compensation—one intended to procure a high valuation of her sexually inferior husband, the other to satisfy over and over again the pride of an ambitious mother. In this type likewise the grief over the lack of a child has a very narcissistic character.

3. The third type is the truly motherly woman: she is the woman who reacts to her own sterility by a readiness to transfer her motherliness to other children or objects. She does not ask who is responsible; if she loves her husband, she conceives the situation thus: "*We* have no child." In their great common frustration, husband and wife are capable, even without the child, of creating the necessary third being in whom the husband gratifies his fatherliness and the wife her motherliness, whether this third one is real or symbolic, physical or spiritual. To repeat what I have said before: The more motherly the woman, the more easily can she satisfy her motherliness even in her frustration.

In childless marriages in which the causes of sterility cannot be ascribed with certainty to either party and where harmony has not been achieved, the marriage may be transformed into a tribunal. Its most important task appears to be the solution of the problem as to whose fault it is, and according to whether masochistic or aggressive forces predominate, the answer is a silent or open self-accusation or a constant hateful reproach of the other partner. The unborn child here too becomes the third corner of the triangle. All the hostile impulses of the two individuals in relation to each other, their whole conflict of ambivalence, all the guilt feelings and disappointment reactions, fuse into this one problem of the unattainable child. And the problem is insoluble because it gradually becomes a vehicle for other conflicts.

According to the woman's personality there are individual reactions here too, fluid levels of transition between the types described. Roughly speaking, the question "How does a woman react to childlessness?" must be answered by two counterquestions: "How genuine is her motherliness? What are the relations between husband and wife?"

The problem of sterility leads us to that of induced abortion, which is often the secondary cause of sterility.

In this connection we must first of all realize that legal and religious imperatives exert an external influence on the psychologic situation. Wherever these imperatives prove to be an irresistible power, either because of the woman's fear of violating the law or because of her loyalty to her faith, the situation is beyond the pale of psychology. It should be noted, however, that the secular and religious laws are sometimes used as rationalizations that conceal deeper psychologic motivations against abortion. In my view, every woman has the right to achieve motherhood and to renounce motherhood, and every normal woman seems to assume this right emotionally, whether it is legal or not.

In a psychologic examination of a woman's reaction to induced abortion before and after it has taken place, it is important to learn for what reasons the elimination of the child was desired and carried out, whether the pregnancy was legitimate or illegitimate, whether it was a first conception or one of many. Economic disabilities, social morality, fear of relatives, objections on the part of the man involved, or inharmonious love relations, are the generally recognized deterrents to extramarital motherhood.

It is obvious that extramarital motherhood must expect social punishment for the "forbidden" intercourse, especially if the social laws are strict and social care inadequate. The inhibiting influence of public morals on motherliness must not be underestimated. There is an unmistakable tendency to grant women, particularly economically independent women, greater sexual freedom—but only if society is not burdened as a result of it. An extramarital child, even in a democracy, is still a moral and social burden. The external appraisal of her motherhood must naturally react on the individual woman's emotional reactions, and she often makes use of the existing opportunity to separate her sexual life from motherhood. Rejection of extramarital motherhood is in a large number of instances the expression of social compulsion and not of absence of the desire to become a mother. For many women this renunciation is very painful and in the course of time disturbs even the strongest love relation. But the compromise may prove bearable as long as the woman is not confronted with the fact of accidental pregnancy.

At that moment the conflict between the instinct of self-preservation and the urge to motherhood is unleashed. The woman's positive attitude toward the child as a promise for the future runs counter to a powerful negative idea, and as a result the child is felt to be a heavy, anxiety-producing burden. There are three typical reactions to this predicament. The first, the "revolutionary" reaction, gives the victory to motherliness in its struggle against society, and the woman decides to take all the consequences and assume social responsibility for the child. The second type of reaction achieves the same result passively: without desiring motherhood, the woman accepts it as an inescapable personal fate, in the face of which she feels helpless. We shall encounter both these types of reaction among unmarried mothers and shall discuss them later.

The third type of reaction—outwardly perhaps the best adjusted to reality—consists in an attempt to eliminate the consequences by abortion. The woman who accepts and the one who rejects pregnancy often have almost identical personality structures; their different reactions are only different aspects of the same psychic orientation. An active-aggressive woman may resist social morality and keep the child or, appealing to the idea of equal rights with men and sexual freedom (like Genia, the fictional protagonist of this attitude discussed in vol. 1), may unhesitatingly eliminate the child. The passive woman will not permit her desire for a child to interfere with the convention and will eliminate it as a matter of course under outside pressure. The more individual differences of behavior can easily be discovered only under a figurative magnifying glass. Thus the motherly woman has her silent ideas about "how nice it would be"; the aggressive woman may be furious about social injustice and toward the man; the woman predisposed to anxiety has fears of death; the woman laden with guilt feelings reproaches herself, etc.

In contrast to the attitudes of unmarried women, fear of social morality plays no part in those of married women. Here the real motives for induced abortion are social difficulties of another kind, such as disturbance of definite plans, the wish (in newly married couples) to remain alone for a time, a feeling of not yet being ready for motherhood, fear of responsibility, and, among more mature couples, the presence of other children, making a further increase of the family undesirable. In both married and unmarried women, the psychologic reactions to abortion depend upon the motives for it. A harmonious-motherly woman who finds sufficient gratification for her motherliness in her previously borne children, reacts to the loss rationally, that is to say, without further emotional complications, provided that she is not neurotic.

The woman who has a compulsion to conceive and give birth repeatedly (cf. above) reacts to an induced abortion that she herself has insisted upon either with severe neurotic manifestations or with an immediately following new conception. The immediate reaction is often very characteristic: it is a kind of triumph over her own compulsion to be pregnant, which she has defeated by abortion. But shortly afterward a depression or a new pregnancy sets in.

Other women feel pregnancy as an external compulsion, as a servitude; they hasten to get rid of their fetters, and once they

are rid of them their first reaction is a blissful feeling of liberation. These are often the same women for whom even marriage
constitutes fetters, and who, ignorant of their inner and unconscious shackles, make external circumstances responsible for
their lack of freedom.

Women prone to excessive guilt reactions use a situation like
abortion for severe self-accusations. Even if such a woman
intellectually claims the right to self-determination, her tyrannic superego does not miss this opportunity, and often the
guilt feeling is revived subsequently, sometimes even after
several years. In climacterical depressions, for instance, the
self-accusation "I am a child murderer" often refers to a long-
forgotten abortion. I once observed an obsessional, conscientious woman, otherwise not pathologic, who was compelled,
because of her physical condition, on two occasions to lose a
3 month fetus. She felt obliged to erect little tombstones for
them, which she treated with great piety. "They would have
become human beings," she maintained, and her ideas on this
subject remained unchanged even after she had given birth to
several children.

Another woman postponed her guilt feelings for only two
years; when she gave birth to a defective child two years after
an abortion, she held her "criminal deed" responsible for her
misfortune. It goes without saying that whether old guilt
feelings are mobilized by removal of a child, as well as the extent
to which they are mobilized, depends on the woman's psychic
disposition—more accurately, upon her outposts of motherhood. The tormenting feeling "I have killed a child" is usually
a reminiscence of the old past when aggressions against her
mother's pregnancy or against younger brothers or sisters
burdened the unconscious with the guilt of having wished
elimination of these siblings.

Closer examination of the inner dynamisms operating in a
large number of cases of induced abortion reveals that at
bottom there is hardly a woman who reacts to it with complete
realism even when the rationalization is the best possible one.
Logically it seems inconsistent that the same woman should

urgently demand an abortion from realistic motives and at the same time reject it. Additional information proves that this contradiction rarely involves an urge to motherhood that has fallen into conflict with reality. We must take into consideration here the inner associative connections of unwanted pregnancy. Despite the conscious opposition, such pregnancies nevertheless fulfill old wishes; these are outposts of motherhood, as we have called them, and for that reason interruption of them must constitute a trauma regardless of reality. On the other hand, an unexpected pregnancy itself is an interruption of an existing psychologic order—a sudden assault of life. But the additional interruption from outside (abortion) also breaks off the psychologic process that accompanies the biologic events and thereby makes it impossible to carry it through to its end.

Thus the psychologic picture is a complicated one: an old wish fulfillment is interrupted, the trauma of the conception is only apparently repaired by the abortion, de facto it is complicated by a new trauma. The social conflict alone can be solved and avoided by abortion. Only subsequently, from the psychologic consequences, do we learn that something has taken place besides the obvious conflict. We learn that pregnancy, especially the first pregancy, is even under the most unfavorable circumstances the experience of an expected fate for which the woman has been psychically prepared for many years. We also understand why the subsequent reaction to an abortion may be stronger than that to separation from the child after it is born. The inner attachment, the identification with the child that we consider characteristic of pregnancy, takes place despite the external circumstances. Even if this attachment lacks the positive cooperation of the normal, joyful maternal ideas of the future, it has that of the woman's whole past in so far as this referred to a child. As a result of the identification process, the removal of the embryo strikes not only at the undesired child, the "endoparasite," but also at a part of the woman's own ego. For this reason the loss reaction must be described less as that of "I have destroyed a child" than as that of "I have destroyed something of myself." At the same time there is a counterdesire to emerge from the situation "unchanged"—but this is not always achieved.

Many young women, after overcoming their early fears, at first display a quite rational attitude; they consider the pregnancy as an accidental result of intercourse, which is an action desired and sanctioned by the ego, and the fetus as a piece of burdensome tissue that must be removed. Only after the fact do they begin to regret their sexual activity, and the reproach is regressively shifted from abortion to sex. Sexual abandon becomes a humiliation through the devaluation of its consequences.

It is noteworthy how often the woman's relation to the man is disturbed by the discovery of undesired pregnancy and the determination to get rid of it. The man is often, and in the most decisive manner, prevented from interfering in the situation; sometimes there is even a tendency to eliminate him altogether from any part in the matter. It is as though the woman were making a special point of settling this difficulty on her own. The stronger the love relation has been, the stronger may be the woman's feeling of being devaluated. In their common fantasies about the future, the two partners considered the child—her child—as something "wonderful"; now it has become something worthless, disturbing, destined to be destroyed. The woman is suddenly confronted with the necessity of destroying what has been her greatest value—often only to enable her husband to preserve his values (career, ambitions, etc.).

Frequently, despite the best understanding between the two partners before the abortion, a change takes place in the woman after it. Even if both have weighed all the pros and cons and taken the decision together, their communion is broken afterward. Suddenly the previous simple reasoning proves wrong; the woman realizes now that her agreement with her husband or lover regarding the abortion had an ambivalent quality. Her suffering and the restriction of her existence, even though for only a short time, for the sake of no positive goal, have produced a change in her. As an after-effect of her physical experience, she feels: "I am not the same as before."

Abortion often signifies an attack upon the woman's narcissistic need that her body be a desired "sanctum" to the man. The common feeling in the young girl that a man loses all respect for her after he has possessed her is reactivated by this new experience. Her emotional reactions are in many cases distinguished by an extraordinary yet only apparent inconsistency. This can be illustrated by the case of a young couple who found themselves helplessly confronting a situation beyond their grasp. They had known and loved each other for several years; a year before the events described here they had begun to have sexual intercourse, both being fairly inexperienced. The girl soon became pregnant and the man immediately declared his willingness to marry her in order to be able to keep the child. But she suggested an abortion, on the ground that his career and ambitions would be impaired by the founding of a family at this time. She had always admired him for his accomplishments and talents and both dreamed of a brilliant future on this basis; the idea of a child had been postponed to a much later date. Both were freethinkers; the girl's morality was strict, but it did not condemn her abortion. When her lover visited her during her subsequent illness, their relation was still warm and tender. But after her recovery she refused to see him, saying that although she did not hate him, she "felt a vacuum" in his presence; she had lost her old feeling for him.

The results of the psychologic observation of this case, briefly summarized, are as follows. The woman voluntarily and spontaneously subordinated herself to her lover's aims and interrupted her pregnancy; but she did not realize the extent of her sacrifice and the fact that the sacrifice would mean more than a bodily discomfort. Later she repented her action—she felt that she should not have sacrificed so much. She also felt that she was spiritually unequal to her lover, her physical and her feminine inferiority strongly invaded her consciousness, because she had been forced to experience something without his sharing it psychologically. One could see how the woman's psychologic processes were interrupted, how her previous identification with him was split by her experience. A new possibility of identification in a family triangle did not come about. She was not quite clear whether she regretted having renounced the child; what she felt was that something of her own self was gone.

The summation of several psychologic reactions produced the neurotic feeling of a vacuum. These reactions consisted of subsequent regret for the sacrifice, the feeling of separation from a physical part of the ego, the feeling of feminine inferiority as a consequence of the biologic process, and, finally, a goodly dose of repressed vengefulness toward her lover. The girl had apparently underestimated the significance of motherhood for her emotional life, for she recovered her former very dynamic ego after she married her lover and gave birth to a child.

The behavior of those women whose path to abortion is paved in advance with all the reactions of shame, fury, and vengefulness toward the man naturally runs a simpler and more normal course. Such a woman recovers from her trauma with particular rapidity and completely disposes of her previous personality. Some aggression and masculinity renders a woman good service in situations in which her femininity comes off badly. Too large a measure of these components, however, can become a continuous, burdensome threat to the man, who does not always succeed in leading the aggressiveness thus provoked into harmless channels.

Ultimately, in so far as the psychic life is concerned, the problem here is to find a balance between the narcissistic and the masochistic forces. Suffering without compensation is difficult to bear and goes beyond the limits of feminine masochistic readiness.

As a whole, the trauma of induced abortion is not irremediable unless it has caused an organic injury. It sometimes happens, especially when the matter is handled by nonprofessionals, that the woman's genital organs lose their capacity for reproduction, so that she becomes sterile. Then the experience becomes fatal and the former relatively good solution of the conflict is no longer adequate. This form of sterility is the most difficult to bear, for it constitutes not only deprivation of a child, but also a constant source of guilt feelings and, above all, of hostile accusations against the man. "Had he been a really loving man he would have mastered the situation," expresses the feeling of such disappointed women. A socially determined renunciation of children always produces more or less resentment against the man; if this renunciation becomes a permanent circumstance no longer controllable by the will, the reproach is intensified and often insurmountable.

My aim has been to show that in woman's life there are definite situations connected with the reproductive function that are so deeply rooted that even when they are solved realistically, without opposition of doubts or counterwishes, the solution is not necessarily successful. Adjustment to reality sometimes involves severe emotional disturbances. Nevertheless, the most advantageous choice between the ambivalent alternative answers to the question "Should I, can I, do I wish to preserve the child?" is the one that seems to involve the lesser immediate dangers; the later dangers may be equally unavoidable whether the decision is positive or negative, and it is impossible to estimate in advance which danger will prove greater in each individual case.

The laws and religious injunctions directed against abortion are, as we have mentioned, complicating factors. Incidentally, it is interesting to note that public opinion, common sense, and normal moral judgment support the woman's human right to be a mother or to avoid being a mother by any of the means at her disposal, according to her wishes. For apart from the attitude of certain groups influenced by the Catholic church, the normal emotional reaction to abortion is overwhelmingly, in the most varied civilizations, to take the woman's part despite any laws to the contrary.

Racial, political, or social interests do not always coincide with the rights of the individual. Perhaps in the near future we shall find a reasonable balance between these two rights of woman—the right to motherhood, strengthened by a greater protection of it, and the right to voluntary control or renunciation of motherhood.

Induced abortion is a more or less voluntary act, often a good adjustment to reality. Spontaneous abortion is a different matter. It frequently expresses a psychic process just as completely uninfluenced by conscious will as the organic process itself.

The advances of endocrinology increasingly enable us to diagnose the somatic forces that tend to produce spontaneous abortion, particularly when no obvious organic disturbance is involved. Today we know that a large percentage of spontaneous abortions and premature deliveries are caused by general endocrine imbalance, primary ovarian deficiency, thyroid and pituitary disturbances, etc. The uterine contractions occurring in abortion and premature labor are the end result of a process that can be traced back to a disturbance of the hormonal supply, but that can doubtless also be inaugurated, provoked, or intensified by emotional factors.

The considerable number of abortions that I have observed were unmistakably so much influenced by psychogenic factors that these latter could be held responsible for the process. Such cases differ from instances of induced abortion in two ways: (1) the inducing agent is in the psyche, and (2) the pregnant woman who resorts to the help of this agent does not act from conscious will or in accordance with conscious wishes. On the contrary, in my opinion it is almost typical of these cases that the unconscious force directed against the pregnancy is in complete opposition to the woman's strong, often even overstrong wish for a child. Future systematic study of spontaneous abortion will probably show whether the body's readiness to react to psychic stimuli in this manner is based on hormonal elements, what part is played by the dispositional expulsion tendencies, etc.

I have not been able to establish psychologic types of women

more predisposed to abortion than others. But I have gained
the impression that, particularly in cases of recurrent abortion,
destructive tendencies directed against the self or against others
are involved.[9] One intelligent patient who had several abortions believed that the term "criminal abortion" denoted
spontaneous abortion, thus revealing her unconscious ideas.

Probably a distinction must also be made between acute
emotional causes operating like shocks, and deeply psychogenic,
dispositional causes. Personally I have observed only the
latter, and in each case I reached the conclusion that multiple
determinants were involved, and that only when combined
could they produce an amount of unconscious anxiety, disability,
and unwillingness sufficient to make the conscious ego, which
wanted the child, unable to resist the unconscious tendencies.
We recall that in Alice (p. 132) earlier expulsion tendencies,
combined with a fear of dependence on her mother, and with
aggressive anger against her husband, produced uterine contractions and a threat of abortion. In other women, pregnancy
became directly the arena of a struggle in which the child was
on the side of the hostile forces, or the self-punishing tendency
had such powerful impetus that to fulfill the ardent wish for a
child was impossible and dangerous.

Mrs. Smith (p. 145) had several abortions because of her fear
of her own inability to become a mother. We understood her
fear when we discovered that she rejected identification with
her own mother.[10]

In many women the idea of the child is so strongly associated
with that of accomplishment that a neurotic inhibition about
accomplishing something in other fields may be transferred to
the child, thus producing a constant fear of failure that expresses
itself in a tendency to abortion.

[9] I am not referring here to cases of habitual abortion in which deep-lying defects in
development of the gametes were found to be the causative factor. I do not know
whether, in addition, psychogenic factors can be found in these cases.
[10] As a rule, such a rejection of mother identification strengthens the girl's wish to be
like her father. This can influence her whole life attitude, all her professional
interests, ambitions, etc., to such a degree as to bring about an increasing conflict
with motherhood—a conflict that assumes the character of a struggle between
femininity and masculinity.

A particularly instructive example of psychogenic abortion is supplied in the history of Mrs. Pecka, who underwent psychoanalytic treatment only in her later years, at the age of 50.

As a young college student she entered into a passionate love relation with one of her teachers, who was only a few years older than she but married and the father of a child. He did not love his wife, but could not free himself from the feeling that he was inseparably tied to her and their child. Their marriage had only a formal character, while his love relation with his pupil was very intense and gratifying. During her treatment the patient realized that at the time she had accepted the status quo, but had always secretly hoped that her lover would eventually divorce his wife for her sake. But in those days she considered herself "above" such bourgeois demands. Her wish for a child by her beloved man grew ever stronger, but her unfree lover, bound by the necessities of his worldly position, comforted her only with promises for the future. At a certain point her wish fantasy seemed to be materializing, for she showed the first symptoms of pregnancy. The two lovers agreed on an abortion; the physician whom they consulted found that the girl was not pregnant and shortly thereafter the symptoms disappeared, as was to be expected.

But the woman's relationship to the man was deeply damaged. She continued in it as though nothing had happened, she ardently yearned for her lover when they were separated, but at the moments of their greatest happiness she would say to him: "When we are both very old, I shall tell you something."

She meant that she would tell him then how unhappy he had made her and how he had destroyed her life by denying her a child. Apparently he too wanted a definitive union with the girl; perhaps he also felt intuitively how strongly she wished for a child, perhaps he feared to lose her. At any rate, he began to speak of a future possibility of marriage. An old heart ailment of his wife's reappeared and the physicians' prognostications were unfavorable. The hope of his wife's death could only be divined in his accounts, for naturally neither of the lovers ventured to have such a wish consciously, much less to express it in words. In the meantime the man did his full duty by his wife and was very much concerned about her health. Then, during a short separation caused by her work, the girl received a letter from her lover informing her that his wife had died suddenly in a sanatorium as a result of her heart ailment.

It was clear that fate had brought her to the threshold of fulfillment. She was supposed to meet her lover a few weeks later, and in her fantasy she began—this time freely—to indulge in future plans. But before she saw him again she fell in love with a young man whom she had known before without having been particularly interested in him. She immediately began a relationship with him and became formally engaged.

When her first lover arrived he was confronted with a *fait accompli*. There followed months of exhausting struggles, during which the widower wooed her violently and she herself swung between her painful yearning for him and absolute indifference to him. Gradually the latter feeling triumphed, she married her fiancé, and was completely happy. But she experienced difficulties in becoming a mother. She wanted to have children, was pregnant several times, but never managed to give birth to a child. Sometimes she had spontaneous abortions, sometimes miscarriages in an advanced stage of pregnancy. Since she was an artist and art meant a great deal to her, and since her relationship with her husband was tender and friendly, she never felt actually unhappy. Her former lover died a heroic death in the first world war. Only during her analysis did my patient understand why her first miscarriage took place immediately after she received the news of his death.

It is true that she wanted to have children, but only by this man who had denied her a child. His death reminded her of the impossibility of realization of this wish. I found that even at the age of 50, long after the events, she had a fantasy that fulfilled her motherly yearnings after her separation from her first lover. She imagined that when, as a young college student, she thought she was pregnant, she really was pregnant, but, feeling that her lover did not want a child, she concealed her condition, went to a foreign country, and gave birth to a magnificent boy, for whom she took full responsibility. In this fantasy she was successful in her work, had many friends, and gathered around her a circle of highly cultured people who worshiped her little boy. Her lover tried to approach her, but she always rejected him. After many years he came to her studio, saw the magnificent young man there, and recognized him as his son. But he was compelled to renounce him, because the mother's offended love stood between father and son.

In her treatment, this patient's love for the unhappily married man, her tenacity in her attachment to him, her inability to renounce the idea of a child by him, her deep need for revenge, etc., could be explained on the basis of profound predetermining motives. Considering that her wish and revenge fantasy survived even her former lover's death, one can imagine the extent of her disappointment and narcissistic mortification. The fact that the man's wife had to die before her love wishes could be fulfilled was unbearable for the girl's self-love.

Our patient recalled very clearly that from the very moment when she had heard that her lover's wife was ill, she feared that the woman might die, because this would deprive her lover of the possibility of proving that he was willing to break all the fetters binding him to his family and to society for the sake of his love for her. She could not renounce this demand upon him. As she said, she herself was willing to sacrifice everything except her demands. Her wish for a child remained attached to the very man who did not give her a child.

The fantasy of the child by this man filled her so completely that she had no room left in her for a real child. This fantasy was intended to gratify an aggressive vengefulness rather than a really maternal yearning. Why she was unable to have a child by her husband, although she consciously wanted one, could never be explained by the gynecologist.

It is noteworthy that her tendency to express psychologic contents in symptoms of the genital apparatus manifested itself even in her youth. In her college days these symptoms fulfilled her wish to have a child; later she resorted to organic means to express her unconscious protest against a child from an unloved man.

Woman's struggle against undesired pregnancy uses other means besides induced or spontaneous abortion. Many women take so strong a psychic attitude against having a child that despite obvious physical changes they deny their pregnancy, apparently in complete good faith, and thus make it psychologically nonexistent in a passive manner. Unwillingness to have a child is not always the motive for denial. In many cases this solution is resorted to in the woman's conflict of strong ambivalence between "I want" and "I do not want," which is thus silenced or postponed. I observed this denial in several obsessional neuroses. In other cases, the woman's emotional reorientation fails to take place because of emotional obtuseness, and she remains under the impression that "nothing new is happening."

In many women, especially very young ones, the denial of pregnancy results from a kind of psychic inertia, an unwillingness to face new complications in life. Such childish women are so far removed from the idea of becoming mothers that they are absolutely unable fully to accept reality. In others, denial is the only way to save a pregnancy threatened by outside reality. "I did not know it," say young unmarried pregnant women at a time when the symptoms are visible to anyone and when it is too late to intervene. Sometimes such women stubbornly deny the facts until they are surprised by labor pains. In many cases the denial arises from unconscious guilt feelings that assume this expression in order to achieve their gratification in the suffering of an unwanted motherhood; the denial serves this masochistic motive by making all outside help impossible. A denied pregnancy can also surprise other persons and thus gratify revenge tendencies to a considerable degree.

Women whose objective self-observation is disturbed by their fear of being unable to bear children can also be found among these who deny their pregnancy, especially when they play a kind of game with fate. "Perhaps nothing will come of this after all, and in that case it is better to protect myself against disappointment," their unconscious seems to say; this is obviously a kind of superstitious fear, akin to the belief that if one boasts of one's happiness it does not materialize.

In summary, unless we are dealing with severe intellectual deficiencies, such as imbecility or idiocy, or with conscious fraud, the failure of a woman to perceive pregnancy in herself results from one of the several psychologic motives described above.

The converse of denied pregnancy is imagined pregnancy, so-called spurious pregnancy or pseudocyesis.

The pubescent girl is full of fears relating to pregnancy, and her excited fantasy sets various "popular" pregnancy symptoms in motion, of which vomiting is the most frequent. Amenorrhea can occur in various age groups, as an isolated symptom or in combination with others (e.g., anorexia nervosa), and it often expresses an unconscious wish for pregnancy. Naturally, a considerable amount of emotional tension must be present; the wish alone is not enough to create the conditions for such a functional disturbance. As a rule what we have here is a summation of psychic motives, among which fear of pregnancy is the element that leads to the overloading of the psychic apparatus and to the physical discharge or inhibition of the function.

It is different with young women who, threatened with sterility, observe their bodies with anxious attention and imagine that they are pregnant. This wish-fulfilling imagination certainly influences the subjective sensations and the organic processes, and suffices to provoke a more or less protracted amenorrhea, morning sickness, and a temporarily inflated intestinal tract. Objective control in the form of medical examination usually prevents the symptoms from stabilizing.

The condition of spurious pregnancy or pseudocyesis goes far beyond these abortive psychogenic pregnancy symptoms.

It asserts itself with all the accompanying bodily manifestations of pregnancy, consistently from beginning to end. A deeper and more complicated psychologic and physiologic mechanism is required to achieve the consequences of a long process, to induce objective changes in the uterus, to start the production of milk in the lacteal glands, etc.[11]

I have had occasion to observe several cases of pseudocyesis. These girls and women developed their symptoms under completely different conditions; nevertheless it was possible to discover similarities among them, suggesting that certain psychic determinants constantly accompany this complicated bodily process.

One case was that of a 25-year-old unmarried woman who was employed as assistant cook in a restaurant. She lived with her parents and numerous brothers and sisters. Her father was chronically ill and she bore almost the entire burden of supporting the family. She had a great deal of work to do and constant worries; her life was difficult and monotonous. For many years she had passively submitted to her fate, and it was clear that she buried herself in her work and in solitude out of fear of life. Later she became aware of the fact that what she most feared was pregnancy: "If an unprotected girl like me ever ventures to go out, she immediately becomes pregnant."

Gradually her existence became unbearable to her, and she felt that she must dare something, but she had no resolution and no initiative. Finally, she tried to break the monotony by force, and against her real wishes joined her comrades in the restaurant in their escapades, which until then she had despised. Now her fear of pregnancy was conscious; it limited her freedom of movement and kept her from all sexual contacts. Then she met a young man. She did not know whether she was in love with him, but "went" with him for one year without having sexual intercourse, although they indulged in "necking" and

[11] Moulton stresses the difference between simple cases of "hysterial mimicking of the external signs of pregnancy, with few endocrine changes," and cases in which the objective symptoms of pregnancy have a profound organic character. Cf. MOULTON, R.: Psychosomatic implications of pseudocyesis. Psychosom. Med. vol. 4, 1942.

he urged her insistently to give herself to him. But she was held back by her fear. She confessed this fear to him and he promised that he would marry her should things "get that far"; he also assured her that he would be careful and that nothing of the kind would happen.

Having apparently grown impatient of her stubborn refusals, he threatened to break off relations with her. She thought that if she now became pregnant he would have to marry her, and that was what she really wanted. But she also felt that this made her a sort of blackmailer, that he would be marrying her only under pressure and not out of love. Gradually, the relation broke off as a result of her continued refusal, and she returned to her former mode of life. The very next month she failed to menstruate and developed the usual pregnancy symptoms. She went through a difficult time trying to conceal her condition, and continued working until she felt labor pains and was taken to the hospital, where pseudocyesis was the finding. She was then transferred to the psychiatric department, where she presented the picture of a woman in the second stage of delivery. Her face and behavior were typical of a woman in travail, her body was arched, there was colostrum in her breasts, and the motions of her intestines were so violent that at first sight they could be taken for the motions of the child.

It is noteworthy that she had never had herself examined by a physician. When her father asked for the name of her seducer, in order to call him to account, she refused to give it; nor had she addressed herself to him. She believed objectively in her pregnancy and at the same time was deeply convinced that she would not have a child. She had no feeling of expectation, she made no preparations, felt no worry about the future of the child, and no fear of the future in general. She had impressively realized her pregnancy wishes in her fantasy in order to protect herself from their actual realization. She put her lover in a position in which he was bound to marry her, but only in her fantasy, and thus she saved herself from the role of blackmailer.

We do not know why she feared real pregnancy, what threats and punishments hung over her in connection with it. It seems that even her fantasied pregnancy brought her much punishment, because she had to suffer a great deal in the course of it; in addition, she had to endure a great disappointment—the lack of the child, a lack for which, it is true, she had been unconsciously prepared. At the same time, we observed that, at least consciously, she breathed with relief when she realized that she had no child.

Another case is that of a woman who had been married for six years without being impregnated. She had two successive imaginary pregnancies lasting several months each, and one is inclined to suppose that with her it was a case of direct wish fulfillment, since to her great despair she was sterile. But, strikingly enough, the climaxes of her pregnancies both times coincided with the yearly reunions of her former schoolmates. During her entire college career she had belonged to a closed group of friends isolated from the other students. They were known as the "inseparable ten" and no one suspected that, despite their friendship, a tension of envious competition prevailed in the group. At first there was emulation in studies, then jealousy among the girls themselves, thus creating unrest in the circle, later erotic rivalry, and in the end competition as to which one of them would marry first and have a child first.

After graduation the friends swore eternal loyalty to each other and decided to have reunions every year at a certain time. The woman of our case, who had always been one of the first in the competition with her friends, soon found herself far behind in the most fascinating race of all, the race for motherhood. The cause of her sterility was an endocrine disorder; at the same time she exploited her peculiar symptoms in order to appear before her old companions as pregnant, thus fulfilling her ardent wish.

It is also notable that in neither of these two attacks of pseudocyesis would she agree to be examined by a physician. Each time she was convinced that she was pregnant, but at the same time she felt that it was not true and did not want to hear the physician's negative verdict. In the psychiatric interview she maintained that her peculiar condition was one of mixed knowledge and ignorance; the influence of her competition with her friends could not be doubted. Incidentally, she very much wanted her circle to accept the plausible explanation that she had had a miscarriage each time. It was obvious that she had also experienced a kind of triumph of the clever one over the stupid ones in having thus slyly deceived her friends. In college she and her circle had competed as to which of them was the most intelligent, and in the given situation she was undoubtedly the winner.

In the earlier mentioned study by Kardiner about the Marquesans we read:

> There was also not infrequent occurrence of feigned pregnancy, which was undoubtedly of neurotic origin and may have been motivated by the desire on the part of the woman to exercise the privilege of control over chief and secondary husbands that went with the state of pregnancy. When the feigned pregnancy failed to materialize it was believed that the child had been carried away by the vehini-hai or that a fanaua was responsible. . . .
> The neurotic manifestation of pseudocyesis is related to the jealousy between women regarding prestige and pregnancy.[12]

If our patient had been a Marquesas woman, she would have had the great advantage of being able to blame the evil spirits. It would have been the fanaua who, at the bidding of one of her nine friends "moved by envy and rivalry," had destroyed her child in her body. Her psychic kinship with the Marquesas women seems to me striking, despite the great cultural differences.

A third case is that of a newly married woman whose chances of becoming pregnant were very dubious as a result of an organic defect of her husband's testicles. She had fallen passionately in love with him and married him despite her parents' protests. Her pseudocyesis lasted for ten months; in the second month her physician gave her a diagnosis of probable pregnancy and she was supposed to consult him again at a definite date to check the diagnosis. She failed to do this, and only the unusual length of her alleged pregnancy forced her to submit to a medical examination, in which her condition was diagnosed as pseudocyesis.

This woman too spoke of the peculiarly ambivalent feeling of belief and disbelief in her condition, and like the others she feared the objective verdict of the physician. In so far as her psychologic motives could be discovered, her pregnancy expressed a heroic struggle for the rehabilitation of her husband, above all in the eyes of her parents, who had opposed her marriage (we were unable to find out whether their opposition was based on their knowledge of her husband's defect). At any rate, by her pregnancy she said: "You see how wrong you have been, he is quite able to beget a child."

But, unconsciously feeling deceived by her husband in relation to her wish for motherhood, she retaliated by the same means: she deceived him with the false promise of a child. By her simultaneous self-deception she negated her suppressed malicious reproach "You cannot give me a child," and thus was in one act both the deceiver and the deceived.

Our fourth case is that of a bereaved mother who after the death of her second child fell into a depression characterized by self-accusations. She reproached herself with having caused the death of this child and turned away from her beloved firstborn, now her only child, evidently in self-punishment: "I am not a mother."

She was urged to become pregnant again and thus to get over her loss. She rejected this advice, but became pregnant in her own way, that is to say, she produced all the typical pregnancy symptoms. She herself denied her pregnancy in a typical melancholy manner and insisted that "nothing would come of it." No one except herself doubted her pregnancy, but it took a long time to convince her that she needed to be examined medically, if only to get rid of her hypochondriac denying idea. The examination showed that she was right, that her pregnancy was spurious. But she herself was deeply shaken and surprised, for somewhere in the depths of her soul she hoped that her denial of pregnancy was really a morbid nihilistic idea of her own.

Here a severe guilt feeling was obviously involved; real pregnancy could not be accepted and the ambivalent wish for it could be realized only in an illusory form, as destructive self-deception.

In each of these cases the psychologic mechanism was different. However, the following factors are common to all of them.

1. There was an ambivalent attitude toward the fact of pregnancy: a simultaneous wanting and not wanting it, a wish for a child, and the fear of its realization or its inner prohibition.

2. The wish for pregnancy did not derive only (or chiefly) from the yearning for motherhood, but from secondary motives, usually of an aggressive, hostile character. The unconsciously expected disappointment was intended to gratify these secondary motives.

3. Sometimes, or perhaps always, a self-punishing intention was fulfilled in addition to the aggression.

4. The simultaneous knowledge and refusal to know that the pregnancy was an illusion were expressed in all our cases by the rejection of a medical examination.

Much in the psychic behavior accompanying pseudocyesis reminds us of pseudology: a lying fantasy is pushed to the fore in order to deny and avoid a more dangerous truth. The intensive character of the fantasy produces in the liar, just as in our symptom-forming women, a feeling of uncertainty: "Is it true or not?" The triumphant feeling of deceiving others often seems in both the pseudologists and the pseudopregnant women to assume the character of revenge: "This time not I am the deceived, but you." The perception "What I am pretending here is quite false" serves in both for self-punishment.

How the psychologic contents assert themselves in the complicated organic processes of pseudocyesis, is a problem for psychosomatic research.

We have seen that some women deny real pregnancy and that others indulge in the illusion that spurious pregnancy is real.

All of these women fear the objective truth because in them motherhood is the victim of a conflict between wanting and not wanting it, between wanting it and being unable to achieve it, between the wish and the fear, the inner command and the inner prohibition. In brief, in all these cases external and internal difficulties prevented the consolidation of a motherly ego.

CHAPTER SEVEN

Delivery

I F delivery were a purely physiologic process, it would probably be subject to far fewer individual variations and cultural influences than it is. In normal organic conditions the process would always be the same. It is the complications of childbirth that supply us with a clue regarding the degree to which it is determined by psychic factors.

Anthropologists have advanced numerous theories to explain the greater or lesser ease of the act of birth in various epochs and in various cultures, peoples, races, etc. Some investigators ascribe the differences to climatic and other environmental influences on the endocrine functions that are important in the act of birth; others stress the importance of a wholesome or unwholesome way of life for the development of the female body and in particular of the genital organs. Still others consider the pelvic muscles, upon the action of which delivery depends, a key factor. According to these latter investigators, the functional efficiency of the pelvic muscles is higher in primitive women because of their more active way of life, while civilization, they think, exerts a disturbing and inhibiting influence on the birth functions. Likewise, primitive women's lesser sensitiveness to labor pains is often emphasized. Their greater tolerance can create the false impression that the process of birth itself proceeds much more easily and rapidly in them. At any rate it is generally considered an established fact that the reproductive process in primitive women is much simpler than in women "degenerated" by civilization. But this question is still largely obscure, and various studies suggest that the relative simplicity or complexity of the process does not always depend upon a higher or lower degree of culture.

Very often we are confronted with modes of reaction that give the outside observer a distorted picture of the facts.

Among primitive peoples as well, severe disturbances of the process of birth occur, especially subsequent invalidism and mortality among the mothers. Nor are the data completely reliable with regard to the length of the process, because we cannot always establish the actual beginning of delivery from the woman's behavior. Partly as a result of faulty observation, and partly because of individual differences in the birth process under identical cultural conditions, the existing data are confusing. Thus, according to several explorers, the duration of the process among Australian tribes (living under the same cultural conditions) varies from a period of a few hours to one of several days. In some tribes the whole confinement period is a matter of minutes. The young mother immediately bathes herself and the newborn infant in the nearest river and returns to her interrupted work as though nothing had happened. If a woman is suddenly seized with labor pains while traveling on land or by water, she resumes her journey immediately after delivery and continues on her way until she reaches her destination.

We learn from an interesting observation made by Kohlbrugge[1] that the delivery of a Teugerresin woman of Java rarely takes more than an hour, but that in scattered individual cases it takes considerably longer, especially in women whose mothers likewise had long deliveries. This fact is explained on the basis of heredity. If we recall the extent to which under our own cultural conditions the process of birth is influenced by the woman's identification with her mother, we can assume that among primitives too the biologic process is not entirely free from psychologic influences.

That deliveries do not take place in accordance with the ideal of natural functioning even among primitives is proved by the fact that many Asiatic peoples, for instance, resort to the help of midwives. Since these women have no idea of modern asepsis and little real knowledge of the birth process, they seem to disturb rather than further it and the rate of mortality during delivery is strikingly high.

[1] Ploss, H., and Bartels, M.: Das Weib. Berlin: Neufeld, 1927, vol. 2, p. 604.

Many prescriptions, rules, and taboos relating to pregnant women suggest that primitives too must have had bad experiences with delivery. These aspects of custom confirm our suspicion that the level of civilization in a given people does not determine the ease or difficulty of functioning in reproduction. It is noteworthy that many customs and superstitions of primitives regarding pregnancy and delivery show a similarity not only to the behavior of neurotic women in our own civilization but also to that of our psychically normal women.

Thus primitive customs relating to the place of delivery are reflected in the very individual preferences of our women in this matter. (Civilized hygienic regulations and institutions usually disregard these preferences, however.) Among some tribes, for instance, parturition takes place in complete solitude in the woods or on a beach. The Maori women of New Zealand give birth to their children in the bushes on a river bank, to which they retire all alone. The Gebrito and Montesca women of the Philippines bring forth their infants without assistance, and the woman is often alone when the labor pains begin. Then she stands up, rests her abdomen against a bamboo stick, and presses hard. The child is received in warm ashes, whereupon the mother lies down beside it and severs the umbilical cord herself.

The Warram Indian woman in British Guiana leaves her village as soon as her time comes. Alone in a hut in the woods, she awaits the birth, which is apparently without danger for her, and then returns to her kin with the newborn child, without having resorted to the help of other people. The women of certain Indian tribes in Guatemala behave in the same way, and similar customs were reported in accounts of early travelers to Virginia.

In our own civilization too many women take refuge in a state of "weakness" immediately after delivery in order to enjoy the baby in peace and solitude, immune from flower-bearing visitors. The need to give birth to the child in solitude and to remain in seclusion with it for a time would manifest itself much more frequently if our cultural customs did not run counter to such a practice.

Among many primitive peoples the woman is considered unclean, even dangerous, during the entire course of her pregnancy. Malevolent demons are thought to people her house and the place of delivery, and we find innumerable customs that are supposed to free her and her intimates from these dangers. The belief in evil spirits that injure the pregnant woman and her fruit is very ancient and deeply rooted; its existence among primitives is another proof that they have had bad experiences with the birth process.

Among many nations the "evil spirit" is embodied in a female being. The malign Labartu of the Semites spread terror and devastation wherever she appeared, and was particularly dangerous to unborn children and their mothers: "She turns over the insides of the woman in labor and tears the child out of the pregnant woman." She caused abortions and miscarriages and threatened death at delivery. The Greek Nereids and the witches of many nations were supposed to possess the same power. The number of these evil female spirits is endless and all of them are, like the vehini-hai of the Marquesans (p. 39), the voice of fear that speaks in the soul of modern woman too: "You will die in childbirth, little mother."

A very ancient custom, widespread among primitive peoples, demands that women should have a special place for delivery separated from their dwellings, a birth hut. Among many peoples the same hut is also used for menstruating women— a proof that the two functions are subject to the same taboos and restrictions.

In this hut the woman in confinement lives in complete seclusion and has contacts only with women friends of the same age as herself who have assisted her in childbirth. In several nations these companions follow her out into the open. For instance, the Niam-Niam woman in Central Africa at the approach of her delivery leaves her husband's house for the neighboring woods, where she gives birth to her child with the help of young women friends. Does not this call up the implication of the frequently heard statement: "My best friend is expecting a baby and will be unhappy if I am not with her." Thus an old promise dating from the period of puberty, when every experience gained its full meaning only if it could be shared with a friend, emerges in the memory of women in our own civilization. At that time the young girls also vowed: "Whoever among us is the first. . . ." Later, the one young woman because she wishes to share the experience by identification, and the other because of her guilt feeling as the happy possessor, go together to the neighboring woods, metamorphosed into the modern maternity hospital. We recall the woman (p. 145), who carried her child within her for all of an extra month in order to be delivered at the same time as her friend. But usually the need for communion expresses itself more simply.

Among primitives, for good and rational reasons, the place of the companions is gradually taken by more mature women with greater experience as birth helpers. The choice of these women is very interesting: among the Maoris of New Zealand,[2] the maternal grandmother assists at the birth of the first child, or, if she cannot come, the paternal grandmother; among other primitives the mother-in-law must deliver the woman in labor. These assistants are obviously chosen not because of their greater experience, but for reasons of kinship, that is to say, emotional reasons. The custom is only gradually transformed into a rational action, and then the place of the "informed" woman is taken by the "knowing" woman and finally by the professional midwife. The art of the midwife develops from primitive usage through transmitted experience to professional and expert assistance in childbirth. The psychologic relation of the birth-giving woman to the midwife is, even in our civilization, very much like that based on the primitive belief that endows an older woman with the power to summon the beneficent spirits and ward off the evil ones.

[2] Op. cit., vol. 2, p. 645.

The "old woman," the wise sorceress, and the modern trained midwife make it possible, more or less, for the woman in labor to escape the curse of female demons among primitives, and the deeply unconscious guilt feeling toward the mother among moderns. Among the former the resort is to incantations, among the latter to more complex psychologic means. By transferring all her feelings against her mother to the midwife, the woman in labor can often discharge her fury, and the influence of the "wise woman" can free her from the fear of childbirth by strengthening her childish belief in the helpful omnipotence of the mother and her substitutes.

Among many primitive peoples the husband must remain at a distance from the woman in labor, for he would be exposed to great harm if he approached the "unclean one." Among certain other more materialistic peoples it is not so much the woman giving birth who is unclean as the matter that is secreted from her genitals during delivery. It is feared that demons dangerous to the husband arise from it. Other men and boys too must avoid all contact with these secretions; otherwise, so run the anxious superstitions of several peoples, their arms and legs will be crippled.

In our modern places of delivery too one sometimes hears curses and execrations against the husband and men in general, which have their far-off source in the belief in evil spirits whose destructive spell is lifted only by the counterspell of the newborn life. The requirements of modern asepsis keep the husband at a distance and simultaneously protect him from the curses of demons.

Not always and not everywhere is the husband excluded from active participation in the birth of his offspring. In many tribes he assumes actual direction and supervision of the birth process, in others he assumes a helper role in a triangle with the midwife and the parturient woman.

Thus it is reported[3] that at Mincopia on the Andaman Islands

[3] Op. cit., vol. 2, p. 656.

When the time of delivery approaches, it is the custom for the husband and a woman friend of the woman in labor to hold her up; the husband holds up her back and presses her when it is desired, while the friend holds a screen of leaves over the lower part of her body and assists her to the best of her ability in the delivery and in removing the afterbirth.

In our civilization these two corners of the triangle are occupied by the nurse and the physician, and this professional and objective division of labor also supplies the emotional tendencies with a favorable outlet: love and hatred, trust and spite, discipline and impatience, can now be transferred to and distributed among these representatives of the childish emotions mobilized in delivery. Thus the active participation of the husband is transferred to the powerful father image of the physician. The husband himself is allowed only to wait outside the door in a kind of couvade, to walk up and down with impatient steps, and to suffer and enjoy his wife's labor pains in his fantasy. The obstetrician has powerful predecessors in the medicine men, sorcerers, and priests, even though the help the latter gave the woman in labor was supernatural and magical. Our modern birth helpers do not suspect that the woman in labor passively yielding to them attributes to them many magic powers, in order to conquer the disturbing fear that has taken possession of her.

We have cursorily stressed some analogies between the birth process among primitives and among civilized peoples. These analogies could be pursued much further, and one has the impression that despite the enormous advances in the field of obstetrics, and the great benefits of exact scientific knowledge, the psychic life of civilized women in labor still contains many elements that bring them close to the fears and superstitions of their primitive sisters.

It is true that with the development of civilization the belief in the participation of supernatural forces in the reproductive function has gradually weakened. Biology, anatomy, and physiology assume full responsibility for the normal or pathologic process. But in this age of greatest scientific advances and of materialist philosophy, the spirits and demons of child birth reappear in a new form. The psychic accompaniments of the biologic function are no longer projected into a demonic world. According to our modern knowledge, the process of birth is not purely somatic, but psychosomatic, and the difficulties arising in the course of it often require the collaboration of psychiatrists for their solution.

One might think that the process of birth unfolds in accordance with specific, inherent, biologically determined conditions, and that it is well protected against external or internal psychologic influences. It is distinguished from other psychosomatic processes accessible to our study by its typical course —that is, the fact that its beginning and end are exactly determined in time—also by its inherently normal character, its clearly determined goal, etc. On the other hand, it is logical to assume that an event involving greatly heightened inner tension and a tremendous physical upheaval will produce important psychic material. Everything suggests that the previously existing inner conflicts become acute in a situation so charged, and that the intensified expectations and fears of pregnancy are further intensified with the beginning of labor.

The psychologic observer soon discovers that all the biologically predetermined functional processes, from the onset until the achievement of the final goal, to wit, real motherhood, are furthered or inhibited by psychic influences. Every single physiologic gesture, every labor pain, as it were, testifies not only to the mutual dependence of the somatic and psychic factors, but also to the fact that in all the biologic functions of reproduction, the woman's whole psychic development and her whole emotional past play a decisive part.

Psychiatrists usually have no opportunity to observe the process of birth directly; they receive their material only subsequently, for the most part in distorted form, imbedded in other contexts. Moreover, the psychic components of childbirth, to an even greater extent than the emotional accompaniments of other female sexual functions (menarche, pregnancy), fall easily into amnesia or are unconsciously falsified.

Objective data about the processes that take place during

childbirth are also unreliable because the perceptions of the woman in labor are to some extent weakened and the area of her awareness is narrowed by her absorption in the progress of the birth. She has an obvious apperceptive insufficiency with regard to all impressions not directly connected with it.

For many years psychiatrists have been interested in the mental states of the newborn child, its traumatic experiences and fears. The first anxiety state arising from its separation from the mother is considered the prototype and cause of all its later anxieties. Strikingly, less attention has been given to the simultaneous processes in the mother. The development of modern obstetrics seems increasingly to reduce the mother's active participation in the process of birth, and the observations recorded in the following paragraphs may appear anachronistic in the near future.

It is valuable therefore to gain an insight into the psychologic reactions of a woman who is delivered spontaneously, that is, into the greatest of all female pleasure-pain experiences, and its accompanying psychologically determined disturbances, before modern technic has deprived psychiatrists of the possibility of doing so. Obstetricians and midwives are too much concerned with physical processes to bother about their patients' psychic experiences. They are usually tired and exhausted, and because they concentrate on the somatic factors, their interest is awakened only when active intervention seems necessary. The obstetrician considers his task completed when the child has emerged unharmed from the mother's body and the mother shows no pathologic symptoms.

Further, modern obstetrics does not wait for an abnormal difficulty in delivery before intervening actively. The hastening of birth by the physician, at the moment when in all probability the child is ready to face all the hardships of extrauterine existence, is increasingly accepted, and it seems that soon there will be no spontaneous biologic process of birth at all.

The following observations are referable in part to a period in obstetric science when the spontaneous process was interfered with only in cases of special necessity. Thus it was possible not only to follow the psychic accompaniments of the physiologic process, but also to track down the psychologic factors of an incipient disturbance. I should like to emphasize the fact that, except when the contrary is indicated, all this material relates to first deliveries. Later deliveries either are repetitions of the first, or have a more individual character determined by the life situation. The typical factors seem most pronounced in the first delivery.

To understand the psychologic situation at the time of birth, we must go back to the last phase of pregnancy. The approach of childbirth is indicated by certain harbingers. Several weeks before the event the uterus drops. At the slightest outside excitation, or altogether spontaneously, it contracts— as though practicing for the labor pains to come. This lowered position of the uterus results in pressures, feelings of tension, and respiratory difficulties, and even the healthiest woman now finds her somatic condition burdensome and uncomfortable. In addition there is a psychic impatience; the harmony between mother and child is disturbed. It is as though nature were seeing to it in advance that the imminent separation from the child should not be too painful (psychologically) for the mother.

We know from numerous experiences that there is hardly any biologic process that is not accompanied and influenced by psychic processes. In the last weeks of pregnancy the mother-child union is disturbed by physiologic factors, and the organic changes produce increasing feelings of discomfort. The physical burden becomes a background for emotional impulses that assume a hostile character with regard to the unity with the child. The mother's inner perception of a pull on her body increasingly transforms the fetus into an alien body, just as it did in the first phase of pregnancy. With the increase of bodily discomfort, the ego of a psychically healthy woman becomes gradually weary of the shrinking of her life contents produced by pregnancy and of her exceptional physical and psychic situation. Apparently the merger of extremes—ego and species—cannot be tolerated for a very long time. The relationship with the child is split: the being in the uterus already has his double, who is the subject of all expectations and fantasied wish fulfillments and whose real existence as a distinct person is gradually approaching. With the end of pregnancy the I-you polarity is simultaneously strengthened, and the psychic management of loving and hostile impulses uses this duality: the enemy must get out in order to reappear as a precious friend in the outside world.

Thus during these last weeks there begins the conflict between the will to retain and the will to expel, and normally it takes place only psychically. The will to retain is above all the expression of narcissistic self-sufficiency that has developed during pregnancy and that refuses to renounce the established unity. The realization, through bodily sensations, of the imminent destruction of this unity, manifests itself in the mother's heightened identification with the child and opposes the expulsive tendencies. On the other hand, the fantasy of the child as an external love object of the very near future has been developed during the whole period of pregnancy and it now joins with the negative emotions of the expulsive tendencies (by negative emotions we mean the effects of the physiologic discomfort). If the conflict between the two tendencies assumes a pathologic character and the expulsive forces win the upper hand, the result may be a premature delivery. But if, in addition to the narcissistic sense of unity, the mother feels concern about the fate threatening the child after it is expelled from its secure shelter, and fears her new responsibility, the retentive tendencies and with them the tendency to prolong pregnancy are intensified. Conservative clinging to the status quo, horror at the idea of splitting a unity woven by many emotional and physical threads, and fear of the pains and dangers of delivery, create resistance to the termination of the condition. The chemically and physiologically determined disharmony between mother and child that manifests itself in the last weeks of pregnancy, is the prelude to the imminent separation that normally marks the victory of the physiologic over the psychic element. It is interesting to note that the sharpening of the two tendencies is revealed in the dream life of the last phase of pregnancy, when the typical pregnancy dreams, in which the expectant mother identifies herself with her future child (the so-called mother-womb fantasy), are increasingly frequent. The mother, who in the dreams of the previous phases of pregnancy often appeared as a little girl swimming in water, now sees herself slipping through narrow cracks, falling from a height, laboriously climbing out of water, striving to reach a far-off goal, etc. In these dreams her own personality can be recognized directly or through associations. Since the question of boy or girl is now more acute, and curiosity about it greatly contributes to the mother's impatient waiting, the child's sex is particularly emphasized in the dreams: the child of the dream is specifically a boy or a girl.

On this point the mother's conscious and unconscious wishes are usually in conflict, and sometimes the wish-fulfilling tendency of the dream adapts itself to hypocritical consciousness, and sometimes to unconscious sincerity. Consciously, very many women, masculine as well as feminine ones, wish for a boy as their first-born. Perhaps in most of them the wish to be reborn as a man plays a great part, but other motives must not be overlooked. I shall disregard here the social motives, and consider rather the individual and psychologic ones. Both the grandfather and the father (or father and husband) wish for and expect a boy, in order to be reborn in him. The feminine woman joins them in this wish and wants to present both of them with a boy as a sign of her love. Moreover, she is motivated by a wish relating to the distant future: in her son she will one day find again a loving and protective man. I shall discuss this wish in detail when I take up the psychology of women in the climacterium.

Deep beneath this wish, deriving from object love, is concealed a feminine-narcissistic aspiration: the woman wishes for a daughter in order to be reborn in her, endowed with all the charm of the new being.[4] It is striking how often the boy

[4] It is this insight into the psyche of the civilized mother that led me to suspect that the Marquesas women devour their newborn girls in order to absorb their youth and charm. This motive is also familiar to us from folklore.

in the dream appears as ugly and the girl as beautiful. Thus the woman's ambivalent relationship to her husband is expressed: "Here is your boy—he is ugly as you are." But the dreamer's own image always appears in the full beauty that she desires for herself and her daughter.

Very often the child in the dream appears not only as already born, but as far advanced in his development, speaking, walking, etc. In this dream the mother fulfills her wish to see her child in the outside world, already freed from the dangers that she herself fears. The dreams are not always so optimistic: the fear of giving birth to a monster is intensified in the last weeks of pregnancy, and cripples, idiots, monsters appear in the pregnant woman's dreams just as in her daytime anxieties. I have observed that the woman who has had an induced abortion, or a spontaneous one for which she feels responsible, is particularly inclined to such self-punishing dreams.

With the intensification of the bodily sensations and the appearance of the so-called preliminary pains, the content of the dreams often reproduces the process taking place in the body: the woman dreams of being hurled in two directions, of being pushed by a more or less personified force, etc. We find all these dreams and nightmares again later during the process of childbirth.

On the eve of her definitive initiation into real motherhood, even the most mature woman is regressively transformed into a child. Just as in puberty (cf. vol. 1), we are confronted here with the peculiar fact that a tremendous advance in existence mobilizes regressive forces. The woman's impatient curiosity in the last weeks of pregnancy reminds us of the childish urge to explore things, which usually expresses sexual curiosity: "How will the child get out?" The adult woman trembles with anxiety just like the child: "How will anything as big as a child get through that little opening?" And repeating her old unconscious desire to look inside the body of her pregnant mother, she is filled with the ardent wish: "If only I could look inside myself once—then I would not mind if the pregnancy

lasted longer." The fear that she had during the first phases
of pregnancy—"Am I really pregnant?"—again comes to the
fore: "Is it really a baby?" If the fetus moves less than before, then something bad must be happening; if it is lively,
then something else is wrong—"it is so restless." The feeling
that her possession is insecure, which accompanies woman
during her entire pregnancy, is now intensified, and she fears
not only for her own life, but even more for that of the child:
"Is it there at all? Will it live? Is it normal? How does it
look? What is its sex?" She is obsessed by worries and
doubts amid her great joy and anticipation.

In all women—the happy and the disappointed, the strong
and the weak, the loving and the hating—the doubts, restlessness, impatience, and joyful expectation all conceal the fear of
delivery, which is increasingly intensified with the approach of
term. What are the sources of this fear? To what extent
is it justified?

Although childbirth is a physiologic phenomenon, a number
of its manifestations border on the pathologic. Even under
the most normal conditions, it is characterized by pain and
bleeding, which otherwise mark only morbid states. Certainly
nature did not intend to make the normal process so difficult,
yet the higher the species in the animal series, the more complicated is the reproductive function, the graver the dangers,
and the worse the pain.

Today we have effective methods of overcoming the dangers
of the birth process. Surgery triumphs over the anatomic
anomalies and chemistry over the powerful physiologic disturbances. In 1847 J. P. Semmelweiss, a young Austrian
physician, made a decisive step in the struggle against the
worst enemy of childbirth, puerperal fever. Convinced that
the real cause of this terrible evil lay in infection of the birth
channels, he created the powerful weapon of obstetric asepsis.
Sir Thomas Watson in England and Oliver Wendell Holmes
in America made great contributions in this field. Through
their work childbirth mortality has gradually been reduced to
a minimum.

However, woman's fear of death has not been eliminated with the real dangers. She has merely transferred her motivation from reality to psychic life. Analytic science can discover only those determinants of fear that spring from the woman's individual life. But we assume that all these fears are only provocations or intensifications of a deep hereditary fear of death that accompanies the new life awakening in the mother's body. Its deepest sources are inaccessible to us. But we know that the fear of separation is one of its chief representatives.

Because of the identification with the child that takes place during pregnancy, the fear of separation is not only that of "I am losing the child," but also that of "The child is losing me." In other words, in birth the child loses the condition of absolute protection and security, that primitive condition of bliss for which all of us yearn. Analyses of pregnant women in the last phase always reveal psychic material in which fearful ideas about delivery correspond completely to the content that we usually interpret as reactions to the birth trauma. In *Inhibition, Symptom, and Anxiety,* Freud says that the earliest infantile anxiety arises with the child's separation from his mother. Rank[5] in particular ascribes great significance to this fear. Through our psychologic reconstructions we are indirectly acquainted with the hypothetic fear of being born; but we are confronted with it really and directly in the fears of the woman approaching delivery.

The fear of separation is also familiar to us from other sources. Perhaps the fright that seizes many children before they move their bowels is comparable to this fear of separation at childbirth. I once had to deal with a young girl who, left alone during her labor, was seized with terrible fear and confusion; in a state of clouded consciousness, as though by compulsion, she brought forth her illegitimate child in the toilet and flushed it down like feces. She was indicted for having murdered her child, and there is no doubt that in her

[5] RANK, O.: The trauma of birth. New York: Harcourt, 1929.

confusion her wish to get rid of it asserted itself. No maternal tenderness or medical care counteracted the excretory mechanisms that were associated with her labor pains and became the motive force of her action.

A similar fear of separation is encountered in neurotic states. For instance, certain sexual disturbances in men are based on the fear of separation from the sperm (ejaculatio tarda), and there are obsessive fears that manifest themselves in the fact that the person who has them does not like to let anything belonging to him drop or lie around. The same fear, varying in intensity according to the individual, accompanies the general fear of childbirth as a reaction to the imminent separation from the content of the body. In women who have not mastered the genital trauma this fear inevitably asserts itself as a component of the fear of delivery. But it is only one component, among others, of a general fear of separation from the child conceived as a part of the woman's own ego, a fear that assumes the character of the fear of death.

Another important source of the fear of death in childbirth lies in an unresolved and guilt-laden relation of the woman to her own mother. We have seen that in all the phases of development toward femininity, in all her love and in all the activities of reproduction that bring woman closer to motherhood, her greatest danger lies in her unresolved guilt feeling toward her own mother. For this makes her incapable of becoming herself a happy mother, free from anxiety. It is clear that this guilt feeling and the anxious tension connected with it are particularly mobilized at childbirth. And the fear has the same content if it is aroused by situations that can be associated with childbirth.

In the overwhelming majority of cases, for women the operation will become a delivery, with all the fears and anxietes pertaining to the birth of a child, and will, like delivery, be quite dependent upon the fate of the patient's relationship to her own mother. Reactions to death wishes against the, mother, particularly against the pregnant and life-giving mother, guilty feelings resulting from the impulse to murder the child already born or in fantasy expected to be born of the mother, may accompany the narcotic sleep and will give content to the anxieties and related symptoms which

precede and follow the general anesthesia. An unsuccessfully resolved relation to the mother contains a still greater, deeper danger. The increased
tie to the mother which develops under the pressure of anxiety and the burden of the feeling of guilt, can receive a new regressive thrust in the moment
of the danger from an operation. The masochistic turning of the agres-
sions against the person's own self then bring about the ominous state of
clinging to the suffering and to the postoperative symptoms.[6]

The foregoing applies to an even greater extent to the real
situation of delivery. It is easy to understand why the custom,
prevalent until recently, of having the patient's mother present
at childbirth, was so important.

In expectant mothers under treatment for neurotic conditions, the former neurotic fear is centered at the end of
pregnancy around the child and assumes a phobic or hypochondriac character. The phobic woman must now avoid
definite anxiety-provoking situations, so that the child may
come into the world easily. The hypochondriac woman
imagines that the child is afflicted with the most terrible ills.
One recognizes in these ideas the same predelivery fears that
can be found in perfectly healthy women, only their amount is
greater. Old neurotic anxieties endowed with definite contents related to birth will re-emerge at the end of pregnancy,
even in patients in whom psychoanalytic treatment has been
successful.

In every pregnant woman the fear of childbirth can receive
reinforcements from other sources. Its content may derive
from the real life situation: for instance, the fear has the character of objective anxiety if the birth takes place under pathologic conditions, or if the woman continues to be worried
during delivery about the possible unfavorable fate of her
child (e.g., when the birth is illegitimate), if her own situation
is more difficult because of the child, etc. This objective
anxiety asserts itself only in the first phase of delivery; later
it gradually yields to the fear associated with the process itself.
The deeply unconscious elemental anxiety that springs from

[6] DEUTSCH, H.: Some psychoanalytic observations in surgery. Psychosom. Med.,
     vol. 4, 1942.

the loss of unity with the child—the fear of separation—is present in delivery from the beginning to the end. It can be intensified by guilt feelings, it can attach itself to former genital anxieties (castration, defloration), and by a detour of the mobilized old infantile mechanisms it can revive anal, urethral, and other fears. For instance, it is extraordinary how often the escape of the amniotic fluid brings the infantile fear of bed wetting to the fore, and how, similarly, the sensations of pressing, pushing, and expulsion of the child from the body mobilize intestinal elements.

The psychologic process is particulary interesting because, in addition to the various individual fears, two opposing fear themes are generally dominant. There is the above mentioned deep and elemental fear of death, which we might call a primal fear; this is accompanied by a more conscious and superficial fear, corresponding to the real dangers to life. The objective character of this fear may be intensified by the fact that the persons around the pregnant woman, those who love her and rejoice in her condition or the imminent consummation of it, are also full of anxious concern during her delivery. All of them, the pregnant woman and her entourage, are intellectually fully aware that neither she nor the child is in danger, that her physical condition leaves nothing to be desired, etc. They fully believe the physician's assurances that everything is in order. They admit that their common fear has absolutely no real basis, and yet they say anxiously: "Often unexpected things happen—one never knows."

This fear does not disturb the optimistic feeling of the psychically healthy pregnant woman and of normal persons around her. Their feeling of joyful expectation is based not only upon their intellectual knowledge that there is no danger but also on their equally elemental faith that life will conquer death. If this inner faith is lacking, the mother is in real danger; she may prove unequal to the possible difficulties of childbirth and its frequent physical surprises. In the polarity of life and death, the optimistic feelings are on the side of life, the anxious-pessimistic ones in the service of death.

In many women, motherhood may fall victim to these unconscious fears much earlier. Some avoid the childbirth fear
by renouncing marriage and children, others forestall it by
sterility or abortion. Still others, however, let their fears be
overpowered by the biologic forces and in their motherhood
find themselves before the gates of a world that seems to them
full of pain and terror. Many are willing to make a sacrifice
of fear and suffering in order to have a child. Only a minority
can accept the biologic process simply for what it is and in the
joyful expectation of a child give up the fear-laden past for
the sake of the future. It seems, however, that this freedom
is only relative; whenever one succeeds in eliminating a part of
the amnesia connected with delivery in both neurotic and
healthy women, one discovers a more or less well managed
fear and an associative connection with previous fears.

This powerful tendency to fear is accompanied by powerful
defense mechanisms. Observations of patients who have
undergone operations prove that psychic preparation for surgical intervention is very important for mastering of the fear
and thus, to a large extent, for the success of the operation.
In other words, it makes a great difference

> Whether the operation was performed as an emergency without the pa-
> tient having a chance to prepare himself or whether the more propitious
> situation obtained and the patient had an opportunity for a longer or shorter
> period of inner preparation. In the first case we have to expect a psychic
> shock reaction in the patient and its influence on the postoperative situation.[7]

The same holds true in relation to childbirth. The long
preparation, for a definite date, certainly helps to accumulate
large reserves of protective forces during the entire pregnancy.
The fear of separation is constantly softened by the euphoric
idea of the child, unless this idea is opposed by unpleasant
counterideas (unwelcomeness of the child, financial worries,
bad marital relations, etc.)

Interestingly enough, this preparation has negative aspects
also. The woman has a feeling, which is intensified at the end

[7] Op. cit.

of her pregnancy, that soon something will take place in her life that, in her subjective estimation, will change the order of the world, that something will come out of her and will exist only by her will, but that nevertheless this something represents a power over which she has no control. Whether she wants to or not, she who has created this new life must obey its power; its rule is expected, yet invisible, implacable. It is inside her and yet it is unknown and irresistible. Because of these very qualities it necessarily produces fear. This knowledge of an event that will happen on a certain date, upon which one depends, and which, nevertheless, one cannot influence, this mixture of power and submission, has something fatal and inevitable about it, like death.

As the end of pregnancy approaches, the woman's restlessness and physical discomfort increase and the child's dual significance is emphasized. The nearer the time of delivery, the greater is the future significance of the child in the mother's emotional life and the stronger the wish to see him in the outside world. This split in the mother's psyche—an interesting and very temporary state—can, as we shall see later, lead to complications. Normally the feeling "Out with the tormentor" is helpful, as it facilitates the separation. Only when this feeling is excessively strong, when the fear of the future attempts to hasten the beginning of this future, when the unconscious counterforce opposes the physiologic commandments and the restless anxiety leads to action, is there danger that the preliminary labor pains may become the real labor and that the fear of separation may paradoxically lead to premature separation. The following observation will illustrate such hastening and delaying influences.

In a woman prone to premature births (she had had four such births), psychotherapeutic treatment had decreased the unconscious anxiety that was the underlying cause; her overexcitability was favorably influenced, and she was able to carry a child to full term. When her labor pains appeared for the first time at the right date, they were so sluggish that

active obstetric intervention was necessary. It was not difficult to gain an insight into her psychic experience, because she
herself developed sufficient introspection to make the process
comprehensible. She was overjoyed at the prospect of giving
birth to a 9 month baby, and, as she said, felt perfectly free of
her old fear. However, during delivery she was seized by a
kind of fear, and in the interval between two labor pains
thought to herself: "What will happen if I again fall into my
old excitable state and throw out the child—will it live then?"

The same fear that formerly excited the innervations now
inhibited them. The same neurotic theme was in the background in both these effects—"I cannot give birth to a living
child."

In many women the restlessness of the last weeks of pregnancy is expressed by intensified activity: they can barely keep
quiet, and have a continual urge to do something, by which
they betray anxious uneasiness even if they are free of conscious fear. The subjectively strengthened sensation of the
uterine contractions induces the woman to go to the hospital
prematurely, while her disappointment at its turning out a
false alarm may make her swing to the opposite extreme,
and, as in the case of the above mentioned patient, her term is
delayed by an inhibiting process. Such subjectively caused
disturbances in the last phases of pregnancy can greatly influence the later process of delivery.

To clarify the psychologic accompaniments of this process, we
shall briefly sketch the physiologic phenomena. We distinguish three stages in a normal birth: those of the dilatation,
the expulsion, and the afterbirth. The dilatation stage often
lasts for several days and is marked by slight contractions of
the uterine muscles, associated with mild drawing pains. For
a woman having her first child they are a signal for preparation,
and almost all women develop a striking activity in this phase.
Only when they are paralyzed by fear do they yield to fate and
let others act for them. Normally this fear is, if not mastered,
at least outweighed by euphoric anticipation: "I shall soon
have a baby."

Naturally, the woman's attitude will from the beginning be determined by her readiness, by the extent to which she has prepared herself, during the last period of pregnancy, for the trauma of separation, or, in other cases, by the extent to which her impatience to get rid of her burden has disturbed the normal process.

This more or less protracted preparatory phase is followed by the first delivery stage, the actual dilatation, so named because the mouth of the uterus is gradually dilated by the violent contractions of the uterine muscles. These contractions draw the neck of the uterus so far upward that its orifice is opened, thus allowing of the passage of the child. While the opening is gradually enlarged, the membranes surrounding the fetus push through, pressing against the orifice, and are ruptured, permitting escape of some of the amniotic fluid.

During the second or expulsion stage of delivery the contractions of the uterus continue; that is to say, the muscles in the neck of the uterus are contracted in a longitudinal direction, then the adjoining section of the muscles contracts in a circular direction. This circular contraction moves constantly higher, and the lower section of the uterus and the vagina become a soft sac through which the child, partly through the driving force of the rhythmic uterine contractions and partly by abdominal pressure, is pushed until its head is protruded through the vagina.

The third stage of parturition, the afterbirth period, usually follows from fifteen to thirty minutes after the birth of the child. In this phase the remaining products of gestation (the placenta) are expelled.

Only the first two stages of delivery are psychologically interesting. The functioning of the uterine muscles, the contractions and dilations, depend upon the innervation. The innervation has three sources: the sympathetic nervous system, which inhibits the expulsion of the fetus; the parasympathetic system, which stimulates the muscles of expulsion; and a local innervation of ganglia within the uterine muscles that participate in expulsive contractions. The normal process of parturition depends upon the harmonious interaction of the various muscles and their innervations. The latter in turn are very much dependent upon internal and external influences. Psychosomatic medicine is familiar with the extraordinary dependence of the sympathetic and the parasympathetic nervous system upon emotional influences; other organs likewise can fail in their functioning under the influence of psychogenically disturbed innervation processes. The task of delivery is thus based upon the antagonistic effects of specific innervations. These effects are automatically regulated: an excessive hastening of the process is opposed by corresponding innervational inhibitions, and vice versa. What is true of the organic processes is also true of the psychic processes. They too, as we have seen, are full of antagonisms; various psychic tendencies and emotional impulses are offset by counterreactions and inhibitions. The autonomic nervous system, which assumes direction of the physiologic process of birth, and likewise the unconscious psychic life, are independent of the conscious will of the woman in labor. The functioning of the autonomic nervous system can be modified by drugs; the psychic unconscious can be influenced more or less indirectly through consciousness. Moreover, the two spheres can enter into a direct but unconscious relationship.

The process of birth, with its boundless anxiety stemming from various sources, offers a particularly propitious soil for the action of psychogenic influences. The mother's attitude toward her child, her readiness for motherhood, the events of her pregnancy, her whole life situation, certainly contribute to the psychic atmosphere of delivery. However, it is striking how many deliveries follow their normal biologic course despite a miserable life situation, despite poverty and worry, fear of social consequences (illegitimacy), an unhappy marriage, etc. Conversely, there are disturbances that cannot be explained either physiologically or psychologically. Their causation lies in the unconscious, and subsequent psychoanalytic reconstruction of such disturbances has given us much insight into the birth process as a whole.

The methods of investigation of the psychologic phenomena that accompany birth are various. Every woman brings to this function definite personality dispositions that color the process. In describing the personality factor, we shall limit ourselves to somewhat schematic definitions. Thus we speak in general terms of the given individual's disposition to passivity and to activity, which puts its stamp upon the delivery. The quantitative degree in which each of these dispositions is present is the next important factor. The third relates to the form in which passivity or activity is manifested.

The difference between the two dispositions is perceptible in the period of the preliminary pains. Many women from the beginning take a completely passive attitude: the physician has promised them that they will not feel anything, that they need not worry about anything, and they base their behavior on that. When seized by sharper pains, they grow very angry and impatient, call for a doctor, demand narcotics, and refuse to give any active cooperation.

As a whole, however, the activity that manifests itself in the final phase of pregnancy is a mechanism of defense against fear. The driving unrest, the urge to activity, is usually rationalized as a method of making the waiting period seem shorter. In actual fact it is a preparation for the active process of birth, produced by the inner urge. Woman's contribution in delivery is manifested not only by the product— the child—but above all by her active participation in the birth. Whether she behaves more actively or more passively is usually, though not always, determined by the nature of her personality as a whole. Some women have turned all their psychic activity to other goals, so that the process of birth is for them only a biologic process to which they submit passively. Conversely, women otherwise more passively disposed are thrown by the first pains into a joyful excited state that spurs them to the greatest activity.

Some women display particularly intense activity at the beginning of childbirth. Mrs. N., whom I observed immediately after her arrival in the hospital, gave me a direct description of the beginning of her delivery. She was a chemist by profession; during her pregnancy she felt very well and continued to perform all her professional duties. The pains began a few days earlier than expected and surprised her while she was engaged in making an important chemical experiment and demonstrating it, with her superior, to a group of students. She worked eagerly while her pains grew increasingly frequent, thinking: "If only we can finish the experiment!" When I asked her why she did not interrupt her work, she said that she did not have the feeling of two separate actions taking place; she felt as though the two were somehow connected and as though her task was to carry them both through to the end. Fortunately, she was delivered only two hours later; she herself was fully convinced that she had herself in hand, and that the birth would come at the right time. Mrs. N. was not a masculine woman, but she fully possessed the degree of activity trend that a woman needs to banish her fear and actually to participate in the birth of her child.

Mrs. N. is naturally only an exaggerated example of pre-delivery activity. In most women this activity is devoted to intensified preparations, in many others it has a more steady character, in still others it constitutes only a short temporary break-through that soon subsides.

A woman with a masculinity complex reacts in various ways to imminent delivery: she takes everything "easily," childbirth is just a biologic process that does not bother her at all, and "naturally" she has had no complaints during her entire pregnancy. She tries to turn the whole process into a minor disturbance of her normal life. She negates her fear and pains and usually asks for narcotics only when things get "too bad." Usually she herself negotiates with physician, hospital, etc.

Another type of masculine woman considers childbirth an indignity imposed upon women by nature, an injustice that must be corrected. Naturally she refuses to endure pains or to participate in the delivery; she feels that it is the task of the modern obstetrician to make everything pass as quickly and painlessly as possible. She puts forward demands and claims only with regard to the child as her product.

The activity of the average normally active woman at the onset of the first pains is somewhat as follows. She herself packs her suitcase, casts a last glance over the nursery to see that everything is in order, wants to have telephone conversations, mostly with her women friends, and often insists upon personally informing her physician, hospital, etc., that her labor has begun. The negation of fear underlying this outbreak of activity is often quite conscious.

Many women fall into a joyful excitation with the beginning of the pains, especially when the pregnancy has been protracted —"I thought I would never have a child." The child has gradually assumed an unreal character, the idea of its existence has become blurred. In others, on the contrary, the reality of the child is so strong at the end of pregnancy that the woman feels as though she were separated from it only by the "curtain" of the abdominal casing, and in her impatient excitement she wants to see it as soon as possible.

During the first stage of childbirth (the dilatation stage), even the most active woman should entirely subordinate herself to the inner forces—a passive, cooperative, patient endurance of the process is her only task. There are women who cannot tolerate this behavior. They want to take the birth into their own hands at once, they want to do something, and refuse to subordinate themselves either to inner forces or to external advice. Like any other manifestation of excessive activity, this behavior may express a primary tendency or a defense against fear. If the innervation processes of the first phase are marked by excessive tension, if the impulses are influenced by fear or an excessive propensity to active participation, the phenomena of labor lose their normal spontaneity, and the process is disturbed. On the other hand, an overpassively submissive attitude toward the innervation forces can prolong the dilatation phase, so that the progressive contractions take place slowly, lazily, or not at all: the birth is stalemated.

In this phase external influence can be very potent. I recall one defiant woman who, upon discovering that she was serving as an object of study for some medical students, immediately interrupted her labor pains, and did it again each time a student approached her. Another woman, who shortly before had been under psychoanalytic treatment, could not continue her labor until she secured confirmation by telephone of the sympathetic interest and proximity of her psychoanalyst. I was unable to learn the motives for the stubbornness of the first woman; as for the second, I discovered that what was in question was not exhortation or encouragement, but deep-rooted transference motives that endowed the analyst with magic powers.

The situation is different in the second or expulsion phase. Now the woman in labor must perform a great physical and psychic task. Abdominal pressure in childbirth is secured only with great effort, and the pain grows steadily worse. The pressure begins rhythmically with the pains; carried forward by the internal physical contractions, her own will power, and external encouragement, the woman in labor consummates her individual act in the service of the species.

Direct observation of women in labor leaves no doubt that childbirth is experienced as a strenuous act of accomplishment and that it requires tremendous mastery over fear and suffering. The shock of the pains and the excitation of the motor apparatus obviously reduce the capacity for receiving external impressions. All former joys and mortifications become pale and unimportant, communication between the ego of the woman in labor and the environment is reduced solely to matters directly connected with the birth process. Her activity is fully taxed, her accomplishment is connected with a tense "listening" to the innervation processes, and everything else, present, past, and future, seems to vanish. Nevertheless, sometimes the sense impressions directly connected with the delivery seem to be excessively sharp, almost paranoic, and the woman in travail has a tendency to misinterpret, mishear, etc.

Despite her anxious concentration on her own ego, the idea of service to the species and concern about the child assert

themselves. Irving, in his book *Safe Deliverance*, calls attention to a peculiar type of behavior[8]:

> Those who have suffered a severe hemorrhage and still remain conscious
> have a strange sense of detachment from reality. They are aware of the
> activities about them and of their meaning, and they sense the anxiety of the
> doctors and nurses who are making every effort to overcome a dangerous
> situation, but they are the least worried of those in the room. Although
> they realize the possibility of death, they have no fear of its event, which
> they face with an almost oriental equanimity. As long as their mental facul-
> ties abide with them, for unconsciousness alone brings restlessness, there is
> no fear, no agony, no frenzy, no struggle to escape.

From women who have gone through very difficult but for
the most part spontaneous deliveries, I have heard that shortly
before taking narcotics and submitting to the necessary intervention they experienced the state described by Irving, but
with the difference that in their complete apathy they were
still strongly preoccupied with the fate of their children and
were tormented by worry about their survival.

The psychoanalyst's contribution to knowledge of the birth
process in this respect is the observation that unconscious
psychic influences have free access to the above mentioned
concentration on an active accomplishment. During this
period of reduced consciousness their influence can be even
stronger than in normal states. It is usually because of them
that a well initiated labor stops, that the contractions become
too strong or too weak, that they do not function at the right
moment, or that they function in a paradoxic way. Instead of
relaxation there is contraction, instead of a pushing forward
there is a closing, barring movement, etc. In some cases one
can observe a sudden cessation of the woman's participation
she protects herself from the rising fear and the pains by letting
herself slip into passivity. Other women want to preserve
their active control to such an extent that they free themselves
from the normal rhythm of the process and cause a kind of
confusion of the contracting activity. The conflict between

[8] IRVING, F. C.: Safe deliverance. Boston: Houghton Mifflin 1942, p. 299.

the active and passive tendencies may also resort to physical phenomena in order to express itself.

If, on the basis of previous analytic knowledge of the woman, later analysis can reconstruct the experiences she communicates as they have emerged from her complete or partial amnesia, the disturbances during her delivery can be fully understood. First of all, it must be mentioned that the restful intervals, the semisleep between two pains, is often filled with dreams and hypnagogic hallucinations. During the interval, unresolved and unmastered psychic tendencies associated with delivery emerge as in a dream and it is usually difficult to discover whether one is dealing with a real dream, a hypnagogic hallucination, or a fantasy. The pain and organic sensations during delivery are obviously connected during the rest pauses with psychic contents. The delivery dream recounted in the following case description of an obsessonal-neurotic patient who had interrupted her analysis immediately before delivery, and resumed it immediately afterward, seems to offer a classic example.

Mrs. Bird was a 25-year-old woman who had been married for three years when she began her analysis. She had a symptomatic obsessional neurosis concerning cleansing and dressing-up ceremonials. She also suffered from headaches that were diagnosed as migraine. She wanted to have children, but neither she nor her husband dared to consider this a possibility because of her neurosis. She clung to her husband, who was included in her ceremonials to the extent that he too was forced to subject himself to certain cleansing procedures. Both were musicians. Mrs. Bird was a talented and ambitious cellist, as well as a teacher of composition and theory.

After a few months of analysis her condition improved to such an extent that she ventured to think of having a baby, and soon afterward became pregnant. Her pregnancy proceeded without the slightest complication; her only complaint from time to time was that she did not have much feeling for the child. My impression was that Mrs. Bird, whose emotional life, in accordance with the emotional constellation of an obsessional neurotic, constantly wavered between love and hatred, did not trust her own feelings, and considered her normal attitude toward a still only fantasied child a sign of her emotional derangement She was overjoyed at the idea of having a child and made all the proper preparations for its birth. But as her pregnancy advanced, her conflicts became more acute. She admitted that the child would not disturb her professional activity, for she could easily give her lessons at home. But would not the child interfere with the development of her talent? Would she be able really to devote herself to her child? Would she have time to devote herself both to her child and to her profession?

Mrs. Bird knew that these problems had nothing in common with the question of time and energy, but arose from the fundamental conflict between her masculinity and her femininity. Up until then she had solved this conflict relatively well because she had sublimated whatever was masculine in her nature by her professional work. Now she justly felt this solution to be threatened.

The beginning of her delivery was normal. She was one of those women who can find an excellent outlet for their active tendencies in delivery. She cooperated energetically without complaining of pains. At one point the midwife told her not to press too much. Just then a longer pause occurred and Mrs. Bird relaxed into a half-sleep, during which she had the following dream. She had a terrible headache, thought that her head was falling apart, and that from it a number of little elves were emerging, who danced around in a circle. Then she awoke under the impact of a new labor pain; from then on her pains grew weaker instead of stronger, her labor was stagnant, and she had to have external help to complete it. She gave birth to a son, experienced all the maternal joys without the slightest emotional derangement, and her obsessional-neurotic symptoms recurred only after several weeks, during the lactation period.

The interpretation of her dream was easy because I knew her psychic situation as a whole. The transfer of the pain from a lower to a higher zone was prefigured in the earlier migraine, which we had even before suspected of concealing birth fantasies. Whether this conjecture was correct is irrelevant; but it was available to be used in the dream, because a few days before her delivery the patient had stated that she had had no headaches for several months, whereupon I remarked facetiously: "You've found another place for the birth."

The direct influence of the analysis on the dream was apparent from the fact that a little while earlier, during her pains, the patient had exhorted herself to be courageous, referring to her analysis and her analyst, and saying that the latter would be proud of her behavior.

The conflict between her masculinity and her femininity was beautifully illustrated by this dream: in it she gave birth through her head, as Zeus bore Athene, i.e., like a man. In her conflict she also tried to achieve the goal of her treatment: what she gave birth to in her dream was not a masculine woman, but tiny, white, tender, very feminine little beings who did not wield a cello but danced around in a circle like women. The substitution of many girls for the one she wished for boy had multiple determinants. The visual impression of a jar of sterile cotton pads at which she looked before falling asleep in the delivery room was one provocatory influence.

Mrs. Bird showed with particular clarity how woman's whole emotional personality is set in motion during the act of birth and how her unconscious asserts its influence despite her intense concentration on the immediate situation. This justifies the assumption that such unconscious tendencies also assert themselves directly in the bodily functions and that they can influence the course of delivery.

Other patients think that they can recall having had flying dreams during delivery; in these all the sexual symbolism familiar from analytic experience is manifested with particular clarity.

Still others tell of persecution dreams, the peculiar characteristic of which is that they are connected with bodily sensations. In such dreams wild beasts chase the dreamer, or a sharp claw or tooth is plunged into some part of her body. She tries to flee, but her persecutors run after her from behind while she faces another danger in front. What is common and typical in all such dreams is the motor excitation in connection with the feeling of being crippled and unable to reach one's goal. My impression is that such dreams actually reproduce the general picture of the birth process. The bodily pain manifests itself in the dream and the motor activity is experienced as flight and inhibition because the woman in labor actually feels dominated by a motor power that she cannot escape. Fear is manifested here even by women who maintain emphatically that they have no fear of childbirth. The projective mechanisms with which we are familiar in the dreams of pregnant women, and in which the child is the mother herself, come to the fore in delivery dreams in another form also. The same mechanisms are familiar to us from the dreams of persons operated upon (before and after operation): they dream that they are witnessing operations performed on other persons. The woman in labor sometimes resorts to the same projective mechanism in order directly to represent delivery, with another person as the chief actor.

Sometimes the dreams represent direct wish fulfillments: the child is seen as already born, and its sex and appearance completely fulfill the mother's fondest expectations.

It must be said that reports about such dreams as direct memories are rare. The whole birth process is for the most part subject to amnesia, and only details are preserved with particular vividness—usually in relation to peripheral facts, not to affective impressions. Sometimes all the external events are preserved in the memory with photographic accuracy, while the woman's emotional experiences are completely buried. These reappear in analysis, like the dreams. Only the temporal sequence is usually entirely lost, and it is often difficult to find out with clarity whether the dream sensation was actually experienced during an interval between pains, at the beginning of the delivery, or later, before or shortly after anes-

thesia if there was any.   Nor can one always establish a de-
marcation between fantasies during half-sleep and real dreams.
But the fact of the psychologic experience and of its relation to
delivery is indisputable.

In Mrs. Bird the time of the dream could be accurately established.   Up until it occurred she had been active in controlling the birth process; she was dominated by the feeling
"I can do it myself" and was fully conscious of her contribution.   Under the violent impact of rising pain and fear, which
she was now forced to admit, she suddenly felt herself seized
by a power stronger than herself.   She had the impression that
she had to yield to a fate, to a feminine fate.   The significance
of childbirth as her own accomplishment, in which she could
experience herself as fully active and masculine, paled; she felt
that she was becoming a weak, yielding creature, a woman.
She wanted to call for the physician's help, after the fashion of
women—"I can't stand it any longer"—and while struggling
against this wish she had her dream.   After delivery she was
ashamed of her weakness and blamed her analytic treatment
for it.   She postponed resuming her treatment, was preoccupied with her now more complicated household, and decided
to resume her analysis only when she began to manifest symptoms in her relationship with her child.   Although she was glad
to have a child, she accused her analyst of having forced her to
become pregnant and thus to have the not only painful but
also "degrading" experience of childbirth.

The fact that she was reborn in her dream as little white
elves was the presage of the later success of analysis in her
case.

Mrs. Bird was a typical representative of the masculine-
active type of woman, who wants her delivery to be an active
accomplishment on her part.   The distortion of feminine activity into masculinity results in complications of childbirth.
The nature of these was easy to distinguish in her case because
they sprang from the same sources as her neurotic symptoms.

At the opposite extreme we find those women who experience childbirth in complete passivity.   Even during preg-

nancy such a woman does not consider herself the possessor of
the child nor responsible for what may happen. She is merely
the bearer of a fruit that will be born from her. Nature, God,
providence will guide the birth, and the powers of the outside
world—the mother and the husband—will see to the necessary
details. These grownups are omniscient; after all, the prospective mother herself cannot know how she should behave.
Many women push this ignorance and passive submission to
such a point that in their eyes it is a mistake to know anything
at all, and they regard all knowledge as disturbing. They
blindly follow other people's instructions and, like children,
are interested only in getting rid of their fear and being subjected to as little pain as possible. Their behavior during
pregnancy is characteristic: they are always with their mothers
(or substitute mothers) or they let their husbands take over
their activity as much as possible. They are happy and
amiable, and only when their passivity is accompanied by a
large amount of infantile narcissism do they become problems:
in the latter case they become very impatient during the last
phase of pregnancy and insist upon hastening delivery, because they cannot control their impatience. The limit of
masochistic tolerance is very low in them, and narcissism
wins the upper hand.

It is interesting to note that all one can learn from such
a woman about her delivery is that "it was something terrible,"
or that "it was magnificent"—she "did not feel anything."
For such a passive and infantile woman the whole act somehow
has a magic character; she simply projects into the outside
world what has been injected into her in coitus. Her ego
secures freedom from fear by subordinating itself from the
beginning to the powers that represent life and death.

The hostility that she, like all girls, once felt toward her
mother no longer threatens her, because from the very beginning she gives the child back to her mother, so to speak—the
same child that she once begrudged her mother or wanted to
take away from her. If such a woman is under analytic treatment, her relation to her analyst shows that her whole personal-

ity is the opposite of that of the aggressive woman. As soon as her labor pains begin, she communicates this fact to her analyst through her closest friend, often through her mother. It is easy to understand why: the analyst is for her another mother substitute who should participate in the birth and in the event of danger help her together with her real mother.

After childbirth she is impatient for the analyst's visit; she wants as soon as possible to show her the baby and express her gratitude. "I owe you the child," she says, even if the psychoanalytic treatment has had little to do with her motherhood.

By their gentle, submissive behavior, these women want to achieve the same two goals in childbirth that the others seek to attain by their active-aggressive behavior: (1) self-preservation, which to them is equivalent to passive avoidance of pain and dangers, and (2) the fulfillment of the wish for a child under conditions that eliminate the old threat "You will have no child." These conditions consist in subordination to the grownups' omnipotence, a subordination that frees them from their sense of guilt and all responsibility.

Some of these women have always displayed an infantile, passive-dependent behavior, and even during pregnancy remain true to this definite type. Despite her great pride in her approaching motherhood and her good physical condition, this woman in pregnancy appears like a little girl playing with dolls. Often she does not disclose the full extent of her passivity during pregnancy and behaves in an adult manner during this period; only the assault of fear at the approach of delivery makes her regress to a passive-infantile behavior.

In the present stage of obstetrics, it is impossible in the case of many of these women to speak of an act of childbirth at all. They are delivered before they have any knowledge of the process, before they have had time to develop fear, let alone master it. Formerly, when it was possible to observe the behavior of such infantile women in spontaneous delivery, one could see that their willingness to yield passively was often accompanied by very aggressive manifestations of protest. The victim of such aggression was usually the mother, as well as her substitute, the midwife. Since this type is apparently frequent, the midwives usually displayed great patience and tolerance toward such women, recognizing the childish character of their behavior.

I directly observed the delivery of a young woman whom I shall call Dolly. A few months before, she had been treated during a brief period for agoraphobia. With every labor pain she had a fit of rage that she expressed by striking the midwife with the wet compress that the latter was holding to her head. This rage was particularly intensified when the midwife spoke encouragingly to her and urged her to bear down. When I entered the room, upon the patient's urgent requests, her behavior changed completely. She suppressed her aggression and behaved in a very grown-up manner. At the same time she began to manifest violent symptoms of fear—sweating, heart pounding, increased urge to move her bowels, etc.

Later, in the course of analysis, I learned that Dolly had wanted to show me how brave and patient she was. She suppressed her aggression only to reveal that it served as a defense against her anxiety: when she gave up this defense her fear broke through. Analysis showed that she developed this vicious circle in other situations too: whenever she was provoked to rage she first suppressed it and felt anxiety instead; then, to get rid of her anxiety, she discharged her aggression in fits of rage. Her relationship with her analyst was so strongly influenced by her old mother relationship that the analyst's visit completely changed the character of her delivery. It so happened that several years before, the analyst had been delivered of a child in the same hospital—a fact that the patient learned from the midwife after the analyst's visit. The midwife was delighted to answer the patient's questions about this delivery in great detail and thus unwittingly caused the patient in the subsequent course of her delivery to imitate the analyst.

Her tendency to passive identification with her mother (or substitute mother) gave Dolly's childbirth a character that had little in common with her own personality. The midwife and the obstetrician thought naïvely that what was involved was a kind of hypnotic suggestion. At that time the phenomena of identification and the strong dependence of all organic processes upon psychic processes were not as well known as they are today.

Many women behave as Dolly did during delivery. They are unable to master the function by themselves, they demand external help, and react with rage or fear to their own helplessness. Their furious reproach against the grownups is twofold: because of the grownups' omnipotence these childish women expect that they will be spared pain and suffering, and because of an equally childish urge to independence they want to carry out the act of childbirth themselves, although they sense from the outset that they cannot. If active help is given them, they fear loss of their independence and grow angry. They sense that childbirth is a task that an adult woman should be able to accomplish by herself and actively, but their childishness makes them incapable of this.

It is interesting that Dolly explained her anger toward the midwife on the ground that the woman's exhortations—"Bear down, make an effort, try"—reminded her of her governess, who had encouraged her in a similar fashion when she was constipated.

Mrs. Bird and Dolly represent two opposite types of women in labor, and their behavior can be understood only with the aid of close analysis. The passive, childish Dolly went through with a normal, active delivery of an adult character after having displayed her real nature only at the beginning. She achieved this by means of identification. The masculine-active Mrs. Bird tried at the very beginning to fight her childbirth fear and pains with her own activity, in order to achieve possession of the child through her own efforts. Since this activity consisted in a masculine-aggressive striving, it conflicted with her femininity and she was unable to complete her efforts successfully.

Another approach to understanding of the psychic processes of delivery is supplied by certain elementary physiologic mechanisms whose significance in all the reproductive functions we mentioned in chapter III. These are the mechanisms of retention and expulsion. This organically determined double direction of the innervations mobilizes associations with functions that relate to other groups of organs—for instance, with excretory functions.

Because of this functional analogy, childbirth awakens the psychic contents that have accompanied the excretory processes at various life periods. It is sufficient to recall the birth fantasies of the little girl observed by Barrett, to understand how easily the process of birth, because of its actual similarity to bowel movements, can revive the earlier situation and its emotional accompaniments. Such secondary, anachronistic revivals of psychic contents connected with early functional activity can easily become the starting point of disturbances in the process of childbirth.

As early as 1923, Eisler,[9] in his article "On Hysterical Phenomena in the Uterus," described a case in which, despite an absolutely normal organic condition and good psychic disposition, the labor was extraordinarily sluggish. After the process had dragged on for three days, the gynecologist made up his mind to intervene. Preparations for use of the forceps were being made when suddenly the delivery began spontaneously. According to Eisler, "it was almost as though the dreaded instrument could be so powerful here because the previous psychic development of the patient had created a definite disposition for such a reaction."

In Eisler's patient, the retention of the fetus could be explained as due to the influence of repressed anal tendencies. At the age of 6, around the time that her younger sister was born, the patient began, quite like the little girl described by Barrett, to suffer from stubborn constipation. She had never entirely given up this symptom and apparently had transferred her constipation to childbirth. However, personal experience has shown repeatedly that such influences upon the innervation processes are never explainable as due to the mere

---

[9] EISLER, J. M.: Über hysterische Erscheinungen im Uterus. Internat. Ztschr. f. Psychoanal., vol. 9, 1923.

repetition of analogous physiologic (in this case intestinal) mechanisms. Some difficulty in the actual life situation or in the emotional relationship to the child, fear of separation, intolerance of labor pains, etc., must be present as *agents provocateurs* to set a preformed mechanism in motion. An intense emotional relationship with the obstetrician, having the character of a transference of old infantile emotions to him, can be particularly suitable for such provocation. Physicians who have taken the time to observe psychologic phenomena know that the threat of intervention can very often—as in the case of Eisler's patient—make the actuality unnecessary and that conversely many women fail to be active in childbirth because they expect external intervention and can, as it were, extort the fulfillment of such a frequently compulsive wish by unconsciously creating difficulties.

One case I observed shows clearly how profoundly repressed memories of former functions can by analogy influence the process of birth. Mrs. White, aged 24, had suffered from hysterical symptoms as a young girl: she thought she had a lump in her throat (globus hystericus), had occasional fits of vomiting and fainting, temporary anxiety states, etc. All these symptoms were of a light and passing nature and gradually disappeared with the help of psychotherapy. She married under favorable conditions, soon became pregnant, and felt very well during her pregnancy. She awaited her delivery with calm and was intellectually well prepared for what was to come. It was a great surprise to her and the persons around her that she was seized with a violent fit of anxiety when her water broke prematurely. In a kind of panic she called her obstetrician, who told her through his assistant that there was nothing to fear, that she should continue to observe her symptoms and communicate with him again. But Mrs. White could not compose herself; her fear increased, making it necessary to resort to sedatives, and her mother insisted upon psychiatric intervention. It was clear to the objective observer that after her water broke she was afraid that she might be delivered too quickly, before the obstetrician got there.

Her belief that without him everything would go badly was determined by the childish character of her relationship to him; yet she felt obliged, because she was a grownup, to repress her intense need of his immediate presence. The psychiatrist recognized the situation and felt that at the moment there was nothing to do but to give in to her wish. However, the rhythm of the delivery was already disturbed, and as a result of insufficient active labor, intervention proved necessary.

A few years later Mrs. White, who since this occurrence had suffered from all sorts of nervous symptoms, decided to be analyzed. Only then was it possible to gain insight into her anxiety at the beginning of her delivery. All her psychic conflicts had begun in prepuberty, when she suffered from enuresis nocturna, which for a period of two years completely spoiled her life. This symptom proved refractory to medical treatment but later spontaneously disappeared, yielding to the other symptoms mentioned above. Pregnancy fantasies typical of puberty contributed to the formation of the symptoms, including her enuresis. Although her real pregnancy was free of regressive elements, the similarity between her old bed wetting and her uncontrollable loss of the amniotic fluid shattered the relatively good superstructure that had been built over her old conflicts and set her old neurotic fears in motion.

Nor was this all. During her pregnancy, the patient's intellectual knowledge about the amniotic fluid mobilized specific old ideas. In this fluid, she thought, the child swims like a fish in water; it feeds on the water and, like a fish, dies when it does not receive enough of its life element. She also referred facetiously to the fetus as "my little goldfish." When the water broke she was afraid that the child would die unless it was rescued without delay.

This fear seems to have been the main reason for the failure of her labor. The inhibition of the autonomic nervous system was comparable to the typical motor inhibition in anxiety states that produce, instead of fast running, absolute inability to move.

Mrs. White was of course neurotically predisposed and her

behavior was certainly abnormal. But if one recalls that the boundary between normal and abnormal is very uncertain precisely in hysterically predisposed persons, and that birth fantasies and infantile theories are always present in feminine psychic life, one can understand how easily the shock and normal fear of delivery provokes the latent old, more or less mastered fears.

Childbirth is even more closely analogous to coitus than to the other bodily functions. The idea that coitus and childbirth are really a single process that begins with intake and retention and terminates with giving and expelling, fits into the framework of the biologic facts. The biologic act begins at the moment of fecundation, continues throughout pregnancy, reaches its climax in labor, and gradually ends in birth.

This dramatic unity predetermined by nature, the progress of events from the first to the last act, the conditioning of one by the other, the continuity of development, are not only biologic but also psychic. The experience of delivery is psychologically prefigured in coitus, the individual reactions during pregnancy foreshadow the nature of the delivery, and the birth itself is only the denouement of the drama.

We have referred more than once to the double task of the female sexual apparatus. To some extent there is a division of labor. The vagina is destined to receive the male germ cells, while the uterus serves as a soil for the fecundated ovum. The vagina receptively opens the gate to life for the child, the uterus supplies the forces to expel it when ripe. The vagina takes over the pleasure of conception, the uterus the torment and pain of delivery. The female rhythm of retention and expulsion dominates both coitus and birth. In coitus this rhythm is set in motion by the active intervention of the male, in delivery by biologic processes of a chemical and mechanical character. Ferenczi[10] calls attention to this fact: "It is striking with what consistency coitus and delivery are represented by

10 FERENCZI, S.: Op. cit.

the same symbol of rescue from danger, especially from water, in dreams, neuroses, myths, folklore."

Rank[11] stresses the identification of bread and the phallus in the formation of myths and also notes: "What is produced in the oven, bread, is also likened to what is produced in the mother's body, the child." This identification relates not only to the functions but also to their instruments and products.

Clinical observation supplies us with rich opportunities to find such analogies. The pain, the fear, the pleasure associated with the pain, the wound suffered and the compensatory prize, the passive yielding and the active mastering, the overcoming of psychic and physical difficulties—all these strengthen the identity of the two acts, an identity that has deep biologic roots.

We have discussed the case of a woman who could enjoy the pleasure of intercourse only if she could at the same time imagine the pains of delivery (Mrs. Andrews). We lack clinical material to illustrate the converse. According to Groddeck,[12] "the harrowing labor pains conceal quantities of pleasure that are denied to man." In my experience—contrary to Groddeck's idea—no evidence of this pleasure can be found in the behavior of women during delivery nor in their conscious memories. But psychoanalysis constantly encounters the identity between the pleasure of coitus and the pain of delivery in associative connections, in dreams, and in neurotic symptoms. To cite a few examples among many: Epileptic and hysterical fits, agoraphobia and claustrophobia, contain both elements as constant determinants, partly in bodily manifestations, partly in fantasies.

The identity of the two experiences can be seen in every feminine woman's later reactions to them: she forgets the pain, retains only the memory of gratification, and yearns for repetition of it.

[11] Rank, O.: Psychoanalytische Beiträge zur Mythenforschung. Vienna: Internat. Psychoanal. Verlag, 1919, p. 27.
[12] Groddeck, G.: The book of the id. New York, 1928.

The value of delivery in the psychic economy can be great in all cases. In Mrs. Bird's and Dolly's, this was proved in the course of later analysis. Mrs. Bird's urge to activity found expression in an accomplishment that formerly was intended to gratify her masculine tendencies. Soon after her delivery the child was no longer the object of her ambitious fantasy ("my" product), but a beloved being whom she could love maternally. The experience of delivery contributed materially to this change of attitude: through it Mrs. Bird realized that she could be active and produce values without being masculine.

It is probable that in the case of Dolly delivery would not have had any psychologic effects without the analytic treatment that followed it. Her passivity deprived her experience of all dynamic force. Only analysis helped her to transform her passive identification with her mother into an advanced, active one. As we have seen, the delivery itself had given Dolly an opportunity to endow her passive identification with a somewhat active character. Her former inability to experience life otherwise than in passive identification was due to the weakness of her ego, to a developmental inhibition, which made her avoid all responsibility and leave it entirely to the grownups because of her faith in their omnipotence. The combined action of two factors helped her to find her way to reality: her analytic treatment strengthened her ego, and her motherhood helped her to overcome her infantile identification with her mother.

The favorable influence of delivery as such can be clearly described. Above all, a cathartic effect inheres in the active mastering of a fear experience, provided that the woman's active participation is sufficiently great. There is also the catharsis through suffering, which certainly can have a considerable effect. During all the preliminary phases of motherhood, the threat "You will not have a child" was present. In delivery the ego, supported by the reality of the child, can ignore this threat, because the old guilt feeling, bribed by the suffering of labor, no longer opposes the enjoyment of the reality.

However, it is not the mere fact of suffering that has such great importance in woman's psychic economy, but rather the activity accompanying the suffering, which pursues its aim in spite of the suffering. Although this activity is outside the domain of the will, it is subjectively experienced as an act of will. Sometimes one has the impression that pain itself—the suffering and the mastering of it—has the effect of a ferment on the emotional life. Yet the chief drawback of freedom from pain consists in the fact that it can be achieved only under conditions that exclude other psychic energies, independent of pain, from the experience. For instance, the transfer of emotions from the woman's own ego to the child as object is prepared even during the act of birth. But in painless deliveries this process is weakened. At bottom, despite her protests and her pleas to be relieved of all pain, the woman wants to fight the birth pains largely with her own resources, and is ready to accept a certain amount of pain for the sake of the fullness of her experience. In some women this desire assumes the form of an idealization of the biblical curse: "I will greatly multiply thy sorrow and thy conception; in sorrow thou shalt bring forth children" (Gen. 3: 16). Similarly the modern German woman, whipped into a state of hysterical fanaticism, asks to be allowed to suffer great pain for her *Führer* when giving birth to her race-dedicated child.

Religious and nationalistic women utilize ideologies to rationalize their masochistic yearning, because it has reached abnormal, destructive proportions. But a moderate amount of masochism is normal and aids in toleration of the pain that woman must undergo in the course of reproduction.

With regard to expressions of pain, women in labor behave in various ways. There are women who from beginning to end do not utter a sound, and there are women who behave like wild beasts. Some later deny that they suffered intensely; others incessantly recount how awful it was. Tolerance or intolerance of pain is certainly highly complex and determined by multiple factors. The well-being or misery of the expectant mother, and her joyful expectation or rejection of the child, undoubtedly influence her limit of tolerance of pain and her readiness to accept it. The highest expression of intolerance is flight into anesthesia through narcotics, with complete loss of consciousness. On the basis of my own experience, I feel that this passive giving up of consciousness is not always an expression of real intolerance of pain but rather an escape from an unbearable fear.

Some women, despite violent pains and the desire of their doctors to relieve them, protest against narcosis even more than against their suffering. Their fear of being physically restricted is intensified, because they feel that while under the influence of narcotics they will completely lose control of their senses and physical functions, that they will be completely at the mercy of arbitrary external powers and unable to defend themselves, that something terrible will be done to them, or that they themselves will be impelled to do something wild. Some carefully watch the preparations for the delivery, others control themselves and worriedly ask upon awakening what they did and said in narcosis.

The threat of loss of consciousness heightens the fear of death. In this respect a woman in labor differs little from women about to be operated upon in a state of narcosis.

Many women misuse the pain they must suffer. A hysterical woman makes a great show of her suffering before the persons attending her and demands compensation for it; an obsessional-neurotic or depressive woman, tormented by guilt feelings, punishes herself by protracting and aggravating her suffering; an aggressive-malicious woman uses her pains to awaken a guilt feeling in her husband: "You have done this." For the husband of such a woman, painless delivery doubtless assures a greater safeguard against this reproach. Feminine-loving women retain no vestige of this reaction after cessation of the pains. But all these are distortions and secondary uses of delivery that have nothing in common with its primary psychologic significance. Incidentally, they often assume considerable therapeutic importance, and cure or alleviation of neurotic ailments through delivery is more common than negative consequences.

Medical science does not content itself with intervening in pathologic phenomena, but is rapidly extending its mastery to the normal physiologic processes. Science endeavors to conquer nature and its imperfections, and to correct whatever damage civilization has done to nature. Even in normal cases, the duration of delivery now depends upon the obstetric technic used, pain is mastered with the help of drugs, and fear is conquered by gradual lessening of the mother's active participation in the process. Her role as birth giver is growing ever more passive.

I question the desirability of this development. Woman's active part in the delivery process, her lasting pride in her accomplishment, the possibility of rapid reunion with her child, and some degree of gratification of that primary feminine quality that assigns pain a place among pleasure experiences in the psychic economy, are precious components of motherhood, and an effort should be made to preserve them.

The psychiatrist and the obstetrician must combine to help nature to the best of their abilities. The obstetrician is usually unable to use his psychologic acuteness and possible interest in psychologic observation. He rarely has the time or the patience to listen to the woman's fragmentary and often irrelevant utterances before, during, and after delivery. He pays little attention to them as a human being and even less as a scientist. He dashes from one delivery to another, often manages his cases so that they coincide in term, in order to be able to let as many women as possible profit from his expert help within a short time, and considers his task well done if everything goes smoothly. An important obstetrician, one of the few who admit the fact of psychologic influences in somatic processes, told me that in the course of his practice he had known only one woman who, upon awakening from her narcosis, refused to acknowledge her child as her own. Yet I knew that four of his patients had had that feeling but had never had the opportunity to communicate the fact to him.

Nevertheless, the relation of the woman in labor to her obstetrician is of the greatest importance. It varies greatly according to the individual and reflects the total personality. But most important is the fact that the mastering of fear, and thereby the whole psychologic fate of the delivery, is often connected with this relationship. Sometimes the woman regards her doctor as an omniscient and omnipotent father figure and believes that nothing evil can happen to her while he is present. She submits blindly and passively to his wishes and orders. In other cases she trembles before his power and concentrates all her fear on his person; an aggressive person makes him the object of her aggression, a woman who needs love expects his sympathy, praise, ministrations, etc. Women show him only that aspect of their feelings which is connected with this relationship. Even if he has a sincere psychologic interest in his patients, their psychic reactions reach him detached from their context, in such a way that his direct observations remain somewhat vague. Therefore such observations cannot reveal the extent to which women's psychologic reactions have a constant significance rooted in biology, the extent to which they are dependent upon the actual, individual situation, etc. Only psychoanalysis can see the the experience of delivery from a distance, place it in the psychic whole, and disclose its real nature. Mrs. White's reaction to her loss of water, for example, was absolutely incomprehensible until psychoanalytic observation gave it meaning. And there are innumerable similar examples. It is difficult to say whether they will eventually convince the gynecologists of the importance of psychologic factors.

If the disturbing elements within and without are well mastered, if the delivery follows a normal, natural course, and if by direct emotional influence or other means the excess of fear and pain is successfully reduced, childbirth is the greatest and most gratifying experience of woman, perhaps of human beings. Two powerful factors make it so: first, the joy in accomplishment that is connected with the mastering of fear and pain and with the woman's own activity; second, the happy relation with the child that begins immediately after delivery. The dynamism of this relationship is clear: the whole psychic energy tied to the labor and withdrawn from the outside world streams toward the child in the moment of delivery, and the newly achieved freedom from pain and fear creates a feeling of triumph and endows the first moment of motherhood with real ecstasy. It is not yet motherliness that characterizes the mother-child relationship—it is only the first foundation stone, perhaps even a reservoir from which springs the gradually developing love for the child.

The last sediments of the deep-rooted anxiety as to whether the child is alive, whether it is normal, must still be rapidly disposed of. The woman's individual wishes and hopes concerning the sex of the expected child often engender impatient curiosity. In almost all types of deliveries, the unmastered concern about the child manifests itself consistently until confrontation with him sets the mother's mind at rest.

A moment later disappointment may begin. Curiously enough, to paraphrase the saying, *Omne animal post coitum triste est*, one might say, *Omnis mulier post partum tristis est*—but as a rule not before she has experienced the ecstasy of motherhood. It is true that sometimes the order is reversed: instead of joy there is first sad disappointment, which only gradually yields to joy; or exhaustion and irritation obscure the positive aspects of a given woman's service to the species. It is not rare for a woman under these circumstances to admit openly that she does not feel anything for her child—that it is alien to her. The motives for this are numerous and not always clear. Apparently even the profound experience of delivery can be disavowed if painful ideas vitiate the realization of motherhood. Later we shall see that unmarried mothers who know that their motherhood will soon end frequently admit absence of feeling rather than experience of grief at the imminent loss of the child. The same is true of unhappily married women who are ready to abandon their husbands and feel the emotional tie to the child as a disturbing element, or of hysterical women who have foreseen all these ecstasies in their luxuriant fantasies and to whom reality seems pale, or of obsessional-neurotic women who have found a refuge from their ambivalent emotions in indifference, or of emotionally blunted, schizoid women who expect a revival of their emotional life from the birth of a child, but are unable to supply the inner capacity necessary for this. A large number of infantile, narcissistic women feel injured by their pains and efforts and hold this fact against the child. Many women are physically and psychically unequal to the great task of child-birth, and exhaustion is not a propitious soil for happiness.

I have mentioned the fact that opportunities for study-ing the psychic processes in spontaneous delivery are becoming rarer. The observer in the room of a woman who has just awakened from anesthesia after being delivered of her child, does not hear any sound of happiness or joy. The last traces of terrific struggle are still visible: the blue marks on her body show that the woman in travail has exchanged the masochistic experience for a break-through of aggression. Under the effect of anesthetics and by the aggression aroused by the motor elements of the delivery process, her masochism is intensified to self-destructive fury, and she becomes likewise a fury against herself and a danger to others. Many women experience the first moment of motherhood after the birth of the child while still tied to their beds. In the room of such a patient one hears the voice of the nurse trying to soothe the mother's ill humor by saying: "You have a magnificent boy."

Whereupon a half-enraged, half-otherworldly voice answers: "Is that so? That's fine, very fine."

Another greets her child with a sad smile: "Poor child, ex-posed to this cold world."

Between her and the child there is usually the barrier of separation, a reaction that has not been completely mastered.

It is impossible to know whether and to what extent this inadequate first contact colors the later relation to the child. Perhaps not at all. Perhaps its only effect is that the woman is poorer for having missed a great experience. Perhaps both mother and child have been denied something profoundly important. Sometimes an introspective, sensitive mother is conscious of this loss. The following letter was put at my disposal by one mother. It should be entitled "One for Many," and runs as follows:

> With two of my children I went through labor with no anesthetic until I was given gas for the last severe pains before delivery. In both cases I regained consciousness, while still in the delivery room, with a sense of elation and achievement. And in both cases I had the normal maternal conviction that I had produced the most superior baby in the hospital, if not in the world.
>
> With the third child I was given an injection of scopolamine and a sedative by mouth at the beginning of labor and remembered nothing from that time until I woke up in my room some hours later. My first reaction was that nothing had happened—it was all to do over again. When I realized that the baby had been born, I could summon up no great interest in seeing or hearing about it and wished only to be left alone so that I could go back to sleep. Even when I actually saw the child I had none of the proper emotions—no particular pride or conviction that this was my baby. I felt only that there was a pathetic little thing for whom I was responsible and before whom I must do my best to counterfeit an affection I did not honestly feel.
>
> As I said before, this feeling—or rather lack of feeling—did not last, and if it had affected only me, I should not consider it of great importance. To be sure, I missed a satisfying emotional experience, but what is of far greater importance is that the child missed an early relationship the importance of which can hardly be overemphasized.
>
> It is hard to believe it was only coincidence that this particular child should have been reserved, shy, and suspicious where the other two were warm, happy, and confident. I cannot but feel that my early lack of interest and affection had a great deal to do with this.

There is an increasing number of women who, without being actually neurotic, nevertheless behave in an unusual fashion after a technically perfect painless delivery. Something has happened during childbirth to disappoint such women and fill them with horror, and this now prevents them from developing love for the newborn. The child remains associated with the horror, a rejected alien object. The mother's unconsciousness and nonpresence have left something unresolved in her. She has experienced the whole process uncreatively, not as giving life to a child, but as an operation that removed something harmful, something that she now confronts in the outside world. Delivery was for her like a trauma, the effects of which extend to the child and prevent her motherliness from flowering. It would be fruitful to subject such cases to a thorough study and to ascertain the relations between the traumatic experience and the existing disposition.

Pathologic reactions after natural, painful deliveries are familiar to us. Confusion and states of excitement degenerating into frenzy and impulse to suicide, destructive attacks on the child's life, and so-called postpartum psychoses that automatically subside after the ebbing of the childbirth excitement, are all well known to psychiatry. Moreover, there are chronic ailments that begin with delivery. In so far as we are not dealing with sickness resulting from states of fever or exhaustion, we must assume that delivery constitutes such a severe and often specific ordeal for the emotional life that it can become a starting point of chronic neurotic and psychotic processes. It is noteworthy that a given experience sometimes has a therapeutic and sometimes a pathogenic effect. For instance, in some cases obsessional-neurotic states become much milder after delivery, in others they become acute; depressions are moderated, or are intensified to the point of becoming clinical conditions.

Schizophrenias and depressions that break out with delivery have a specific content and character, even when only a provocation or hastening of a chronic process due to an existing disposition is involved. Zilboorg has studied the relation between psychotic illnesses and the instinctual-dynamic and ego-psychologic processes in the reproductive function.[18] All these observations were made independently of the type of delivery. However, one cannot help feeling that in some cases the abnormal reactions can be explained by the fact that the delivery took place in a state of unconsciousness. As I have said, I have observed women who after a prolonged delivery in

[18] ZILBOORG, G.: Malignant psychoses related to childbirth. Am. J. Obst. & Gynec., vol. 15, 1928. IDEM: The dynamics of schizophrenic reactions related to pregnancy and childbirth. Am. J. Psychiat., vol. 8, 1929.

narcotic sleep declared that the children presented to them were not theirs, that they had been interchanged with those of other women.

In such cases the women are soon set right intellectually, but their emotional estrangement persists for a longer time. In two instances accessible to my analytic observation, severe obsessional neuroses were involved. In both there was a fully preserved sense of reality. In both cases anesthetics were administered immediately after the beginning of the labor pains. Both women were primiparas, happy at the prospect of having a child; their pregnancies had been favorable. Their weak emotional natures proved unable to bear the vacuum created between their expectation of the child and their first contact with it. Their estrangement from the child was too strong, and their disappointment at having missed the experience expected by every woman produced in them the feeling "This cannot be my child, otherwise I would feel more for him." Such feelings of estrangement are also familiar to us in schizoid women.

In the 2 cases discussed here, the emotional derangement was, in my opinion, caused by the type of delivery. What seems to take place in this process is that as a result of the woman's unconsciousness, the expected objectivization of the child's existence, its projection into the outside world, is slowed up and, so to speak, detached from the context of the experience as a whole. The dynamism of the mother-child relationship is disturbed, because the child experienced in the outside world does not necessarily coincide with the child that was in the mother's womb; this is why the mother has the feeling "It is not my child." Such a strong reaction to the violation of continuity naturally takes place only in women whose emotional disposition was deranged before, but, even so, such pathologic distortions are very instructive and deserve careful study.

The history of anesthesia is one of ever expanding progress. Interestingly enough, it was used for the first time in the same year that Semmelweis made his epochal stand for obstetric asepsis. In 1847 Sir James Simpson first used ether in obstetrics and soon replaced it with chloroform. In America, the new conquest of death by asepsis and of labor pains by anesthesia began in Boston. There Channing was the first to adopt Simpson's innovation.

In the last hundred years science has not rested in its efforts to spare women suffering. Nitrous oxide and oxygen, ether and quinine, morphine and magnesium sulfate, in various combinations, quantities, and manners of application, are all used. An ingenious combination of drugs can even achieve amnesia for the whole painful process. Scopolamine and morphine given hypodermically produce a kind of twilight sleep and complete amnesia, even though the pains are felt during the contractions. Amytal combined with scopolamine, codeine, or morphine seems to have a similar effect. Recently much use has been made of pernoston injected intramuscularly and intravenously, and satisfactory results seem to have been achieved with avertin. But the states of excitation produced by all these drugs justify the psychiatrist in questioning their absolute value from the point of view of psychic health.

In the current attempts to find a method of delivery that eliminates all pain without affecting consciousness, some obstetricians employ lumbar or spinal anesthesia—so-called continuous caudal anesthesia—and paravertebral block. I have investigated the experiences of several women with these methods. All of them have the same feeling of an impersonal experience: "It was as though it were happening in the movies." They were happy over the births of their children, felt strong and well, but "something" was missing. One intelligent woman was able to give me a detailed description of her experience. During the entire period of delivery she had a tense and oppressive feeling that, she said, was like a vague fear. She had great confidence in her physician's ability and watched his efforts with some degree of objectivity. She compared her experience with a scene at a railroad station: somebody is waiting for the train, the railroad workers do their best to see to it that the train comes in on schedule, that it arrives without accident; perhaps it will be a little late. I asked her whether she had a happy feeling of expectation, as before the arrival of a beloved friend or relative. Curiously enough, this was not the case. The joyful realization that she was expecting a child had been lost somewhere in the course of her anesthesia and all her psychic energy was devoted to tense observation. Thus, although the process was analogous to a spontaneous birth, the attention was concentrated on other people's activity.

After the birth she was overjoyed at having the child. But the ecstasy of happiness was lacking, and she had a general feeling that she had missed something. Another woman who had been delivered under caudal anesthesia felt distinctly that her experience of delivery was disappointing and empty.

From the psychologic point of view, this type of delivery has the advantage of rapid reunion with the child and freedom from the aftermath of narcosis. But the absence of the feeling of accomplishment is very marked. It is noteworthy that the woman usually does not realize this till later.

I must add that I have heard of exactly identical reactions to very painful and exhausting deliveries. In these cases the pain and effort taxed the psychic energies to such a degree that the joyful reflux could not take place. It would be worth while systematically to examine a larger number of similar cases.

Grantly Dick Read,[14] an English physician, is following an entirely different path. He is seeking a method of delivery that would assure a natural birth with as little pain as possible. He too holds fear responsible for all the troubles women suffer as a result of childbirth, and by means of systematic instruction, preparation, and intelligent assistance he tries to keep the patient in labor free from fear and pain but lucidly and actively participating in the process. This method seems particularly favorable from a psychologic point of view, although the theoretic assumptions of Dr. Read's impressive obstetric technic need correction. By attributing labor pains

---

[14] READ, G. D.: Childbirth without fear. New York: Harper, 1944.

to fear alone—"panic is caused by tension and tension by fear"—he underestimates their organic causes.

Nor does the fear of delivery arise from misinformation or inadequate preparation or training. Dr. Read takes a too realistic attitude toward this fear; he attributes it to bad environmental influences and thus falls into the same error as those who believe that the young girl's fear of menstruation can be eliminated by education (cf. vol. 1). Enlightenment plays the same important but not decisive part in childbirth as in menstruation. Occasionally intellectual insight dispels some of the fear, but not the deeply rooted inner anxiety. We have seen that this fear is determined by profound and multiple factors; the psychologic task of a woman in labor is to master it in a favorable manner, and Dr. Read's great merit is that he has shown a way toward this end through the woman's active participation in delivery, through increasing her optimism as to the future and her willingness joyfully to make the sacrifice of pain for her hope of the child. However, Dr. Read underestimates the great importance of his personal influence, which is so powerful only because his patients feel that the obstetrician deeply understands their psychic needs. Impressive as his method may be, I doubt that it can be developed into a standard technic.

Medical technic continues to advance, and nothing can stop its forward march. But it is possible to try to perfect this technic in such a way that the dynamism of feminine psychic life is fully taken into account. Women often avidly accept the blessing of painless birth in complete ignorance of the fact that they are thereby renouncing the experience of birth and the ecstasy of the first contact with the child. The point of view of the woman's conscious ego, which represents reality, is: "I want to have a child and I want to achieve this end with the least possible suffering and cost of energy." The obstetrician is in alliance with this conscious ego, and the noblest aspect of his profession is his struggle to protect the woman and the child from danger and to reduce the mother's pain as much as possible. His cold objectivity, which is concerned only with physical processes and disregards the psychologic condition, is perhaps better than an understanding that can help only very little and disturbs the objective, organic orientation. If psychogenic disturbances intervene in the physical process, psychologic help can come only from intuitive understanding or detailed objective knowledge of the given individual's personality as a whole. Intuition is not everyone's gift, and the obstetrician has no time for and usually no interest in detailed psychologic knowledge. The psychiatrist's task is to communicate his knowledge to the obstetrician and to make useful suggestions to him. In the present stage of obstetrics, these suggestions are: (1) to find a technic of delivery in which the psychic value of the mother's active participation in the process is taken into account, and (2) to reunite mother and child as soon as possible after birth.

It seems that the method of caudal anesthesia elaborated by Lull and Hingson[16] meets the second requirement. As for the first, the authors are trying to create a substitute for physical activity by diverting the parturient woman's interest (listening to radio, conversation, etc.). Though childbirth becomes less painful, we must not forget that the psychic dynamism is adversely affected by an omission of performance. The question requires further study. On the other hand, our psychologic suggestions should not conflict with the efforts to spare women suffering and to prevent the destructive effects of pain and fear.

I am afraid that our youngest mothers, the very ones who are most eager to take advantage of modern technic and renounce the birth experience, are least able to cope with the negative aspects of this technic. Their development toward motherhood has met with difficulties from the beginning. And while our first concern here is with women, we must not forget that our science is not yet able to say whether the mother's experience of childbirth is not the first foundation stone in the child's future psychic life.

[16] LULL, C. B., AND HINGSON, R. A.: Control of pain in childbirth. Philadelphia: Lippincott, 1944.

We have limited our observation to women giving birth to their first children. There is no doubt that for the woman who has already passed through the purgatory of experience and consolidated her motherliness with a previous child, the emotional dangers are less than for one who is being delivered for the first time. But even such women are painfully aware of the difference between the experience of spontaneous delivery and that of technically controlled delivery, as shown by the letter quoted above.

It is possible that the demands of the psychiatrists in this regard are anachronistic and absurd. Undoubtedly obstetrics will continue to make technical advances regardless of psychology, and woman's psychic behavior will adjust itself to the cultural developments. Her active productive contribution will turn to other goals that have nothing to do with motherhood. Man's traditional disadvantage, the fact that his fatherhood is uncertain (*pater incertus est*), now has its much weaker counterpart in the young mother's surprised question: "Is this my child?"

Man's repressed infantile wish to give birth to a child of his own gestation is symbolized in the tale of a homunculus begotten without a woman's participation. Modern obstetrics, a masterpiece of masculine efficiency, deprives woman of her active participation in delivery, and thus in a certain sense deprives her of her monopoly in this field. Perhaps man is thus unwittingly driving woman into those spheres of activity that he once claimed as his own, and is contributing to the progressive wiping out of sex differences.

CHAPTER EIGHT

Confinement and Lactation: First Relations with the Child

WITH the separation from the child through birth, a new world opens for the mother. But the continuity of the psychologic elements of the various stages of motherhood (conception, pregnancy, delivery, lactation) is preserved throughout. These elements may assert themselves with varying intensity: in one stage they may recede into the background or move within normal limits, in another they may increase to a pathologic degree. They may have analogous forms of expression in each stage or conceal themselves behind defense mechanisms that produce phenomena seemingly opposite to the previous ones. The psychologic relation to the fetus can even outlast the biologic phase of pregnancy and continue for a shorter or longer time in the relation to the child; or the pregnant woman's joy and interest in the content of her own body can swing to the opposite pole with the birth of the child, and this can lead to various difficulties in the mother-child relationship. The pregnancy fears may be overcome in the act of birth or they may continue in the form of excessive anxiety about the child.

In my general remarks on the psychology of motherhood I have referred to the differences between the instinctual actions of animals and the relationship between the human mother and her child. Direct observation of this relationship reveals these differences very clearly; but from time to time we are struck by certain analogies to instinctual behavior.

First of all we shall recall the fundamental difference: the primitive instinctual actions of animal mothers often lead them with great certainty to achieve goals that they do not pursue emotionally or intellectually. In human mothers—perhaps also in intelligent animals—the relationship to the child is accompanied by emotions and ideas. These may be combined with conscious and unconscious affective representations that largely divert this relationship from following a straight line. It can even be said that such affective representations are always present in some degree.

An unmotherly attitude, opposed to the conscious wish tendencies of the woman, may sometimes become very strong and assert itself in the very biologic functions that we assume to be dominated by the maternal instinct. In discussing pregnancy we have already mentioned the curious fact that a woman may have all the maternal qualities as well as the sincere desire to conceive, bear, and nurse a child, and yet be compelled to terminate her course, as it were, at one of these way stations of motherhood. Thus it is clear that psychologic motherhood is a very complicated structure in which we can find our way only by applying several methods of investigation, and even then only to a very limited extent. I shall begin my discussion by describing the biologic events.

Biologically, woman up to her delivery plays the role of a passive bearer of the future, and only her fantasy life permits her to perceive this future with maternal and creative joy. During pregnancy all the mother's organic processes are adjusted to the physiologic needs of the fruit ripening in her womb. The organic relationship between the fetus and the maternal organism is very much like that between a parasite and its host. Only the fantasy directed toward the future, and the emotional charge of this fantasy, make the fruit of the body a beloved being. Many women turn so strongly to this future that even during pregnancy they give up all their other interests, their whole intellectual life, and become absorbed in the gratifying fantasies of future motherhood. Others from the beginning take a defensive position, and even try to strengthen their interests outside motherhood, or directly use the child to heighten their self-assurance and feeling of individuality.

The upheavals we have observed in woman's psychic life during pregnancy are partly an expression of the tremendous changes taking place in all her organic functions, and partly the direct result of the expectation of a child and of the emergence of hitherto latent psychic contents.

I have spoken of the physical and psychic shock of delivery. During the period immediately following it, woman is not yet by any means freed from the chain of physical burdens imposed upon her as a result of sexual intercourse and the fecundation of her germ cells. We must clearly keep in mind the complicated physiologic work that takes place in the body of a woman who has borne a fetus to full term. The overdilated uterus of pregnancy, which has displaced all the other internal organs, begins to return to its normal size, and the other organs resume their place. The processes of renewal tax all the forces of the organism. When a woman joyfully states after delivery that, as she puts it, she is herself again, she is mistaken: for while the organism is strenuously progressing toward return to its normal state, new constructive work in the service of the reproductive function begins, in the activity of the lacteal glands. Preparation for this new organic task takes place during pregnancy: the lacteal apparatus begins to function in this period, owing to the chemical influences of the endocrine organs on the lacteal glands, and at the time of delivery the production of milk reaches its highest point.

Thus we see the continuity of the organic processes that serve the reproductive function. The physical separation from the fetus does not—for the time being—interrupt this continuity. The organism no sooner recovers from the great physiologic shock of delivery than it must assume a new physiologic function, suckling the child. From the first stages of the reproductive function, the whole physiologic apparatus of the maternal body works altruistically, giving in favor of the child, and woman's whole body adapts itself to the great task of motherhood—first to the fetal existence of the baby, then to its extra-uterine existence. After delivery the largest share of the bodily energies goes into the stream that flows from the mother's body to the child now outside her.

What, then, is woman's psychic behavior during this new stage of the reproductive function? How does the parallelism between the physical and psychic processes manifest itself in this case? And, above all, what are the mother's emotional reactions to the shock and trauma of separation?

During delivery the woman experiences an "end of the world" feeling as a result of having withdrawn for a time from all her relationships to the outside environment; this feeling is partly prepared during pregnancy by the centering of her life interest on her condition. Now, after delivery, she rebuilds the world around the child, and her abandoned relationships with the environment are gradually restored through him.

It is possible to speak of three acts of this reconstruction. The first coincides with the last moment of delivery, in which there is an influx of ecstatic feelings for the baby. The reaction of separation is compensated by a kind of rediscovery of the child. In women who have been delivered under narcosis, this reaction is postponed and can never be as intense and gratifying as when the child is immediately welcomed after the performance of the birth task.

The second act is the confinement period: this is a very gratifying time, according to the individuality of the mother and her whole life situation, though sometimes disapppointment reactions take place even then. Despite her joy over the child, the woman's orientation is still extremely narcissistic. For some time the world is still identical with her own ego, the mother feels herself at the center of all loving attention, and her child is above all regarded as her product, her achievement. Only gradually does he assert his own demands, rights, and needs, and only gradually does the mother's relationship to him assume the character of an object relationship. Before it has become stabilized as such, there are relationships to the child that, properly speaking, are not yet identical with the later maternal love but are rather preliminary phases of it. Joy and pride on the one hand, disappointment on the other, are in conflict, and many motherly women admit later that they felt the child as alien and repulsive, and were conscious that their feelings were a mixture of joy, fear, and sometimes even a curious indifference.

Observations of women who immediately after delivery have lost their joyfully expected children, or who have given birth to dead babies, show that the reactions to such a loss do not have the character of real grief such as one suffers after the death of a beloved object. They correspond to the effects of nonfulfillment of a wish fantasy, of mobilized guilt feelings or accusations against others, etc. In such cases readiness for a new pregnancy sets in strongly and very soon. The situation is different if the child is lost after an interval of time during which the mother cared for him, especially if she suckled him successfully. Then there is real mourning; readiness for a new conception develops slowly and only after the grief for the lost child has subsided. These differences are interesting because they illustrate the relations between "maternal instinct," which is expected to hold sway immediately after delivery, and maternal love, which develops only gradually.

The confinement period is characterized by a preliminary phase of motherliness. At its center is the problem of lactation, to which we shall return later. The psychic processes of confinement as a whole naturally depend on the entourage, the real life situation, the customs in the given country, family, etc. A woman of restricted means, plagued by financial worries, concerned about the loss of her earnings or her absence from home, afraid of the difficulties that await her when she returns with the additional burden, will experience the period of confinement in a manner different from that in which it is experienced by a well-to-do young woman who can joyfully indulge in the "glory" of her new estate. In addition there is the relation to the husband and the whole emotional situation.

Cultural influences are responsible for the external details of confinement, although here too we repeatedly recognize the return of familiar themes in different forms. Among a large number of primitive peoples, men are absolutely forbidden access to the room of the confined woman. In more civilized, even patriarchal nations of past times, men, although they were allowed to enter the room, usually lost all authority there. This was woman's domain; only her word, opinions, and ideas were respected.   In our own culture, woman has won the right to have her say in the most important cultural and social institutions, but she has largely been forced out of the room of the confined woman as adviser or aid.   The mother of the recently delivered woman has yielded to her son-in-law; the wise women, friends, etc., have given way to the physician.

Many peoples regard the woman in childbed as unclean and taboo, others regard her as sacred.   In certain primitive groups, she must be isolated, because, according to irrational beliefs, she is thought to be a danger to others.   In our own society, strangers are kept at a distance as much as possible in order to protect the new mother from the rationally known dangers of infection.

To make congratulatory visits to young mothers is an old and widespread custom.   In the Middle Ages and well into modern times, the occasion called for a great display of pomp.

Confinement was the period during which it was proper for women to show the valuables of their homes and their most beautiful adornments to their women friends, acquaintances, and neighbors. . . . Feminine vanity was taken into account.   Since the confined woman received the visits of her women friends and neighbors, she herself tried to adorn herself, her newborn infant, and her room as richly and splendidly as possible, in order to arouse not only the admiration but if possible also the envy of her female visitors.[1]

Apparently the narcissistic element in the woman who is not yet absorbed in her love for the child, manifests itself not only in our own but also in other, less developed cultures.

The "wicked" woman, the witch, dangerous to mother and child, often emerges in the confinement room; among the Jews her classic representative is Lilith.   Jewish women hang up amulets and inscriptions with Hebrew phrases containing the following magic spell:

In the name of the great and formidable God of Israel!   The prophet Elijah once met a specter named Lilith and her escort. . . . She said: "I

---

[1] Ploss and Bartels: Op. cit., vol. 3, p. 155.

am going to the house of the confined woman N. to make her sleep with the sleep of the dead, to take her newborn child, that I may satiate myself on his blood, suck out the marrow of his limbs, and leave only his corpse."

This is apparently another vehini-hai, tormenting our confined women in their fears.

The third act in the reconstruction of the woman's relationship with the environment corresponds to her urgent need to emerge from her narcissistic limits and once again emotionally to occupy a place in the outside world. There are two means of achieving this—through the child and through the outside environment.

I have previously tried to define the various emotional elements in the mother's relationship with the child conceived as an outside object, elements that in their totality are called motherliness. We have reduced them to three main components—tenderness, altruism, and a specifically colored activity. Taken together, they form, in our view, the psychic atmosphere of motherliness. Maternal altruism is based on the fact that with regard to the child the mother is completely selfless and willing to sacrifice everything, including her life. The essence of maternal love is that it demands nothing, sets no limits, and makes no reservations. It is complementary to the child's first attitude toward the mother, when she is for him a reservoir for the satisfaction of all his needs, a being who, he feels, has no interests outside him. The only direct compensation the mother can expect from the child is something that is inherent in maternal love itself—joy in his existence and well-being. This relationship develops directly, paralleling the bodily processes, out of the mother-child unity during pregnancy.

It is true that the cutting of the umbilical cord results in a reorganization of the bodily functions and partly dissolves the mutual dependence of mother and child. This dissolution gives the child the possibility of replacing his mother with another object in case of need, and returns to the mother a relatively greater freedom of movement. But in so far as the psychic-emotional existence of mother and child is in question, this liberation has only a very relative, almost purely theoretic value, especially for the mother: maternal love—that is to say, the emotional tie to the child—creates a *psychic umbilical cord* that only the Parcae, the Fates, the goddesses of life and death, can cut. The symbolic meaning of the allegorical "thread of life," as representing the umbilical cord, is clear to anyone who understands maternal love.

With the cutting of the physical umbilical cord the intra-uterine mother-child unity is destroyed, and the mother receives a real substitute for what until then has been only a fantasy, an illusion. But in order to realize the unique position of maternal love among all other human emotional relationships, one must understand the following fact. Side by side with the progressive tendencies of motherhood, which strive to adjust themselves to the child's development, a regressive tendency asserts itself in every mother, seeking the restoration of the prenatal unity. We have mentioned the instinctual tie of the animal mother to her young and the physiologically determined separation reactions. In the human mother the separation reactions are transferred from the physiologic to the psychic domain and, as we have said, survive the physical and even the social dependence of the child upon her. They are an expression of the psychic umbilical cord.

The fact that maternal love is rooted in the condition in which the split between the ego and the nonego does not yet exist, creates the emotional situation that can be observed in some forms of being in love: "The object has, so to speak, consumed the ego. Traits of humility, of the limitation of narcissism, and of self-injury, occur in every case of being in love."[2] Freud considers only men capable of this selfless love; in his view women do not need to love but only to be loved, and whenever they love in a selfless manner, they are loving "according to the masculine type."

I shall not reopen the discussion of this question here (cf. vol. 1, p. 190). It seems to me that the form of relationship

[2] FREUD, S.: Group psychology and the analysis of the ego. London: Hogarth, 1940.

that appears temporarily in being in love is a permanent characteristic of genuine maternal love. As this love develops at the expense of self-love, it may impoverish the mother's ego, despite the far reaching identification between mother and child. Every woman has desires and aspirations that have nothing in common with the reproductive function. She has her own personal ego, which strives for expression, enlargement, gratification, experience. If she does not succeed in gratifying her ego within the framework of the reproductive function and her relation to the child, a conflict must break out between the polarities reproduction-ego and ego-child.

We have seen what forms this conflict takes in pregnancy and what possibilities of solution exist in that stage. After the unity has been split, two tendencies are present in the mother—one progressive, aiming at helping her ego to regain its rights, the other regressive, aiming at reunion with the child and the preservation of the psychic umbilical cord. The latter tendency, so close to the organic aspect, is perhaps the expression of the "maternal instinct."

Even if we assume that maternal love is set in operation by the organic processes of the reproductive function, there is no doubt that in the life of each individual it receives accretions from various sources and that it is subject to changes in the course of time. In the newly arisen conflict between the ego interests and the reproductive functions, maternal love is a bridge. The pride in the child, his dependence upon his mother's love, the still existing identification with him, and the fantasies about his future, are compensations at the disposal of the endangered ego. They can serve it only if maternal love is present.

The ego reacts in various directions. First of all, in every case, there is an automatic, reflex-like defense against the strong burden laid upon the ego interest, which sees in motherhood—and, as we have shown, justly so—a danger of impoverishment. Then come the more specific loss reactions—the woman's feeling that her freedom of movement is restricted, which becomes a danger particularly in youthful mothers. There is also the woman's fear of having her physical beauty impaired—often with strong emphasis on the breasts. There is the competition between motherliness and eroticism, between intellectual aspirations and maternal duties, and the danger felt by the woman's ego in having to give up her own infantile ties in favor of the adult status that motherhood imposes upon her, or, conversely, the danger of falling back, through motherhood, into earlier more or less loosened ties.

Another danger for the ego lies in the fact that the existence of many women consists in a successful structure of defense mechanisms and sublimations that may be shaken by the experience of motherhood. All these dangers become more serious under conditions that may be generally described as ego weakness. In other words, the woman's ego does not feel equal to the tasks of motherhood, and reacts to this danger with fear and attempts to escape. In addition, many women feel incapable of producing the amount of emotion they consider necessary for the well-being of the newborn child, or fear that they will be exposed to a new and unbearably ambivalent conflict in their emotions.

The mother's tendency to preserve her unity with the child, an instinctual wish to keep him within or with herself, counteracts these ego dangers. The fear accompanying this tendency has the character of the fear of loss; it is an inheritance, a continuation of the fear of separation that in its most intense form accompanies delivery.

The fate of motherliness thus depends upon the result of the conflict of these opposite forces. An excess of fear of ego impoverishment produces flight from the child, failure of the bodily functions in the reproductive service, and inability to experience motherliness. On the other hand, excessive fear of losing the child will result in excessive devotion to him, too drastic turning away from other interests, and a disposition to neurotic fears about the child.

Paradoxically enough, we can observe in many women a strengthening of narcissistic self-love, not only as the first

reaction after the birth of the child, but also during the altruistic phase that follows. Some of these women have particularly strong masochistic tendencies. Reactive narcissism
is here mobilized as a defense against excessive masochistic
altruism. We are familiar with this process, so important in
feminine psychology, in other contexts (cf. vol. 1).

Such a strengthening of secondary narcissism takes place
especially in women whose emotional life is unable to produce
enough motherly joy over the child to compensate for the
sacrifices involved in motherhood. This is the case in every
emotional derangement that is accompanied by sensations of
emptiness and impoverishment. Such a reaction is very
typical of schizoid affective disturbances. Women who are
aware of such affects in themselves expect the child to release
them from their inner rigidity and coldness, and are greatly
disappointed when this does not happen. They complain
openly of their lack of feeling for the child or rush to find other
compensations. They also join the contingent of women
subject to compulsive motherhood and try to achieve the full
experience of motherhood by begetting a new child again and
again.

Women who rush into motherhood out of an inner feeling of
solitude experience the same disappointment. They expect
from the child the love they do not get otherwise or the fulfillment of a longing for a repressed object to which they still
unconsciously cling. It goes without saying that the child
does not come up to this expectation, for he demands of his
mother the very thing that she herself wants to receive—
boundless love given in selfless devotion.

If the birth of the child mobilizes the woman's destructive
tendencies against him and her own ego, as is the case in pathologic conditions, the mother's turning toward other interests
means salvation not only for her own ego but also for the child
threatened by these destructive tendencies.

Women who are under the constant pressure of lurking
guilt feelings, and prone to obsessional-neurotic and depressive
reactions, often allow their children to develop tyrannic claims

from the beginning of their lives and actually to oppress them by their demands: we are familiar with the idea of "His Majesty the child." Later the mother's ego desperately seeks some means of regaining its lost freedom. These means lie outside motherhood, often in a turn to masculinity.

A woman who has unconsciously considered her entire pregnancy a substitute for the lack of a penis, and for whom the child signifies a compensation for this lack, develops typical reactions that partly consist in demands upon the child and partly are supposed to give proof of her own accomplishment. In such cases, the anxiety over the child may very well be a repetition of the familiar genital loss reaction.

When the birth of the child is experienced not as a compensation, but as a new genital trauma, the masculinity complex is directly strengthened. The simplest expression of this process is a turn away from motherhood to accomplishments in other fields. In some women the birth of a child paradoxically results in a generally heightened creativity. Accurate psychologic observation discovers that the motive force behind the heightened creative urge is disappointment in and flight from motherhood. J. Lampl–de Groot[3] gives masculinity an important place in motherhood: "Just as the little girl satisfies her activity in her play with dolls, so the woman utilizes a bit of her masculinity in nourishing and caring for her child and later in educating it." I think that this observation is correct, but valid only as regards a certain type of woman.

The stronger the woman's masculine tendencies, the more resolutely can her ego turn away from the tasks of motherhood; on the other hand, the more passive and masochistic she feels, the greater can be her fear of dependence upon the child and the more determined her flight into masculine activity. This explains why a strengthening of masculine tendencies after childbirth can be observed particularly in women who were previously passive. A masculine ego will of course be more efficient in repelling the new dangers than a feminine-passive one.

[3] LAMPL–DE GROOT, J.: Problems of femininity. Psychoanalyt. Quart., vol. 2, 1933.

Zilboorg,[4] referring to his postpartum schizophrenic patients, says: "The child, it appears, has for these women more the value of a lost male organ than anything else. . . . Childbirth being a castration, the psychotic reaction to it is a recrudescence of the penis-envy." It is particularly interesting that his patients turned to masculinity because of their inadequate affective motherly relation to the child, and mobilized a previously existing disposition in the psychosis not after giving birth to the first child, but only several years later, after having another child. I have found that the pathologic reactions of emotionally deranged, schizoid (not psychotic) women are very often postponed and centered on later born children. It seems that in these women the psychic balance is harder to preserve when the maternal relationship must be spread to several children than when it is concentrated on one child. In many women all of motherhood—especially its prerequisite, the sexual act—is permanently connected with guilt feelings; therefore they can experience themselves as mothers only in suffering, and provoke suffering continually. In them the *mater dolorosa* attitude is carried to the extreme.

In others, the idea of their own rebirth emerges in connection with delivery. For them pain has functioned as an atonement for unconscious crimes, and now they are free of sin, newborn. The popular expression "If I should come into the world again" is realized in their emotions, and they seem to think: "Now I have arrived again, and I want to organize my life in such a way that I may make up for everything I have neglected heretofore."

The knowledge that the new world belongs to the child and not to her can cause great difficulties in the development of motherliness in such a woman. Only through identification with the child can the mother build the new wish-fulfilling fantasies about the future.

Several phenomena that we have observed in pregnancy persist after childbirth. For instance, pleasure in pregnancy,

[4] ZILBOORG, G.: The dynamics of schizophrenic reactions related to pregnancy and childbirth. Am. J. Psychiat., vol. 8, 1929.

which we have observed in infantile types, can now continue in a particularly infantile relation to the child. Such women do not achieve the expected development toward reality, they do not renounce the fantasy relationship with the child, and they play at motherhood like prepuberal girls. They are very proud of their children, want to show them to all their friends, have a certain triumphant feeling with regard to their own mothers, are overjoyed at the gifts they receive, are impatient for the first visit, etc. When the game becomes serious, and the infant begins to make demands upon his mother's selflessness, the first difficulties arise. The reactions of these women are then something like this: "How can such a thing happen to me? After all, I am the one who has the right to make demands!" This woman is the "sweetest little mother" while confined, and an excellent nurse—for a few weeks. Then she is seized by the fear of having her freedom restricted, of being dependent upon the child, and of impoverishing her ego, which, being still in need of development, is really in danger. She has not yet reached the stage at which she can feel secure and grown up; she is actually not ready for motherhood. Because her infantilism is usually connected with her childish relationship to her own mother, her motherhood is only a new opportunity for her to intensify her dependence upon her mother and her conflict with the latter.

Sometimes a woman grows gradually into the role of mother, or can fulfill her duties only by sharing them with her husband. We have previously mentioned a type that we called assistant mother (p. 73). But then we were speaking of girls and women whose puberty was interrupted by actual motherhood and who remained in the stage of motherhood typical of puberty. Now we are referring to women who, as far as their chronologic age is concerned, have long ago left puberty behind them, but who, because of a fixed infantile structure, cannot develop further and assume the role of independent mother. Unfortunately we encounter this type very often at present, as one of the consequences of the war. Women who previously functioned well must appeal for help to social agencies and child centers, because, now that their husbands have been drafted, they are collapsing under the burden of their maternal duties. They energetically demand the return of their mates and childishly consider the war situation as a personal affront to them. Sometimes the husband can be replaced by appropriate assistance, but often such women begin to suffer from previously latent neurosis. The psychiatrist who gains insight into the underlying psychic situation in such cases soon discovers that what is in question is not the woman's erotic longing, or the absence of the father as family supporter, but the motherliness of the husband, without whose active help that of the wife cannot function. In the life stories of such mothers one always discovers a strong infantile dependence upon their own mothers that has been transferred to their husbands.[5]

It is striking how much the woman's need for a mother substitute increases in the period immediately following childbirth, even if she has rejected her own mother. For instance, women with deranged emotional lives try to find mother figures in their entourage in order to cover their own lack of motherliness by identifying themselves with these. Even then they do not have much feeling for the child, but they imitate the attitude of a loving mother so well that they themselves and the persons around them think that their motherliness is genuine. I have called such women the "as if" type.[6]

Others do the same thing in order to keep themselves free of compulsive identification with their own "wicked" mothers, and to replace the latter by an ideal figure. Often such a woman manifests a longing to reconcile herself with her mother and thus free herself from her neurotic fear of losing her child. Sometimes there emerges the unconscious memory of the time when the mother and not the little girl was the real "owner" of the child. This leads to a conflict with the mother over the child. Or else the young woman has the feeling that

---

[5] A number of war neuroses of the character here described have been observed at the Psychiatry Clinic of the Boston Psychoanalytic Institute.

[6] DEUTSCH, H.: Some forms of emotional disturbances and their relationship to schizophrenia. Psychoanalyt. Quart., vol. 9, 1942.

another woman—usually the nurse—wants to win the child away from her. This conflict is hard to solve because on the one hand the young mother does not feel equal to full responsibility, while on the other she yearns for independent motherhood. One woman in childbed precipitated a paranoic psychosis with the delirious idea that her nurse wanted to take away her child.

It remains for future observations to discover what influence modern marriage, built as it is on companionship, exerts on the development of women toward motherliness. In contrast to the situation in the previous generations, when the young woman's mother was present at the delivery, she is here usually eliminated as unnecessary, and if she is admitted to the room where her daughter is confined, or to the nursery, it is more or less out of kindness; she is not needed, because "the child is our own affair." Yet the daughter's real liberation from her mother may be only simulated rather than real.

Mature women likewise can often turn their motherliness only to a little helpless baby. Their feelings are closest to the maternal instinct of animals, which operates only as long as their young are directly dependent upon them. I have observed this relation to the child in the most varied, almost opposite types of women; I have seen it in erotic, very feminine women, greatly in need of love, whose tender feelings move between eroticism and the baby. They do not long to be in love as long as the baby is small, but later they become impatient and turn to eroticism with greater intensity of need. Apparently the child plays a great role for these women as an erotic toy (Freud), but they can permit themselves to indulge in this behavior only while it is very young. Such a relationship to the child is gratifying for them and often also protective; for that reason they always want a new baby and thus join the group of women subject to compulsive motherhood.

A masculine-aggressive woman prefers a baby to an older child for entirely different reasons. Upon him she can impose unrestricted domination without meeting opposition. She thinks she is educating while in reality she is only ruling.

Many women prefer the baby to the child because in the relation with the baby their fear of separation is eased and their sense of responsibility more secure. It is easier to keep a baby in close physical proximity, removed from the dangers of the environment, than a child who gets about independently.

All such women usually feel particularly well during pregnancy and would gladly continue the unity with the baby now outside them.

In contrast to such women there are others who, in a more masculine manner, do not know what to do with a baby. They have no feminine intuition, they cannot feel with another being, they cannot translate the baby's reactions, his seemingly irrational needs, into intellectual language, and they remain alien to him. They make the greatest efforts, read all the books they can find on the care of infants, attend lectures on the subject, and take part in discussions. Such a mother scrupulously does everything she is supposed to do, but becomes genuinely participant only when the child can communicate his experiences in a way that reaches her intellect. As a rule such women are intellectualizing rather than intellectual. In them the intellect plays the part of a defense mechanism in every condition of life: where an emotion is expected, an idea appears. Many intellectual women are actually only fugitives with impoverished emotions.

Many young mothers defy the discipline of modern infant care just as they defied every other discipline. Others follow the rules meticulously and pedantically because of uncertainty and fear. The matriarchal-active mother and the feminine-intuitive woman know how to find their way around all the rules. The former persuades the pediatrician, the latter charms him or cheats him a little. The baby fares well with either—with the former because she loves him and does not yet make any ideal demands upon him, with the latter because she lovingly understands or, more accurately, senses him.

Usually definite individual motives influence the first mother-child relation. Much of this relation is prepared during pregnancy, much of it depends on the individual capacity for love and the personal method of mastering fear. Just as is the case in pregnancy, the mother relation is conditioned from the beginning by various psychologic influences of her own childhood development, upbringing, and cultural environment. The position of the child is a factor connected with many other factors; it is a link in the varied play of interacting events, it is an object of neurotic reactions, etc.

I observed a young war mother who immediately after delivery became unfaithful to her soldier-husband and lived promiscuously; she tossed her child into her mother-in-law's lap without bothering about him further. This peculiar behavior could be explained only as arising from a combination of motives. During her pregnancy the girl was very happy and prepared herself for the undivided possession of her child. She also wanted to prove to her husband that he was wrong in considering her childish and unreliable. When he wrote his mother from the front asking her to take care of the child, his wife became very angry, and no maternal love could protect the the husband from her strong revenge impulses. This seemed plausible, and we could assume that she deliberately oversatisfied her husband's wish by definitively giving her child to his mother and then acted out her revenge in unfaithfulness. But gradually we discovered that the young mother had begun to fear her own aggression and that in giving her child to her mother-in-law she was protecting him from herself. "Do you know that she has ten children, each stronger than the other?" she once said in passing, not in order to rationalize her own actions. Obviously, she could love her child only in a triangle, and when she became angry with her husband she warned herself: "Put the child in better hands, otherwise something may happen to him."

This rejecting mother was thus actually a protecting mother. I did not learn what motives in her past predetermined her reaction.

Occasionally we see war mothers who married for so-called war reasons (cf. vol. 1). This hasty action achieves full reality only with the birth of a child, when all of a sudden the young woman realizes that at bottom she does not wish to have the given man either as a husband or as a father of her child. She would like best of all to erase the whole business, patriotism notwithstanding, but now a kind of living corpus delicti is present that prevents such a solution. The child is drawn into the process of disavowal and an otherwise warm and certainly motherly woman complains that she feels no maternal love for him. She behaves like many unmarried mothers who do not let their motherliness flow freely because they know that they must part from their children. Emotional uncertainty about the real future, in which the child is a link in a chain of events, can nip maternal love in the bud and absolutely negate any effective relationship with him. It is extremely character-istic that such affective denials and repressions set in at the very beginning of the confinement period, before maternal love has a chance to develop. Apparently in such cases the sway of "instinct" in the human female is too weak and her narcissis-tic self-defense too strong to leave the way open to maternal love.

Many young mothers exaggerate their devotion to the in-fant, neglecting all other interests and their own persons for him; they are ready to renounce everything they valued before. This devotion may from the beginning be an overcompensa-tion, which then usually makes room for a negative attitude toward the child, or else creates hostile feelings toward him only secondarily and reactively.

I have known cases in which the mother even during preg-nancy used the child to consolidate and steady her own ego or her marriage, which was built on weak foundations. The motherliness of such a woman often depends upon whether the child has served to achieve her purpose in having him or not.

Quite a number of mothers lie in childbed, freed from their pain and the physical burden, but not from the pregnancy fear that "it will be a monster" or that "it will not live." One mother told me that she spent her first night after delivery in a half-sitting position, to keep herself awake so that she might look at her baby again and again. (She would not have been allowed to do this in a modern hospital.) She felt compelled constantly to confirm to herself the reality of the child and her happiness in really having him. She also told me that these hours were the happiest of her life—and I believe her. I also believe that in the past there were many mothers who would have agreed with her on the basis of their own experience, and I hope that there will be many to do so in the future.

In modern hospitals the mother listens anxiously to outside noises, she tries to recognize the little voice of her baby among those of the other babies, and whispers to her visitors that she has succeeded in bribing the nurse by flattery or some subterfuge to let her child stay with her a few minutes longer than is prescribed. "Isn't that lovely?" she asks. This situation may very well arouse concern; one wonders whether hygiene and psychology are not in conflict here. But since we know that in all fields of life progress is connected with regressive tendencies, let us comfort ourselves with the hope that science will regain the old insight that the mother-child unity must be dissolved only gradually. What was once obvious must now be rediscovered by experimental science.[7] The phrase "rejecting mother," which is so current today, will take on an entirely different meaning, for in the majority of cases the rejecting mother is first a frustrated mother.

While the continuity of motherhood, from conception on through all the stages of the reproductive function, up to the relationship with the real child, is assured, motherliness, that is, the emotional relationship to the child, assumes different forms according to the mother's individuality and the phase of the child's development. Thus we must clearly distinguish between the mother's relation to her completely helpless baby and her relation to her child. The relation to the suckling baby is different in childbed from what it is when the mother gets up; later, breast feeding produces reactions in the mother different from those produced when she is feeding with formulas, etc.

[7] A strong trend in this direction is already visible. Cf. RIBBLE, M. A.: The rights of infants. New York: Columbia Univ. Press, 1943.

We must consider the confinement period as an area intermediate between pregnancy and normal life, in which the separation trauma is mastered by the beginning maternal relation to the child. However, it seems that the longing for reunion is from the beginning in conflict with the urge for liberation. The fear that manifests itself now applies to the separation from the child and now to loss of the ego; now the child is endangered by life, now the mother by the child. The interplay of self-love and concern for the child is unmistakable and clear during the happy but anxious days of confinement.

This interplay partly determines the fate of nursing. All the conflict of the first life period of the newborn infant focuses in the vital problem of nursing. Thus the psychology of the confinement period is from the outset connected with the problem of lactation·

Psychoanalysis has long been trying to investigate the suckling period in normal and pathologic individuals, and the importance of the weaning trauma and its relation to neurosis and psychosis have been clearly demonstrated in rich clinical material. More than to anyone else we owe to Abraham[8] important discoveries about the so-called oral phase of instinctual development. Modern psychologically minded pediatricians observe the processes directly at their source, and interest in the nursing mother is increasing with interest in the infant.

Freud was familiar with the influence of emotional forces on the physiologic process of lactation as early as 1892.[9] At that time he still used hypnosis as a therapeutic method. In this period he was able to observe a young woman who after her first delivery suffered from various obviously hysterical symptoms that forced here to give up nursing her child. At first she lacked appetite and felt pains in her breasts, then secretion of milk stopped completely. "When these obstacles recently

[8] ABRAHAM, K.: Selected papers. London: Hogarth, 1929.
[9] FREUD, S.: Ein Fall von hypnotischer Heilung. Ztschr. f. Hypnot., Suggestionstherap., Suggestionsl., vol. 1, 1892.

occurred again after a second childbirth, they were eliminated by two profound hypnoses with countersuggestions, so that the lying-in woman became an excellent nursing mother": thus, for the first time, I believe, the dependence of the nursing capacity upon psychic influences was demonstrated as though in a controlled experiment.

Many years ago I chanced to observe a curious disturbance of lactation. A young obsessional-neurotic mother, who had transferred her emotional ambivalence also to her newborn child, was compelled to give up nursing after a few weeks, although she wished to nurse her child and her breasts were full of milk. In the intervals between her child's feedings, her milk flowed out in streams, so that her breasts were empty when they were to be given to the child. The methods to which the young woman resorted in order to circumvent this unfortunate state of affairs were reminiscent of the behavior of a man suffering from ejaculatio praecox who tries to hasten the sexual act but is always foiled by his precipitance. She tried to advance the time of the feedings, but the result was always the same: it was too late.

A Polish wet nurse, whose psychic life was much less complicated than that of the patient just mentioned, showed the psychosomatic connection just as clearly. For this poor, illiterate girl, one of the greatest advantages of her vocation consisted in the fact that she was supposed to drink a quart of beer a day, in order to increase her secretion of milk. The favorable influence of beer on the glandular activity, which was considered an indubitable fact in former times, yielded her a pleasure prize that she turned into an obligation for her employers. One day, on the recommendation of a physician, her employers tried to give her less beer and her production of milk stopped at once. It began again when she was given the full quota of beer. So far as I can remember, at that time everyone about her was much more impressed by the miraculous virtue of the beer than by that of the nurse's defiant protest.

An educated young woman reacted almost in the same way to

the visits of her mother, who, being a motherly woman herself, expected her daughter to perform her maternal duties, that is to say, to nurse her child. The young woman, seized by fear like that of a schoolgirl on the eve of examinations, stopped producing milk every time her mother appeared.

Today, the fact that the secretory activity of the lacteal glands oscillates under psychic influences is accepted even by skeptics, and every worker in the field of infant welfare and feeding is familiar with cases as obvious as those cited above. But further observations are still needed to prove that the flow of milk produced in the woman's body has its normal second source in her emotional life. Personally I am convinced that by far the greatest part of nursing difficulties are psychogenic. Middlemore says correctly[10] that the process in the child and the processes in the mother combine into a unity in which "it is scarcely possible for one partner of the nursing couple to be in trouble without involving the other." I believe that in the nursing period the psychic umbilical cord connects the mother's breast and the child's mouth, and that it runs through the arena of the conflict between the egoistic tendencies and the altruistic forces of motherhood. The result of this conflict determines whether the nursing is a success or a failure.

It would seem that among primitives the biologic tendency to suckle and the "maternal instinct" connected with it triumphantly assert themselves, so that no conflict arises at all. According to most anthropologists, nursing by the mother is a general and unquestioned custom among primitive and half-civilized peoples; wherever the mother avoids this duty, we are in the presence of quite civilized tribes. It must be noted, however, that more recent research shows that this theory is not universally valid (cf. Marquesas culture).

Closer examination of the anthropologists' findings leads us to suspect that even among primitives psychic influences cause nursing difficulties. The means of magic and religion are often successfully used to insure an abundant flow of milk.

[10] MIDDLEMORE, M. P.: The nursing couple. London: Hamish Hamilton Med. Bks., 1941, pp. 6 ff.

In many of the mysterious formulas and magic rites that are reported, we recognize defense weapons against the same fears of primitives that we have seen in connection with pregnancy: the mother's milk may dry up because a "wicked" woman (or her child) has sucked the breasts empty, or an envious woman has procured magic spells from the medicine men to spoil the milk, etc. In many East African tribes a woman who is unable to nurse her child loses her man's love; he turns to another woman whose breasts are full. An East African savage, fearing the loss of her man, may fall into a condition unfavorable for the production of milk. A civilized woman fears impairment of her slenderness and sexual attractiveness and unconsciously inhibits the maternal function that she is consciously willing to perform. The savage and the civilized woman achieve analogous end results, that is to say, lactation difficulties, despite the difference between their purposes and cultures.

From time to time social fashion decrees that woman shall not nurse, so that her beauty, freedom, comfort, etc.,[11] shall not be impaired. This frees her from conflict but at the same time deprives her of a source of pleasure.

Our own modern society tries to help woman to achieve a compromise solution. Although it recommends that she nurse her child, it tries to find a *modus vivendi* between mother and child that allows the mother to protect her ego interest to a large extent and simultaneously to preserve the biologic mother-child relationship. Today we are witnessing an interesting cultural conflict in this field. Woman is offered increasingly great opportunities for developing her ego outside the reproductive function, while the ideology of active motherliness is exalted. As a result, woman's psychic energies can neither completely concentrate on the interests of her own individuality nor flow unhampered toward the being dependent upon her. Thus society furthers the inner conflict: woman is asked to agree to a partial renunciation now in one direction, now in another. The discipline of regulated nursing of the

[11] MALINOWSKI, A.: Op. cit.

infant, the placing of the child in hygienic isolation, the tolerance toward complete or relative inability to nurse, are on
the side of the individualistic ego. But objectively the mother
is a vital emotional necessity for the child, and her knowledge
of this fact places the child between the mother and the rest
of the world as a kind of screen that acts to intercept her
other emotional and intellectual interests. Moreover, outside
all cultural influences, there are the mother's deep longing for a
more intimate relationship with her child, her justified concern about his emotional development, her feeling of guilt for
neglecting him—in brief, motherliness. These forces are on
the side of the reproductive function in its conflict with the ego.

Ferenczi[12] justly avers that the suckling infant "can be
prevented from sliding back into nonbeing only by an enormous expenditure of tenderness and love. . . . If love and solicitude are lacking, the destructive drives are soon aroused."
Recent observations seem largely to confirm these views, formulated several years ago. There is an increasing suspicion that
many of the child's oral aggressions, his lack of desire to suck,
about which there is so much discussion today, his constant
falling asleep at the breast, and his restlessness when he is
supposed to sleep, express a dissatisfied "sliding back" induced
by his failure to receive a sufficient "expenditure of love."

The conflict discussed here will perhaps be clarified if we
divide it into its components and illustrate it by examples.

In Seifulina's novel *Verinea*, the primal forces of the nursing
mother are briefly but brilliantly described. The action takes
place during the Russian revolution. Verinea, a former
prostitute, expects a child. But she has important social
tasks to perform, she is a revolutionary commander and her
comrades need her. She returns home in the midst of her
labor pains, does not complain, but only clenches her teeth.

"I want my child to come into this world in joy. I have waited for it a
long time. . . . I will not cry out, I wish it to have an easy birth."

And she uttered only one single cry, a loud, strong one. It did not seem

---

[12] FERENCZI, S.: Das unwillkommene Kind und sein Todestrieb. Internat. Ztschr. f.
Psychoanal., vol. 15, 1929.

to be a cry of pain, but one of joy. And then her body was pierced by an indescribably sweet, light sensation and she heard the marvelously lusty voice of the newborn child.

"Show it to me! A son?"

The revolution knocks at her window, Verinea must leave her child to help his father and her other comrades. Cossacks break into the house but they find only the midwife and the child and search in vain for Verinea. Then the foxy old Antip says: "Leave the child and the midwife here. Then the mother will return by herself. The milk in her breasts will drive her to her baby."

And, true enough,

> A woman's figure rose from the vegetable garden. . . . Verinea approached with the light, alert step of a wild animal. Like a she-wolf she slunk toward her young. It was as though she scented the track with stretched neck, as though she were attracted by her own smell, the smell of the blood taken from her veins, to nurse and rescue her young.

Verinea, who was once a prostitute, loves. She loves the revolution because she loves suffering humanity and wants to help it. She loves her husband because he has given her an opportunity to express herself, she loves her child with instinctual, elemental force, "like a she-wolf." And she dies like a mother, altruistically turned toward her child, free of the fear of death, because she has mastered it by virtue of her solicitude for her child.

Here again we seem to fall into a contradiction. Previously I referred to a conflict between the mother's individualistic ego tendencies and her motherliness. If Verinea were only a primitive mother dominated by the instinctual forces, she would testify to the fact that such motherhood presupposes an unconditional concentration of all vital interest on the child. This is not the case. We know that Verinea loves other things too; she not only grasps the revolution emotionally but knows its goals and methods. Verinea is a woman of insight and understanding. But because she is capable of love and free of fear, she is free of conflict between her ego and her motherliness. This brings us to the decisive point of our problem.

The women with whom we have previously dealt do not have sufficient strength and freedom from fear to bear the decentralization of their strivings without difficulty. Or, expressing it differently, their social goals and individual strivings are too far removed from the sources that give motherliness its strength. If this were not the case, the cultural developments and new adjustments would be accompanied also by a better kind of regulation, just as in the case of Verinea, who, with her breasts full of milk and her heart full of maternal love, nevertheless dies for the revolution, a victim of her enthusiasm for a social cause and of her love for her husband. The Cossacks have prevented her at a given moment from being only a mother. She herself was ready for it, free of conflict, like a she-wolf.

Let us now return to our observations of lactation.

The psychoanalyst, who is not in a position to watch the nursing pair directly on the spot, compensates this disadvantage by his concentrated and objective study of the psychic content mobilized in the course of the nursing process. He is also better equipped to relate his observations to broader events indirectly connected with the problem. Thus he sees again and again that the psychologic manifestations of lactation are part of a more general behavior within the framework of motherhood as a whole. The aim of our observation is to integrate the special phenomena into the general process.

Women who really devote themselves to nursing their children, and who do not experience this function as a secondary duty, maintain that they feel particularly contented during the nursing period. According to them, this contentment has a direct and primitive character. Interestingly enough, almost all of them use practically the same terms to express this condition: "I felt like a comfortable, well fed cow." At bottom, these women during the lactation period are not preoccupied introspectively with themselves, and their contentment is entirely tied up with the well-being of their infants. They may at the same time largely continue to pursue their old interests, but they frankly admit that they do not devote as much time and energy—libido is really the correct term here—to these as before. Usually they must even force themselves to persist automatically in their previous activities. We can understand these women: their psychic energy flows toward the child together with the stream of milk; that is why they feel like cows. They also maintain that during the lactation period they are psychically taxed by the reproductive functions to a greater degree than during pregnancy. This too is understandable. During pregnancy their preoccupation was with something more like a fantasy, now it is real love. Formerly the pull was to introversion, now it is to a real act of unselfish devotion.

Physiologic and psychologic giving coincide in these women. Their general behavior corresponds to the character of their lactation. They are either feminine-passive in eroticism and giving in motherliness, or they are matriarchally active givers and demanders in all of their life conduct (vol. 1). For these two types, pregnancy is usually a positive expectation, and lactation a source of joy.

Paradoxically, the masculine-aggressive woman, whom we have elsewhere contrasted with the feminine woman, is very often an excellent nurse, and her conflicts with her children begin only with their independence. Lactation is an accomplishment of which she is proud, and the dependence of her children upon her gives her the kind of satisfaction she desires. During the period of active service for reproduction she is even inclined to renounce "temporarily" many other gratifications. I have met several women who really enjoyed changing their activity from scientific work to producing children. Later, when their children grew older, they became most exacting and impatient mothers, and the fact that psychically their children nevertheless remained strikingly healthy proves perhaps that the first life period is the most important.

For another type of woman, the feeling of being a cow is an attack on her inner security. Her ego is not strong enough to bear the change of interests and the cessation of the usual control over the emotional processes without tension and fear.

She feels the biologic function, the infant's demands, and the need for a new adjustment as dangers, and resorts to defensive measures. The vector mechanisms that are set in motion in the function of giving also manifest themselves as a tendency to retain, and nursing difficulties arise. This leads to a conflict between maternal love and maternal duties on the one hand, and attempts at escape on the other. Maternal love refuses to renounce the unity with the child, the woman's sense of guilt reminds her of the child's needs, and she makes overcompensated, usually unsuccessful attempts to continue nursing him. A vicious circle results for the nursing couple: the child reacts with suckling difficulties to the mother's attempts at escape, whereupon the mother reacts by an intensification of her own nursing inhibition. Furthermore, a mother unable to continue nursing her child because of "lack of milk" is often inclined to deprive him of other proofs of maternal love. Her inability to nurse is a trauma for her, and she runs away from her whole relationship with him. This sometimes happens also in the case of the woman who is unable to nurse for physiologic or allegedly physiologic reasons. Frustrated in her expectation of the joy of nursing, she takes revenge on the child and herself, lets other persons feed him, and limits her care of him to merely the absolutely essential.

The mother's feeling that her ego is endangered can make her regard her child as an enemy and his oral needs as aggressions. The ego's sensitiveness to the danger may manifest itself in a fear: the child's sucking is felt as devouring, and thus the naïve infantile idea that the child devours the mother is experienced emotionally. If this feeling reaches awareness, the mother complains that her child throws himself upon her like a beast, or she has a sensation of a physical loss that must somehow be compensated. One mother whom I observed had the peculiar habit of eating something salty before each breast feeding in order later to replace what her child had taken from her by drinking a great deal. Another felt compelled to eat during the nursing in order not to be eaten, so to speak. My hypothesis concerning the Marquesas women's fear of being devoured by their sucklings is partly based on my observations of the type of woman just described.

Verinea has been likened to a she-wolf. I am convinced that if she could have held her child securely in her arms, she would have been transformed into a blissful cow.

If a woman's emotional life is full of fear of the little devouring beast and if this fear is accompanied by an aggressive reaction, or if the child is primarily the object of aggressive rejection rather than of tender love, his role as a dangerous beast is more profound. The mother's own aggression is projected in the child and her anxious excitation perhaps sends him unconscious signals that provoke a kind of reflex in him. This expresses itself in simple refusal to take the breast, or, if the child's aggressive tendencies are stronger, in painful biting of the mother.

Psychoanalysis of women who have suffered from nursing difficulties often reveals that because they inwardly perceived their own aggressions, they felt themselves to be like wild beasts during lactation. The failure of the suckling function represented an attempt to escape, not in order to protect their own persons, but chiefly in order to protect the child against the dangers of their aggressions.

This observation led me to speculate about the origin of several myths. All existing interpretations of myths assume them to be products of masculine fantasy, and masculine-minded science overlooks the fact that women have always had a reputation as seeresses, clairvoyantes, fairy tale tellers, etc. Perhaps many myths owe their origin to definite feminine psychic impulses, and their content, if closely examined, might give us an insight into these impulses.

A feminine-minded approach brings up the following problem. If the attempt to establish a close connection between dreams and myths is methodologically correct,[13] could we not use feminine dreams and fears expressing the lactation conflict to explain certain myths strikingly analogous to these

[12] ABRAHAM, K.: Traum und Mythus. Leipzig, 1909.

dreams and fears? If so, may we not venture to assume that Romulus and Remus, in the myth, were exposed on the hillside because their mother's fear and exhaustion had transformed her into a wicked she-wolf?[14] And perhaps it is later she herself who reappears as a good she-wolf and rescuer, in order to give her children the breasts she had previously denied them. The she-wolf often appears in fairy tales and dreams as a mother animal. Perhaps we might also say that the mother of Moses exposed her infant to protect him not only from a dangerous father but also from possible other dangers that threatened him directly from his mother in the stress of her lactation conflicts. For she too, like the she-wolf in the myth of the founding of Rome, reappears in order to give her milk to the son whom she had previously exposed.

And when she could not longer hide him, she took for him an ark of bullrushes, and daubed it with slime and with pitch, and put the child therein; and she laid it in the flags by the river's brink. And his sister stood afar off to wit what would be done to him. And the daughter of Pharaoh came down to wash herself at the river; and her maidens walked along by the river's side; and when she saw the ark among the flags, she sent her maid to fetch it. And when she opened it, she saw the child, and behold the babe wept. And she had compassion on him, and said, This is one of the Hebrews' children. Then said his sister to Pharaoh's daughter, Shall I go and call to thee a nurse of the Hebrew women, that she may nurse the child for thee? . . . And Pharaoh's daughter said unto her, Take this child away, and nurse it for me, and I will give thee thy wages. And the woman took the child, and nursed it [Exod. 2].

The unconscious aggressions of the nursing mother move between her fear of being devoured and her impulse to destroy the child by the oral way. The sources of the fear and the motives for intensification of her aggressive rejection of the child may vary individually; usually they are overdetermined. The dispositional background lies in the reality-determined and culturally strengthened split between the poles of ego and

[14] In analyzing all these tales of exposure, Rank and Freud deal with the safeguarding of the child from destruction by the father. The father is warned in some way that his newborn son will be a danger to him. The relation of such myths to the Oedipus complex is obvious. Cf. RANK, O.: Myth of the birth of the hero, Nerv. & Ment. Dis. Monog. 18, New York: Nerv. & Ment. Dis. Pub. Co., 1914; FREUD, S.: Moses and monotheism, New York: Knopf, 1939.

reproductive service.   A weak ego cannot defend itself against
the danger otherwise than by renouncing the reproductive
service.

If this split is accompanied by another, rooted in the mother's
ambivalent feelings for the child, the conflict becomes more
intense, and the consciously experienced fear, the aggression,
and the defense mechanisms assume the character of a neurosis
or psychosis.

One is sometimes surprised to hear a sweet young mother
who wanted to have a child, and who thinks that she loves the
infant, declare that she cannot help having a feeling of disgust
when she nurses him: "he is so animal, so shameful and dirty,
when he lies like that at the bare breast."

Probably this represents an overdetermination of the process;
a specific component of disgust seems to be present in many
cases—all the more so because nursing is connected with a
constant nervous excitation rooted in the physiologic processes.
We know that the sucking stimulus is transferred to the genital
apparatus in a reflex-like manner, thus performing a great and
important biologic function, for it causes the smooth muscles
of the uterus to contract, as a result of which the uterus decreases in size, the bleedings after delivery cease, and the whole
process of recovery is furthered.   This favorable secondary
function of nursing brings certain dangers in its train.   The
contraction of the uterus is often painful, and the joy of nursing
may be disturbed by these painful sensations.   Moreover,
the physical reflex connection between the breasts and the
genitals is accompanied by an associative sexual stimulation.
Even apart from the lactation, the nipples play a prominent
role as an erogenous zone, and thus sexual sensations can be
aroused during lactation.   The excitation felt in the genitals
can also disturb the joy of nursing.   For the nursing mother
can bear almost anything more easily than the confusion of
conscious sexual emotions with the tender, loving action of
nursing.   As soon as such sensations begin, repression begins
too, and with it disgust and loathing with regard to the child,
as reactive formations.   The repression of the sexual compo-

nent can include the feeding function, and thus the latter is disavowed too. The result is then incapacity for nursing that often is refractory to all influences. Motherly-loving women do not shy away from these sensations; they incorporate them into the totality of the positive experience, consciously or unconsciously.

Among some primitive peoples, if a nursing mother dies, her living infant is put on her breast and burned with her, so it may continue to suck her milk in the after-life. Among others, the child is slain if the mother dies in childbirth or during the lactation period. These usages derive partly from the belief that a child deprived of its mother's milk and care must perish miserably. They also express the belief that such a child will grow up into a terrible and dangerous individual. Sometimes this belief is based on the idea that the misfortune of the dead mother is transferred to the child and makes him fatal to others. These primitive beliefs have some similarity to our modern knowledge about the influence of maternal love on the child's psychic development, about the identification of mother and child with each other, etc. Seen more realistically, the difference between our culture and that of primitives is that we can create a substitute for the maternal food and also for maternal love. Nevertheless, "ghosts" are still effective in this sphere.

Lactation is certainly one of those physiologic processes that, like menstruation and every other phenomenon connected with the female reproductive functions, is extraordinarily exposed to psychic influences. I also think that there is a union between the nursing mother and her suckling, a union so deep and delicate that we cannot always grasp it.

In order to thrive, the baby needs his mother and the mother needs her baby. But psychic processes cannot be induced by violence, and when they are unconscious, not even by good will. For that reason I believe that the blessing of "mothering" (a term very popular in the modern nursery) cannot always be achieved by the mere observance of the "mothering" regulations. We must always keep in mind that the modern

woman is strongly entangled in a conflict between her ego
interests and her motherhood, that her tendency to develop
anxiety has greatly increased, and that intellectual knowledge
and conscious will are rarely decisive in the field of motherhood.
I know excellent women who succeeded in pursuing some vocation with the greatest efficiency, at least on a part time basis,
and yet were ready exactly on the minute to give suck to their
babies. But these modern sucklings! They do not like
punctuality, and at the mother's slightest gesture of impatience, her furtive glance at the clock, for instance, they react
as though she were a wicked she-wolf.

Many women express their fear of motherhood by becoming
functionally incapable of it; others do not permit themselves
any freedom without guilt feelings. Whenever they are away
from their children, they are seized by a peculiar and irrational feeling of restlessness and worry; sometimes they describe it as "longing." It is akin to the feeling in childbed
that I describe as "listening"; it is the natural pull at the
psychic umbilical cord. The younger the child, the shorter
the cord, and the more the pull is burdened by neurotic additions and excessive dutifulness, the more painful it is.

This kind of longing is not comparable to any other emotion; it is neither pure dutifulness nor love, and probably
parallels the instinctive background, the primary mother-
child relation. I believe that the number of rejecting mothers
will considerably decrease if we can further the free development of maternal emotions by regulating the functions less
and by favorably influencing the fear. The psychic umbilical
cord will then do what is necessary.

Very often the situation can be mastered only by means of a
compromise. Women whose whole life has assumed certain
forms and whose sublimations have become an irrevocable
component of their psychic life, can be good and loving mothers
only if motherhood does not become a danger to their solidly
rooted life values. Such women are no doubt ready to sacrifice for the child everything that can be consciously influenced.
But the capacity for nursing, the constant and honest readiness

to be there only for the child, cannot be achieved by this method. The task of the psychologic adviser is to give these women permission to compromise and eventually to renounce nursing. They themselves must accept as a necessary result of the compromise the fact that by reason of it they are missing something important.

The confinement period usually supplies an important basis for motherliness. It gradually passes into the puerperium, that is to say, into the phase in which the woman is not yet in full possession of her bodily ego. The psychologic adjustment to the child can in normal cases be divided into three periods: (1) the hospital stay, (2) the first period after the return home, and (3) the stage of recovered freedom of movement with the end of the puerperium.

For many women the stay in the hospital signifies a pleasant freedom from responsibility, for others it is a prison term during which they must hold in check their own desires and ideas, the whole active urge of motherhood. From this difference of attitudes later differences result: mothers who blossom and rejoice over the child in the hospital, are subject to more or less mild depressions or states of anxiety after the return home, while other mothers awaken from an inhibited state to joyful activity when they begin to feel themselves the mothers of their own children in their own houses. Many ask for help and instruction, others want to take all the difficulties upon themselves, in order to build solid, reliable foundations for their motherliness, and they find that their first relation to the child, untroubled by the interference of others, is the most reliable. In the light of this experience, we feel that mothers and their newborn children should be left to themselves more than they usually are.

CHAPTER NINE

The Mother-Child Relation

THE main problems of motherhood make their appearance at the beginning of the reproductive function, and, as we have seen, continue, with the birth of the child, in the mother's relation to him. One of these problems is rooted in the inevitable conflict between the interests of the individual and those of the species. Woman's two greatest tasks as a mother are to shape her unity with the child in a harmonious manner and later to dissolve it harmoniously.

If motherhood as the psychologic expression of woman's service to the species filled her psychic life solely and exclusively, she would lose her individual attributes, she would become immersed in motherliness, so to speak. At least in our civilization, with its regulated births, woman has wide opportunities for making compromises between motherhood and her other, more personal needs, drives, and interests. As a result, there are as many variations in the psychology of motherhood as there are mothers. The capacity for these compromises is based chiefly, apart from reference to the cultural opportunities, upon the fact that woman's motherliness and femininity are not the only wellsprings of her psychic forces.

Those tasks of motherhood that serve the preservation of the species correspond to the developmental stages of the child. For instance, all of the mother's interests during the child's first life period are chiefly directed to the goal of his physical thriving. Her activity at this time is applied to his feeding and bodily care. At this stage the mother's urge to preserve the unity with the child is strongest and the possibility of gratifying it greatest: the child's helplessness during the suckling period furthers this unity. We have already spoken of the mother's conflict between the fear of separation—we may now call it the tendency to persist—and her urge for liberation in this first phase of the child's life.

The mother's next tasks are those of upbringing; besides her attention to bodily care, she is now concerned with the child's psychic well-being and his adjustment to reality and its inevitable frustrations. Above all, the mother must now teach her child to control his instincts, and the better her own instinctual life is controlled, the better does she succeed in this task. She must not be too mild in her methods of training, for excessive indulgence involves the danger of the child's remaining undisciplined and dominated by his instincts. Nor must she forbid too much, for excessive inhibition exposes the child to the danger of neurotic illness. In brief, it is difficult to rear a child, and we must admit that today even psychoanalysis does not offer an absolutely reliable preparation for the mother's tasks. The only thing on which we can rely in this respect is the woman's own inner harmony and her intuition, which will give her greater insight into the child's emotional processes than pedagogic or even psychologic training alone. But she must exercise her intuitive understanding intelligently. Here instruction from outside is possible, and help from a psychoanalytically minded adviser can be particularly fruitful. Thus the psychologist who aims at purposeful rearing of the child must gain insight into the mother's processes, not only in order to be able to give her expert assistance, but also because his own pedagogic success in many cases can be achieved only if he simultaneously influences the parents, especially the mother. It is now generally recognized that the child's difficulties are often those of the parents. The fact that knowledge of the mother's psychologic processes has become an important part of modern pedagogy has led to consideration of the mother indirectly through the medium of her child. In contrast to this, the psychoanalyst is in a position to approach the mother's psychic life directly and to consider the child only as a factor in the mother's experience.

Most important, the psychoanalyst is in a position to discover the influence of the unconscious on the psychology of motherhood and to ascertain that it is determined not only by cultural and environmental factors but also by the unsolved conflicts of the mother's past—conflicts that now seek their solution and gratification in motherhood. Whether a satisfactory way out is found or not, depends upon the nature and strength of these conflicts.

Another significant discovery is the fact that many forces of the unconscious contribute to enrich psychologic motherhood. In a normal development toward motherliness, these forces are subject to sublimation. Instinctual tendencies of a sexual nature are transformed into motherly tenderness, in analogy with the process of development in the child; aggressiveness is transformed into protective activity, the excessive narcissistic need to be loved is actively gratified in maternal love, and the masochistic tendencies are gratified in the mother's willingness to sacrifice.

The correct course of this transformation is one of the prerequisites of normal motherhood, and the mother's relation to her child is often a touchstone of her normality.

The methods followed by the mother in solving her tasks are various. Her best guide is the emotional complex of maternal love. The active application of this love grows increasingly difficult in the course of time. The child, at first a part of her own ego, now confronts her as an increasingly independent individual with all sorts of individual demands, with a great number of typical and accidental difficulties, with his progressing psychic development, his fantasy life so difficult to fathom, and the changing manifestations of his emotional life. Every gesture of the child expresses an important development, and the mother's task is to be constantly on the alert and to enter into her child's feelings, for only thus can she achieve the inner certainty that enables her to grasp the volatile expressions of childish life and to intervene now in a reflex manner, now with critical deliberation, to inhibit or to further.

Such intuitive empathy in the child's psychic life is the continuation and psychologic expression of the mother-child unity. This unity was previously physiologic, established through the umbilical cord; now it continues in the mother's capacity for deeply identifying with her child. The concept of the psychologic umbilical cord (cf. chap. VIII) seems best suited to denote this transformation of the unity from a physical into a psychic one.

Dorothy Burlingham[1] communicates very interesting observations on the effect of the mother's conscious and unconscious emotional reactions to the child's psychic problems. In these observations the child is the receptor and acting part in the interplay of affects and ideas between mother and child, while the mother is a sending station emanating affective impulses. Burlingham believes that we are here confronted with extremely sharp observation on the part of the child.

My own observations are of the mother as receiving station for the child's affective impulses, and I think that mother and child gradually develop each a gift for observation that is based upon a deep community between mother and child. Even the suckling displays reactions to his mother's conscious and unconscious impulses—reactions that certainly do not result from a particular gift for observation, but rather from very acute, instinct-like sensitivity. Recalling the refined instinctual relations between the animal mother and her young, we are justified in assuming that the intuitive achievements of the human mother are also closer to instinct than to the intellectual gift of observation. The great "wisdom" of mothers results from the blending of two functions, the affective-intuitive and the intellectual.

The mother's identification with the child may also assume distorted forms. For instance, egoistic self-love does not allow some mothers any identification except that of the child with their own ego. Accordingly they strive through educational measures to achieve an identification of the child with their own persons and love only themselves in their children, without suspecting that by this method they can create only

[1] BURLINGHAM, D. T.: Die Einfühlung des Kleinkindes in die Mutter. Imago, vol. 21, 1935.

external similarity. Inwardly, the child will not have the slightest kinship with his mother, for no successful identification can be achieved in this manner. Such children will later imitate other models with ease, but will be able neither to love nor to develop independent personalities.

Another type of mother seeks in and expects from her child something that she misses in herself. Since she intuitively realizes that her child builds his personality on models, and since she herself does not want to renounce serving as his model, she makes a great effort to pretend before him to be what she is not. As is well known, children are extremely sensitive to those actions of adults that run counter to the actions expected of themselves. But they are even more sensitive to a mother's inner untruthfulness, to her simulation before herself, her child, and the rest of the world of something that she is not but that she wants her child to be. If the mother fails in this undertaking, her love for the child is transformed into hostility and becomes a danger for him. A good case in point is that of a mother who turned from her 8-year old son out of moral indignation because he was a liar, while she herself was "a fanatic for the truth." Now we know that fanaticism for the truth usually conceals untruthfulness.

Other mothers unable to achieve empathic maternal love replace it by a miserable scheme of intellectually contrived ideal education and try later also to maintain their relation to the child, their unity with him, through the medium of such ideals. The setting up of an ideal is supposed here to replace the lack of warm emotions in the mother or to help to resolve her permanent ambivalence conflict; as a rule the children do not agree to such a proposal and do not live up to what is expected of them.

A particularly instructive example of this is the life story of an Italian working woman who for a number of years required he help of a social agency. Mrs. Mazzetti first came to seek financial assistance, a step that she obviously took only after long hesitation and with a feeling of injured pride. Her husband was an alcoholic, her marital situation was very unsatisfactory, she had a number of small children, and she became pregnant again and again.

In the course of her contact with the agency she finally separated from her husband after many quarrels and reconciliations, but she continued to require the help of the agency. Now it was her children who caused her difficulties, all of them, one after the other.

Personal contact with Mrs. Mazzetti soon revealed that although she sought help it was difficult to influence her. She bore herself like a well controlled, superior person who was above the situation and simply could not understand how she came to be closely associated with such people as her husband and several of her children.

Her entire bearing was more like that of an emotionally controlled New England bourgeoise than of an Italian working woman. It turned out that this bearing was consistently used only in face of the outside world, but that within the limits of her emotional ties, that is to say, in relations with her family, she gave way to uncontrolled emotional outbursts. This inconsistency in her personality called forth detrimental reactions from the members of her family.

From her life story we learned that, coming from a poor, uncultured milieu, she had always had the urge to become something "better." At an early age she had to contribute to the support of her family, but she always attended night schools and would perhaps have achieved something in harmony with her aspirations if she had not met her husband. He was the opposite of her ideal but obviously exerted an irresistible sexual attraction upon her. At the age of 16 she had sexual relations with him, soon became pregnant, and found herself compelled to marry him.

It seems that when her lofty ambitions for herself were shaken by her sexual attraction to her future husband, she fell into confusion. She continually tried to raise herself again but chose methods that were obviously unsuitable. She went to night school, studied, took examinations, but at the same time created an impossible situation at home. From her husband's reactions it was clear that she blamed him for her degradation and thus created a vicious circle. The man was a first class workman, employed the year round and very well liked at his place of employment. Mrs. Mazzetti evidently had emphasized her superiority to him in a very aggressive way, which drove this simple man to vengeful reactions and was one of the reasons for his alcoholism. He began to neglect his work and developed a common attitude that can be expressed thus: "If you think I am good for nothing, I shall prove that you are right." He tried to devaluate his wife's superiority by admonishing her to look after the house and the children, by hindering her ambitions outside the family sphere, and apparently also by making her repeatedly pregnant.

For her part the wife, after having mistreated her husband, appeared to develop a reaction that is also typical: she was very contrite for a time and adopted a passive, submissive attitude, humbly making her peace with him and accepting the pregnancy. At the time of her last contact with the agency she had seven children, three adolescent daughters and four sons.

After her separation from her husband she turned all her emotions to the children, and began to treat them as she had treated her husband. She demanded a great deal of them in the spirit of her earlier ideals. As long as the children were small she appeared to be attaining her goal. They were very ambitious, successful in school, etc.

When Louise, the oldest child, approached the age of sexual maturity, her mother seems to have fallen into a state of anxiety that was based upon her own past experiences. This anxiety was expressed in heightened watchfulness and strictness, to which Louise reacted with protests. The result was that the girl identified with her mother—though not with the maternal ideal but with the "fallen" mother. She repeated her mother's experience and at the age of 16 had an illegitimate child. Mrs. Mazzetti reacted not like a loving mother sympathizing with her daughter's unhappiness, but like an aggressive mother who felt injured in her ambition to have a respectable family.

Then she demanded that Louise be motherly toward her baby; the young girl was naturally unable to fulfill this demand because she did not feel motherly. It was impossible to make Mrs. Mazzetti tolerant of her 16-year-old daughter; she was full of moral demands upon her and did not display any maternal warmth. She seemed to have the same dual attitude toward her children that she had toward her husband: thus, after having made Louise suffer sufficiently, she became too indulgent and was unable to enforce any discipline.

The role of superior, authoritative mother that Mrs. Mazzetti so much wanted to play was made particularly difficult by one factor. She had attempted—and for a while with success—to convince her children of her own superiority and to devaluate their father. However, because she accepted their father sexually and repeatedly became pregnant by him, she seems to have contributed to her own devaluation in their eyes. As a result she could not succeed in bringing up her children according to the moral standards that she imposed upon them. Presumably too the children were more dependent emotionally upon their tender, warm father than upon their mother, tormented as she was by ambition and worries about prestige. They took their mother's side verbally, but emotionally they clung to their father and were against their mother.

Another psychologic difficulty in the children's upbringing lay in Mrs. Mazzetti's emotional ambivalence, particularly in the forms it took. She could never be kind to more than one of her older children at a time, and always indulged her negative, aggressive emotions at the expense of the others. Since the children thus alternated as objects of her love, the child who had just been loved, only to be rejected in favor of another, was driven to rage, jealousy, and revenge. This took place repeatedly among the three older girls. The children realized that their mother's love was unreliable and that its variations did not at all depend upon their behavior; thus they could not take the mother's ideal demands seriously. As a result, one daughter after another became promiscuous, they brought syphilis and illegitimate children into the home, the little boys began to steal, and Mrs. Mazzetti could not understand why her younger children, who had only a short time before been obedient and exemplary, began one after the other to follow in the footsteps of their older, good-for-nothing siblings. She failed to realize that there are two things above all others that children cannot stand in a mother—ideal demands instead of tender harmony, and ambivalence instead of evenness of emotions.

Thus the proper utilization of the existing unity between mother and child, that is to say, of identification, is one of woman's tasks as a mother. Another involves what I call the tragedy of motherhood, for it consists in mastering the painful breaking of this unity, the cutting of the psychic umbilical cord that ties the mother to the child. The problem concerns both members of the union, but their aims are opposite: the child strives for the breaking of the tie, the mother for its preservation. As soon as the child is born, the mother must learn that her relation to him is only a temporary stage in his existence. While this stage largely determines his future, nevertheless some day it will become a thing of the past, in connection with which (at the best) he retains reminiscences and tenderness. He can develop into a free adult personality only if he transcends his intimate relation to his mother, his unity with her.

For the mother, however, there is no past in her relation to the child, nothing has gone by, everything remains timelessly present, the wish to preserve the tie is inherent in motherliness. The intuitive understanding that she must and should renounce this tie in favor of her child is at bottom a self-violation, a blow to her maternal feelings. Because of this conflict, the mother can remain free from neurotic difficulties in relation to her children only under especially favorable conditions. Or, to put it differently, the stronger the neurotic disposition, the greater the mother's intolerance of her child's struggle for emancipation, and the greater her tendency to react with unhappiness and anxiety to his progressive separation from her.

From analytic observations of women of various ages, one

inevitably gathers the impression that their inner readiness for anxiety has different contents than that of men, and, in contrast to what takes place in men, goes through a definite process of transformation. While in man the fear of castration is at the center of all anxieties, woman's anxiety is gradually transformed from the genital fear through the fear of defloration and rape into the fear of childbirth or death. This process follows biologically determined paths. It goes without saying that the inner readiness for anxiety becomes conscious experience of fear only through various reinforcements and provocations.

If we follow the fate of this anxiety preparedness, we see that a greater or lesser part of it is transferred to the child as object. The fear of separation, which we have seen to be an accompaniment of the reproductive functions, changes into concern about the child, and as the child grows up this concern is transformed into the tragic emotional conflict of motherhood. The old anxiety preparedness continues in this conflict, and the latter, if intensified, easily leads to neurotic complications. The idea of the "anxious mother" is a comprehensive concept that can include everything from tender solicitude, the need to know that the child is always close, painful longing on every separation from him, hypochondriac worry about his physical and psychic well-being, to real anxiety states and phobias. We consider fear intensified beyond a certain limit to be morbid, and where it exists we assume that the anxiety preparedness has been quantitatively and qualitatively changed by the addition of new or old elements.

In a certain type of hysterical, infantile woman who was excessively tied to her own mother, the fear is a direct reaction to separation. Such a mother is otherwise free of fear, does not worry hypochondriacally about the child, is uniformly tender and perhaps somewhat extravagant in her manifestations of love for him. But when the child goes out of her sight, she is seized with anxiety. In milder cases, the knowledge of where the child is, or that he is being well cared for, is sufficient to decrease the inner tension.

Many women otherwise normal and mature are seized by a

painful longing that readily develops into fear when the child is not physically near them. Mothers who are engaged in intellectual or artistic work often declare that they can concentrate on their tasks only if they know that the child is safe at home, or within sight from a window. As the child grows up, these anxious mothers free themselves gradually from their inner anxiety or fall into the above mentioned tragic conflict, in which they suffer more than normally because of the child's tendency to liberate himself.

One sensitive mother very much attached to her son intensified her awareness of him to such an extent that in later life she had an almost paranoic feeling that a tie continued to exist between herself and her son, although he lived in another city, and thanks to this tie she knew by telepathy whether all was well with him or whether he was in trouble. She felt the psychic umbilical cord in a very realistic manner, and her paranoic feeling reflected a gift for empathy intensified by longing; she had developed this sensitivity in relation to her son from his early childhood on, and it enabled her in later life as well to interpret correctly any sign from him, even the most insignificant one.

We have said that fear is intensified when it receives increments from various sources. In women with hysterical dispositions one often finds a thread deriving from old guilt feelings: "You will lose your child." This is a continuation of the old threat of pregnancy: "You will die in childbirth."

Obsessional-neurotic women display less of this kind of fear. The conflict of ambivalence in the relation to the child often leads to a cooling off of the emotional relation and to replacement of it by a very strict and careful education, with accompanying demands of perfection on the mother as well as on the child. In other cases, the pressure of the existing aggressions leads to their overcompensation and the formation of reactive overtenderness or overprotection, as described by D. Levy.[2]

[2] Levy, D. M.: Op. cit.

Rado[3] has given a brilliant description of an overanxious mother, showing in an extraordinarily clear-cut fashion the inability of certain women to escape from the mother-child unity.

The scene was the beach of a small and quiet seaside resort. One day there appeared close to where I was lying a young woman with a little boy perhaps five years old. They were strangers and I never came to know them personally, but for several weeks I was an involuntary eye-witness and auditor of their behaviour. The little boy behaved just like the other children who thronged the beach. He played in the sand, ran about, fetched water in little buckets from the sea to his sand-castles, and so forth. The mother lay in a deck-chair; now and then she read a book or a newspaper and, for the rest, she passed the time with needlework. She was generally sunk in her phantasies, and only occasionally chatted a little with the other women. But whatever she was doing, she glanced up anxiously every few minutes, sought her boy with a look of concern, and if she could not immediately detect his where-abouts, began to call in a despairing manner, "Ma-a-a-ssimo, Ma-a-a-ssimo." If the child had strayed just a few paces from her, or if he was anywhere near the water's edge (he never went further, for he was plainly timid about the sea), she flew after him, seized his arm and dragged him back again to her. If he quarrelled with the other boys, or tried to resist his mother, she generally scolded him or gave him a sound slap, only to overwhelm him with violent kisses if he began to cry. So it went on, all day long: with the punctuality of clock work, the perpetual cry of "Ma-a-a-ssimo, Ma-a-a-ssimo" made itself heard.

Rado assumes that we have here a reactive formation in which the mother

Loved and hated the child at one and the same time, but she had repressed her hate out of her consciousness by an extreme overaccentuation of her devoted tenderness, and so put an end to the inner discord.

Rado goes beyond this assumption and points out that

The mother behaved as if her boy, playing on the beach, were threatened with some unknown dangers, and must be shielded from some harm. . . . The objective observer then judges the mother's apprehension to be exaggerated beyond all measure, for in reality there could be no question of such dangers as she feared . . . . She was compelled to protect him from herself, to direct her precautions against her own person.

---

[3] RADO, S.: An anxious mother: A contribution to the analysis of the ego. Internat. J. Psycho-Analysis, vol. 9, 1928.

It is quite possible that in all anxious mothers repressed hostility toward the child plays a part. Perhaps there is no human relation, not even that of mother to child, that is free of such impulses. But the anxiety preparedness results from the mother's deep need to preserve her unity with the child, and the mechanism of reactive formation operates through her great love for the child, which does not permit the hatred to manifest itself otherwise than through overcompensation producing new love.

In most of the cases of such excessive fear for the child that I have observed, the children involved were sons. Freud[4] says:

> The only thing that brings a mother undiluted satisfaction is her relation to a son; it is quite the most complete relationship between human beings, and the one that is the most free of ambivalence.

There are mothers whose pathologic emotional life blights even the love for a son, and mothers unfortunate enough to be compelled for some motive to repress and disavow this love. But because the separation from the son signifies a loss of the most valued part of the mother's ego and her most loved object, the fear of loss is constantly lurking, and is constantly ready to mobilize. Freud also says:

> The mother can transfer to the son the ambition that she was compelled to repress in herself, she expects him to gratify everything that has remained in her of her own masculinity complex.

This favorable method of mastering the masculinity complex is not always utilized. There are mothers who transfer their aggressive, envious hatred of men to their own sons. They emasculate their sons by inhibiting their boyish urge to motor activity and drive them into a passive, feminine orientation. In glaring cases the mother is completely conscious of her dislike of her son's sexual organ: she refuses to clean it, teaches the boy to urinate as girls do it, etc.

In my opinion the highest stage of maternal love, motherliness, is achieved only when all masculine wishes have been

[4] FREUD, S.: New introductory lectures on psychoanalysis. New York: Norton, 1933.

given up or sublimated into other goals. If "the old factor of lack of a penis has not yet forfeited its power,"[5] complete motherliness remains still to be achieved.

The mother's fear of separation from the little daughter who moves away from her expresses itself in the same way as her fear with regard to the son only while the children are little. Later, intuition warns the mother much more urgently of the dangers involved in her longing for her son, and this longing is opposed by the proscription "You may not." Probably her fear of incest, the dark foreboding of erotic dangers for herself and her son, also operates here. Avoidance of the "sissy" danger and of the son's identification with herself, which might make him feminine and passive, seems just as necessary to the intuitive mother as to the little boy himself. It is different as regards the daughter. In her case the homosexual component of the mother's libido sends out warning signals much more rarely, and only if it is excessively intense; further, her attempts to seduce and tie the daughter are much more active, free, and direct. Moreover, identification with the mother is much less dangerous for the daughter; in fact, as we have seen, the mother is a necessary model for the daughter's later femininity.

Only gradually does a protest arise in the girl against her infantile dependence upon her mother. This protest usually degenerates into hostility that during puberty is strengthened by the daughter's rivalry with the mother for the father's love. The mother feels abandoned, and as a result of her fear of losing her daughter, together with her fear of the consequences of her daughter's independence, she intensifies her wooing or attempts to exert an authoritarian power over her. The mother's memory of her own temptations and puberal experiences constitutes a specific factor in her relation to her pubescent daughter. Sometimes the bad experience of her own youth casts its shadow on the daughter's life, and the mother tries, successfully or not, to protect her daughter from repeating her own fate. In her distrust she projects her own repressed striving

[5] FREUD, S.: Op. cit.

to her daughter. "You must not become as I am," says her self-devaluating guilt feeling. Such attempts often drive the daughter into greater rebellion and provoke the feared eventuality. Mrs. Mazzetti offers a good example of this. A masculine woman often seeks in her daughter the perfect femininity that she herself lacks, or tries through her daughter to achieve the masculinity that she herself has been denied. In her inner confusion, she tries to make her daughter a man, and to devaluate masculinity in her son.

We can often observe how the woman's own unmastered tie to her mother drives her to compulsive repetition. In these cases the anxious mother accompanies her daughter in all her undertakings—with a display of tenderness of course. She wants the girl to communicate all her experiences and introduce all her friends to her, and sleeps in one bed with her, without regard for her husband. When on occasion I have professionally objected to such behavior, I have several times been assured: "I myself slept with my mother until my marriage."

In one case, the mother, who was otherwise normal, could be convinced only by her daughter's attempt at suicide that the latter was desperate because she saw no way out of the fetters of maternal love except through death. Another mother thought that her love for her daughter was all-sufficient and that the latter's love marriage and happy motherhood were an unnatural crime. She made not the slightest attempt to adapt herself to the new reality. When she failed to dissolve her daughter's marriage, she fell ill with a depression.

I observed an even more morbid intensification of the mother tie to a daughter while treating a neurotic girl psychoanalytically.[6] The patient was 20 years old, the only child of rich parents. Her father had little interest in family life and was more like a guest in his home than a parent. From the very beginning the mother had bestowed the full measure of her frustrated love on the child. The infantile mother-child relationship had been successfully maintained to such an extent

---

[6] DEUTSCH, H.: Psychoanalysis of the neuroses. London: Hogarth, 1932.

that at the time of her treatment the girl slept with her mother and sucked the mother's breast or finger regularly before going to sleep.

As a result of this training by her mother and the maintenance of their unity, the daughter began in puberty to suffer from anxiety states when her mother left the house, giving as her reason the fear that something might happen to the mother —"she might for instance be run over." She would wait for her mother by the window, with an expression of intense anxiety on her face, which would light up with relief when she saw her return home alive. It seemed that here the process had ended by reversing itself. At first the mother had refused to be separated from her daughter, then the daughter took over the continuation of this behavior. The anxious mother now had an overanxious daughter. The normal puberal drive to liberation from such a tie had been intensified into a hostile rejection of the mother. But instead of freedom there came intensified fear of separation, with the character of an overcompensation of hate for the mother.

Long before, the grandmother of this phobic patient had inaugurated the process by attaching her daughter (the patient's mother) to herself, and this daughter's unfortunate marriage had intensified the tie. It is noteworthy that the homosexuality aroused or sanctioned without repugnance by the grandmother—though its sexual component did not become conscious—continued in the mother. In this case (as in almost all cases) the daughter's bed was not only the place of gratification of the mother-daughter love, but also served as an escape from the relation with the rejecting or rejected husband.

Although one cannot impute a typical character to such an open and immoderate mother-daughter relation, such situations occur quite frequently. Especially in puberty, the mother's fear of losing her daughter, added to the daughter's overcompensated hatred, results in an excessively strong tie between them.

It might be expected that hostile competition would develop

between a still young mother and her adolescent daughter. My own observations suggest that the mother-daughter relation is much more frequently characterized by altruistic renunciations on the part of the mother, and by a tendency to identify with her daughter's joys and sorrows, than by competition. The oft-quoted phrase from one of Madame de Sevigné's letters to her daughter—*La bise de Grignan me fait mal dans votre poitrine* ("The icy blasts of Grignan hurt me in your chest")—is a beautiful illustration if this.

As we have said, the relation to the son is almost never as direct and clear in its purpose. The unconscious seduction by the mother's love and tenderness occurs much earlier, when the boy, in her opinion, cannot as yet have any sexual desires. Later the mother uses other means in her desperate attempt to keep him. These consist usually in continuations of the earlier infantile community between mother and son and in methods of upbringing aimed at preserving the psychic umbilical cord by means of permanent emotional dependence. Many of these methods are used upon children of either sex. In my opinion, maternal overprotection, in its numerous forms and variations, as carefully observed by D. Levy with the aid of rich material, ultimately serves the purpose of preserving the child's dependence and of averting the separation trauma for the mother. The most direct means to this end is infantilization, that is, the tendency to keep the child childishly helpless as long as possible. The form of mother-daughter tie described above seems in most cases to fit this scheme.

The overindulgent mother who subjects herself completely to her children's tyranny, and who exerts her overprotection in this more passive way, is certainly a woman whose inner fear springs from masochistic guilt-laden sources. The opposite type is represented in the domineering mother who drives the child into passivity and dependence by her own active attitude, and who exerts her overprotection with the help of aggressions. All these means lead to the same end, that is, the dependence of the child, and naturally tally with the characterologic and affective total personality of the mother.

However, I consider Levy's view[7] that "all maternal over-protection can be regarded as compensatory of unconscious hostility" an excessive generalization. There is a longing, together with a deep-rooted fear of loss, that springs from the positive sources of maternal love. Overprotection can therefore also serve as a defense mechanism in avoiding separation.

There are, however, more refined, less blatant methods that work quietly, indirectly, and all the more powerfully. They also prove more reliable for the preservation of the mother-child tie than the coarse methods that sooner or later arouse the child's protest.

There is the common fantasy life, the accord between the conscious and unconscious impulses in the mother and child. Sometimes the fantasies conceal the unconscious personal element in a cloak of the humdrum and banal, sometimes they dress it in a mask of the supernatural and remote. Sometimes they directly reveal their nature in dreams and only slightly veiled actions. Abraham[8] has recorded an observation that suggests such an unconscious accord between mother and son:

A young man whom I was psychoanalytically treating had observed since his early youth that his mother was betraying his father with a friend. He connected with this fact typical fantasies of a Hamlet character: he imagined that his mother and her friend would kill his father. One day his mother told him a dream she had had: in it a stranger made her an object of ridicule and deprecated her abilities and qualities. So she threw him out with the help of Mr. X [her friend]. My patient pricked up his ears when he heard his mother tell this dream and understood at once that the stranger could be none other than his father, whom his mother together with her friend "threw out"—that is, did away with. He justly concluded that his mother's fantasy was preoccupied with the same outrageous idea as his own. The agreement even extended to details. He too had often reproached his father in his fantasies for not sufficiently respecting his wife's valuable qualities. She herself justified her abandonment of her husband on the same pretext.

In Abraham's case the father is a man who does not know how to value the mother. Such a discovery on the part of

[7] Levy, D. M.: Op. cit.
[8] Abraham, K.: Koinzidierende Phantasien bei Mutter und Sohn. Internat. Ztschr. f. Psychoanal., vol. 11, 1925.

both mother and son can be the prelude to common feelings, and the early infantile unity between mother and child develops into a life attachment.

In the son's fantasy the father is never as good as the mother. But a father who mistreats his wife unwittingly strengthens a now indissoluble unity between mother and son.

Poets and novelists know this. In *Sons and Lovers* by D. H. Lawrence, Mrs. Morel's sons experience the hell in which their mother lives. Her own love disappointment becomes her sons' fate. They must fulfill the ideal demands of their mother that their father failed to meet: "she was afraid of her sons' going the same way as their father." They become teetotalers because their father was a drunkard. William, the first-born, begins this process.

> All the things that men do—the decent things—William did. He could run like the wind. When he was twelve, he won the first prize in a race. It stood proudly on the dresser and gave Mrs. Morel a keen pleasure. The boy only ran for her. He flew home with his anvil, breathless, with a "Look, Mother!" That was the first tribute to herself. She took it like a queen.

All mothers want to be queens to whom sons pay tribute.

And when the sons leave home to seek success in life, they do not know, just as William did not know, that they are inflicting pain on the mother by pulling at the psychic umbilical cord.

> It never occurred to him that she might be more hurt at his going away than glad of his success. Indeed, as the days drew nearer for departure, her heart began to close and grow dreary with despair. She loved him so much. More than that, she hoped in him so much. Almost she lived by him. She liked to do things for him; she liked to put a cup for his tea and to iron his collar, of which he was so proud. Now she would not do it for him. Now he was going away. She felt almost as if he were going as well out of her heart. He did not seem to leave her inhabited with himself. That was the grief and the pain to her. He took nearly all himself away.

The poet thus helps us to describe what we have called the tragic destiny of motherhood.

The even more tragic thing is that William, like every son who through the mother's deep, painful longing remains tied to her, perishes because of this tie. Mrs. Morel mourns William's death just as all mothers mourn: "If only it could have been me." She is sincere: all mothers would prefer to die themselves.

I have known mothers who lost their sons in the first world war. The deaths of their grandsons in the second world war reopened wounds in them that had never been healed. "Comfort yourself with your other children," say their friends, thus revealing their ignorance of the curious fact that the loss of one child estranges the mother for a long time from her other children. Pain and suffering are the most powerful components of the psychic umbilical cord, especially when the first-born is involved.

Mrs. Morel mourns William while completely neglecting Paul, her second-born. Only when he falls ill with pneumonia, as though to emulate the dead William, and when the danger arouses her fear and guilt feelings, does she turn toward him.

"I will die, Mother," he cried.
She lifted him up, crying in a small voice: "Oh, my son, my son!"

This was the same cry she once had for William.

That brought him to. He realized her. His whole will rose up and arrested him.... The two knitted together in perfect intimacy. Mrs. Morel's life now rooted itself in Paul.

The sons are different and their mother's unconscious methods of tying them to her are likewise different in regard to each.

She was a woman who waited for her children to grow up. And William occupied her chiefly. But when William was not so much at home, the mother made a companion of Paul. He hunted far and wide for blackberries and brought her the best he could find.

And when she, the earth-bound mother who struggles through reality, gives free rein to her fantasy and reaches out for beauty, it is Paul who understands her:

"I am a wicked, extravagant woman, I know, I shall come to want." She unfolded another lump of newspaper and disclosed some roots of pansies and of crimson daisies. . . .
"But lovely," he cried.

"Aren't they!" she exclaimed, giving way to pure joy. "Paul, look at this yellow one, isn't it—and a face just like an old man!"

"Just," cried Paul, "and smells that nice! But he's a bit splashed."

Then he told her the budget of the day. His life story, like an Arabian Nights, was told night after night to his mother. It was almost as if it were her own life.

It is noteworthy that in the mother-son alliance, Paul Morel's everyday life stories became a kind of Arabian Nights tale, a life-long common fantasy world.

In Ibsen's *Peer Gynt*, Peer and his mother Aase, who live in the distant north under completely different cultural conditions, are like doubles of Mrs. Morel, the English miner's wife, and her son Paul. Aase tells her little son fairy tales while the father drinks:

> Then both of us sat home
> And sought to forget our misery
> . . . .
> One wants sometimes to get rid of one's cares
> And discard the evil thoughts;
> Some need brandy, others need lies.

Aase, that terribly overindulgent mother, calls Peer a liar, but in silent community with him is ready to experience lies as truth—for this is the only thing that gives meaning to their common life, which is full of privations. The tie knit by herself out of common fantasies keeps them together until death, and Aase dies in her son's arms believing his lies—the happy mother in fairy tale land.

Many mothers in their attempts to tie their children to themselves appeal cleverly and consistently to their guilt feelings: "You will abandon me, who have suffered so much?" Others manage to occupy the place of the ego ideal so deeply and permanently that any weakening of the child's relation to the mother is felt by him to be dangerous for his inner morality. A domineering, matriarchal woman often achieves rule over her children by setting up a common ideology, thus gratifying her tendency to dominate. In many families the pressure of tradition proves irresistible because it is exerted by a beloved and admired mother. New England offers many examples of such situations.

Gorky, who has a profound knowledge of the Russian people, shows us another woman's tragic love for her son in his novel *The Mother*. Like Mrs. Morel and Aase, she has been insulted, mistreated, and dishonored by her alcoholic husband. She is all alone in this miserable world with her son Pavel. It is a sad and difficult life: the mother is completely devoted to her son, while he, like most sons, in his heart is far removed from his mother's lot, insensitive to her suffering, absorbed in his own inner unhappiness. Then he is seized by the fire of the Russian revolution, and Pelagia Vlassova, the half-dead, tormented woman, with her body debilitated and her spirit numbed by long years of toil and her husband's blows, becomes a great heroine of the movement of liberation, because of her deep and passionate love for her son—through him, for him, with him.

Aase can hold her son in her arms in her hour of death because she believes his stories and thus strengthens his self-confidence. Pelagia lends ear to the new things her son tells her: at first they are perhaps only a fairy tale for her. "Pavel came closer to her and made his first speech about the truth he had grasped straight into her face dampened by tears." Proud of his knowledge and filled with ardent faith in its truth, he spoke of what he had just learned to understand.

He spoke less for his mother than to test himself. . . . He pitied his mother, he began to speak again, but now about herself, her life. . . . It was the first time she heard such words about herself and her life. . . . But now her son sat before her, and what his eyes, his face, and his words said, moved her heart, filled it with pride in her son who understood his mother's life, spoke to her about her sufferings, and sympathized with her. . . .

Pavel saw the smile on his mother's lips, her attentive face, the love in her eyes. It was as though he had succeeded in making her understand the truth of what he said, and youthful pride in the force of his words strengthened him in his faith in himself.

Thus far, these three mothers and their sons, although they live in different places, are like translations of the same text into three completely different languages—Paul's Arabian

Nights tales, Peer Gynt's tall stories, and Pavel's revelation
of new truths. The sons draw self-confidence from the eternal
faith of the mother and gratify the mother's deepest life purpose—to preserve her son, or to have the illusion of preserving
him. Pelagia Vlassova is the only one among them who goes
farther, by making her son's ideals her own and really helping
him in his hard and dangerous struggle: "The words of my
son are the pure words of a worker, of an incorruptible heart!
Learn to recognize the incorruptible by his fearlessness!"

She dies with faith in her son, united with him in faith in the
revolution, just as Aase dies in Peer Gynt's arms.

Reviewing the various methods of preserving the mother-
child relationship, we see that they follow a certain law. They
are adapted to the successive phases of the child's development.
First, the mother gratifies the child's instinctual needs, participating in his pleasure. Then the child achieves a sublimated, tender relation to his mother, who enjoys his need to
lean on her and his tenderness, and responds to them. In the
end, the mother, as a result of educational and emotional influences, becomes a part of his ego ideal and thus is reunited
with him.

Every phase of the child's development ends with intensified
tendencies to liberate himself. The mother—every mother—
tries to keep him attached to herself and opposes the actions
that tend to dissolve the tie. She continues these attempts
anachronistically later as well. The question is: To what phase
of development do the methods correspond—do they serve
intensified gratification of instincts (pampering), tolerant and
emphatic tenderness, or stronger and continued influence of
the superego?

In order to achieve her goal, the mother must fulfill certain
conditions. She must keep away from what is forbidden and
guilt-laden, or this must be well concealed and masked. It is
possible that a tender relation like that between Mrs. Morel
and Paul conceals the guilt feeling caused by a common death
wish with regard to the devaluated father. The fantastic
relationship between Aase and Peer Gynt conceals their com-

mon disavowal of Peer Gynt's inferiority. Such an alliance can be seen frequently in a less fantastic garb. Also, one often has the impression that such an admixture of concealed motives greatly contributes to strengthening the mother-child relation.

Pelagia Vlassova perhaps found the most reliable method: she entered into her son's life interests and through her love for him learned to love something impersonal, the idea of social emancipation.

The struggle for ideals is not taken up by every son and daughter. The gray prose of everyday life also offers the mother opportunities to achieve understanding identification with her child, instead of making demands upon him, particularly if she succeeds in assimilating the life interests of her child that are outside her own and in exchanging her own horizons for his. A feminine-intuitive mother finds possibilities for such an identification, for in a kind of tragic awareness she knows that this is the only method of keeping her child. If she lacks the inner capacity for this, she must rely upon compensations outside motherhood and remains a sad (or embittered) orphan mother.

About women as mothers, Freud[9] says: "In the child they gave birth to, they are confronted with a part of their own body, as an alien object to which they can now give full object love from their narcissism."

The whole complexity of psychologic motherhood is expressed in these words. When we see the mother's relationship to her growing children under the magnifying glass of psychoanalysis, we realize that we are dealing with something unique. Some components of the maternal affective complex are familiar to us from other relationships and conditions: in being in love there is similar overvaluation of the object; in mourning there is similar restriction of all other life interests; in people tormented by guilt feelings there is a like masochistic readiness for sacrifice; in melancholy we find such a far reaching identification with another person that

[9] FREUD, S.: On narcissism: An introduction. Collected Papers, vol. 4.

everything imputed to him in the patient's unconscious turns against the patient's own ego.

A mother who lives in the constant and anxious awareness that she will have to give up her children piece by piece, as it were, in favor of their further development, behaves—controlling herself more or less—like someone who must give up an important, valuable, indispensable part of his own personality together with his beloved object. Her apprehensions about the child who is becoming independent often sound like the complaints of a hypochondriac who is overworried about himself, and her willingness to sacrifice exceeds that of the normal masochistic lover. Above all, we find in many mothers a mode of reaction that seems to be explainable only on the basis of a particular strengthening of motherliness as such. Such a mother is often willing—sincerely willing—joyfully to sacrifice everything for her children, especially for her only child. At the same time she imposes an implacable condition on life: her child must be well and happy. On this point she has no tolerance, no social sense. Her child is the center of the world, and the seamy side of life, which all humans must know, must be kept far from him.

Such a mother also feels the psychic umbilical cord with particular intensity: she bears separation from her child very badly, she must be informed of his condition at every moment of his life, and her happiness and wretchedness depend completely upon him. Her psychic life is an emotional echo of his experiences. She shows social and other interests only when her mind is free of worry about her child, and then these interests can be warm and rich.

When analyzing such women, we learn that while they were very narcissistic before their motherhood, this narcissism usually had a definite character: it expressed itself in formation of a high ideal, in an emotional reserve that bespoke not so much an emotional poverty as great demands upon the object. They have learned the really sacrificing, selfless, tolerant love that is entirely absorbed in the object, in their relation to their own children only. If such a woman has a disposition to pessisimism and self-torture, her apprehensions and worries as to the future apply to the child, and her fear of the dangers of life concerns her own person less than his.

I realize that I am describing here a neurotic mother. But her neurosis is only a distortion—perhaps a very slight one—of the general maternal fate. Maternal love is a peculiar mixture of narcissism and object love, and at bottom the child never confronts his mother as "an alien object." The love she gives him is paradoxically the most selfless self-love. That is why the task of separation from him is psychically so difficult.

The child, as his mother's love object, is supposed to achieve an independent existence in another sense too. The relationship to him is a new acquisition that in large part utilizes and transfers old relationships. For this reason he is threatened with the danger of being identified with other objects, so that all the affects that are or were applied to the others flow to him. In the triangular situation, the child should not become part of one or the other parent but an independent member. We have already pointed out the dangers involved in the mother's striving to have her child identify with herself. This identification may relate to a definite past period in the mother's life that in her fantasy strives for repetition in the child. Usually experiences of the mother's own childhood are involved here. Next to the wish "You shall be happier than I was," the repetition asserts itself in some form, and the child is assigned a definite role that has nothing to do with his own wishes and aspirations.

An example of this is a mother about whom analysis revealed the following. She had an only little son whom she loved very much. She was intelligent and intuitive and believed that she was not making any educational mistakes. She devoted much of her free time to her child and would tell him true and imagined tales about her life in Russia, where she was born. The untrue stories were always recognized as such by common agreement. One of these, usually told to the child while he was being fed, ran as follows: "I have three grown-up sons over there [in Russia]. They are three giants. They eat a whole ox and a pot of spinach as big as this room for every meal. They are enormously strong and perform all kinds of exploits."

The accomplishments of these characters were described in detail, and the mother and son were greatly amused by them. The attitude of these three powerful but stupid fellows toward the little boy was naturally not very good, for they knew perfectly well that the mother loved him alone. Then the mother would tell him why she loved him so much, in such a special way, in contrast to her feeling for the others: he was intelligent and refined and tender, and things of the spirit were as close and precious to him as they were to her.

Sometimes the three brothers appeared as competitors, but naturally they were always rejected by the mother and forced to return to Russia without having gained anything. There was nothing they could do. For the mother loved only him, the little one, and her stories always returned to this refrain. She herself experienced enormous joy and a feeling of triumph over the "big fellows" because of her warm and gratifying emotions toward her beloved little son. She was somewhat concerned over the fact that he did not eat well and obviously had fears at night. But she saw no danger in her stories.

Analysis showed that she herself was a child born a long time after her two sisters and her brother. She was her father's favorite, and the typical relationship to the third daughter developed: she was the only one among the children who shared the father's intellectual interests and took up his profession. The others were three giants, but she achieved the triumph of being the best loved and the chosen one. Now, as a mother, she wanted to re-experience this triumph and let her beloved little son share in it: "He shall be as happy with me as I was with my father."

But she overlooked one psychologic fact. If her grown-up sisters and brother had been a solved problem for her, she would not have needed to experience her triumph again and again. Actually they were still there, those giant fellows;

they involved a danger for her and had to be conquered again and again. She recalled that despite her father's love for her she had felt very insignificant in her littleness and had been very jealous of the strength, accomplishments, and potentialities of her older sisters and brother. They also often tormented her and she was physically afraid of them. Since she had repressed that part of her memories in the stories she told her little son, she did not know that he refused to eat because he could not, after all, compete with boys who ate a whole ox, and that at night he was afraid because if they should come they would prove stronger than he. Thus the little boy sensed more of the mother's unconscious than she did herself, and against her will identified himself with the anxious component of it.

Another mother presented a similar case. She told her pampered, talented little daughter, to whom she knew that she would give the best possible upbringing and education, that she would eventually be apprenticed to a poor little shoemaker and would suffer many privations in his house. These plans had a happy ending because here too both mother and child were aware of the parent's love and solicitude. But the mother unconsciously had to gratify her own masochism in her stories before she could allow her little daughter, whom she identified with herself, to be happy.

Even greater danger menaces a child who is diminished in his own existence by identification with other objects. If the child becomes the likeness of his father, previously devaluated by his mother, he is subjected to all his mother's disappointment reactions. If he is identified with a still loved husband, he is later all the more pressed in his competition with him. If marriage and the child have served to overcome the mother's unhappy love for another man, and if the unloved husband's features reappear in the child, he is in danger of losing his mother's love.

As I have said, the directness of the mother's relation to the child can also be disturbed outside the triangle, by the

unconscious affective transference of her old ties still striving
to be realized. Personally I have never seen a mother repeat an unsolved childhood conflict in her relationship to her
own child unless an emotional and neurotic motive or a particular life situation provoked her to do so. I shall illustrate
this point by an example.

A mother asked for help from a social agency because she
was no longer in a position to maintain her home and support
her children. Her difficulties were intensified by the fact that
her husband was in the Army, but they had a character different from those of the other war mothers we have discussed.

Mrs. K. was the mother of two girls aged 7 and 4, and of a
1-year-old boy. At the age of 20 she had married a 22-year-old
man whom she had met in college. Because of the couple's
decision to found a family the girl was compelled to interrupt
her studies, which she did without the slightest regret. Her
husband graduated from college with honors, and with some
help from his parents and the girl's was soon able to support
his family and increase it in accordance with his wishes. Up to
the birth of her youngest child, Mrs. K. had been an energetic,
healthy, and independent housewife and mother. She easily
mastered all the difficulties, bad habits, etc., of her two girls
and always had enough time left to gratify her own intellectual
interests.

Soon after the birth of her boy she became ill with a gallbladder inflammation caused by gallstones, from which she had
begun to suffer during her last pregnancy. Since that time she
had been unable to manage her household and her life; she
could not finish anything, she neglected her home, her children
grew increasingly wild, and the little boy caused her the greatest difficulties of all. She had been an excellent nurse to her
two girls, but she could suckle her boy only for a short time,
because of her illness. Nevertheless, he was very well physically, but in contrast to the little girls brought great disquiet
and tension into the home. From his sixth month on he
cried all night long, lost his appetite from time to time, and
constantly presented his mother with new problems: now it

was an inflammation of the throat, now teething troubles, a cold, digestive difficulties, etc. The pediatrician said that Franky was "a splendid boy," that the mother was "nervous."

In the course of the interviews it gradually became clear that Mrs. K. unconsciously hated her boy, that from the very beginning she had tried to suppress her hatred by means of excessive care of him, and that this suppression cost her a great deal of energy. As a result she was tired, neglected the household, and was unable to continue the previously good upbringing of her little girls. She exaggerated all the boy's minor indispositions, and in her concern about him there was always an element of hypochondriac fear for her own person. "After all, I'm sick. Just look at me, I'm going to collapse," she said again and again. She said that at night she went to bed with an anxious expectation: "Will he disturb me again?" By her anxious listening, her leaving the doors open, etc., she obviously helped to create a restless atmosphere around the child. During the day she often found herself compelled to punish the boy as well as her daughters, who reacted to their mother's anxiety with anxiety on their own part. Mrs. K. maintained that her little girls had been "angels" before the birth of Franky.

Mr. K., who was exempt from the draft, had enlisted because he could no longer bear the atmosphere at home. Attempts were made to obtain the help of women members of the family, above all Mrs. K.'s mother, but they failed because Mrs. K. refused to give up her own position of authority with regard to her children.

In the end she ceased suppressing her hatred against the boy; she admitted it and asked in despair whence it came. She now had to make up her mind to place him in a children's home.

Up to her eighth year Mrs. K. had been an only child, pampered and idolized. Then her mother gave birth to a little son to whom, naturally enough, all the attention of the family now turned. Mrs. K. had never accepted the usual appeasement offered by mothers: "Now you are going to have

a little brother whom you can take care of and play with."
She tried to draw attention to herself and from that time on
became a sickly child. Her hypochondriac mother surrounded
her with doctors and nurses and trembled at every little symptom she showed. As a result of her mother's behavior, the
girl herself became hypochondriac, and one summer when she
was sent to camp she annoyed everyone around her with her
complaints. However, just at that time, when she was 12,
she had an impulse, under the influence of a camp counselor
with whom she became infatuated, to liberate herself from her
conflicts. She gave up her competition with her brother,
freed herself from her dependence upon her parents and her
hypochondriac symptoms, and developed various interests and
good, positive relations with other people. At 20, she fell in
love with her future husband and, as we have said, remained
healthy until the birth of her boy.

Through Mrs. K.'s whole life story ran the thread of more
than normal self-love. She had always loved to be loved,
she had worked for success, she had renounced her career
because she justly believed in her husband's great future. Her
pregnancies were good and her two "blonde angels" gratified
her maternal pride. She had also wished for and expected a
son. Her gallbladder inflammation, an unpleasant, protracted,
and chronic illness, constituted a strong attack on her narcissistic inner world, which until then had had all gratification. She bore a grudge against the boy because he disturbed
her contentment just as her little brother had once done.
At that earlier time she had felt frustrated in her need of love
and had reacted with physical illnesses. Now her physical
illness became for her a signal to expect additional love in a
life period in which actually more devotion was expected from
her as the mother of a new child. In other words, she had an
intensified need to take at a time when her task consisted in
giving. To the narcissistic mortification of her physical illness she reacted just as in childhood with an increase of self-
love, hypochondriac self-observation, and aggression against
the environment, especially that part of it which made demands
upon her.

This exacting and hostile environment was her little boy. He was the origin of her illness and he demanded nourishment, care, and tenderness from her. The conflict between the heightened demands of her ego and the reproductive service, or its product, resulted in increased disharmony. Her purposes became contradictory. Her maternal willingness to sacrifice failed completely in favor of the hypochondriac turn toward the ego, and she removed her maternal love not only from her boy but partly also from her other children. Little Franky would perhaps have been a normal child, easy to bring up, like his sisters, if he had not become the object of his mother's hostility. This hostility asserted itself probably in a number of small actions of which Mrs. K. was unaware, but to which Franky reacted with the usual sensitivity of little children. Her behavior probably resulted from the summation of negative stimuli—her own illness, the reactivation of her former emotions toward her brother because of his sex, probably also the fact that her husband had diverted his interest to the impersonal tasks of the war. These factors seemed quite sufficient to induce her gradual collapse.

Many mothers can bear the personal sacrifice they must make for the child only if it does not involve an injury to their narcissism; in such women the transfer of the various ego interests to the reproductive function upsets the psychic economy, except under certain favorable conditions. The narcissistic forces of self-preservation and the masochistic functions of motherhood must come to a harmonious agreement. The merging of self-love and object love for the child is the prerequisite of the maternal experience. If one of these basic elements of the feminine psyche is overburdened, emotional disorders and their pathologic manifestations appear.

In Mrs. K. the organic illness and the excessive demands of the newborn infant overburdened the masochistic element; as a result, the narcissistic counterforces were intensified and at once resorted to the means they had employed in the past—hypochondria, self-love, and, in connection with this, hateful aggression against the *agent provocateur* of her difficulties. The old guardian of her narcissism previously developed by her environment, especially by her mother, prevented her from masochistically intensifying her love for her little son as a "child of sorrow" (Freud).

It is clear that a whole chain of inner experiences was required to make her transfer her old brother relation to her little son and to mobilize her hostility in connection with this transfer.

A mother must not strive to achieve any other goals through her child but those of his existence, otherwise she runs the risk of failing in her purpose and of being cheated of the experience of motherhood. One woman who had voluntarily remained childless for five years after her marriage made up her mind to become pregnant in order "finally" to liberate herself from her dependence upon her mother, who had dissuaded her from having a child because of the financial difficulties involved, the uncertain political situation, etc. She felt her mother's advice to be a prohibition and decided to violate it with the conscious idea "A child will give me my freedom." Her pregnancy was normal, but soon after childbirth difficulties set in. She was unable to suckle her child, complained of having no feeling for him, and developed a depression. The child played a role that was the opposite of that which he was supposed to play: instead of liberating his mother from her fetters he imposed a new burden upon her—a feeling of guilt for having transgressed her mother's prohibition—and increased her dependence upon her mother. Even after the end of her depression, this woman long remained hostile toward her child, and only psychoanalytic treatment could reconcile her with him.

We recall that in many women pregnancy itself is supposed to serve definite purposes alien to motherhood. These purposes are now transferred to the child. They are often banal and superficial: for instance, the husband wants an heir, a proof of his masculinity, or feels obliged to abide by the family tradition, or is tired of leading a restless life and desires to found a stable home; his wife yields to his wishes without being ready for motherhood. Or she notices signs of un-faithfulness in her husband and wants to bind him to herself by having a child. Or her life lacks content, she is aware of its emptiness and decides to become a mother out of boredom, so to speak. There are innumerable such motives of a coarsely realistic character; there are unconscious motives, some even of a compulsive nature.

We have previously introduced the term compulsive mother-hood. It applies to all those women who repeatedly become pregnant and have many children without being mothers in the full sense of the word. Many of them, like Mrs. Andrews, cannot enjoy sexuality unless it implies impregnation. Others want to atone by pregnancy for an unconscious guilt, and only burden themselves thereby with additional guilt. In such compulsively repeated pregnancy there is often a fatal chain of guilt and atonement, the one provoking the other. Some women want to enjoy the pride of motherhood, others its suf-ferings, masochistically. Some want to appease a neurotic feeling that they have injured their bodies through masturba-tion, by proving that they can give birth to a child. Some want only to be pregnant, and accept the child as a necessary consequence; others want only a baby, always a new baby. Some do not feel themselves to be mothers and try to make up for this lack through another child. Others suffer when they discover their own infantilism and hope to grow up through having a child—and if one child does not produce the desired result, by having many children. Thus the child becomes only a means, not an end in itself, and in such cases biologic motherhood does not lead to motherliness.

Sometimes a motive that is at first of secondary importance comes to stand between mother and child; then gradually the balance is shifted and the secondary motive becomes primary. For instance, a mother who loved her child suddenly dis-covered that she had sacrificed her beauty to her motherhood. She tried to recoup her loss by using her child to enhance her beauty. Like the French painter, Madame Vigée-Lebrun, she played the part of the Madonna in the numerous Madonna and Child photographs that she had taken. In society, in the streets, etc., she was always seen with her little daughter: glorification of maternal beauty became the objective of her relation to her child. When the young girl grew up she naturally rebelled against this unity and attributed to her mother the role the latter had predetermined—that of the wicked woman in the fairy tale who questions the mirror. The situation was hopeless, for the mother could not behave like a normally aging mother, especially since beauty had once been very important to her. In normal cases, the jealous competition of the mother subsides because of her loving identification with her daughter, whose successes she makes her own and thus enjoys indirectly. In this case, the daughter justly disbelieved her mother and, jealous of the latter's well preserved beauty, projected her jealousy into the mother and hated her with a hatred that became fatal to herself.

This process of identification of the ambitious mother with the ambitious successes of her children, of the vain mother with the beauty of her daughter, is one of the anchors of salvation every mother has at her disposal. As a rule, a mother who competes with her own child is rare; her alleged jealousy is usually a projection of the child's typical conflict to the mother.

Another displacement of roles resulting from secondary causes arises from the tendency of mothers to follow a definite model in their relation to their children. Next to such models fixed in childhood (representing members of the family) there are new acquisitions in later life that also press unconsciously for repetition. In women with hysterical multiple personality or of the "as if" type, this process is very clear. Their motherliness goes through the same vicissitudes as their personalities as a whole: as mothers they are now one, now another person.

A model that a given woman considers inaccessible in other fields may seem accessible to her as a mother and thus lead her to peculiar behavior. A German socialist woman of the 1890's found a political ego ideal in the famous agitator Lily Braun, in whose shadow she with her own modest talent was compelled to remain. In her relation to her son she imitated Lily Braun's relation (as described in her memoirs) to her son, a man of genius who died young. The robust nonintellectual son of this woman, who later became my patient, was driven to gangsterism by his mother's attitude toward him.

Neurotic mothers easily include their children in the pathologic process. The neurotic emotional conflict attacks the sanctum sanctorum of motherliness. The child loses his original meaning and is subjected to emotional impulses that were not meant to concern him. As the grandson of a hated grandfather, as the son or daughter of a rejected father, as the memory of an undesired, perhaps "sinful" action, and often as a part of his own mother, who directs toward her child her masochistic fury against herself, he is hated or rejected, neglected or maltreated.

When the pressure of reality becomes unbearable in the conflict between the self-preservation tendencies and motherhood, the mother, in order to spare herself, often renounces a love relationship with her child and prefers to reject him. Much oftener, the emotional relation to the child remains suspended in the subjectively felt void, because an inner prohibition has succeeded in thwarting and isolating the emotional experience before it had a chance to develop fully. Very young or unmarried mothers often accuse themselves of "not feeling anything for the child." The same is true of women whose entire motherhood from pregnancy through childbirth to the later relationship with the child is marked by prohibitions and threats of punishment. One young woman maintained stubbornly that her child was completely alien to her, and persisted in this assertion until she discovered that her motherhood had been under her dead father's "curse": he had been against her marriage with the child's father. Similarly, an atheist mother became estranged from her child because, according to her obedient unconscious, just as according to her religious parents, he was a "bastard," because the marriage of his parents had not been solemnized by a religious ceremony.

Childishness carried into motherhood—and I have often

had occasion to deal with this—creates a bad soil for the difficult and serious emotional tasks of this estate. The performance is successful only intermittently: now and then the
little girl grows into her maternal garb, but usually she is
helpless, becomes confused in her emotions, and escapes into
negation of them through hatred. One very young mother
came close to strangling her baby: "It cried so much and I
did not know why."

Mothers always fear for their children and sometimes fear
them. The fear of the lactation period—"He is devouring
me"—the mother's justified fear of having to give up her ego
for the child, often expressed in concern over her personal
ambitions, beauty, etc., can lead to hostility and reactive
formations. Mothers with this attitude cannot endure the
normal aggressions directed by children of both sexes against
their mothers. Above all, they provoke these very aggressions. This leads to those long chains of difficulties between
mother and child in which the primary and secondary factors
are almost indistinguishable. It is not possible to say, in many
cases, why mothers behave as though their motherhood lacked
a kind of immunization against the dangers common to their
condition. Sometimes one has the impression that they present
a kind of inhibited development in which passivity prevails
and the active elements of motherhood are absent.

The children's intuitive sense and their aggressive drives
combine to exploit the mother's inhibiting anxiety and she
becomes their tormented victim, constantly wavering between self-defense and masochistic surrender.

Casting a retrospective glance at the psychologic processes
of motherhood, we see that this seemingly obvious and natural
biologic process involves difficult tasks for woman. We find
in it a world of polarities—ego interests and service to the
species, the mother's tendency to preserve her unity with
the child and the child's drive to freedom, love and hostility,
and a large number of personal, frequently neurotic conflicts.

The methods used to solve all these problems vary with the individuals. Probably the path traced by nature is the most successful: having many children is the best protection against the tragic loss. They make the psychologic umbilical cord more real and facilitate its management. This path is largely barred as a result of cultural influences. The strengthening of the ego interests in the forms of social, intellectual, and professional tasks, while creating new conflicts for woman, also creates new opportunities of solution. Woman's ego might contend that in fact there is no such thing as pure motherliness, just as there is no absolute femininity or absolute masculinity. We have earlier opposed the distinction so frequently made between mother and prostitute, by our reference to the motherly prostitute (p. 38). Erotic women, perhaps even those who have certain qualities of the prostitute, often bring more warmth into their maternal feelings than ascetic women; masculine components may supply a useful addition to maternal activity, etc. Every single maternal quality can have disturbing effects if exaggerated, the mask of motherliness may conceal thoroughly unmotherly qualities, motherliness can be used for indirect goals, etc.

The definition of the specific qualities of motherhood consists in demonstrating a motherly core, around which the secondary admixtures are grouped in varying measure. The presence of the latter is just as much a prerequisite of motherliness as the presence of the core. Methodologically, the procedure is the same here as that which I followed in defining the feminine core (vol. 1), with consistent care to take important secondary components into account.

CHAPTER TEN

Unmarried Mothers

O UR social morality casts a dark shadow on the motherliness of a considerable number of women. Illegitimate motherhood is above all a social problem
and is judged differently in different societies. Without
entering into all the complexities, we shall point out that even
in our own civilization the moral judgments passed upon it
vary with the milieu. In some classes economic pressure
hinders the founding of families and thus furthers illegitimate
motherhood. Among European peasants the inheritance
customs have always prevented early marriages. Among
the lower classes, both in the country and in the city, pre-
marital intercourse is fairly widespread, but monogamy is
often maintained even without marriage and the illegitimate
child enjoys the same rights in the family as the later born
legitimate children, especially where the love relationship
results in marriage. In these cases illegitimacy is not morally
condemned; it is part of a sexual order sanctioned by custom.

It is true that social developments in the last decades have
brought about a change in the attitude toward illegitimate
children in all civilized countries. The idea that mothers who
have given birth to children without the sanction of marriage
are sinners is obsolete, and generalized condemnation has
given place to the tendency to consider unmarried mothers a
social symptom, resulting from specific economic and sexual
conditions. The existing social order is considered inadequate
in its treatment of illegitimate motherhood. It is hardly
possible to estimate objectively the influence of this trend upon
the deeply rooted social prejudices against illegitimacy. Indirect evidence casts a glaring light on the prevalent ideas on
this subject. In June 1944 the following note was published
in *Medical Economics:*

A proposal for withholding from the press the list of births now available at all registrars' offices has been abandoned by the New York State Department of Health. Immediately after a meeting to consider the proposal, the department said the state's Attorney-General had ruled that it had no authority to adopt such a regulation.

The plan had been suggested primarily to protect unmarried mothers and illegitimate children from publicity, but the New York State Publishers' Association had argued that if it were approved, other departments of the state might also attempt to regulate publication of official information. Most newspapers throughout the state have been voluntarily withholding publication of illegitimate births, and their counsel said they would continue to do so.

It is tactful of the newspapers voluntarily to refrain from announcing illegitimate births, and those who made the proposal to withold the lists of births from the press were certainly motivated by charitable considerations. That the attorney-general could not sanction this proposal, and that the publishers' association refused officially to renounce its rights, does not concern us here. But the fact that such protection of unmarried mothers and illegitimate children resting on the tactful discretion of the newspapers is necessary, shows that our society still regards such motherhood as a disgrace that must be shielded from all publicity.

Medical science today enables women to bring their children into the world almost painlessly. It believes that it is thus increasing women's willingness to give birth to children and thereby fulfilling an important social task. But is not this technologic progress devaluated by the fact that it has taken place in a social order that holds that motherhood must be concealed as a disgrace unless it fits into a definite social pattern?

Psychologic considerations are very important in any attempt to clarify the problem of illegitimacy, because there is a far reaching interaction between the social and psychologic determinants of this phenomenon. Where social condemnation is less strong and illegitimate children are not considered a grave mistake, the emotional reactions of unmarried mothers are not the same as they are where illegitimate motherhood is mercilessly stigmatized by law and public opinion.

However, the psychologic factors lie deep in the soul of the mother and illegitimate motherhood has its own specific emotional points of departure. The social factors constitute the background and are assimilated by the psychologic ones: certain emotional reactions are set fully in motion only by the social obstacles. We know that under normal circumstances unmarried women have great difficulty in overcoming their sexual inhibitions because of their fear of pregnancy. Next to the fear of defloration, the threat of conception is the most powerful guardian of the young girl's virtue. Fear of motherhood accompanies woman's psychic life in marriage too, and the difference between the normal and morbid manifestations of this fear is quantitative, and noticeable only when it leads to difficulties affecting the reproductive function. The social prohibition against illegitimate motherhood plays the part of an ally of this deep-rooted fear; it rationalizes this fear and thus furthers adjustment to reality. On the other hand, we have the sexuality of the unmarried woman, who is not always able to escape the physiologic consequences of the sexual act. The conscious or unconscious wish for a child can prove stronger than the rational arguments opposing it.

Thus we have a definite distribution of strength as between the wish tendencies and the defense tendencies. The psychic processes do not always mechanically follow the pattern of this distribution of strength. The inner prohibition may give rise to a defense; but the same prohibition can set in motion a compulsion to violate it. Similarly, there may arise a strong psychologically determined protest against the external prohibitions. In sexual intercourse, the wish for pregnancy, which is not always equivalent to the wish for a child, may assert itself. I have pointed out before that the urge to motherhood is not necessarily the expression of an instinctual force and does not necessarily serve real motherliness. I have dealt with this psychologic phenomenon in legitimate motherhood, and it will confront us even more clearly in illegitimate motherhood. Thus the psychology of illegitimate motherhood will prove to be only partially a reaction to social difficulties.

Two questions must be considered in this connection: (1) the psychologic prerequisites of illegitimate pregnancy, especially where it could have been prevented or where it is repeated several times despite its destructive effects on the mother's life and despite the fact that consciously she does not want it, and (2) the woman's subsequent reactions to her illegitimate motherhood.

I have pointed out that pregnancy has a psychologic meaning of its own apart from the fact that it is a prelude to motherhood. We have seen that some women compulsively become pregnant several times in order to gratify psychologic tendencies that are not directly connected with the wish for a child. But since motherhood is a consequence of pregnancy, it is difficult psychologically to separate the condition and the result. This makes it impossible to avoid some repetition in our discussion.

The type of unmarried mother most frequently encountered, because she is most frequently in need of public assistance, is the young girl still in the throes of adolescence. We have seen how immature sexual play can become a serious matter, and how the tragedy of unmarried motherhood may result from secondary psychologic motives. Any excessive charge of puberal conflicts can operate as such a motive. The motive may be that of flight from incest fantasies into unrestrained self-abandonment to the first man encountered (many men to replace the one and only), with or without fulfillment of the immature fantasy "I want a child"; it may arise from an unfavorable identification (e.g., with a pregnant mother, sister, friend, etc.), from vengefulness toward the family, from a tendency to self-punishment, etc. Sometimes a complicated combination of psychic motives is present, and sometimes simple sexual curiosity suffices to confront a young and immature girl with the very adult task of motherhood.

The adolescent feeling of solitude that I have previously mentioned (vol. 1) is sometimes intensified into a depression and a feeling of vacuum, and the girl seeks refuge from this in life, excitement, and forbidden pleasures. Especially those young girls whose feeling of solitude is increased by lack of tenderness in their environment, are prone to such uncontrolled sexual indulgence leading to motherhood. They misinterpret man's sexual lust for tenderness, and their own need for tenderness creates the readiness for motherhood, with its wonderful opportunities for gratification of the most tender of all feelings. Motherly unmarried mothers are often women who respond with complete abandon to the first sexual assault, as a result of their need for tenderness.

One such woman was Louise, a handsome 17-year old girl whose relatives came to a social agency asking for help and advice in the difficulties the girl had created for them. Her mother had died a few years before and her father lived in Texas with another woman, but partly supported Louise. Mrs. L., who took care of the girl, was her mother's first cousin. She was a kindly woman of about 50 and showed obvious loving solicitude for her young relative. She lived with her husband and her married daughter's family on a farm in New England. Louise was learning millinery in a near-by town. Four months before her case came to the social agency she had been delivered of a boy and had returned to the farm with him. Her cousin had not known about her pregnancy, although she had heard that Louise was going out a great deal with young men. Louise denied this and her cousin, greatly taxed with her own family, could not devote much attention to the girl: "Louise knows that we will always help her when she needs us." The difficulty was now that Louise refused to separate from her child and generally behaved in a very defiant and disagreeable manner. As a child she had always been good, but seclusive and absorbed in her dreams.

Louise was very tender toward her child, but refused to suckle it for more than six weeks, alleging that the nurse in the hospital had said that the child did not need his mother's milk for more than six weeks. The aunt found the girl completely changed. She had been timid and reserved; now she went out with boys and returned home late at night. She did almost no work but constantly carried her child in her arms and pampered it. She took it into her own bed at night, and since she often returned home late, the child wailed and demanded to be carried. The relatives thought that Louise should also think of her future; they were willing to keep the child and give Louise an opportunity to continue her apprenticeship. Otherwise, they thought, she should work in a factory; idleness did not seem to be doing her any good.

Louise agreed to all their proposals. She realized that she should learn a trade and work, but under no circumstances would she leave her child. When told that it would be better for him to be brought up in the country, and that if she kept him she would be unable to watch him during working hours, she answered with great emphasis: "But I will be with him in the evening and at night." During the daytime, she said, her neighbors would help her if the child cried.

"What neighbors?"

Oh, she would find a room in a nice neighborhood, and everyone, she said, "will love Billy—he is such a wonderful child."

The statements of the relatives and Louise's peculiar disregard for reality aroused the suspicion that her intelligence was of a low order. But prolonged contact with her showed that she had a good mind and that her pseudostupidity was connected with her introverted daydreaming. She had a powerful imagination and the ability to transport herself into a world which belonged to her and in which everything went as she wished. She had always wanted a child and was very happy to have the baby. She had never imagined that it would be an illegitimate child. She had also hoped and yearned for a home of her own and had not even conceived that it could be otherwise. Now she no longer expected her hopes to be fulfilled. What life could give her she already had—her child. She no longer believed in the other things: what had been her self-evident future, from which she was now cut off, could be fulfilled only in her fantasy.

She refused to give additional information about the child's father. She had gone out with him to amuse herself; he was tender and sweet and she did not think that he wanted to have sexual intercourse with her. When he made such proposals to her, they appeared absurd—such things were done only when one was married. Once he took her out and was so passionate and desirous that she could not defend herself. She became a passive object and could not say "No." This was repeated several times, and each time the whole thing seemed somehow absurd, unexpected, and yet inevitable. She did not think that she could become pregnant, and by the time she realized that she was, her boy friend had joined the Army and she thought it proper not to burden him with the news, and also to conceal it from other people, and to make up her own mind about the whole thing. She had no worries about the future, she knew that things would be settled somehow, and when she was advised in the hospital to appeal to her relatives, she did so without hesitation. Everyone was good and kind to her. She knew that she now had a great responsibility in life and sometimes she was very much afraid of it. This fear seized her, for instance, when she suckled her child. Then she had the feeling that she was tied, helplessly entangled in a crushing situation. It was because of this anxiety that she had stopped nursing her child, although it had been "lovely to hold him so close and tenderly." She also went out at night, she said, because she wanted to liberate herself from this oppressive anxiety. She had no interest in the boys with whom she went out now, but whenever one of them was very tender with her, she grew weak and allowed him to do things that still seemed to her absurd.

Louise was the youngest child in her own family, the only child of her father's second wife. Her older brothers and sisters married and left the parental home when she was still small. Her mother, who could not have any more children, pampered her boundlessly, and her father too was very loving toward her. She lost her mother at the age of 10, and her father moved to the home of his eldest daughter in Texas. Louise went to her cousin's farm and expected that in time her father would send for her. Now he was writing to her and sending her money, but she no longer thought of joining him. She was happy at her aunt's, although somewhat lonely and left to her fantasy life. Her cousins were older and not interested in her. When she came to the city she could not bear her solitude and, like the other young girls in her shop, went out with young men. She had had intimate sexual relations only with Eric; she declared in the hospital that she did not know whether she loved him, but she would gladly have married him on account of the child. He did not seem to care too much about her; he had left her with a tender promise, just like her father.

It is clear that Louise's motherhood resulted from two motives—passivity, inability to say "No," and the need for tenderness, which she had once enjoyed abundantly and which had ceased for her after her mother's death. In her uncontrolled sexual surrender, these two motives could be served. It is very likely that her longing for the absent father who had disappointed her made her love frustration unbearable and that she escaped from her fantasy life into reality. Louise, as a type, would have made an excellent wife and mother in an orderly family life, and her warm motherliness would have flowered in a triangle consolidated by marriage. She lacked the active component of motherhood in which the child as an object of her tenderness could satisfy her emotional needs. She loved the child tenderly, but her passive need to be loved remained unsatisfied. For this reason she compulsively ran away from her child to new experiences, while at the same time she clung to him with all her genuine but immature mother love. She obscurely sensed the dangers of the future and the threat of repetition tendencies. She wanted her child to be with her to protect her from these new dangers; rootless mothers often and usually unsuccessfully impose such a role on their children. Louise's inadequate sense of reality, and a definite optimistic component of her fantasy life that made her believe, despite her disappointments, that "someone will be found among the neighbors," constituted great dangers for her future, from which her child and her previous experience would not suffice to protect her.

Louise was so fearful of the dangers provoked by her psychic life that she was completely unaware of the social difficulties that would gradually arise for her and her child. This situation endangered her social adjustment and she might easily have become asocial, a burden to society, an object of public assistance, and a candidate for repeated illegitimate motherhood. Louise is typical of many unmarried mothers who become pregnant compulsively again and again. But she is only one of many types, and in my opinion not the most difficult. In other types, other unconscious motives that were at play during the first pregnancy, press for repetitions. In such cases the first bad experience paradoxically fails to create a protection but operates instead as a provocation and intensifies the tendency to repetition. The fear of pregnancy becomes a motive for it, just as the fear of death, the unbearable tension of expectation, can become a motive for suicide.

In the case of all such immature young mothers, we say that the ego is too weak to escape the dangers and temptations of the outside world or to achieve more favorable conditions under which to satisfy the urge for motherhood. The numerous cases I have encountered have always involved a weakness of the ego that made it unable to resist the strong psychic dangers otherwise than by transference of them to the outside world. Such an immature woman's motherly demand for a child is often only the child's demand for a mother. Every experienced psychiatrist or social worker knows that in such a case of compulsory motherhood she can often save the girl by being a substitute mother to her.

Not unlike Louise was Mrs. Olson, a 27-year-old married woman of Norwegian origin, the mother of two children. She came to a social agency to ask for help in placing her children.

Her older child, a 4-year-old girl, was the illegitimate child of a man named Robert, with whom she had had a short-lived affair. He was the first man who had ever paid any attention to her. After a homeless and loveless childhood, she found herself in the position of an unattractive and inhibited girl tormented by feelings of inferiority, without prospects of love or happiness. Robert had met her at the same time as Sidney, her present husband, and it was obvious that she had become Robert's and not Sidney's lover by mere accident. Robert was rather brutal and aggressive; she gave herself sexually with an automatic passivity, out of gratitude and enthusiasm over the fact that someone cared for her, and became pregnant at once Her mother took care of the newborn child, but Mrs. Olson, one year later, wanted to place the child for adoption, because she did not like to be dependent upon her mother

Several months after the birth of this first child she began a relationship with Sidney and this time too became pregnant at once. After she had given birth to a boy, for whom Sidney conceived a tremendous liking, he asked her to marry him, and she gladly consented. He adopted both children and was a tender father to them. Then he was drafted and sent to Virginia. For some time Mrs. Olson remained where she was; then she broke up her home and followed her husband, taking her children with her. The climate and food in the new locale were dreadful and both parents felt that it was impossible for the children to remain there. Mrs. Olson returned to Boston to place the children. She was very restless and wanted to have her children placed at once, in order to return to her husband alone. If she were free, she explained, she could immediately find a job in Virginia and work close by to her husband, but she must go, and as soon as possible, for her husband was calling her and needed her urgently. She could not and would not, she said, take her children with her, because she needed freedom of movement; should Sidney be transferred, she wanted to be in position to follow him. If conditions were favorable, she explained, she might send for her children; she had no ties in Boston and it did not matter where she resettled. If Sidney should be sent abroad, she could return to Boston, but now she was anxious to get to Virginia. She felt that she had an obligation toward her husband because he had always been so good to her and helped her when she needed someone; that was why she wanted to join him when he needed her. She felt that he was angry with her, as he had written to her wondering why she had not come back to Virginia to join him. She displayed panicky impatience in her interviews and repeated, in a defiant, childish manner: "I want to place the children and go to Virginia."

She declared that she herself had had a very sad childhood. Soon after she was born, her parents were divorced and she was placed in a foster home. Although she expressed bitterness at having been placed as a child, she did not seem to have the same feeling about placing her own children. Her relation to her own mother seemed to play a part in her haste to place them. It was obvious that Mrs. Olson violently protested against being dependent upon her mother and jealously guarded against letting her take the love and dependence of her own children away from her. Whenever the mother or a social worker proposed that the children be left with the mother, Mrs. Olson reacted violently, saying to her mother, "No, that would be too much for you," or to the social worker, "Oh no, mother is just like a stranger to me; besides, she spoils the children"—and would immediately add, expressing her old hateful reproach against her mother, "She placed her own children; I know what she is like." She felt compelled to act toward her children as her mother had acted toward her. But at the same time she negated this identification, and as though to defend her attitude said: "I want to place the children only for a year or so; it does not matter when they are so young."

This identification manifested itself in still other ways. She deprived her children of their home and father, as her mother had done; the two women further had in common a tendency to dominate and an attitude of reserved coldness toward their children.

Mrs. Olson's hostility toward her mother and simultaneous dependence upon her played an important part in her psychic life. For instance, she hated to receive financial help from her mother, yet she could not make herself free of it. Each time her mother gave her money she made her feel "as though she were the boss." At the same time she praised her mother: "She protects me, manages my affairs, and is so helpful with the children."

Mrs. Olson's childhood had been almost completely devoid of tenderness and love. She was fatherless and held her mother responsible for this. And yet her mother remained the only being to whom she was emotionally attached, though this was against her conscious will. Just like Louise, she yielded to the first man she encountered because of her emotional hunger. In Louise, it was the sudden loss of the rich love she had received from her parents, and sudden fatherlessness, that made her a passive object, giving everything for tenderness; Mrs. Olson was driven to undesired motherhood by the emotional privations of her entire childhood, by her premature fatherlessness, and above all by her flight from her mother.

Mrs. Olson described her life with her children after her return from Virginia. She could bear the day, but at night she was seized by restlessness and despair that drove her out of her home. She read all night long, could not sleep, drank coffee, and waited for the morning. She thought and thought, she said, and could not help remembering the time when she was an unmarried mother. Even though she was married now, she still felt terrible about it. "I guess neither of my children can feel that one is better than the other, for they are both illegitimate," she said.

She referred to her organic constitution as being "of iron," meaning that she easily became pregnant—and immediately resumed her demand that her children be placed, so that she could be under her husband's protection as soon as possible. She also cited reasons why she never wanted to return to Boston except to take the children. People there knew about Mary's illegitimacy, she said, and she met Robert there sometimes, and meeting Robert only created an unpleasant situation, although she did not intend to be unfaithful to her husband— "He has been so good to me." If her husband should be sent abroad she would go with her children to another state, for example South Carolina, and work there—"any place is better than Boston." And again and again, as though in a panic, she insisted on placement of her children and on her liberation.

To protect herself against her nocturnal restlessness she took a night job and left the children alone. When she was told that it was not good for them to be left alone, she grew very angry, as though she were being unjustly scolded: "Why, I would go crazy if I had to sit inside these four walls all the time."

Evidently Mrs. Olson felt that her children could not protect her from her feeling of loneliness, her longing, and the dangers threatening her. When left alone with them she was probably seized at night by the same anxious restlessness and longing as Louise, who went out with boys to avoid the fear of the very dangers that she conjured up unconsciously by her association with boys. But Louise thought that her child would protect her from these dangers—this was the reason why she insisted on having him with her. Mrs. Olson had learned from experience that this does not hold. Louise was only an anxiety-filled dreamer, while Mrs. Olson seemed to suffer from deep depressions, from which she took flight in excessive activity.

Her feeling that her husband needed her gave her gratification, and her motherly tenderness toward him obviously gave her greater protection than her relationship with her children. He was rather dependent on her, she explained. "When he was at home," she said, "he seemed happy just to be with me; he never cared to go out. He appeared to be enjoying himself just being at home."

Observing the relation of the couple during Mr. Olson's visit to Boston, one could see clearly that the man was completely under the domination of his wife, who was in full control of the situation. From Mrs. Olson's anxious remarks about her former lover, it seemed that she was not yet quite free from him. The passive-masochistic component of her personality, under the mask of need for love, had made her give herself to an aggressive man in her masochistic readiness for illegitimate motherhood. This mask was simultaneously the true face of that component of her psychic life which made her yearn for love. She had escaped from these dangerous tendencies to her passive, lovable husband, and now insisted violently upon reunion with him because she felt herself again threatened.

This passive-masochistic tendency probably characterizes a large proportion of unmarried mothers; it is a feminine tendency, intensified by guilt feelings, that, once cruelly gratified through illegitimate motherhood, seeks repetitions of the same situation.

Interestingly enough, Mrs. Olson's story ended differently from the manner in which she had forevisioned it in her South Carolina fantasy. These plans were abandoned when she found that she was again pregnant. Protected now by legitimate pregnancy, she was no longer threatened with illegitimate pregnancy, and she could devote herself entirely to her children.

Mrs. Olson hated her mother and was at the same time dependent upon her. Louise's mother had died. What these two women had in common was fatherlessness, a yearning to be loved, passive-masochistic tendencies, guilt feelings about their illegitimate motherhood, fear of its repetition, and a compulsive tendency to this repetition.

Mrs. Olson was completely conscious of her guilt feeling as a reaction to her illegitimate motherhood, while in Louise we have the right to take it for granted. Mrs. Olson handled this guilt feeling in a paradoxic way: it is as though she feared the repetition of illegitimate motherhood as a punishment for the previous one, and as such, something that might be provoked by herself.

The same was probably true of Louise, who seemed to be exposed to just such a danger, and is true of many other women, who again and again bring illegitimate children into the world not in order to experience maternal happiness but in order to punish themselves by being disgraced.

Ida was a 17-year-old girl whom I met through her employer, Mrs. Driver. She was a friend of Mrs. Driver's niece, who had recommended her for the post of governess to Mrs. Driver's three children. Ida took the job because her resources were insufficient to enable her to realize her most ardent desire, namely, to become a kindergarten teacher. Mrs. Driver was enthusiastic about Ida's gentleness and her excellent manner with the children, and was ready to do everything to help the young girl. Two months after Ida took her position with Mrs. Driver, she began to have fits of dizziness and vomiting. Mrs. Driver thought that these symptoms were neurotic, and the fact that Ida refused to see her parents or accept any support from them strengthened this conviction. Mrs. Driver knew that her governess was the only child of a well-to-do minister and assumed that her conflict with her parents would eventually be solved.

When Ida was brought to me she did not impress me as a neurotic. She looked somewhat childish, being dressed like a 12-year-old girl, and her unconcern with the events of her own life was striking. At first she was secretive, but gradually she became confiding and told me that a year and a half before she had met a young man four years older than herself in a summer camp. They fell in love and planned to continue their relationship after the summer vacation. Ida wanted to attend a school for kindergarten teachers; George intended to learn a trade as soon as possible; later they would become engaged and then married.

Before these plans could materialize, however, George was drafted for military service. The young couple decided to marry before he joined the Army. Ida's parents absolutely opposed this plan, because they were conservative Protestants and George was a Jew. Ida began an energetic struggle against her parents and in the end persuaded her somewhat passive friend to elope with her. They met in the village where they had spent the previous summer and, thinking that they would soon be married, began to have sexual intercourse. Soon Ida, who had been ardently in love, cooled in regard to George; her feelings were now a mixture of passion and sudden fits of indifference, and one day, without giving him any explanation, she ran away and joined a girl friend in Boston. She told this friend that she no longer wanted to have anything to do with George and that her only wish now was to carry out her previous plan of attending a kindergarten training school, but without financial support from her parents.

The character of Ida's neurotic symptoms made me suspect that she was pregnant. She admitted that since her flight from home her periods had ceased. Although this had never happened to her before, and although she was completely enlightened about sex, she began to think that she was pregnant only after I had pointed out this possibility.

My conjecture proved correct. After the first shock, however, Ida remained extraordinarily self-controlled. She made very realistic plans for her future, figured out carefully to what extent her condition interfered with her other projects, began to save money to cover the expenses connected with it, and referred to her child as a foreign body that must first be removed and later established somewhere else. She took it for granted that her child would be placed for adoption and no longer worried about it. She sympathized with her parents but felt no need to make up her quarrel with them; her interest in George had completely vanished; she said that she was glad that he had been drafted and would never learn anything about the whole affair. She was worried only about the fact that the people among whom she would later live and work might some day learn that she had given birth to an illegitimate child. She confided to Mrs. Driver and me that she had made up her mind to confess the truth to her parents when this became unavoidable, and prepared herself in a matter-of-fact way to solve her problem.

Mrs. Driver kept Ida in her home as long as her condition could be concealed; then she helped her to arrange for the delivery of her child and for its placement in a foster home.

When I saw Ida several weeks after her delivery, she gradually admitted that her matter-of-factness had not been genuine. She had had terrible fears before her delivery; she had been sure that she would die, and had even begun to pray, although for the last few years she had been an atheist and never went to her father's church.

Almost until the end she thought of her child as something foreign, of which she would rid herself as soon as possible. Only after having moved out of Mrs. Driver's home, when she was alone, as it were, with her unborn baby, did she begin to fantasy about how nice it would be to have a baby. The content of her fantasies was tender, but she considered realization of them impossible. She obviously condemned herself to renunciation. Occasionally she had the idea of keeping the child and returning to her parental home with him. She said that both her father and mother loved children and that they would surely find a solution for her problem. Then she rejected this idea as absurd and again sought refuge in her indifference and matter-of-fact adjustment to reality. In the maternity hospital she declared that she would not nurse her child and would place it for adoption at once.

After his birth, she found her little boy extraordinarily "cute" and began to nurse him, but following each manifestation of maternal joy, she demanded that her child be taken away from her as soon as possible, since she could not keep him in any case; she said that she did not want to have anything to do with him, that he did not mean anything to her, and that she feared that he could mean something. But at the same time she considered postponing the placement of her child. As the date of her discharge from the hospital approached, she felt weaker and had fits of fever; it was clear that she was loth to return to the world, where she would be confronted with reality and compelled to renounce her boy in favor of it. She wanted to stay with her baby as long as possible. In the hospital she felt secure; life was centered around herself and her baby. It was obvious that she now wanted to keep him but realized the difficulties that this involved. She showed keen interest in the fate of her child and in the kind of home he would have; she wanted to make sure that it would be a good one and that he would be properly cared for.

With Mrs. Driver's help she made up her mind to give up

the idea of adoption for the time being, and the child was placed in a foster home. Ida visited him there and became very much upset; she declared with tears in her eyes that she missed him terribly, that she wanted to keep him, but that she did not see how she could.

At this point Mrs. Driver, a truly motherly woman, proposed taking the child into her home and thus satisfying Ida's motherliness by proximity to her child. Mrs. Driver thought that later Ida might decide to create a home for her boy herself. Ida's reaction was very peculiar. She emphatically rejected her employer's proposal and refused even to discuss it, declaring that this would be like giving her child to her own mother. Thus she would not only lose him but herself fall into a new dependence.

This reaction is understandable if we take Ida's total situation into account. Her case is one among hundreds, a fundamentally banal story of illegitimacy. But its very banality casts much light on the psychology of what is perhaps the most frequent type of juvenile unmarried mother. Like all of them, Ida was young and inexperienced, at an age when sexual curiosity and the feeling "Something like that cannot happen to me" constitute the greatest dangers for the young girl.

In Ida, as in other unmarried mothers, the rebellious struggle against her mother and her mother's moral commands and prohibitions acted as a powerful motive in the choice of her love object, her elopement, and her intercourse with her lover. A hateful protest against the mother often contains revenge tendencies, and when a young girl becomes promiscuous, a prostitute, or an unmarried mother, she often both fulfills a fantasy and punishes herself. Ida's father was a clergyman; her mother, the daughter of a reactionary minister, was a fanatically devout bigot; even earlier she had suffered from Ida's atheism and justly interpreted it as a malicious aggression against herself and her husband, masked as freethinking. The parents opposed Ida's marriage with George not because of racial prejudice but for religious reasons. Ida made no attempt to win her parents over, as for instance by promising that George would be converted; she eloped, less to consummate her passion for George than to gratify her aggressive feeling toward her parents. To emphasize her emancipation, she entered into a sexual relationship before marrying, on the pretext that she would soon be married anyhow. Actually she remained obedient to her mother, for her sexuality was inhibited; anxiety and repentance accompanied her sexual gesture, so that she remained completely frigid. After she had carried out her unsuccessful attempt to emancipate herself, George's role changed; the man formerly loved now became an accomplice in her struggle against her parents, especially her mother. The pressure of her guilt feeling made her love a crime, and Ida had to repudiate George just as a criminal on the stand repudiates his accomplice in crime.

Ida continually showed maternal feelings but disavowed them just as violently as she disavowed her love for George. Confronted with Mrs. Driver's proposal to take her child, Ida found herself entangled in a deep and genuine conflict. If she kept the child and accepted Mrs. Driver as a foster mother, she would have to share him with the woman who was a complete mother substitute to her. Ida quite rightly felt that the resulting emotional situation would only sharpen her puberal conflicts with her own mother, that her sense of guilt with regard to her mother would be intensified, and above all that she had no more right to gratify her love for her child than her love for George. She was also worried about her work in the profession for which she and her parents had such high regard, about her future as a kindergarten teacher, and about the reactions of her new milieu, the milieu of her ambitions and aspirations, to her illegimate motherhood. George wrote to her from his Army post proposing to come and marry her, without even knowing of his fatherhood. Ida refused this proposal with curious haste. If she married him now she would be doing it only as a sacrifice for her child. Tormented by social fears, neurotically disavowing her relationship with George, and striving to fulfill her mother's old wish that she become a kindergarten teacher, Ida renounced her child with a heavy heart and comforted herself with the thought that she could marry later and bring legitimate children into the world.

Even after her child had been placed in a foster home, she insisted repeatedly that she did not have any feeling for him and renewed her demands to have him adopted. She now considered her child, just as she had considered him during her pregnancy, a burden that she must get rid of; she had not the slightest sympathy for George and often left his letters unopened for days.

Such a reaction to illegitimate motherhood often takes place in young girls like Ida, and for similar reasons. The furious reproach against the man—"You have got me into this state"— usually arises when he avoids responsibility or when the relation has cooled off previously and is continued against the will of the girl and contrary to her emotional needs as a result of pregnancy. It was completely different in the case of Ida. From the beginning she resorted to a very frequent defense mechanism, that of denial; she denied any emotional relation to George, repressed all her affective life, and appeared seemingly cold and unconcerned—a little schoolgirl with bare knees who could not be a mother because she was still a child.

The concealment of motherhood from the father of the child usually has two motives—denial of a positive emotional relation to him, often for reasons similar to Ida's, and narcissistic fear of being rejected and condemned by him. Moreover, how could Ida, at a moment when she was so full of repentance with regard to her parents, admit a love whose most important motivation had been her defiant violation of parental prohibitions? To some extent Ida was also a war mother. The typical motive for wartime motherhood that we have mentioned before perhaps operated in her too: it is difficult to resist the demands of a hero exposed to the danger of death. Just like the other war mothers, she declared that she had yielded to his pleas that she elope with him because he was about to be drafted; however, we have seen that Ida's willingness to risk illegitimate motherhood had also been fed by other sources.

The case of Ida shows us with particular clarity how much the relation of the mother to her child depends upon her psychologic situation as a whole. A young mother who expects her child in an atmosphere of love is completely and joyfully filled by his organic presence. Ida, who, so to speak, trained herself for separation from her child immediately after his birth, and for having him adopted, forestalled the trauma of separation by assuming toward him the attitude one has toward a burdensome parasite, a kind of growth from which she would free herself at a given moment. This behavior is characteristic of expectant mothers who from the beginning resort to the radical defense mechanism "I have no child and I do not want a child," in order to prepare themselves for the necessary renunciation. Nor can the child's movements within the body arouse motherly feelings in the customary manner if they are opposed and inhibited by the idea of future discomfort.

External influences can intensify the ideas of discomfort on the one hand and mobilize the girl's still childish yearning for motherhood on the other. Seeing babies in the hospital, Ida reacted as any normal young girl would react and said: "They are so cute!"

Perhaps she also sensed a current of motherly happiness in the other mothers in the hospital; perhaps her wish to keep the child in spite of everything was later accompanied by other, less conscious psychologic motives. Her substitute mother declared herself ready to take the child, and the typical childhood fear "My mother will have the child" reawakened, as well as the deeply rooted wish "It should belong to me." It is noteworthy how Ida's motherliness was chilled by the argument that if she kept her child she would still have to share it with another woman. Her fear that her dependence upon Mrs. Driver would be strengthened certainly played a large part in her considerations. Ida felt extremely guilty toward her parents, particularly her mother. She tried to bribe her sense of guilt by various means, first by deserting her forbidden lover. In her *post factum* obedience to her parents she emotionally denied any interest in him. In the end she decided upon a solution that had been predetermined in her mother's plans for her: she gave up her lover and the "child of sin" in order to devote herself to a profession that to her parents was the symbol of ideal aspirations as opposed to the "taint" of sexuality.

When she had finally made up her mind to desert George and the child, Ida plunged into her work. But her behavior revealed that despite her renunciation, she had not achieved her goal of liberating herself from her sense of guilt. She lived in perpetual fear that someone might discover that she was an unmarried mother. She was tense and worried for fear that she would not be accepted in the better schools. She often displayed a tendency to betray her secret in the very quarters where she most wanted to conceal it. She made excellent progress in her work, won the respect of her schoolmates and teachers, and received a scholarship; yet every step forward in her career was accompanied by the constantly lurking fear of what would happen if her secret should become known. She behaved like a hunted criminal.

An inexperienced observer might have been taken in by Ida's own rationalization of her psychologic conflict. Illegitimate motherhood is a social complication and the sense of social guilt is strongly mobilized, especially in a milieu like that of Ida's parents. Yet not even the most reactionary milieu would have condemned her to such an extent as she constantly feared. Her immediate milieu was extremely tolerant and Ida was well aware that her "disgrace" was not a disgrace at all in the eyes of the people with whom she worked. Nor were her elaborate precautions necessary, for no one ever suspected her. Indeed, even her reactionary parents turned out to be much more tolerant and forgiving than she herself. Ida felt like a condemned criminal not because she had had an illegitimate child, but because the reckoning of her guilt was triply weighted. First, she had acted out her hostility by an aggressive act against her parents, by eloping with a man whom they rejected as a possible husband for her. Then she had tried to make up for her first offense by disavowing her love for George and deserting him. Thus she had defeated her purpose, because she had burdened her conscience with a new and perhaps even greater guilt by sinning against her own love and against George. Her third guilt related to her motherliness, which she denied to herself and her child.

Ida successfully repressed all these themes of guilt and characteristically transferred her guilt feeling to society. She constantly tried to convince Mrs. Driver that she needed her help only to conceal her illegitimate motherhood and thus master her social difficulties. But Ida was fortunate in the choice of her confidant. Mrs. Driver, a sensitive and intuitive woman, grasped the situation and was not misled by Ida's brilliant professional success. She knew that it was much more important for the young woman's future to bring order into her confused and repressed emotional life than to insure her material success. Instead of supporting her in her efforts at concealment, she showed Ida that her guilt feelings had another source and that her fear of society was only the result of transference. She insisted that Ida summon courage enough not to break with George until after she had seen him once more, and that she postpone adoption for her child. Thanks to Mrs. Driver's enlightened help, Ida eventually became a happy wife and mother. Such happy endings do not always come to pass; often the best solution is escape into socially valuable activity. But cases like Ida's should always be subjected to thorough psychologic examination before the social factor is taken as the key to the situation.

Virginia was a good-looking 19-year old girl, petite, shy, soft, and attractive. Her physical appearance was rather infantile and there was nothing motherly about her. When she got in touch with the social agency her child was 2½ months old. Up until then Virginia had been in a maternity home, caring for her little boy herself and clinging to him with the greatest tenderness.

Before the baby was born she displayed the typical attitude

of the unmarried mother: she would have liked best to have an abortion, and when this could not be done, she enthusiastically accepted the proposal to have her child adopted.

Her childhood situation was similar to that of Louise: she had lost her mother at the age of 6, her father had married another woman who did not get along with Virginia, and her relationship to him was one of estrangement. Her contact with the father of her child was most casual, according to her. She had met Anton at a restaurant, and claimed that she had had intercourse with him only once. She was terribly excited after this experience and from the beginning was afraid of impregnation.

For seven years, from her early puberty on, Virginia had been employed as maid in the house of the W. family. Mrs. W. was the mother of four children, two of whom were born while Virginia was in her service. The girl's position in the household was between that of a member of the family and a servant. Mrs. W. showed her much motherly solicitude, knew all about her life, and enjoyed the girl's confidence. Yet Virginia's love life had its locale in restaurants and dance halls. Probably, like any girl even in a more normal mother-daughter relationship, Virginia had her sexual secrets, into which she initiated Mrs. W. only when she justly considered herself in danger. Mrs. W. at once advised adoption for the illegitimate child. She kept Virginia in her home until the final state of her pregnancy and in a motherly way helped her to conceal her condition from the neighbors. Virginia had adjusted her moral standards to the demands of the neighborhood and did not want anyone to learn of her mistake. She thought that despite the events that had taken place, it would be possible, after her confinement and the placement of her child, to return to her job under the previous emotional conditions. She considered the W. home her own and Mrs. W. a beloved and loving mother.

Her plans changed when, like a motherly little girl, she took care of her child and performed her motherly functions, even though at first just obligatorily. Soon she declared: "If you have to take this baby away from me, you'd better do it very soon, because I am getting very fond of it."

She found her little Tommy "cute," smiled warmly when she spoke about him, and proudly showed him to her visitors. She said quite frankly that she did not know what she was going to do when she left the maternity home. Mrs. W. was willing to have her back, but not with the baby, and Virginia would not give up Tommy now "for anything." She thought of going to her grandmother, but she did not know what the latter's reaction to the baby would be. If she went there she could take a job and her grandmother could look after the baby; but she was afraid that this plan would not work out.

We saw Virginia torn between contradictory desires. Her entire plan derived from the fact that she still thought of herself as a little girl clinging to her mother, depending upon her, and wanting to stay with her. She had lost her own mother at an early age, had had bad experiences with her stepmother, and was happy to have found a substitute mother. It is very significant that the attachment to a substitute, following a childhood full of emotional privations, is often more tenacious and lasting than the original mother tie, which weakens under normal circumstances. The professional persons in authority who were now in charge of the girl justly assumed that her unfortunate and premature motherhood could help to mature her quickly, and that therefore her final decision about her own and her child's future should be postponed. They felt that she could never resume her former place, because she was different now—she was a mother and no longer a little girl. But Virginia herself continued in her dilemma: should she return to her mother as a little girl or stay with her beloved baby as a dutiful mother?

Motherly women around Virginia, perceiving these signs of motherliness, encouraged the new feelings awakening in her. Under suitable external and internal conditions, genuine motherliness develops from such immature stimulations, which we have referred to as outposts of motherhood. Thus, under very active external influence, Virginia, the little girl, who yearned terribly for her substitute home and substitute mother, made up her mind to renounce her girlish role and assume the duties of an adult mother. This decision was put into effect with the help of the social agency, which tried to find a job for her under conditions that would permit her to keep her baby. The wisdom of her returning to Mrs. W.'s home seemed questionable under any circumstances, since it was learned that Mrs. W. was even more emotional than Virginia; it was reported that she wept without any self-control at little Tommy's christening.

A job was found for the girl in a pleasant home with three little children. Virginia and her baby were to be together. But from the beginning the girl displayed resistance. Although she accepted all the arrangements made for her without any criticism, she was evidently worried about her status, and planned to tell her employers that she was married and that her husband was in the service.

Within a short time Virginia was extremely unhappy. She called on Mrs. W. and complained that her room was dark and cold, without sunlight for the baby. She was ready to adjust herself, but it became increasingly evident that no matter what her surroundings might be, she would probably react with fear, remorse, and unhappiness to any new place. Soon she decided that she could not continue in her position, that she would give up the baby and return to Mrs. W.'s. "After all," Virginia said, "hers is the only home I know."

She wanted to place the baby for adoption because she did not think that she herself could give him all the material benefits and care that he needed.

During her stay in her new surroundings, pleasant yet alien to her, Virginia, according to her own description, was "all tied up in knots," unable to do the right thing for Tommy and not interested in him as she had been before. But when she realized that she could return to Mrs. W.'s, she melted and spoke warmly about her baby. She "wouldn't think of having him adopted now," she wanted only to find a temporary home for him. Perhaps some day she would marry and then she would be able to have Tommy live with her. Her attachment to the baby increased as the time for parting from him drew near. She became more active in doing things for him, at the same time energetically looking for a foster home, and was more independent than ever in her behavior. Apparently she had decided to return to Mrs. W. under any circumstances, and this decision freed her from anxiety, gave her inner security, and allowed her to feel and act for the child. She could be an active, solicitous mother when she felt that she herself was loved and protected by a mother. When she returned to Mrs. W.'s house she shouted at the top of her voice: "I'm home."

Her new difficulties soon began. Virginia herself did not know whether she would rather have her child with her in Mrs. W.'s home or not. At last she decided she would rather not—for she wanted to be one of Mrs. W.'s children, just as before, and how could she claim that status if she were the mother of a child in the house?

Mrs. W., who was apparently a kind and motherly woman, finally took the child also into her home. After all, Virginia was not really her daughter; she was a kindly treated youthful servant. As an unmarried mother, Virginia probably sank in the social scale, and the solution of the problem arising from this fact was uncertain. However, under the circumstances, it seemed best for Virginia to return to her former dependence. It would have been an error to follow a routine formula and to try to break her infantile ties by violent means, especially at a moment in her life when her psychic tasks and her problems in face of socio-economic reality were very difficult ones.

The case of Virginia is much less complicated than those of Louise and Ida. Psychologically she was perhaps more like the girls whom I have termed assistant mothers (Lydia, Mrs. Baron). A girl of this type can be tender and solicitous but is unable to assume the active responsibilities of a mature mother, especially when her own premature motherhood is opposed by the condemning attitude of her social milieu. We need not look too far for the motives of Virginia's "mistake." The normal inhibitions of young girlhood were perhaps too easy to overcome in her case not because she was particularly excitable sexually or because there were particular weaknesses in her ego, but because she was in a sense neglected, in that she lived in a milieu that accepted her only partially and from the beginning considered her as inferior and not really belonging. The statistics of illegitimate motherhood in various European countries show that servant girls supply the highest percentage of unmarried mothers. Apparently the same psychologic motive is operative: close contact with a higher social stratum that enjoys a larger share of the pleasures of life prepares a fertile soil for the seduction of the excluded ones. Other contributing factors are certainly the economic insecurity and habitual ill treatment of servant girls and the monotony of their work. In Virginia's case the center of the problem lay perhaps in the fact that, as a motherless and homeless child, she longed all the more for identification with her new milieu and unconsciously suffered from being rejected by it. We felt that this provocative motive would probably continue to operate throughout Virginia's life with the family in which she stayed a servant girl. Ida's danger had an internal source, Virginia's an external one. They represent completely different types of illegitimate motherhood.

Elsie was 23 years old; she came to the agency directly from the hospital where her illegitimate baby was born. She was accompanied by her parents. Her mother was a domineering person who had solved the problem in advance: the main thing was "not to advertise the story." In this respect she was strongly reminiscent of Ida's mother and of many others whose middle class morality suffers a heavy blow from their daughters' illegitimate motherhood, and whose main concern is to preserve the family's social prestige. The baby was for the time being placed in a foster home and was naturally destined for adoption: that had been decided from the beginning.

Elsie was an amiable and intelligent person, but according to the foster mother and everyone who had been in contact with her, she was unable to express her feelings easily. She had not seen her baby and was in quite a conflict about it. She was afraid to see it lest she should be unable to part from it.

She came from a little western town, where she was a school-teacher. She had been completing her education in an institution in New York and there she became pregnant. Then she went back home and managed to conceal her condition. It became apparent only during the last month of her pregnancy and at that time she was on a farm with her parents.

Asked whether she had seen her baby, she answered that she had not seen the little girl and that she felt as though she had never had the child, though sometimes she felt that she would like to see her. When she was asked to give the name and address of the father, she vehemently refused. When told that this was a necessary formality in arranging for adoption, she declared: "That is impossible. He does not know about the baby and is in New York."

She said that she would take full responsibility financially for the baby's care and was sure that everything would turn out all right. Once she was very pensive and said: "I never thought this could happen to me."

This is a typical utterance of girls in her situation.

Elsie was doubtless far beyond adolescence, but the whole atmosphere in her home contributed to making her seem somewhat juvenile. She planned to go back to the farm with her parents, eventually to take her teacher examinations in New York, and then to return home to work.

She refused persistently to give the father's name. He was a teacher and lived in New York. She assured us that there should be no difficulty in having the child adopted—his family were very good stock. She decided to leave Boston without seeing the baby, as she believed that this was the best thing to do. She would of course like to know how it was getting along.

She described how she had come back from school pregnant but told her mother nothing until her condition was obvious. She was very reticent about the whole matter and her parents did not know anything about the father of the child.

According to her mother, she had always been determined and stubborn, but all the family were fond of her.   Everyone in the agency was amazed at how cheerful and unconcerned she seemed—on the surface she took the situation too complacently. In a letter to the foster mother she wrote: "The baby has not been given a name.   I have no ideas about it . . . .   I would appreciate it if you would choose one."   She thus emphasized her emotional unconcern about the baby, who remained in the foster home until it was adoped.

After the summer vacation Elsie returned to Boston and told us what a good time she had had on the farm.   She had stayed with her parents and they had treated her "just grand."   They were neither oversolicitous nor evasive, but just as they had always been.   She had passed in her teacher examinations. She said laughingly: "I managed to keep myself busy."   When told that the baby had blue eyes she said in a gay but very impersonal and matter-of-fact manner, "I guess all babies have blue eyes."

Under pressure of the investigation necessary for arranging the adoption, she answered questions.   The father of her baby was a teacher in the school where she had taken her courses. She had known him for two years; she did not know very much about his family.   She had been attracted to him by his gay personality.   She had never told him about the baby, fearing that he would want her to have an abortion, and this, she felt, would have been scandalous and would have impaired her health.   They had never used contraceptives.   When it was pointed out that perhaps she really wanted a baby, she shyly admitted this.   On the other hand, she had rejected the idea of marriage because she would "never, never want to tie him down."

She did not think that he had very much money; he was ambitious, greatly interested in his career, and hoped to win a scholarship and continue his training.   He felt that his parents had done enough for him.   Asked whether she really thought that she would have tied him down, she answered in a thoughtful manner: "I don't really know."

An exact computation of her earnings and expenses made by herself showed that she would have nothing left for herself if she assumed the entire responsibility of the child. She said that it would not be too hard for her, she had it all planned out. Suddenly she said: "I would like to see the baby."

During the summer, when she had received word that the little girl was ill, she was so anxious about her that she had made up her mind to see the child when she got back to Boston.

She agreed that she had an inhibition against talking about her troubles: "I know there is some block that keeps me from talking about myself. I guess it might have been due to the way I was brought up. . . . I guess the real reason that I never confide in anybody is because I never really trusted anybody. It's my puritanical family—the way I was brought up. It's just that one must not display too much emotion or affection for anything. One realizes that it is there, but one does not express it . . . . I love my brothers and parents dearly, but I never express my affection for them. . . . Whenever I am depressed I play solitaire and try to think it through myself." All the time she preserved her quiet, friendly manner, and was very attractive and charming; she impressed everyone by her matter-of-factness. She insisted on adoption and responded to the baby on her visit to the foster home in a typical, detached fashion.

Elsie had never been able to confide in anyone. She had always been popular, but had never had any real friends. She was always changing schools and easily made new friends.

She described her family situation. She had a sister twelve years older than herself and long married, who rarely visited her parents and her four brothers. Elsie was the youngest in the family. Her brothers, she said, were "wonderful," and her parents were proud of them. In fact, she was the only girl at home and she knew that she was very much loved.

Her life had always been very easy, her parents and brothers had been so good to her, they had perhaps babied her a little.

Her sisters-in-law were not so inhibited and readily showed their emotions. She admitted eventually her jealousy of her sisters-in-law. Two of them had had babies at about the time when Elsie was pregnant.

Her mother had always told her that whatever happened, she could always come home. She felt very sorry for her parents—they had tried to be so nice to her. She had returned home when she was pregnant because, she said, "I always knew that whatever trouble any of us ever had, my parents would always want us to come to them."

She had not told her mother of her pregnancy immediately because she wanted to go back to school and finish her examinations, and felt that her mother would not let her continue if she knew of her condition. Her mother discovered it when it was no longer concealable and only then was the matter discussed. Concealment of the fact was the main concern and adoption was decided upon at once.

Elsie's attitude toward the father remained unchanged. She was always very unemotional when she talked about him. She said that when she found out that she was pregnant, she felt that she wanted never to see him again. She didn't know just why. She didn't want to get more deeply involved with him because she knew she didn't want to marry him. "I suppose some girls would think about it and worry," she said, "but I'm not that kind. I made up my mind what was to be done and did it."

She referred to the man as very attractive, "very outgoing with people, keen mentally . . . rather superficial." Here she stopped and refused to elaborate. Asked whether this trait had anything to do with her not going to him when she knew she was pregnant, she blurted out that she knew he would suggest only one thing—abortion—and that was absolutely against her principles. She agreed that not using contraceptives was "pretty dumb." She should have known better. She could not explain it.

She had no social grounds for not marrying the man. His family was just as good as hers. It was just that she didn't know whether he would want to marry her, and she supposed that "there was a lot of pride mixed up in it" somehow. She certainly wouldn't want to have him give up his work, as he might have to, if they married in order to keep the baby. She didn't want him to give that up for her.

She had never thought much of petting or carrying on with men. She had felt very guilty ever since her first intimate experience with Frank. She had never felt serious about anyone before she met him. He had often spoken to her of marriage: he would always say that when he finished this and this—then he would get married. Once during the interview she admitted that she had thought at one time that "it would be fine to marry him." But she felt that she did not want to marry him then when she was pregnant.

"Why?"

"Oh, I guess it would interfere with his plans. Besides, I did not care to marry him any more myself."

Asked whether she had thought at all about Frank's possible reaction to having a child, and whether she could approach him to help facilitate the adoption proceedings for the baby's sake, she answered that she had thought about this, but the answer still remained the same: she still wanted the adoption but did not want to approach him.

During the whole formal procedure of adoption, Elsie exhibited no sign of emotion. She usually spoke flatly and objectively about her relationship to the alleged father and to the child.

Before discussing the question of Elsie's illegitimate motherhood, it is necessary to arrive at a better understanding of her personality. She was an emotionally inhibited, cold person. She herself complained of her inability to show feelings, and denied having any. She was a lonely girl who longed to find not love but security and satisfaction in her own strength and independence. The deep causes of her emotional inhibition are unknown to us; we have only the scanty statements that she herself made about it. She referred to her background, and we can believe that she came from a milieu in which the parents love their children and declare themselves ready to do everything for them, but obviously avoid any display of tenderness in order not to make them soft. Elsie refused to express her feelings because of her disposition or probably as a result of her upbringing. Compelled from her earliest childhood strongly to repress (i.e., hide) her emotions, she later became unable to produce any or to enter into warm emotional contact with others. Up to her twenty-third year Elsie had never been in love and had had no intimate friends. Because she rejected all emotions, because she branded every emotional expression as exaggeration or weakness, she developed a strong inhibition of her entire emotional life that survived her childhood. Elsie compensated the lack of a warm feminine emotional life by overemphasizing her self-assurance and will power, and intensified her recourse to these qualities especially when she felt affected and endangered in her narcissistic self-love. In such instances she fought behind the bastion of her self-assurance after an even more radical emotional withdrawal from the outside world.

Elsie was a completely narcissistic person, bent upon proving shrewd and efficient in the struggle for existence. She considered herself independent and had the necessary self-confidence for proving her independence.

She was a scanty giver but a very exacting taker. She wanted to be sure that she was loved, but since she was wretchedly ignorant of emotional experience, she measured emotions by their objective proofs. And here I think was the root of her feminine and human misfortune. The situation in her home, where, after her sister married, she spent many years as the only girl and the youngest child, with several successful brothers, produced in her a double desire. She wanted to be strong like her brothers, to have a career as they did, and at the same time to be especially loved as the youngest and as a girl. Her feminine position at home was somewhat shaken by her sisters-in-law and she probably reacted to this by an intensified hunger for stronger, objective proofs of love.

Although she did not fall in love—she was unable to—she gladly let herself be loved by an intelligent and attractive man. Completely unawakened sexually, she had the typical attitude:

nothing could happen to her. The fact that she expected the man to take full responsibility for contraception shows that here her infantile narcissism won the upper hand over her proud self-reliance. In a moment of frankness, she admitted that she expected pregnancy (we can even conjecture that she provoked it). What were her motives? On the basis of our impression of her whole personality, we are entitled to assume that it was not the feminine, motherly longing of a loving woman but rather self-love that influenced her in this, as later in all her other decisions. We must not forget that two of her sisters-in-law expected babies when she became pregnant. Probably her first sexual relationship had given a definite content to her previously existing envy; she wanted to have a child too, and pregnancy would supply her with an objective yardstick for measuring the extent to which she was loved.

From the very beginning the voice of motherliness had been drowned out in Elsie by egoistic motives, for what she wanted was proof of being loved, rather than the fulfillment of her desire for motherhood. Narcissism is extremely sensitive in its processes, and Elsie, even before she thought of informing her lover of her pregnancy, perceived that in the circumstances she could not proudly march into marriage. The man loved his ambitious plans more than he loved her. Upon realizing this humiliating fact, she proudly withdrew into herself, and in a typical fashion enjoyed a narcissistic gratification by the detour of her sacrifice for him. Such concealment of pregnancy from the father of the child in order to be spared the deep humiliation of rejection is a frequent occurrence and a typical narcissistic reaction. The suggestion of an abortion on the part of the man is often felt by the woman as a severe and deep mortification, and many girls save their future relation to the man, and often to the male sex as a whole, by avoiding such a suggestion and choosing the difficult fate of an unmarried mother rather than abortion. Elsie consciously admitted this avoidance by referring to her "principles."

Elsie showed that she had brought her competition with her brothers into her love relation when she observed with a certain irony that she "wouldn't want to have him give up his work, as he might have to," if they married in order to keep the baby. She was unwilling to renounce her future plans for the sake of a motherhood that no longer gave her any narcissistic compensations, but only a baby. By her unconsciously desired pregnancy Elsie also achieved another goal that was perhaps more important for her at the moment. Since in her eyes love was measured by objective proofs, she gave her parents an opportunity to show that their promise with reference to "whatever trouble any of us ever had" was sincere. It is also very characteristic that in all these troubles she unswervingly followed her own plans.

Elsie was not incapable of maternal love. For brief moments a glimmer of femininity showed itself in her behavior; for instance, she was afraid of the danger of letting the child come close to her, and ran away from it.

The solution that a more materal and less egocentric woman would have found did not exist for Elsie. This solution would have been to value the possession of the child and its well-being more than the gratification of being boundlessly and self-sacrificingly loved by a man. This would have led to marriage and compromise.

We knew that Elsie's defensive mechanisms functioned so well that she would soon overcome the episode of her illegitimate motherhood; she was one of the very few women who can overcome such experiences without guilt feelings. She would silence such feelings by strictly fulfilling her duties, and without repentance. If she married she would be a model mother. The atmosphere around her child would be cold. Elsie's background would operate like a hereditary evil; in fact, her child would repeat the experience of her own childhood. It was because of this experience that she could so easily renounce her illegitimate child; and because of it, she would bestow tenderness upon a legitimate child only with reserve.

A less complicated example of a narcissistic reaction in an unmarried mother is offered by a comical episode that I witnessed personally. The incident took place in a European court. A middle-aged man, very highly placed socially, the respectable father of three grown-up children, was suddenly sued for support by a young man about 20 years of age. According to his mother's statements, the defendant was his natural father. The latter, a small, weak intellectual, appeared timid and inhibited. Almost paralyzed with surprise, he was confronted by an enormous fellow, a typical healthy peasant, twice as big as himself, who threw himself at his feet and said: "Little father, don't you want to recognize me?"

The alleged father's surprise seemed genuine.

The young man's mother, a healthy, aggressive peasant woman, stated that twenty-one years earlier she had been a servant girl in the city, that the defendant had visited her employer's son, that he had come to her room at night and there had had intercourse with her. As a result of this relationship, her son was born. Now, she said, she wanted to give this son an opportunity to be trained in a city trade, because he disliked life in the country as a laborer. She herself was happily married, the mother of two healthy legitimate children, and her husband thought it proper that not he but the natural father should take care of her first-born. The woman's attitude gave the impression that she was quite convinced of the justice of her case. She had obviously remembered the alleged father under the pressure of new life problems and had initiated a suit for support because of her ignorance of the statute of limitations. Although the defendant could not recall this episode of his youth, he was honest enough to admit that "it was after all possible that something like that had taken place." The judge asked the plaintiff the natural question: "If you were convinced at that time that this man was the father of your child, why did you not sue for support at once?"

Whereupon the robust woman exclaimed indignantly: "I did not want that son of a b—— to think that I needed him or his money."

The offended narcissism of a servant girl emotionally hurt

had made her assume the burden of supporting an illegitimate child in preference to appealing for help to a man who had used her only as an object of pleasure.

The character of a woman's reaction to her illegitimate child depends upon her outposts, the preparatory acts that have taken place in the preceding development. Legitimate motherhood too originates emotionally in the past. The psychologic conditions secondarily created by illegitimacy or primarily leading to it usually strengthen these outposts. The tendency of the young mother to "give back" the child to her own mother can be more easily gratified in an illegitimate situation. In some social circles the parental home is a depot for the daughters' illegitimate children, and the grandmothers in such homes consider it natural that they should take care of these children without any feeling of resentment over their illegitimate birth.

An illegitimate child fathered by a married man fits readily into the frame of the Oedipus complex. The realization of the masochistic fantasy about being left "on the street" with the illegitimate child of a seducer, is a very frequent variation of the puberal prostitution fantasy. Psychoanalysis shows us that the little girl's wish for a child has many components and each of them can be reactivated and lead to realization under certain circumstances.

The masochistic wish to be abandoned with the child has an aggressive counterpart in the wish to deprive the man of the child begotten by him, as an act of revenge. The wish for revenge is a consequence of the frustration experienced at the hands of the father in the past, which is now transferred to another man. The fantasy of the illegitimate child is extraordinarily frequent, and its determinants are many and varied: there is the masochistic Cinderella, who punishes herself as a deserted mother; we meet the vindictive "strong woman," who takes the child away from the man, and also the bisexual individual who does not even take the man into consideration in her parthenogenetic fantasies. All these individual motivations can later result in the conception of an illegitimate child or in definite reactions to the birth of such a child.

When we pointed out that adolescent fantasy life involves the danger of a break-through in the direction of acting out, we emphasized the fact that fantasies nevertheless usually manifest themselves in neurotic symptoms rather than in direct realizations. Many young girls dream of rape, suffer from hysterical vomiting or anorexia nervosa as expressions of pregnancy fantasies, insist upon being operated on, etc. Much more rarely are they raped, impregnated, etc., as a result of their own provocations, and this occurs only when their fantasies are accompanied by a real, emotionally irresistible motive or by a number of motives.

A mother's or an older sister's real pregnancy may provide the final stimulus to a premature or illegitimate realization of the wish for a child in a young girl, but only when destructive-sadistic motives in reference to the mother or sister, or masochistic motives directed against the self, break through the normal inhibitions and defense mechanisms.

Evelyn, whose difficult adolescence we have examined in detail (vol.1), was unable to halt the morbid acting out that had been provoked in her by definite events. After her prostitution escapades, her sleepless Cinderella nights on the stairs, her protest against her mother's new pregnancy, and her expressed intention to appropriate the child expected by her mother, she had an urge to make herself independent and to take indisputable and exclusive possession of the child. "I will be the first," she said, for her ambition was always to precede her older sisters in every experience.

We lost sight of Evelyn for many months. She hid herself from everyone who wanted to guard her against her evil fate, and she was able, driven by the fatalistic power of the unconscious, to transform her puberal fantasies into a masochistic orgy. She re-emerged only shortly before her delivery, when she dragged herself from the neighborhood of a military camp in California all the way back to her parents' home in Massachusetts. The father of her child was probably one man among many, "a guy named Joe," who could, however, easily be replaced by another Joe. All these real and yet unreal fathers, assuming their roles simultaneously or successively, combine into one inaccessible father.

Evelyn was placed in a maternity home; she had been enriched by a bitter experience, yet she remained the same as before. According to her, the girls at home wanted to talk to her about their boy friends as if she knew all about everything. She supposed it was because of the baby, but she was far from knowing everything about men. There was the danger that Evelyn would again run away blindly in order to "know everything."

"Funny how things have changed," she said. She felt like a stranger at home, even though they had been "so darn nice" to her—she knew that she had changed so much, but she was "dumb" about the others. She had not asked to come home; her mother had asked her to come back, she said.

The thing that worried her so, she said, was that, being in a maternity home, she would have to take care of her baby for five weeks. She did not want to keep the baby, but she was afraid that she would get so fond of it during that time that she would not be able to give it up. Her father and mother had told her that she could bring the baby home and that they would help her to take care of it, if that was what she wanted to do. She thought it was "swell" of them, but she took the attitude that as she was only 16 she "had no business being mother to a baby . . . "it wouldn't be fair to the baby." But she had thought so much about having a baby, and was always so crazy about the babies in her family, that she was afraid of this "five weeks business." There did not seem to be any way out of it, but it worried her.

Of course, said Evelyn, her mother was willing to take care of the baby, but that didn't seem right. Evelyn felt that the child belonged to her, but at home even with her own child she would be only an assistant mother, because she was not yet ready to be a real mother.

The last weeks of Evelyn's pregnancy were those of any

woman having her first child—full of impatience and increasing although denied fear. Asked whether she was afraid,
she sighed and said that she was not, then smiled sadly and
amended: "Very."

The fact of illegitimacy adds specific fears to the general
fears: in addition to the antithesis of death and life, and that
of hero and monster, there is the question: Shall I fulfill my
yearning or deny it? Let us recall Ida and Elsie, who simultaneously denied and admitted their yearning by choosing, like
Evelyn, to renounce the confrontation with their children in
order to avoid the danger of maternal feelings. We were able
to follow Evelyn's course before she became an unmarried
mother, and we know that all her behavior—her restlessness,
her flights from home, and finally her pregnancy—were the
results of severe puberal conflicts.

She wanted to be more experienced than her older sisters,
and, in competition with her mother, to have her own child.
She achieved this goal; she had a child, and her mother was
willing to take care of him. Evelyn consented and brought
her child home. Her motherhood failed to influence her
puberal behavior to any great extent; she soon began again
to wage her old hostile struggle against her mother. She was
still torn between two contradictory tendencies—the wish to
be free, and the wish to be a mother bound to her child.

Evelyn is particularly instructive for us, because we often
indulge in the deceptive hope that motherhood can favorably
influence the morbid acting-out tendencies of immature girls,
overlooking the fact that in such cases motherhood itself is
only part of the acting-out behavior. We know many unmarried mothers of Evelyn's type. Common to all of them
is the compulsive, blind realization of the immature wish for
a child. If this unconscious wish proves stronger than the
protective inhibitions, the girl is easily driven to biologic
motherhood without being psychologically capable of motherliness.

Some girls are from birth destined to be unmarried mothers.
It is a family tradition: grandmother, mother, aunts, sisters,

one after the other, have brought illegitimate children into the world and scattered them in foster homes or brought them to the grandmother.

Although there is usually no lack of respect for the grandmother, who also has had personal experience with illegitimacy, as a rule there is contempt for the mother. The girl's own nonachieved ego ideal says: "I shall not bring a bastard home." At an even younger age than her mother did it, barely on the threshold of adolescence, she becomes illegitimately pregnant, although she consciously rejects identification with her mother. If the bodily symptoms of an illness were involved, heredity could be held responsible; here one is inclined to speak of educational influences. I observed the fate of a family of very high social standing in which the dreadful *faux pas* occurred in three generations. My patient, who belonged to the last of these generations, and who was brought up in a convent school, had no idea that her mother and grandmother had perpetrated the same misdeed, and it was only in the course of a long analysis that the secret that she had guessed all her life was revealed as preconscious knowledge of the "family disgrace." In this case it was certainly not the educational influence of the environment but an ineluctable identification with the mother that entangled the girl in the same fate.

A girl of poor, proletarian family in which illegitimate motherhood had been traditional for generations, was very proud of the fact that she alone, among all the feminine members of her clan, married at the age of 25 without having given birth to an illegitimate child. She remained sterile for eight years after her marriage, and only gynecologic treatment enabled her to become pregnant. Whether she owed her unique position in her family to an organic deficiency, or whether her psychic defense extended even beyond the desired boundaries, is difficult to say.

F. Clothier[1] cites a case in which the girl's fateful identification with her mother led her with mathematical certainty to illegitimate motherhood.

[1] CLOTHIER, F.: Psychological implications of unmarried parenthood. Am. J. Orthopsychiat., vol. 13, 1943.

In some cases, the path that leads from fantasy to realization is very short, and the events that ordinarily take place in fantasies are starkly acted out in reality. Conception takes place under specific conditions that have nothing to do with love or sexual excitement. The psychic state of these girls excludes every possibility of self-control, so much so that one might say that they fall into a twilight state. In many cases there is even amnesia of the event, the girl denies her pregnancy or maintains in good faith that she has no idea how it happened. I know of a young minor who at first refused to hear of her pregnancy and later stated in court that she had been impregnated by the respectable father of her schoolmate. The accusation was revealed to be pseudologic, but the girl had a real gap in her memory as far as her impregnation was concerned, and "felt" that it was this man who was responsible. It is hard to say whether her pseudology was caused by a dark reminiscence of what is usually experienced in childhood as seduction by the father. It is noteworthy that in a real seduction by an older man, whom the seduced girl naturally identifies with her own father, the fact of pregnancy is denied with particular stubbornness and often until the last moment, as though the youngster wanted to say: "One cannot have a child by one's father."[2]

The morbid acting out, which unfortunately has inevitable biologic consequences, tends to be repeated, and a not inconsiderable number of cases of illegitimate motherhood with multiple pregnancies owe their existence to a blueprint fidelity in the repetition of the situation that leads to pregnancy. The event is then endowed with the character of a hysterical fit, sometimes even of a psychotic episode. Some of the cases observed by Beata Rank[3] seem to belong to this category.

In such cases the social agencies must cope with almost insurmountable difficulties. The fact that social-cultural prob-

---

[2] In an examination of sixteen unmarried mothers, Kasanin found various neurotic traits leading to neurotic acting out and illegitimate motherhood. Cf. KASANIN, J. AND HANDSCHIN, S.: Psychodynamic factors in illegitimacy. Am. J. Orthopsychiat., vol. II, 1941.

[3] RANK, B.: Unpublished.

lems are here mixed up with biologic, psychologic, and psycho-pathologic problems is responsible for these difficulties, and so far the progress accomplished in this field has been far from satisfactory.

The psychologic approach cannot change the fact that un-married mothers must also fight on a front that lies outside psychology. The social prejudices against the mother and child make it difficult to solve the psychologic conflict and to create the preconditions for a gratifying motherhood ex-perience. Thus the debate takes place between two tendencies. One represents the view that social assistance must first of all take the child into account and simultaneously free the mother from the social and psychologic burden of illegitimacy; the other strives to educate the illegitimate mother for mother-hood and to secure for her the most favorable conditions for achieving this goal. Clothier supports the first view, which is certainly more in harmony with reality.[4]

She justly criticizes the "rigid attitude among social workers that the baby should remain with the mother *at all costs*." She also questions the value of the trial period of several months during which the mother "must be given every op-portunity to decide herself whether or not to retain custody of her baby." As she states the case,

> By urging the mother to nurse her baby and permitting a mother-child relationship to develop, we put tremendous pressure on the mother to keep her baby .... The mother who after 1–6 months gives up her baby loses not only the product of her conception and whatever it may have stood for in her fantasy, but she also loses a baby with whose personality her own has become inextricably interwoven. Suckling, fondling, and caring for a baby have made it more consciously a part of her than ever it was in the uterus. Compare the loss of the mother whose baby dies at or within a few hours of birth with the bereavement of the mother who loses her baby during or after the nursing period.

Where the mother-child relation has followed a straight line of development, Clothier's argument can be accepted without reservations. But the psychology of motherhood under socially

[4] CLOTHIER, F.: Problems of illegitimacy. Ment. Hyg., vol. 30, 1941.

normal conditions has shown us that this relationship is often more complicated. We know that in the legitimate situation the child's position in the mother's emotional life is often influenced by the unconscious, and this is even more true in the illegitimate situation, which itself is often produced by unconscious motives. The unconscious also partly determines the role that the child will play after it has become a reality. The child's position in the mother's psychic life can turn out to be negative or positive; even under the most favorable conditions, the child may in the end be felt as a negative element, and in that event the mother's relationship to him is full of guilt feelings that arise from her unconscious hatred and protest against his existence. Similarly, both the unmarried and the married mother can enjoy the proud feeling of productivity and gratifying tenderness despite unfavorable conditions. Such a relationship with the child can overcome the conflicts arising from the struggle against the outside world and the fear created by it, if the mother has the requisite time and opportunities. Tactfulness and experience on the part of those who give help play a great part here.

The woman's real readiness to adjust herself to a difficult reality in favor of maternal love must not be confused with infantile ignorance of reality and denial of its difficulties. The least matu reamong unmarried mothers are the very ones who often fight to keep their children. Theirs is a struggle for a possession, not very different from that for a desired toy. In such cases the child is removed from the center of the emotional life after the first excitement of the will to possess has died down, and like a toy it is desired again after it has been taken away. Many a repetition of pregnancy in a youthful mother whose child has been taken away arises from this protest: "But I want my child after all."

Many young mothers are helpless and undecided about their motherhood and fall into even greater helplessness when they are given the freedom and right to decide. In all such cases, as in all the actions of children, external authority must step in, to assume not only responsibility for the child's subsequent real fate, but also responsibility before the inner court of the mother's immature personality. This assumption of responsibility is, psychologically speaking, equivalent to the creation of an ego ideal in the outside world to which the youthful ego can submit itself. The situation is the same as that in all the conflict-ridden puberal experiences in which the young struggle for independence, yet would gladly leave all the responsible decisions to the grownups. The fact that the young girl has gone through the purgatory of a serious experience does not always make her mature, and motherhood creates only a possibility of maturity, not maturity itself. The solution here should follow the path of an identification with an authoritative person. In this case command or advice is not sufficient; the outside influence is effective only as a direct offer of opportunity of identification for the weak ego.

Another group of unmarried mothers, while recognizing the real difficulties, are ready to tackle them in order to keep their children as possessions. They are the same aggressive women who, as married mothers, become overindulgent; with this feminine detour they gratify their aggressive masculinity through the child. They put into effect the parthenogenetic puberal fantasy to which I have repeatedly drawn attention: "I have a child born of me alone, I am its mother and father. I do not need or want a man for the begetting of a child."

I have also mentioned unmarried mothers who are fully conscious of this tendency (vol. 1, p. 123) and who give themselves the luxury of producing a child on their own, reducing the man's role to begetting. But in most cases this process is unconscious, and these very women often pursue the child's father with hostile demands, not out of their emotional need for a solicitous father for their children, but out of revenge and fury at the fact that he exists and was indispensable. It is just as impossible for understanding outsiders to influence the fate of the unfortunate child here as it is in the case of married mothers of this type.

Broadly speaking, the conflict of illegitimate motherhood

is fought out on two fronts. The first front is that of the relation to the immediate and the remote milieu. The social structure and the degree of the girl's and of her family's dependence are the decisive factors here. A *faux pas* in a respectable middle class family does not have the same implications as it has in a proletarian milieu; it is not the same when committed by an artist as it is when committed by a schoolteacher, etc.

The second front is the unmarried mother's inner life. Very often such women transfer the center of gravity of the conflict to outward reality and attempt to resolve it by renouncing the child. Here the inner world is disavowed, the woman is guided by the outside world, and she imagines that by adjusting herself to its demands she can achieve the *status quo ante*. This disavowal of the inner world is not always permanently successful, and often the principle of reality can be applied advantageously only if the woman has gone through the full conscious experience of frustration, disappointment, and renunciation. Otherwise she is exposed to the danger of a subsequent reaction such as we see in the following case.

Mr. Valentin, a well-to-do and cultivated business man, asked me to give psychiatric assistance to his 34-year-old wife, who refused to consult a psychiatrist herself. She maintained that she herself would eventually master the nervousness caused by her emotions, and, according to the physician who treated her, by her extreme physical exhaustion. Six months before, she had given birth to a healthy girl and had nursed the child for several weeks. Later, however, she was compelled to stop nursing the child as a result of her nervousness. She had had a number of sleepless nights and displayed increasing signs of agitation.

Mr. Valentin had married Lina, the patient, eight years before, as a widower and father of four children ranging in age from 6 to 12. The bride was a calm, well mannered girl who was employed as a bookkeeper in his office and was an excellent worker. Mr. Valentin was fifteen years older than his wife; when he met her he had been a widower for three years, and he felt that Lina could be a good mother to his children. Throughout their years together he had considered his marriage to be a blessing for all his family. Lina willingly gave up her job and devoted herself to the children, who clung to her as to their own mother. She was perhaps a little too soft and pampered them. She had never expressed a wish to have a child of her own and was glad that she had not become pregnant, because this might have disturbed the harmonious relationship between her and her stepchildren. But seven years after her marriage she did become pregnant, and the whole family looked forward with eagerness to the birth of her child. Her pregnancy and delivery were completely normal. But even during her confinement she displayed restlessness and impatience, refused to give her breasts to the child, and seemed completely changed toward her husband. After returning home she resumed her housekeeping duties. Her attitude toward the newborn baby was most peculiar. She refused to see it, neglected it completely, and, according to the statements of her neighbors and the older children, let the infant cry for hours without paying any attention to it. Mr. Valentin took care of it at night, because he felt that his wife needed rest, and when she slept, she slept very heavily right through the night. Mr. Valentin mentioned incidentally that before her marriage his wife had had an illegitimate child, but that she had long since solved this problem and that it played no role in their common life.

Finally Mrs. Valentin was induced to submit to psychotherapy and I was able to learn the psychologic motives of her depressive agitation.

She had been seduced at the age of 18, had given birth to a child, and had placed it for adoption immediately after delivery. The father was a young man whom she had known for several years. He had wooed her for a long time, and immediately after achieving his sexual goal and impregnating her, had deserted her. She considered her fate sealed, refused to get married when opportunities offered, and responded only to the wooing of the widower with children, feeling that in

marrying him she would be doing a good deed.   She informed
Mr. Valentin of her past and by his liberal attitude toward it
he earned her gratitude and respect.   She was very happy in
her marriage, loved her stepchildren as her own, and did not
think of the possibility of becoming pregnant.   She was overjoyed, however, when it became clear that she was about to
have a baby.   What tormented her now was that from the
beginning she had felt hatred and aversion for the newborn
child; she was unable to overcome her antipathy to it, and
feared that some day she would "do something" to it.   She
telt that it would be best for the "poor thing" if she left her
home until she recovered from her peculiar exhaustion.

The psychologic solution of the problem seemed obvious:
the birth of her new child mobilized the buried memories of
the past, and the guilt feelings associated with having given
away her illegitimate child prevented her from being a good
mother to the new one.   This interpretation tallied with the
real situation: she now wanted her legitimate and desired
child to suffer the same fate that had perhaps befallen her
illegitimate one.   She was a good stepmother to another
woman's children and a bad mother to her own child.   Her
guilt feeling derived its strength from the renewal of the old
situation.   Does this not indicate that the biologic tie between
mother and child cannot be dissolved with impunity?   It would
be incorrect to think that every woman who disavows her child
—as many young unmarried mothers do, under the pressure of
social demands—is exposed to this danger of psychic punishment.   Usually, the birth of a legitimate child erases the last
vestiges of the traumatic experience.   Such an experience
creates only a disposition to guilt feelings, or intensifies a
previously existing or subsequently acquired guilt.   The
woman's consciously good intention to secure a good future not
only for herself but also for her child through having him
adopted, can give rise to the unconscious idea "I have destroyed, killed my child."

Analysis proved clearly that in Mrs. Valentin's case the
guilt feelings were tenacious and inexorable because behind

her disavowed motherhood there was a heavy burden of previous guilt. She had been the oldest child in a family with many children. Her mother, as a result of a heart ailment, became crippled after giving birth to her last child and urgently needed the help of her oldest daughter. At first Mrs. Valentin had been a loving mother substitute, but her relation with her father did not develop very favorably. Soon her relation with her mother deteriorated too, and she decided to leave her parental home and become independent. Her love affair and her illegitimate motherhood constituted an initial repentance and self-punishment. The psychic gods of vengeance often like to transform atonement into a new guilt, and that very thing happened to Mrs. Valentin. Her marriage to the widower gave her an opportunity to repeat and correct the old situation of her girlhood: this time the motherless children found her a good mother. But here too fate pursued her, for her repentance became a new guilt: she was unconsciously reminded of the fact that she would have remained in her parents' home if her mother had cleared the way for her activities as substitute mother by dying, just as her husband's first wife had done. With such a heavy burden of guilt, she managed to preserve her psychic balance until her deepest wish—the wish to have her own child—was fulfilled; then the psychic line of toleration was crossed and she collapsed under the weight of her guilt feelings, again creating a new guilt by her act of self-punishment, for in her depression she justly accused herself of being a bad mother.

Mrs. Valentin adjusted herself excellently to the demand imposed by her struggle on the first front, i.e., that of reality, but postponed the solution of her struggle on the second front. This second front is that of the woman's own ego. In unmarried mothers there is a conflict between self-preservation and awakened motherhood. Although pregnancy and its fantasy experiences have not yet produced maternal feelings, they have, even under unfavorable conditions, mobilized a certain tender readiness that the woman's ego cannot renounce without a sacrifice. Clothier is quite right in thinking that motherliness grows with the care bestowed upon the child, and that the trauma of separation is the more intense, the longer the relation with the child has subsisted. But we must not overlook an important factor: we know how often confrontation with the bitterest reality is borne more easily than a psychic burden. Ida, Elsie, and Evelyn avoided contact with their children because, as they confessed, separation would otherwise have been too difficult for them: by this very fact they revealed the existence of emotions that they at the same time denied. The insight we have gained regarding abortion should also teach us to be cautious here: the separation from a child not really experienced in the outside world may constitute for the mother the loss of a part of her own ego.

The actually existent child from whom the mother has separated is and remains hourly and daily a real object whose fate is uncertain, and for which she may feel responsible unless she has completed her liberation. All kinds of guilt feelings— that constant burden of the human soul—are ready to be activated under suitable stimulation, and such a stimulation is supplied by an unresolved conflict about a child. It goes without saying that separation from the child will be the harder for the renouncing mother, the more love ties have been created between them. On the other hand, the later guilt reactions are the more effective in proportion as the mother has felt hateful and aggressive toward the undesired child. A mother who killed her child immediately after its birth, in a premeditated act prompted by social fear, stated before the court that she now felt great love for the child and wished to call it back to life in order to hold it in her arms and press it to herself: "I don't care what happens to me, for the child can't be given back to me."

She also frankly described the fury and hatred she had felt for the expected child and for the newborn infant before its death.

Under given circumstances it may be better for the mother to separate from a known and loved child than from an unknown and hated "something" that only subsequently, after separation, assumes concrete form in her imagination.

A decision in favor of motherhood nevertheless does not always guarantee a harmonious solution even if it has been taken after mature deliberation and realistically. The case of Mrs. Nawska, unmarried mother of a little girl, confirms this. I was able to follow her fate for several years. She lived in a Catholic town in Europe, and came of the petty nobility, among whom an illegitimate child represented the worst possible disgrace. She led a curiously isolated existence. The only teacher of French in her town, she gradually lost all her pupils from the good families, gave lessons to pupils of obscure origin, and earned her living partly as a fortune teller to servant girls. For many years she was seen wearing the same black dress, which gradually became green with age, while her little girl was always dressed with the greatest elegance. Up to her puberty, little Stella had the best that could be had in toys, dresses, etc. In public parks the mother and child always huddled close together, and Mrs. Nawska was very careful that her little ostracized Stella should not receive any social rebuff. Children willingly played with her, especially because the room that Mrs. Nawska occupied with her child was a place forbidden to the children by their parents. Moreover, Stella always had the best toys and the best books, and her mother took care of her and her friends much more tenderly and interestingly than did the other mothers. Mrs. Nawska always had the most delicious sweets, knew the most interesting fairy tales and the most exciting games. She herself seemed to be suffering from hunger, but she always gave alms to beggars with the words, "Pray for the soul of Otto Retlow."

The most striking fact about her was that she painted her face with white paint, through which custom she earned the nickname of "the pale countess." Otherwise her behavior was full of tact and dignity and showed no symptom of psychotic trouble. The ban put upon her by the little town and her social isolation gradually turned her into an eccentric.

Mrs. Nawska told me her story herself and I was able to

verify it. At the age of 18 she had met a young Austrian officer at a ball given by a Polish noble and soon developed a love relation with him. Since she was unable to produce the large sum of money demanded by the military hierarchy as a condition of her marriage to him, he decided to give up his military career. Meanwhile, fully certain of their common future, they continued their relation quite openly and as a result the girl's reactionary family threw her out of the parental home. She immediately made use of her good education to earn her living and became a teacher of languages.

Everything went according to plan, until one day the young man's mother summoned her and declared that if she really loved her son, she must for the time being renounce the idea of becoming his wife, because marriage would lay a burden upon him to which his weak constitution was unequal. She, as his mother, felt it her duty to protect her son. The young girl calmly accepted this declaration: the word "mother" deeply impressed her. It created in her the conviction that the other woman was acting for the highest interest of her son, and she immediately promised to separate from him. She did not wish to cause complications by telling him what had happened, and, taxing all her psychic strength, forced herself to declare to her beloved that she no longer loved him. She was then in the fourth month of her pregnancy, and told him that she was not sure that the child was his.

In view of the fact that Mrs. Nawska seems to have had an extraordinary fantasy life, we may assume that she found the strength for this masochistic renunciation by identifying herself with a heroic character in a novel. But the fact remains that, standing on her own feet, she struggled through her very hard life with her illegitimate child, that she preserved the most faithful and romantic love for her lover, that she worshiped her child and was always a self-sacrificing mother to her. Endowed with great feminine intuition, she wanted to bring up her child in the greatest respect for her father, which is so important for femininity. The fact that she had left him with a heroic gesture, and that he had not left her in disgrace, probably became for her a source of lifelong narcissistic gratification.

On one of our two fronts, Mrs. Nawska made a peace: she was happy in her motherhood and gave her illegitimate child the best that she could muster. On the second front (the social) her struggle continued throughout her life: she paid unremittingly for her transgression of the social commands, for her social guilt feeling, by her masochistic fate. She could surely have led a more dignified existence if she had moved to another town; she could also have made friends in a more liberal milieu. But she chose not only passively to yield to her fate as an outcast; she also actively emphasized her isolation by the pale mask she wore on her face like a badge.

As illustrating another unsuccessful attempt at resolving the conflict, we may instance the history of a contrasting type of illegitimate motherhood. Mrs. Rowley was a married woman of Italian descent, with many children. Owing to the extreme poverty of her family, she was for many years in contact with a social agency. During her numerous pregnancies Mrs. Rowley was often gravely ill with toxemia, high blood pressure, gallbladder infections, states of exhaustion, and other consequences of complete neglect of prenatal care. Her children were continually sick and the unfortunate mother sacrificed herself completely for them. Mr. Rowley too was often ill, usually at moments when the family situation was somewhat better. Although he was employed steadily, he was hardly adequate as a family supporter and filled a very modest job without making any effort to improve his earning opportunities. Apparently he completely lacked the urge to do so.

According to the records, Irma, the oldest child, aged 14 when her problem came up, was illegitimate. Her alleged father had deserted the mother and child to marry another woman. Very characteristically, the problem of Irma emerged only after several years of contact between Mrs. Rowley and the social agency. When the social worker gently broached the matter of Irma's paternity, Mrs. Rowley was embarrassed for a moment, then with a sigh of relief went on to tell the social worker what she had never dared to tell anyone else. She had been deeply concerned about Irma, who, it seemed, went to school under the name of Irma Arnold. At one time Mr. Rowley talked about adopting her, and Mrs. Rowley very much wanted him to do this, but the matter was repeatedly postponed, because Mr. Rowley said that he did not have the money to do it. She regretted that it had not been done earlier, and believed that Irma was now self-conscious and wondered about her name. Mrs. Rowley had never given her any explanation about it, although all the time the whole problem had weighed like a stone on her heart. She did not know what to do about it, but frankly admitted that she was very much worried about her first-born.

For one thing, Irma was a very quiet child, not care-free and happy like other girls of her age. The mother tried in every way possible to make her feel no different from her sisters and brothers, but she thought that Mr. Rowley, although he probably did not mean it to be so, was less fond of Irma than of the other children. This hurt Mrs. Rowley and as she talked about it the tears welled up in her eyes; she said that when Irma was small, she had had a chance to "give her away," but she loved her so much that she preferred to keep her. Although she liked all her children equally, she had to admit that if she had a favorite, it was Irma. She felt unhappy because she could not get Irma the clothes she needed to go back to school, but she had so many children to provide for that she couldn't see her way clear to getting Irma the things she ought to have. Irma had begun to show symptoms of the usual puberal rebellion, which was complicated by her knowledge or surmise of her illegitimacy. Not long before, some children had asked her whether her mother was married when she was born. Irma had not been able to answer this and had asked her mother about it. Mrs. Rowley's reply had been: "These children would do better to mind their own business."

When Mrs. Rowley talked about Irma, she kept her hand over her heart and wept on and off. She confessed that throughout the years she had shed many tears about Irma—she thought a lot about her and had always been anxious to change her name to Rowley. Irma had questioned her several times as to why her name was Arnold. Mrs. Rowley's only answer had been, "Well, aren't you the curious one."

She would like to change Irma's name now without talking to her about it, because she was so terribly afraid that Irma would run away from home if she found out that Mr. Rowley was not her father. Irma would often talk about children who had stepfathers and how mean they were to them; she said that she would never remain in a home with a stepfather. Mr. Rowley had always been very kind to Irma and treated her no differently from the other children. Mrs. Rowley felt that Irma should know the truth, but could not make up her mind to reveal it to her; she discouraged the girl from questioning her, and postponed the whole thing to some future date.

Mrs. Rowley worried a great deal about Irma's future. She was obviously obsessed by the fear that the girl would not be able to find a job with her telltale name, that it would make a difference to her future husband, etc. She would hate to have Irma unhappy because of something *she* had done. More than anything in the world, she wanted Irma to be happy. She suspected that many people knew the truth, and she did not know what they thought of Irma. Perhaps it would have been better to have had the girl adopted when she was a baby. But as soon as Irma was born and she saw the baby, she knew that she wanted to keep it. She was sure that she would always try to do the best she could for Irma. Now she wondered whether the girl was worrying about something, whether she was sad. Irma did not stay out late at night and was always careful to do just as her mother told her. Mrs. Rowley was thankful for that, as she would not want Irma to get into the difficulty that she herself had got into.

Mrs. Rowley's relation with Irma's father had gone over several years; they had always planned to get married, but they never had done so. When she met Mr. Rowley she told him about Irma, because she thought it best to have that settled beforehand. She knew a great many other women who had not told their husbands about such things and later there were all sorts of marital difficulties. She wanted to avoid this if possible.

She did not know whether they could afford to have Irma's name changed, but she would like to have it done as soon as possible. It was suggested to her that the best way of getting Irma's name changed was that of having Mr. Rowley to adopt her. The fee for this was only $5. At this Mrs. Rowley began to withdraw, asking whether it would be necessary to appear in court and to tell Irma about changing her name. She did not care about herself, Irma was the important one; she could not bear to see her daughter unhappy.

She knew that it was her guilty conscience that made her wonder so often how many people knew about Irma. She had worried about her daughter for so many years; when she went to the hospital because of illness, Irma was on her mind constantly. She was concerned lest her husband might not treat Irma as nicely then as he did when the mother was there. Sometimes she thought that she had become sick from worrying about all these things.

Sometimes she thought that her own mother's death was God's punishment visited upon her for becoming pregnant with Irma; her mother had died just before Irma was born. She thought that God had continued to punish her all through the years and that was why she had had so much trouble in her life. She felt that it was God's punishment that her children were always getting sick and that she never had enough money to live on.

Mrs. Rowley could not accept the idea of telling Irma the truth—even though she knew that this was the best thing to do. She feared that Irma would take a hateful, revengeful attitude. She confessed that she had had a thought that she would not dare to reveal even to her husband; the only person to whom she would tell it was the social worker. The thought

was that it was too bad that Irma had not died when she was
a little baby, because she was like a little angel then. If the
girl had died as a baby, she would not be facing all this now.

Then Mrs. Rowley started to speak about her repeated
pregnancies. She had told her husband that she did not
want another child, and he did not bother her very much. She
did not enjoy sexual relations particularly, because she was
always worried about having a baby. They never used any
means of contraception, nor did she ever do anything to herself after she became pregnant. She told how sick and fragile
her children were, complained about her misery, and returned
obsessively to her most burning problem, Irma. She was afraid
that some day quarrels might arise between her and Irma and
she might ask the girl to get out of the house, when actually
her resentment toward Irma was only because of the worry she
caused her. "Do you mean I really hate Irma?" she once
asked.

Mrs. Rowley also had other guilt reactions; everything she
did was under the sign of a bad conscience. She was always
apologetic and asked over and over whether this or that act of
hers had been right or wrong. She had no personal life, neglected her appearance and health, and was entirely absorbed
in her worries about her children, her pregnancies, and procurement of food for her family. She went to church at night so
that nobody would see her, because she was ashamed of the
way she looked; she felt that this was God's punishment for
what she had done in the past. There was always someone
sick in the family and she lived in constant fear that one of her
children would die. She also said she was worried for fear
that something might happen to Irma.

Whenever she began to recover a little from the family's
recurring economic crises, she became pregnant, sick, and then
neglected herself physically; whenever their financial situation
improved a little, either her husband or one of her children fell
ill; their expenses increased and her worries along with them.
She was threatened now with a new pregnancy and declared

that she was afraid that she would not be able to live through it; she had suffered too much during her previous pregnancies. When she actually became pregnant, she felt very much ashamed because, she said, it was wrong for her to have more children when they were already having such a difficult time. But still the problem of Irma preoccupied her most of all.

This is the story of a mother who thought that she had solved the problem of her illegitimate child. At the outset there is the mother's conscious or unconscious death wish against the "poor fatherless child . . . the poor angel." Her decision to have the child adopted would make the death wish unnecessary, but in the mother's guilt feeling placement for adoption can have the same meaning—"I have destroyed my child." We have seen how often a motherly feeling appears in unmarried mothers: it is perhaps accompanied by an old wish fantasy, perhaps the voice of conscience becomes very loud, perhaps a summation of motives leads the mother to decide in favor of the child: "I want to keep it." Then comes the life struggle, as in the case of Mrs. Nawska, although not always in such a grotesque form, or a favorable marriage solves the conflict and the illegitimate child has a chance to become a member of a legitimate family, as in Mrs. Rowley's case. In many cases, however, the shadow of the past hangs over the child's existence and it turns out that the solution of the conflict was only apparent.

The vital question is always: Does my husband really love my child? A living symbol reminds the mother of something she has consigned to oblivion, and the effects of the relinquished love for the father or of the subsequent hatred of him cannot easily come to rest, because the corpus delicti in the person of the illegitimate child constantly reopens the old wound. The now respectable mother is reminded of her disavowed past and anxiously tries to find in the heritage of her bad past a sign of an identity with the rejected part of her own ego. Mrs. Rowley feared that her daughter would become a runaway, thus expressing her worry that the girl would have an illegitimate child just as had happened to herself. She, like many others, believed in divine punishment. In Mrs. Rowley another guilt feeling accompanied the guilt of sexual sin: she thought that she had killed her mother by having an illegitimate child. The grandmother does not always die shortly before the birth of an illegitimate granddaughter, as in the case of Mrs. Rowley, but very often the blow inflicted upon the woman's mother by the disgrace weighs just as heavily in the daughter's guilt feelings.

Mrs. Rowley was caught between her conscious love for Irma and her constantly lurking hate feelings toward her; for this reason she was unable to tell her the truth and carried her oppressive secret as a constant burden.

She became pregnant repeatedly, and a strict taboo against birth control ruled over her conceptions and pregnancies. Hers were compulsive pregnancies to make her pay, by the misery of her legitimate motherhood, for having had an illegitimate child. She evidently used religious motives as a rationalization against birth control (although she had not feared to enter into an illegitimate relation with her first mate). In her unconscious she was a child murderer, and she refused to perpetrate a new sin by murdering other children (through birth control or abortion). Thus she used motherhood as a painful atonement, and since this did not effect much change in her hatred of her illegitimate child, she was compelled to be pregnant again and again. Her maternal joys were smothered under her worries, and the constant illnesses of her undernourished children only intensified her motherly guilt feelings instead of weakening them.

The fate of an illegitimate child accepted by the mother is not always as full of subsequent negations as in Mrs. Rowley's case, nor are the guilt reactions of the mother always so strong and the method of the struggle so bound up with the functions of motherhood. But in a great number of cases, the conflict between the self-preservation tendency and motherhood is made more acute and complicated by the ambivalence of the feelings for the illegitimate child.

Mrs. Valentin had her child adopted, and we have seen the severe conflict that flared up after several years as a result of this. Mrs. Nawska kept her child, paying for her maternal happiness with social misery. Mrs. Rowley struggled incessantly to transform her decision to keep her illegitimate child into maternal love.

We must admit that our psychologic understanding is still very incomplete; we never know how a decision that seems wise and in harmony with reality at the beginning will work out later.

A good solution should take both aspects into consideration —adjustment to outside reality, and understanding of the psychic forces. One should not try to adjust the woman to reality by making her yield to outside compulsion and renounce the child. Nor should one insist on the ideology of happiness through motherhood if the woman is psychically incapable of such realization under the given conditions. Since motherhood, as we have seen, is a complex psychologic problem that includes many components, those who are called upon to give social aid must take these components into consideration.

And we must not forget a truth that experience has taught us. In addition to the social problems of illegitimate motherhood, there is woman's profound need to love her child in a family triangle. For this reason it will not be enough to give social protection to unmarried mothers and to change social morality. A feminine woman needs this triangle, and if it is lacking, all the other emotional conflicts, on whatever front their solution is attempted, are intensified.

CHAPTER ELEVEN

Adoptive Mothers

I F the emotional experience of motherliness presupposed biologic motherhood, the psychic misery of a motherly woman yearning for motherhood though her body has proved sterile, would indeed be insurmountable. The somatic factor would triumph over the psychic, and as a result the existence of the barren woman would necessarily be one of constant and bitter frustration. We have pointed out in an earlier chapter that a genuinely motherly woman has the opportunity to divert her feelings from the immediate goal to another, sublimated end. The shortest way to achieve this is to substitute for the fruit of one's own body a helpless human being in need of maternal love and protection. An adoptive mother can be the full equivalent of a real mother in so far as the child is concerned, and whatever difficulties he may experience later are of secondary psychologic importance, if he is assured a sufficient amount of biologically determined gratifications and adequate emotional atmosphere. The biblical concept "bone of my bone and flesh of my flesh" has great power when the mother's relation to the child is determined less by the feelings of motherliness than by her narcissistic wish to continue in him her own physical ego. This wish, which is materialized in the enlargement of pregnancy, is frustrated in the mother whose child is not born of her own body. For the gratification of maternal love, however, and for expression of tender feeling toward a human being who needs it, as well as for exercise of the masochistic-feminine willingness to sacrifice, the adoption of a child affords a complete opportunity.

The woman's narcissistic pride in the product of her body can easily be transferred to the success she achieves through tender care, education, and personal influence in her relation with another woman's child. Love and continuous contact can make the adopted child her own as it were, and the fact that it is not of her blood can be forgotten after a relatively short time. Especially does a child adopted during the first months of his life, who from the beginning has been freed from the conditions in which he was born, who has not enjoyed any other maternal love than that given him by his adoptive mother, who has learned to think and feel as she does, cease to be a stranger for the motherly woman; he becomes a part of her own ego, just as precious and loved as if she had engendered him.

More particularly, a "child of sorrow," a child for whose life she must fight, a sickly child whom she has "saved," has all the chances of a child of the flesh with a motherly woman. A moving example of this is that of a young foster mother who found it so hard to separate from the child in her care that she induced the mother to let her adopt him. When someone protested to her that she could have her own children, she answered emphatically:"What do I care for children as yet unborn, when I love this child?"

The family triangle too, the foundations of which are normally laid in the act of fecundation, can be fully formed on the basis of mutually valued developmental goals, shared hopes for the future, and community in the care of an adopted child. The biologic disadvantage of his not being of his parents' own flesh and blood can be neutralized later by appropriate educational influences.

Our direct observations for the most part refer to situations that were optimal for the adoptive mother. Historically, a tremendous change has occurred in the procedure of adoption. It is amazing that in the past the will to motherhood by adoption of a child was undaunted by the tremendous difficulties that had to be overcome. When we recall that in the last century in Germany a woman was not permitted to adopt a child before she was 50 years of age, that in France a child could be adopted only after reaching the age of 21, and that in America the anonymity of the natural and of the adoptive parents has been safeguarded only in recent years, we realize what enormous progress has been made. Today we can secure the most favorable conditions for adoption by study of the subtle psychologic processes in both the parents and the children involved.

Much has been said and written about the psychology of the adopted child, less about the psychology of the adoptive mother. Yet the primary cause of the adopted child's psychologic reactions lies not so much in the circumstances of his birth as in the effects of this reality on his environment, above all on his adoptive mother; only from her does the influence extend secondarily to the child.

To understand the adoptive mother as an individual and as a type, two factors must be considered—the woman's capacities for motherliness in her relations with the adoptive child, and her motives for adoption. It goes without saying that we are here disregarding all motives of a practical or social character and are interested only in those cases in which a purely emotional motive is present.

When a woman's longing to be a mother is not gratified by children of her own, and when she seeks a substitute by the most natural method, namely, adoption, the question arises as to why she has no children of her own. In the course of our discussion we have met various types of women who long for children but are unable to gratify this longing directly, owing to unresolved psychic conflicts. We have seen the midwife (chap. 11) who out of fear of the biologic functions was obliged to content herself with presiding over the delivery of other women's children, and Unamuno's Aunt Tula, who despised sexuality to such an extent that she could gratify her ardent motherliness only by exploiting the sexual service of other women. We have seen the androgynous woman who withdraws from female reproductive tasks and yet wants to create and shape a human being after her own image, and the woman whose eroticism has remained fixed in homosexuality and whose yearning for a child derives from the profound source of her own mother relationship. Many such women renounce men, but gratify the wish for a child by adoption.

Among these single adoptive mothers there are some excellent women who are so tactful and have so much insight for the needs of the child that they find ways and means to bridge socially and emotionally a situation that is abnormal for the child. Their position is like that of unmarried mothers, with the difference that the latter are condemned by society, while the former are only considered dubious. The amount of neurotic tension that produces this socially and emotionally unfinished situation determines the child's fate. Those cases in which the motive of the adoption is rooted in the parthenogenetic fantasy "I do not need a man for that" usually end, so far as I have been able to observe, in relinquishment of the child as soon as he begins to make stronger demands on the mother. Unfortunately, the financial, intellectual, and ethical standards of the prospective adoptive mother are more carefully considered than her emotional balance when her fitness for adopting a child is being judged.

The situation is different when an unmarried woman adopts a child not primarily because of her own urge to do so but because a motherless child needs her as a mother substitute. An aging spinster who out of pity undertakes to care for an orphaned child is completely unlike the bachelor girl who wants to have a child. The danger of a woman of the "motherly aunt" type often lies in the extravagance of her motherly happiness. She regards the adopted child as an unexpected gift of fate, and because of this feeling of gratitude or obligation she creates an excessively soft and tolerant atmosphere for her charge.

Sometimes two women friends who live together are psychologically so much like a married couple that they need to be complemented and to form a triangle. I have observed several cases of sublimated relationship between two women friends whose feminine longing, combined with their masculine urge for a permanent accomplishment, led to the adoption of one or more children. The allocation of roles was not clear and apparently the two women played both roles, those of father and mother, just as is often the case in unsublimated overt homosexual relationships in which both partners are bisexual. My personal impression is that the masculine principle in such family units is represented by the excessive intellectualization of the relationship to the child. These female couples engage in psychologic-pedagogic observations and experiments, aspire to give their adopted child a perfect education, and the outsider has often the paradoxic and slightly comical impression that their manless menage lacks a feminine member.

The largest proportion of adoptive parents, however, is recruited from among sterile married couples. Here the psychology of the adoptive mother is largely determined by the psychologic motives for sterility (if any) and by the woman's reaction to her renunciation. Has her fear of the reproductive function proved stronger than her wish to be a mother? Is she still so much a child that she cannot emotionally and unconsciously decide to assume the responsible role of mother? Is she so much absorbed emotionally in other life tasks that she fears motherhood? Is her relationship with her husband so gratifying and fulfilling that she fears a change in the *status quo*? Does she think that her husband should not be burdened with the tasks of real fatherhood? Does the threatening and forbidding voice of her mother speak from the depths of her old guilt feelings? Does she think that her body has been injured by forbidden actions? Does she hold her husband responsible for her childlessness? Does a deeply unconscious curse of heredity burden all her motherly wish fantasies? And, above all, has the sterile woman overcome the narcissistic mortification of her inferiority as a woman to such an extent that she is willing to give the child, as object, full maternal love?

If a woman has consciously made up her mind to adopt a child all these questions are unimportant, and she is only later confronted with the task of overcoming all the remaining unconscious obstacles. Many women mature to the stage of motherhood only when they have a child; many, even in relations with children of their own, struggle against unconscious difficulties that have not hindered the reproductive functions but nevertheless have created either physiologic or psychic disturbances.

The hopes, fears, and worries of the adoptive mother are largely the same as those of the natural mother: she wants her own ideals and wishes fulfilled in the child, she wants to make real the "hero birth myth." In both cases, the disappointments are absorbed in maternal love, and the demands in regard to the child's destiny grow more modest. If the mother's narcissism remains uncompromising and the demands upon the child are not reduced, the adoptive mother's disappointment reactions are more ready to manifest themselves than the natural mother's in the attempt to blame reality for her disappointment: "It is not my child."

The natural mother's fear of heredity can have an actual physiologic basis in a family that is really tainted. If the woman is predisposed to emphasize the pessimistic aspects of life, her joy in the child is disturbed by her fears of bad heredity and these fears often exert an unfavorable influence on the child's free development. This fear can also have a psychologic source: the mother's hostile feelings toward members of her family, especially toward her husband, create in her a tendency to be on the alert for expressions of hereditary traits; indeed, she will try to discover and often will provoke manifestation of them in her own child. Sometimes the familiar fear of giving birth to a monster, accompanies—in a very mild form—the mother's relation to a normal child and in her hypochondriac fantasies makes him the innocent victim of her unconscious sins. From similar psychologic motives, more deeply rooted and without foundation in reality, the adoptive mother will anxiously watch for signs of bad heredity in her adoptive child. All the fears and worries that would, in a different form and without apparent justification, relate to a child of her own, will now lead to the seemingly justified question: "How can we know?"

An aggressive mother who tends to suppress every urge to independent, spontaneous activity in her child, will justify her attitude by her fear of the unknown in the adopted child and claim that every manifestation of a foreign will must be promptly suppressed. A masochistic mother allows the adopted child to develop his aggressions without restraint, in order perhaps to bring nearer to realization a deeply rooted fantasy— that of being "killed" by the father and now by the son. She experiences this self-provoked aggression as the effect of a hereditary curse in the adopted child. A woman whom I knew to be very masochistic was really murdered by her sister's illegitimate son, whom she had adopted. Later it was discovered that her upbringing of the boy had been faulty, because it was based on her masochism and her constant fear of his heredity. In another case, the mother of a vigorous and kind adopted son had a severe anxiety neurosis because of a dream of the boy's that he imprudently recounted to her; in the dream an unknown man attacked his mother with a knife. This dream confirmed her long-nursed fears: "one never knows." And although she had never been superstitious, the woman saw in this dream, so typical from the psychoanalytic viewpoint, a portent that her son would slay her, his adoptive mother.

All the difficulties of children that adults usually do not understand, and for which every mother seeks an explanation, are endowed, where adopted children are concerned, with the character of something inborn. Why does the child have fears at night? Why does he have fits of anger? Later comes the problem that is the most difficult for the mother to accept and understand: "Why does he hate me, when I am so good to him?" The child's normal conflicts of liberation, accompanied by hostility toward the parents, are interpreted as signs that he does not "belong" to the family. The adopted child's insecurity is fed by the mother's insecurity, and a vicious circle arises, in which the mother's anxious question— "Does he love me as my own child would?"—is answered by a similar question on the part of the child: "Who are my real parents? Am I loved like a blood child?"

"Blood is thicker than water," says the adoptive mother. She does not realize that it is only her fantasy that leads her to interpret the child's behavior, under the magnifying glass of her fears, as a manifestation of bad heredity. Actually this

behavior is mobilized in the child by the suggestive force of
her suspicion, and he driven by that force to a kind of compulsive acting out.

Such an interaction between the horrified, anxiously watchful
attitude of the adoptive mother and the reactions of her adopted
child is illustrated by the following case.

Mrs. Asman, aged 26, of Russian-Jewish descent, came to a
social agency for help in finding a domestic to stay with her
three children, Anne, aged 7, Helen, aged 6, and John, who
was 4, while she went to work in a dyeing establishment. She
looked somewhat hard-boiled, sullen, inarticulate, and unhappy. She said that it was necessary for her to work
because her husband, from whom she had separated two years
before, gave her very little financial support. However, she
would have preferred to be at home with the children, as she
worried about them while at work.

When the social service index was mentioned she asked for
help in learning about her own mother. At the time of her
marriage she and Mr. Asman had gone to the city hall for
birth certificates and she had learned only then that she had
been adopted and that she was the illegitimate child of an
unidentified soldier. Her adoptive mother had died two years
before she came to the agency and her adoptive father some
years earlier. She described her life with her adoptive parents,
who were Russians, as unhappy, because her mother was so
strict. She left high school against her mother's advice and
went to work in a candy shop, where she stayed several years.
Her mother did not allow her to enjoy normal recreation and
freedom and watched and escorted her carefully. Occasionally,
Mrs. Asman suspected that she was an adopted child, but
this was always denied by her parents.

At 21 she married Mr. Asman, whom she had never loved
or found attractive. Her adoptive mother did not approve
of him, but she married him "for freedom" and in order to have
a good time "going places." For a brief time she was happy
to be going out so much, but gradually her husband went back
to his street corner gang, gambled, and left her alone frequently

in the evening. When the children came Mrs. Asman became absorbed in them. Some years later she met an Irishman named George, an unemployed waiter, who was also unhappily married. She fell in love with him and after a few months arranged a separation from her husband. It was clear to Mr. Asman that she did not care for him, and he left the house but continued to support the children.

After some months George and Mrs. Asman were arrested in the latter's home, having been reported to the police by George's wife and brought into court. Mrs. Asman was sullen before the judge and received a suspended sentence on an adultery charge and on a second charge of neglecting her children. The latter was based on angry statements made in court by Mr. Asman about her leaving the children alone in the house, etc. She was placed on probation, warned to stay away from George, and custody of the children was given to Mr. Asman.

Mrs. Asman later obtained the custody of her children, as they were improperly cared for by her husband. She went to work again, since her husband gave her only slight financial support, and hired a domestic to care for the children. Her husband refused to divorce her. She said that she still loved George and would marry him if he were free, but she denied that she was continuing her relationship with him. The social worker realized that Mrs. Asman could not confide in her because she was, in the woman's eyes, a representative of the law.

Mrs. Asman had given birth to a baby boy and had planned to conceal this from her husband and from the court, but Mr. Asman had discovered it and gone to the judge. In court his wife stated that the child was his, though it was not. Her probation was continued. George was still very much in the picture and was the baby's father.

Mr. Asman was rather limited both in intelligence and in character; he was impulsive and somewhat immature. However, he behaved extremely well and generously, in view of the whole situation. He had always suffered from the fact that his wife did not want him. He was still fond of her and would have resumed living with her if she had desired it. He said of her: "I've got nothing against her, she's a good kid and a good mother, but the girl just can't keep out of trouble. Help her out of one fix and she'll get into another. She doesn't know how to take care of herself."

George was also a problem. He was sincere in his feelings toward Mrs. Asman, but very much confused because of his deep love for his own children, whom his wife threatened to keep from him in the event of a divorce. She refused to give him a divorce, at least for the moment, and at the time when Mrs. Asman returned to the agency he was living with his wife and spending less time than formerly at Mrs. Asman's home. He appeared to have little initiative or ability to straighten out the whole affair, being a rather gentle and somewhat passive person.

Mrs. Asman's relationship to her children was interesting. She had a fierce determination to keep them with her, seemed to love them very much, gave them excellent care, and handled them quite well. She had some fears about possible delinquency in them, owing to her uncertain heredity, and asked again and again what would be best for them. She reiterated frequently that her husband was never interested in the children, and said that she first became interested in George because of the interest he showed in her children.

Mrs. Asman seemed to be somewhat confused and at first it was difficult to understand her. Only gradually was it possible to get behind her confusion. As a child, she said, when she did not know that she was an adopted daughter, she found something strange in her mother's behavior. Her mother was too strict with her, practically never allowed her to go out with other girls and boys, and watched over her as though she were a bad girl. "She distrusted me, although there was no reason for her to do so," said Mrs. Asman.

No other mother whom she knew wanted to have her daughter's love and attention as much as her mother did. She was not permitted to have friendships with other girls and was prevented from having contacts with boys: "She wanted me all to herself—she was kind of jealous."

When the girl was 12 years old, her cousin told her that she was an adopted child, but her mother emphatically denied this. The child accepted the denial but somewhere inside her a suspicion remained, and from then on mother and daughter constantly watched each other. The mother had fears about the daughter's behavior, and the girl, obscurely understanding her mother, believed her cousin's statement because she had suspected the facts before.

From then on she interpreted everything her mother wanted to do for her not as a sign of love, but as a compulsion, and she protested against it with defiance and hatred. The adoptive mother had apparently conceived an educational ideal formed in opposition to the character of the girl's natural mother: she wanted to make her a virtuous, cultivated little lady, and was ready to make any sacrifice to give her a higher education. The child was not lazy, but she left school, refused to continue her education, and brutally destroyed her adoptive mother's educational program. She felt cheated, responded to distrust with distrust and, out of protest, became the opposite of what the mother wanted and expected her to be—all this not because it was "in her blood," but because her mother's anxious, suspicious behavior drove her to it. She married the first boy she met, not because she loved him, but because she wanted to be free from the compulsion to which she was subjected in her home—and perhaps in order to protect herself quickly from the fate that her adoptive mother feared so much.

In the depths of her mistrust the girl must have sensed why her adoptive mother watched her every step with such strictness, "although it wasn't necessary." Perhaps the child had at an early date formed her idea of her natural mother as embodying a contrast to her adoptive mother's educational tendencies, and in her defiant rebellion identified herself with the imagined mother, in opposition to her adoptive mother. Later, when she was "accidentally" confronted with the real facts, her suspicions received a most realistic confirmation, for she found out she was the daughter of nameless soldier and a prostitute.

When she came to the agency she was a tender and loving mother, but she had to leave her children in order compulsively to repeat her own history with regard to them. She said herself that she knew it was better for the children "to have their father and mother together," but she was unable to achieve this.

She had a legitimate husband, yet she could not avoid the fate of bringing an illegitimate child into the world. Characteristically, for this birth she gave her own name in the maternity hospital, although she had the right to use her husband's name. She was torn between her genuine wish to have a home, a regular married life, and a socially adjusted existence, and the wish to lead an unsheltered and harried illegitimate existence. She sought help from the social service workers, who were kind to her, but felt compelled to repeat in relation to them her fatal game with her adoptive mother: she distrusted them, lied to them, concealed her self-destructive intentions, and opposed their counsel, although she subsequently realized that it would have been much better if she had earlier followed her adoptive mother's advice and now the social workers'.

The hereditary trend appeared to be continuing. Mrs. Asman was well on her way to repeating, with her children, her own experience as a child abandoned by its mother; but in her double identification she also imitated her adoptive mother and began to express concern that her children might become "criminal," like herself and her natural mother.

The life story of this adopted daughter who fell into psychic confusion casts retrospective light on the psychology of her adoptive mother who, because of her own watchful anxiety, had driven the girl into "heredity," in this case into identification with her natural mother. The concealment of the truth and its accidental disclosure seem to be responsible for Mrs. Asman's fate.

In other cases the hereditary evil feared and observed by the worried adoptive mother turns out to be only a projection of her own repressed tendencies. She identifies the child with a rejected part of her ego and naïvely refers to it as a trait inherited from an unknown mother. The following case offers an interesting illustration of this.

Martha, a 12-year-old girl, was referred to a social agency by her adoptive mother. For the application interview, Mrs. Brooks came with a woman friend. She gave her name at the switchboard as Julia Brooks and was announced to the worker as Miss Brooks. Several times during the interview the social worker called her Miss Brooks and was not corrected. Mrs. Brooks never referred to the adoptive father except as "he." All these factors, the girl's problem, and an indefinable quality about the woman, led the social worker to believe that she was not married, so that the worker when filling out the application blank was surprised to learn that she had a husband. Mrs. Brooks seemed very anxious about the girl's problem and thoroughly cooperative. She stated that the girl was subject to violent temper tantrums and frequently beat up the children in the neighborhood, particularly the boys. She was erratic in her school work and her teachers felt that her mind was not on her studies. In the application interview Mrs. Brooks told of sex play between Martha and a neighbor, Kate, aged 14. She observed it particularly on a night that Kate spent in their house, sleeping in the same bed with Martha. Mrs. Brooks heard some evidently harmless words that made her suspect that the two girls were masturbating. Later she learned that for some time Martha had been the instigator of considerable voyeuristic activity in the woods back of the house, with both boys and girls. The girl had displayed herself to the boys and had persuaded them to do the same, saying: "I'll show you that we are no different."

Mrs. Brooks was very cooperative and seemed to face the problems that emerged very well, and to be making a great effort to deal wisely with the situation. Martha never had a close relationship with the woman psychiatrist and never trusted her. This was rather characteristic of her, for on the whole she did not form close attachments, except for her occasional crushes. Mrs Brooks thought that she was most fond of her maternal grandmother. Martha knew that she could rely upon her adoptive parents' affection for her, but never really reciprocated her adoptive father's strong love.

Mrs. Brooks was the second oldest of five children; she had one older sister and three younger brothers. She described her mother as of less cultured family than her father and as a domineering, aggressive woman who wanted to keep control of all her children. Mrs. Brooks said that in her childhood she was occasionally furiously angry with her mother and at such times went to sit outdoors until her anger cooled.

Neither Mrs. Brooks nor her sister ever succeeded in becoming pregnant, and each of them adopted two children. Mrs. Brooks had gone to Radcliffe for two years and wanted to continue, but her mother was opposed to spending the required money, so she went to work in a factory and took night courses to complete her college education. She was very bitter toward her mother for this attitude, saying of her: "She tried to ruin my life." The mother was also opposed to this daughter's marriage, and Mrs. Brooks said that once when she was ill during her engagement she overheard her mother say: "I'll make her give him up. I've always controlled her and I always will."

At this point Mrs. Brooks made up her mind that even "if Mr. Brooks had been coal black" she would have married him. They were married for nine years before they adopted Martha; Mrs. Brooks had tried various devices prescribed by doctors in the hope of becoming pregnant. It was she who particularly wanted to adopt a child. They looked for a baby to adopt for quite a long while, both of them being determined to have a girl.

The child was the illegitimate daughter of a French mother. Mrs. Brooks refused to let the people who placed the child tell her anything about its background, and also tried to keep the maternal grandmother from finding out anything about it. She insisted upon putting through the adoption papers three or four months after she took the baby, instead of waiting the customary length of time. It was in court at the time of the adoption that Mrs. Brooks saw the girl's own name for the first time—Lafontaine. She suddenly realized that the little girl's features were French and was quite stunned at the discovery that the child was of different nationality. She was upset and depressed over the matter for two days, but after that time felt no real difference between herself and the girl. However, she wished that occasionally she were better equipped to understand Martha's temperament. About a month after the adoption, Mrs. Brooks was buying a dress in a cheap little dress store and saw a young factory worker with French features looking at dresses. Suddenly the thought came to her, "This might be the mother of my child."

This was an isolated instance in her experience. She was unaware of having had similar feelings at any other time.

In the course of the interviews, Mrs. Brooks talked a great deal about various women friends of hers and about her outside interests. She frequently mentioned one of these friends, a teacher, who accompanied her at the time of the application. She also had a woman friend who was a responsible official in one of the state institutions, whose advice she had often asked. She told an involved story about a Canadian girl who came down for the summer and made advances to a girl whom they all knew. This was the first time that Mrs. Brooks became aware that there is such a thing as homosexuality. She later told of a nurse, a friend of hers, who had visited frequently in her home and who was very peculiar. This nurse was the first person who told her about masturbation. Mrs. Brooks had many outside interests, was very active in a feminist organization, was chairwoman of various clubs, etc. Sometimes her husband was annoyed with her for devoting so much time to things outside the home.

In the first interview Mrs. Brooks said that the children had been told about their adoption and that neither of them had shown any particular reaction to it or referred to it since. The social worker in her interview with Martha mentioned the fact of Martha's being adopted. Martha was as if struck by a bomb. Gasping, she asked: "What are you talking about?"

When questioned, Mrs. Brooks said that she did not use the word "adopted," and that Martha, puzzled about where babies come from, had merely assumed that most babies come from a store and that Mrs. Brooks had bought her at a hospital. However, after this talk Mrs. Brooks made a clean breast of the situation and answered every question Martha asked. The girl reacted very well and was overjoyed to learn that her cousins were also adopted.

During all the interviews Mrs. Brooks blamed her own mother for everything. She described her mother not only as aggressive, but also as very masculine and "very possessive—she wanted to possess her children, body and soul." She also said that her mother had always wanted her to sleep with her. She also willingly took her granddaughter Martha into her bed. Mrs. Brooks had disliked this, although she still liked to sleep with her mother. She wanted to know why people want to sleep with their mothers.

Mrs. Brooks had obviously fled from her mother dependence into marriage. Her mother's character, as she described it, was largely identical with her own: there was the same aggressiveness, masculine behavior, and possessiveness with regard to the children, and above all there was the physical attachment of the daughter to the mother. Mrs. Brooks slept with Martha, just as her own mother had slept with her. She felt that this was not the right thing to do, but continued to do it even after she was advised not to.

She was in a panic about her adopted daughter because the latter was boyish. The Damocles' sword of homosexuality constantly hung over the girl's head, and sexual curiosity, exhibitionism, and above all masturbation were the mortal sins from which Mrs. Brooks wanted to protect her soul.

All the material she presented proved unmistakably that she projected her fear of her own homosexuality into the child and that her own guilt feeling about masturbation made her spy upon Martha. She noticed little things, just like a paranoic, and interpreted them in a manner that fitted in with her fears.

Some years before, she had observed a homosexual relationship between two girls, which horrified and disgusted her. She had the impression that there was a certain "strange," aggressive quality in the friendship of Martha and Kate. She was disturbed also because "sometimes Martha looked at boys with a very queer expression." She was also alarmed by the fact that Martha had boyish tendencies, played like a boy, etc. She said that she had once known someone who was like that (obviously herself).

Mrs. Brooks carefully watched the development of Martha's sexuality, and it was interesting to note how closely she associated the two problems of adoption and sexuality. Thus she enlightened the child about both things simultaneously, as though they were related.

She struggled against Martha's masturbation, told her that "her body was a sacred thing and must not be played with." It was sacred because at some time she would have a baby. Shortly before that, Mrs. Brooks told Martha that she had waited eight years for a baby and that God had not given it to her. In this, she obviously made an unconscious confession of her own "destructive" play with her body. There was no doubt that Mrs. Brooks had her own ideal of chastity, that she was frigid, and that her sterility was connected with the idea that she had destroyed her femininity by masturbation. She blamed her own mother for Martha's sins: "They are very close—they are two of a kind."

During her interviews she constantly returned to the theme of her adopted daughter's foreign origin. Obviously she thought that the girl's own background played a great part in her abnormal behavior. She also constantly revealed her accusations against her own mother, and her feelings of guilt—a striking illustration of the projection of the mother's own repressed tendencies into her child. But in the background there lurked the idea of heredity, of the French mother who had had an illegitimate child, who abused her body for sexual things, and from whom Martha had inherited some of her traits. Mrs. Brooks had not yet clearly formulated this anxious accusation; she still divided the responsibility for the bad influences between her own mother and the child's illegitimate mother. But many adoptive mothers consciously direct all their accusations and morbid fears against the "stranger," whoever she may be.

Another case of adoption shows clearly how the whole situation can be influenced by the adoptive mother's unconscious tendencies. As usual, we gained an insight into this mother's problems when she asked for aid with regard to her adopted child. Mrs. Slutsky came to the agency asking for help in controlling her "niece," aged 12. She reported that the girl stole money, refused to obey, was sulky, played like a boy, and wanted to wear boy's clothing. The school commented that though the aunt was seeking help for Rose, she was in definite need of it herself. Rose's school work was satisfactory, the teachers reported that she was a quiet, inconspicuous girl who, when the visiting teacher talked to her, refused to admit any difficulties but was willing to see the social worker. The girl tended to minimize the problem and talked a great deal about her aunt's illness, fatigue, and efforts to "dose herself."

Mrs. Slutsky was a pleasant, sociable person. She had adopted Rose, who was her sister's child, as a baby. For twenty years Mrs. Slutsky managed a cafeteria not far from Boston, and her parents lived with her. She spoke with particular feeling about her mother, who had died three years before, describing her as a "beautiful, kind person who adored Rose also, and actually breathed for her, she was so fond of her." She also said that her mother was an independent person, and that their relationship was extremely close. After her mother died she kept the cafeteria till her father died—this had occurred some months before she came to the agency—and then she moved to another house in another suburb of Boston to give Rose a new home.

Her marriage to Mr. Slutsky took place soon after her mother's death. She revealed that she had been engaged for ten years to another suitor, but could not marry while her mother was still alive. Her fiancé was a sociable person who liked good times, and she had been afraid that if she did marry him things would be difficult in regard to Rose. He had told her that she would have to get someone to take care of Rose and she did not see how she could do this, since she had accepted the girl as her responsibility. Therefore she decided to marry Mr. Slutsky instead of her fiancé, because he seemed a quiet, home-loving type of man and in living with him she could give Rose more time and a better home life. Mr. Slutsky was twenty years older and had proved to be a good friend, but Mrs. Slutsky now felt that the marriage was a mistake as far as Rose was concerned, because her husband was too reserved with her and evidently wanted her out of the way.

Mrs. Slutsky's description of her marriage and its effect on Rose showed that Rose was upset and cried considerably. For that reason, she continued after her marriage to share a room with Rose, except at the very first; however, during this short period she went to sleep with Rose first, and then left her to go to her husband's room. She was worried about the tension in the home and described herself as being in a difficult position "trying to keep them both satisfied." Then she spoke of her nervousness and illnesses. She had been ill ever since her baby girl was born a year before, and in the last several months had suddenly lost 26 pounds. The doctors called it "nervous exhaustion" and said that she would have to get her situation settled and her nerves calmed before she could feel well. She had always prided herself on keeping her emotions to herself and supposed that she "took it out" on herself. The housekeeping and care of the child were left largely to her husband.

Mrs. Slutsky gave the following information about her life and family. Rose's mother, who was divorced when Rose was 6 months old, was a "brilliant woman...a great musician," and extremely successful in her professional work. She was not a home body or a maternal person. She also had a son by this first marriage, whom she had kept with her. She had remarried and now had several other children. According

to Mrs. Slutsky, Rose's father was "no good"; he was a drunkard, and his son was causing her sister much trouble now because of traits inherited from his father. Very frequently
Mrs. Slutsky spoke of Rose's bad traits as likewise having been
inherited from her father. Rose's mother had no feeling for
her, but Mrs. Slutsky wrote her in emergencies, and whenever
the girl visited her mother she behaved well in contrast to the
way in which she behaved with Mrs. Slutsky, which evidently
hurt and offended the adoptive mother.

Mrs. Slutsky stated that she had had a younger brother who
died as a child. Of the two sisters, it was Rose's mother who
had enjoyed the education that Mrs. Slutsky had wished for
herself. She had wanted to go to college like her sister, to
have a career; in everything she wanted to be exactly like her
sister. This wish was not fulfilled and she had to devote
herself to a more domestic career. Her sister was her father's
favorite, but he had never liked Rose, although she was the child
of this favorite daughter.

When the adoptive mother discussed her problems in relation
to Rose, it was evident that she was worried about the girl's
interest in boys, about her not picking the right friends, and
about the girl's definite antagonism toward both herself and
her husband. Sometimes they feared that Rose would harm
their baby. Mrs. Slutsky's chief concern was that her relationship with Rose had changed, and that after all her efforts
to make a home for the girl, things had gone from bad to worse.
Rose had resented the marriage and the baby.

Rose, now in the midst of her puberal difficulties, was in
a critical situation. It was clear to the social agency that
Mrs. Slutsky could not give her a feeling of security and that
the young girl felt neglected and deserted. Having up until
then had two mothers, she now felt threatened with having none.
Her own mother had a large new family and her adoptive
mother had a husband and a new baby. At Rose's age girls
have difficulties even under normal conditions. She was already having fantasies of having a baby, yet did not want to
give up her position as her adoptive mother's only child.

Mrs. Slutsky stated that Rose had asked directly to be allowed to tend the baby, but that she had revealed so much aggressiveness and hostility toward it that the parents were afraid to leave her alone with the child. We can understand that the young girl became rebellious, that she defied all discipline, and that she fled into boyishness. She demanded additional proofs of love from Mrs. Slutsky and clearly revealed the longing of an adopted child who feels abandoned and unloved and turns in fantasy to the "other" mother. Rose revealed this fantasy in a story she told: she brought a fictitious report from school that the teacher had said that Mrs. Slutsky was uncooperative and that Rose's own mother should be approached to send her to another school. When questioned about this tale, Rose admitted that it was largely imaginary, "but the teacher might just as well have said it."

The psychology of Rose's adoptive mother was more complicated than Rose's. Mrs. Slutsky's motherhood was entirely conditioned by her relationship with her sister. She wanted to have everything that the sister had, but since she could not, she had to make compromises. Her sister was loved by her father; Mrs. Slutsky had renounced him, turned to her mother, and remained tied in this relationship all her life. The sister had a career; Mrs. Slutsky was willing to renounce this and to assume the role of woman and mother: "My sister was not a mother."

But she succeeded in all this only under definitely neurotic conditions. She wanted her sister's child and adopted it. Since she remained emotionally tied to her mother, she built her life on the triangle of her mother, herself, and the child. From the very beginning Mrs. Slutsky seems very consciously to have given her life and her motherliness the character that we commonly assume in that of two women friends adopting a child. She even built her triangle on two bases, for she did not cease sharing the child with her sister, let herself be called "aunt," and whenever any difficulty arose concerning the girl addressed herself to "Rose's mother."

She could have led a normal life and had children of her

own; a man wooed her for ten years and she felt attracted to him, but she renounced him consciously in favor of Rose, unconsciously in favor of her triangle. Only after her mother's death did she build a new home for Rose. She married a man much older than herself who was intended to take her mother's role in the triangle, and it was not part of her life program that he should still be a man and make her a real mother. When he did, she inevitably collapsed. She did not keep her unexpressed promise to Rose not to have any children of her own. Out of guilt she did not permit herself to be a real mother and emotionally neglected her own child. But her relationship with Rose became complicated, and she was unable to master the new difficulties.

Only now did she show the typical reactions of an adoptive mother. She blamed Rose's difficulties on heredity—in this case the father's—and presented her, not directly but emotionally, with a retrospective bill, a demand for gratitude: "I have sacrificed so much for you." No such debt exists in a really motherly relation of a mother to her beloved child. But since adoptive motherhood is not in itself motherliness and only offers an opportunity for motherliness, it became in this case an arena of various emotional experiences, gratifications, and frustrations that have nothing in common with motherliness. If Rose's fantasies had come true, Mrs. Slutsky would have lost her contest with her sister at the very moment when life forced biologic motherhood upon her instead of adoptive motherhood.

An understanding of Mrs. Slutsky's situation reveals many typical elements in the psychology of adoptive mothers. These usually do not appear as clearly and directly as they do in this instance, but nevertheless reveal their existence in various ways.

Having thus examined the difficulties of adoptive motherhood, I can restate my main point: The motherliness of the adoptive mother can be enriched by the same joys and sorrows that fall to natural motherhood. The fact that the adopted child comes into the mother's life under abnormal conditions, that the heredity of another mother casts its shadow on the nursery, etc., merely intensifies the readiness for difficulties that may arise in the natural situation too, but that usually assumes another form and is less easily rationalized.

I have repeatedly stressed that aspect of motherhood which is still closely bound up with the woman's old mother relationship. This relationship is a curse if it perpetuates the old conflicts, hatreds, jealousies, depreciations, and fears of retaliation; it is a blessing if the woman's old tenderness for her mother is free of fetters of dependence and if it can flourish anew in relation to the child.

The adoptive mother must prove herself even more free from old dependencies, if she is to get rid of tormenting ideas, no longer animistic but really justified, about the robbed, competing, devaluated, and, above all, "unknown" natural mother. This is one of the fundamental conditions of her success as the mother of an adopted child. We have also seen that women readily transfer their own repressed conflicts to an adopted child. Mrs. Brooks's fear of her own homosexuality assumed the form of fear of bad heredity.

A fairly frequent motive for adoption is that of replacement of the loss of a beloved child. Adoption is resorted to especially in cases in which the mother is no longer able to have another natural child. But often the adoption of a homeless child is supposed to serve as atonement for unfaithfulness to the lost child. Sexual begetting is unconsciously regarded as a sin and rejected by the mourning mother. Often the adoption represents an attempt to interrupt the mourning violently—a mistake that is usually followed by bad consequences. For during the period of mourning even the woman's own children are deprived of love and exposed to the painful silent reproach: "Why did you not die instead of the other?"

The mother's guilt feeling with regard to the the dead child does not permit her to turn to other objects, especially to new ones; the child adopted as a comforter has very poor chances of conquering the mother's heart. Under certain conditions the mourning mother is sometimes ready to give another child her love—as when the child is an unfortunate orphan, bereft of his own mother. Such a child becomes a companion in mourning and pity for him sanctions the new relationship.

The rescue fantasy plays an important role in adoption. The symbolic expression of birth in dreams and in folklore assumes a real and important meaning for the adoptive mother. Her egoistic action assumes the moral and altruistic character of a good deed, and her guilt-laden scruples can be silenced more easily. It is better to rescue a child than to steal one from another woman.

In discussing the psychology of the adopted child, many authors have pointed out that his situation is like the realization of the fantasy called the family romance. The most general conscious content of this fantasy runs as follows: "I am not the child of my parents" (or "of my mother," or "of my father"). This negative component is accompanied by a positive one that is supposed to answer the question "Then whose child am I?" Here we have two recurrent typical answers. The more frequent one is, "I am of higher origin." The other—"I am of lower origin"—is much rarer, but it does occur. These fantasies result from complications in the child's relationship with the parents, which often becomes so contradictory that it arouses in the immature child a feeling that he has two kinds of parents.

The adopted child can give this fantasy a conscious and reality-adjusted character, because he actually has two sets of parents. He can manage his ambivalence, his unfulfilled longings, his hatred, and his excessive need for love within the framework of this dual formation. According to his psychic needs, he can endow his origin with a higher or lower quality. Even true information given him does not usually satisfy him and leaves room for speculative fantasies.

It must be assumed that for the adoptive mother the way is paved for the revival of her own infantile family romance in a completely modified form. She too is usually confronted with the problem "Who are the real parents of my child?" In one case,[1] analysis revealed how the infantile family romance influenced the mother's later relationship with the child. The patient, who was of upper class family, related that in her early childhood she was convinced for a long time that she was the daughter of a dirty peasant. She connected this conviction with a jocular remark made by a member of her family, that if she were naughty one Michel Noxen would come and carry her away in a bag just as he had brought her. She knew this terrible Michel Noxen. He was an uncouth peasant whom she had frequently seen in her father's office. Her belief that she was his daughter had no other basis than the casual jest she had heard. At the time this remark was made, the patient ardently worshiped her father. It was even then a tender, sublimated alliance in which she persisted all her life. She consciously formed her ego ideal after the model of her highly esteemed father, who at that time and later was equal to all her demands.

The reason for her stubborn persistence in the belief that she was the daughter of the uncouth Michel Noxen was discovered by analysis. The young girl, in addition to her adoring, sublimated attitude toward her father, had preserved an unconscious fantasy from an earlier period of her childhood. This fantasy originated in her interest in the sexual relations between her parents. The role she ascribed to her father corresponded to her sadistic interpretation of coitus and represented him as cruel, mysterious, and "dirty." The dirty Michel corresponded to her unconscious version of her beloved father, and she thus accepted him in one component of her psychic life as her "true" father.

What interests us here is that the girl included this family romance in her own motherhood. Married young, she always had an ardent desire to have a son who would resemble her revered father—who would be intellectually distinguished, of lofty morality, etc.

When her yearned-for son was born, she gave him a name

[1] DEUTSCH, H.: Zur Genese des Familienromans. Internat. Ztschr. f. Psychoanal., vol. 16, 1930.

unusual in her circle—Sepp, a typical Austrian peasant name. She herself did not realize how she had happened to come upon this name. She rationalized her action by thinking that the name Sepp had an implication of sturdy quality, and that she wanted her son to be adjusted to the coarser aspects of life. During her analysis she recalled the following event. As a little girl, she was once sitting on a stool near her father's desk, as she often did. Her father, a lawyer, was dictating to his secretary: "Michel Noxen bequeathes his farm and all his belongings to his only son, Sepp."

Now everything became clear to our patient. Behind her conscious wish to have a son like her respected father there was concealed the old fantasy of the brutal, low class father, which asserted itself in her naming of her son. Thus after many years her family romance had its epilogue.

Although this patient was not an adoptive mother, her case shows that the family romance can be preserved for a long time, to be revived at an appropriate moment in adult life. The psychologic situation of adoption, with its often unanswered question as to who the real parents are, can supply a mighty impulse for fantasies in the mother and child. I had occasion to observe a well known actress, mother of an adolescent son, who adopted a little girl. The adoption was arranged privately and all she learned about the child was that it was of superior, perhaps even aristocratic parentage. This otherwise sensible and not appreciably neurotic woman immediately built a real family romance around the child. She fantasied that the little girl was of very special origin, that Prince X, who was notorious for his many love affairs, would one day appear on the scene as the father, fall in love with his little daughter, and richly reward her kindly adoptive mother. This fantasy was developed in every detail; it became increasingly unrealistic, and absorbed the woman more than her real relationship with the adopted child. Finally she herself began to feel that the situation was uncanny.

This woman's mother was a minor actress who, after separating from her insignificant husband, had a love relationship with a wealthy and influential man. This man took care of his mistress' daughter, and my patient owed to him her careful professional education and career. The little girl knew and loved her own father; nevertheless she was not free from the fantasy that her mother's lover was her real father. With her adoption of a little girl, this fantasy revived, and my patient experienced a new edition, so to speak, of the original fantasy. Using means different from those used by Sepp's mother, she realized her family romance after postponement for a generation.

Another adoptive mother followed her little adopted son like a shadow. If he had been her own, we would easily have recognized in her the type of neurotically overanxious mother with whom we have dealt earlier (e.g., the mother of Massimo). But she rationalized her fears of separation and left us in the dark as to whether her fears were occasioned by the real situation or whether she would have behaved in the same way toward a child of her own. She was fully conscious of the content of her fears: she was afraid that the unknown mother of the child would kidnap him. She accepted only intellectually all my arguments that this mother was probably glad to be rid of the child; she felt that "one can never know." She was tormented by anxiety dreams, in all of which the other woman persecuted her, took revenge upon her, stole the child, etc. We know such anxiety dreams in other women. The symbolic vehini-hai usually aims at the blood children of the Marquesas women. But here the vehini-hai was the real mother of the child, who had really lost the child, and who might really try to claim him as her own.

This anxious adoptive mother had a child of her own several years later; she paid much less attention to him. Her excessive anxiety with regard to her adopted child bore evil fruits, as we could have predicted. This handsome and very gifted boy became a chronic runaway in his puberty. Even under normal conditions boys run away from an excessive attachment to their mothers and unconsciously seek another mother whom they have the right to love without committing incest. They not only imagine a family romance, they act it out. But, in connection with the fantasy of our anxious adoptive mother, the behavior of her adopted son confirmed her eternal suspicion that he yearned for his real mother.

Another such mother, a somewhat hypochondriac woman, was obsessed by the idea that her adopted son would become mentally ill. She fearfully observed him and saw in each of his gestures the first symptom of illness, for "one can never know" —he might have had insane ancestors.

The idea of heredity, in which we see irrational but deeply rooted motives, is tenacious in all such cases, and the struggle against the rationalization "One can never know" is very difficult. The test of reality, the only court to which we ascribe the full right of a decision in a dubious situation, is here largely on the side of the afflicted mother. Everything that has been preformed and determined in the deep anxieties of her psychic life is now in the realm of real possibility. The relation between reality and fantasy is displaced; much that otherwise would be recognized as the pure product of fantasy activity is here stimulated, intensified, and endowed with a real character by external events.

Adoptive mothers whose motive for adoption is sterility are particularly prone to such overestimation of the real situation. We must not forget that in such cases adoption constitutes an attempt to remedy a severe trauma, and that this trauma must be overcome before motherliness with its gratifications can fully develop. What kind of trauma it is, and the woman's reaction to the necessary renunciation of the hope of giving birth to a child, depend very much, as we have seen, upon the cause of sterility. The emotional difficulties of adoption may originate in the very conditions that have led to sterility, and the ghosts that were supposed to be banished by the renunciation of the reproductive function can under different circumstances re-emerge in the adoptive mother in a new form. The fear "I cannot have a child" will, for instance, assume the form that we have seen in our last case: "The child will be taken away from me." The adopted child can become the bearer of all the problems that have led to sterility, as well as of those that normally pertain to a child of one's own. The only difference is that here the conflicts have a more real background.

As I have said, childlessness is probably the most frequent motive for adoption. Relative childlessness, that is to say, when the adoptive parents have begotten one or several children without attaining the intended number, is similarly a motive. Especially parents with one child will often manifest an intense yearning to have more children. A woman who has given birth to a child, especially a woman who has enjoyably tested her motherliness on her own children, will make a more reliable adoptive mother than one who longingly pursues her frustrated desire for an unknown experience. The prospects for all participants are particularly favorable if the differences in age and sex between the adoptive mother's own child and the adopted child are such that she does not fall into the conflict of preferring one to the other, and such that the older child is well prepared to accept the child from outside in a friendly way. An obsessional-neurotic mother with a tendency to guilt feelings will naturally be exposed to the danger of attentively "listening to her heart" in order always to be fair to the adopted child. In her self-distrust she often overcompensates her emotions in favor of the adopted child and thus puts him in the exceptional position that she properly wants to avoid. This is particularly true of the adoptive mother who unexpectedly gives birth to the child whose place the adopted child was supposed to fill. The power of natural forces, the "voice of blood," the stronger attachment to the child she herself has borne, do not necessarily outweigh the prior right of the adopted child who was loved first. The manner in which the mother manages her ambivalence conflicts and guilt feelings will determine the decision in favor of one or the other.

I have spoken of mothers who have a sort of passion for pregnancies or for babies. Others want to have a definite number of children, still others desire large families. The same, perhaps to a higher degree, is true of adoptive mothers.

There are women—I might call them female Pied Pipers—
who use the bait of a cozy home and motherly care to lure
children out of social institutions without regard for their
nature, driven by a strong psychic urge to help children, to
foster fledglings in their nests, and to hear the name "Mother"
uttered by as many mouths as possible. They have both
their own and other women's children; what is important to
them is the number and the results. If they have no children
of their own, one suspects that in them too the quantitative
mechanism "many for one" is at play. But even in women
who enjoy their own capacity to bear offspring, an unstilled
yearning for one unachieved child may lead to reaching out
again and again for a new child, and as soon as they have it,
to looking for another. There was a female eccentric in New
York who devoted her fortune and energy to looking for
homeless cats; she was an adoptive mother with unsocial
aims.

A masked kidnaperism may often lead a kind and reasonable woman to undertake the grandiose social task of becoming
a replacing mother of the abandoned or neglected children
of many mothers. I have heard such an addict of adoption
speak with the greatest energy against social assistance to
children: a child—every child—needs one mother, *the* mother.
And she offered herself as such a mother to society.

Many women have a quantitative ideal of a family and strive
to achieve it. The number they want is the number their
parents' families had, or, more frequently, an improvement
upon that number. If such women do not acquire the number
of children they want by giving birth to them, they resort
to adoption. In other cases, the woman is not satisfied with
the sex of her children, and adopts a child to fill the place of
the boy or girl she lacks.

One of my patients was moved to multiple adoption by a
curious infantile idea that had become fixed in her unconscious.
When she was 8 years of age, her mother became pregnant.
She had two little brothers, and she was prepared for the arrival
of the new baby by being told that a little sister was going to be

bought for her. She had been enlightened about the process of birth by her nurse before the arrival of one of her little brothers, but she completely ignored the nurse's explanation and expected the new baby as a gift that would be bought for her. She now imagined that there were two kinds of children: those who were born and did not belong to her, and those who were bought outside the home and were her legitimate possessions. Later, after she married, she gave birth to three boys in succession, and after each of these births she adopted a girl, feeling that the boys were for her husband, but the girls belonged really to her. She tried to explain this curious behavior by the child's sex—"girls belong to the mother"; only later did she realize her true motive.

It is certain that similar individual motives, which remain completely unconscious, operate in adoptions. Thus in the psychology of adoptive motherhood we are confronted with two different sets of problems. The first relate to women condemned to absolute or relative sterility who nevertheless refuse to renounce motherhood. The second relate to mothers who for one reason or another try to add to the number of their own children by adoption. Sometimes adoption is used to solve financial or other practical problems.

Referring to the group of sterile women, I shall again raise the question: What privations must the sterile adoptive mother endure, and what are her opportunities for gratification? The privations consist above all in the foregoing of the emotional experiences that accompany the biologic process of motherhood. The *dolce far niente*, the gratifying introversion of pregnancy, with its absorption in the promising future, the gradual maturation of the fantasy of a child to its reality, the uncomfortable and yet satisfying yielding of the woman's own organs to prepare a dwelling place for something that is only developing, the exemption from obligations and the joyful postponement of ordinary life problems to a later date, the fantasies about what sort of being the child will be, the active and joyful preparation of a nest, all are denied to the adoptive mother. The adoptive mother who has never had any children of her own is also deprived of the means of freeing herself from anxiety by the cathartic experience of the fear of birth, of the discharge of her guilt feelings through suffering, of the painful-joyful experience of delivery, of the repossession of the child after being separated from him, of the narcissistic gratifications of the confinement period, and of the reunion with the newborn through lactation.

An interesting representation of adoption can be found in the Etruscan statues of Hera, the adoptive mother of Hercules, who is shown giving the already grown boy her breasts to suck, in order to perform, belatedly at least, this basic task of motherhood.

The adoptive mother is spared the fears of expectation, the piece by piece fighting out of the inner conflict between the polarities of self-preservation and service to the species, of life and death. She remains free from the regressive affects that are provoked by the biologic processes of the reproductive function. She is also spared the bodily pains, the fears, the conflict between retaining and giving, the real and fantasied death threat, the ensuing void, the often slavish service to the species. But here as elsewhere, deep in the unconscious, there remains the unsatisfied longing for the masochistic experience she must miss and the reproach directed against the ego for having avoided this function. Both the woman and the man are deprived of the realization of the narcissistic wish for physical immortality.

The altruistic, object-loving component of motherliness, the tender joy in the child's growth, all the emotional threads that are woven between mother and child and father and child during the whole period of childhood, can be fully realized by adoptive parents.

If the narcissistic wish for a child as the product of one's own body is predominant, and if the importance of the child as object recedes, adoption will bring only disappointments. I observed one young woman who, prevented from conceiving by an organic illness, adopted a child and was an excellent, loving, and dutiful mother to him. But every time she saw a pregnant woman, or was informed that one of her friends was expecting a child, she reacted with even greater despair than in the period before the adoption. Her maternal emotions toward the little boy, whose illnesses and development gave her all the motherly cares and joys that she reveled in, could not compensate her for the inability to experience woman's natural pride in the fruit of her own body.

It is well known that the gratification of one psychic need often causes increased tension regarding another, which disturbs the gratification. Behind the emotion "He is a lovely child, I love him as my own," the disappointment "But he is not mine" may become more intense and disturb the joy. In several cases I have observed more or less stubborn depressions, temporary rejections of the adopted child, and feelings of hatred—"He is not mine"—directed against the child, despite the adoptive mother's tender maternal love for him.

We have also seen that the motives for adoption can be very different, and that the emotional reactions of the adoptive mother depend upon the structure of her personality and are determined by earlier events. The important facts of woman's earlier life history are usually revealed to us only by psychoanalysis. But as in other aspects of life, we can here likewise often discover the past from its repetition in the present. With sufficient insight, we can reconstruct past experiences from present behavior, although when the problems of motherhood are involved we must keep two things in mind—the woman's deep biologically and psychologically determined need to be a mother, and the demand of reality, which often drives her into motherhood even when her unconscious is opposed to it.

In addition to her many frustrations, the adoptive mother is faced with a particularly difficult task: she must explain to the adopted child that she is not his real mother, she must revive the ghosts that she tries painfully to chase away from her own psychic life, unleash again the pain and estrangement that she mastered or still must master. She fears the burden that she must impose upon the child, his disappointment, his subsequent questions and explorations. Usually this obligation is imposed upon the mother from outside; she is told that it is practically inevitable that the child will eventually learn the truth from others, that it is difficult to keep a secret known by other people, and that under any circumstance it is preferable to protect the child from an almost certain surprise revelation by telling him the truth.

The mother herself often has the greatest difficulty in accepting this necessity. Why should she tell the child? How will she do it? Her love for the child is the same as that of a natural mother and is valuable to her because of this very identity. She is naturally unwilling to expose this relationship to danger.

Usually she cannot find a suitable opportunity, postpones the ordeal, burdens herself with an unfulfilled task, and by this postponement releases an ever growing resistance to a sacrificial duty that she does not fully recognize. Something in this resistance is reminiscent of the task, so hard for many women, of enlightening their children sexually. How and when to tell the facts to the child, is a burning question that often continues to seem insurmountable.

We have learned a great deal from the experience of psychoanalytically trained teachers on the question of sexual enlightenment; it is now generally recognized that the child should be guided gradually, and that at each stage the explanations should be adjusted to his intellectual capacity. In addition we know that only persons who can feel with the child will find the right way and the right moment. The time of the explanation, and the amount of information that the child can receive without a traumatic reaction, cannot be determined on the basis of his intellectual or somatic maturity alone. It is thus impossible to satisfy the oft-reiterated demand for precise indications as to the age levels at which the various phases of the explanation can be given.

The same is true of enlightenment on other matters that are difficult to assimilate. How much of the truth to tell is a problem of tact and cannot be gaged in any rules. One thing is certain as regards all situations of this kind: if one is not emotionally influenced, it is not difficult to determine the degree of the child's intellectual development, that is, how much he can understand and assimilate.

The insight into the child's emotional life, the determination of the moment when he is emotionally able to receive the information favorably, is even more a matter of tact and sympathy. The child spins his own family romance according to his love-hatred relationship to his parents. The mother who, as he imagines, did not give birth to him—in this phase she often is a malicious, powerful witch in his fantasy—will strengthen this idea in him by enlightening him at this time. But if enlightenment takes place when the child is filled with a sense of security and of being loved by his mother, the question of who gave birth to him seems to him highly unimportant, and nothing will change in his tender relationship to his mother. The alleged daughter of Michel Noxen was very happy and proud when she was told that her father had bought her from the dirty peasant. At that time she was so certain of her father's love that she saw a particular proof of this love in the fact that he had bought her. He was compelled to accept his other children because they were born to him. But he bought her because he liked her so much—out of love.

It goes without saying that the adopted child will also use the knowledge of his origin against his adoptive parents, according to the ambivalence of his feelings toward them. If he is disappointed in them he makes use of the fact of his adoption discharge the guilt feelings originating in his hostile impulses. Similarly, the adopted child will seek the answer to the riddle of his own psychic life in the riddle of his birth. And yet there is no doubt that the solution of these difficulties can be just as difficult or easy in a situation in which the psychic accent is not centered on the problem of adoption.

Despite the differences in the real situations, the analogy between the predicament of the adoptive mother and that of the mother who must give sexual enlightenment to her child and wants to escape this task, is very striking. In both cases the psychology of the mother plays an important part. In both cases, it is necessary for her to have freed herself from her own prejudices and fears if she is to achieve the desired reaction in the child. We recall Mrs. Brooks, who so clearly associated these problems of sexuality and adoption, which were both taboo for her.

This point can be illustrated by the following incident. A very intelligent woman asked an authority on early childhood education to give a thorough and scientific explanation of sex to her very clever 8-year-old boy. She had done the best she could, but each time the boy asked for detailed information she felt so inhibited and ashamed that she found it best to seek the cooperation of the expert. The latter spoke to the boy, found him very well instructed, and discovered why the mother was unable to overcome a definite difficulty. The child absolutely refused to accept the fact that his mother, whom he so honored, could have anything to do with such things. When the facts were made clear to him, he became very thoughtful and sad, and when he was leaving he turned at the door and said to the expert with a very pleading look: "But the First Lady, Mrs. Roosevelt, she doesn't do that!"

We understand very well the meaning of this remark: if his own mother is so debased, he may still find a feminine figure somewhere in this world to whom he can transfer his earlier belief in his own mother, and so salvage it.

The psychology of this boy's mother will make it clear why she found it so difficult to answer his questions satisfactorily. She wanted to avoid the danger of losing the "first lady" aura that the child had built around her. The love of the child tried to keep the mother far removed from every sexual involvement, and the mother did not want to give up the position the child attributed to her. The fact that natural things had become devaluated for the child resulted from his mother's own inner lack of freedom.

The same is true of adoptive mothers; they too find it difficult to give explanations, because they themselves are not free of prejudice against their artificial motherhood and their adopted children's origin. They want to deny the facts to themselves, to preserve the illusion that they are connected with the adopted child by a complete experience of motherhood, and to find a confirmation of this illusion in the child. If a mother frees herself from the devaluation of her adoptive motherhood and enjoys her motherliness in relation to her adopted child without inhibition or restriction, she will find the right moment intuitively.

The realization that evolves from the following episode, taken from the records of a social agency, may help her in this task. A Negro girl was brought up in a Catholic convent from her earliest childhood as the only colored child there. She called her favorite nun "Mother" and refused to accept the explanation that she was not the latter's child. She was unaware of her dark color until she was 6, when she was sent to her parents' home. She noticed that there was a physical difference between her mother and her beloved nun, and only then did she notice the color of her own skin. She then made desperate attempts to get rid of her color by constant rubbing and washing, not because she was aware of racial prejudice, but because she did not want to accept the real facts. She wanted to remain the child of her beloved woman, regardless of who had given birth to her. Every loving and loved adopted child wants to do this.

In choosing the right moment one must consider the persons in the environment, who are less inhibited than the mother and recklessly precede her in enlightening the child. The fear of such a possibility and a certain fanaticism for the truth often induce the mother to show unnecessary haste in introducing the child to knowledge that he is absolutely unable to digest. The result may be just as bad as the hesitation described above, because under all circumstances it is necessary to know the whole psychologic situation of the child in order to do the right thing.

I have said that the psychologic motives responsible for sterility can also disturb adoptive motherhood. Conversely, the adoption of a child can, interestingly and fortunately, mobilize so many defensive forces against the psychic enemies of motherhood that the latter must leave the field; as a result, earlier sterility may be corrected. This phenomenon has often been observed, but so far it does not seem to have received a satisfactory explanation. Many more concrete observations are needed to go beyond current speculative assumptions. In this connection I am submitting the scanty material at my disposal.

A young, motherly, and introspective woman tried to explain to me why she became pregnant just when she was about to adopt a child. For a long time she had refused to take another woman's child and even after eight years of childless marriage clung to the hope of having her own child. Finally, however, she decided that she had to renounce it and began to look for a suitable baby. Just as she was about to adopt it, she became pregnant. This is what she said: "During the first three years of our marriage we were tense at every coitus, trying to avoid conception; during the following five years we were tense trying to achieve it. Only in the last six months had we given up all attempts and become free from anxious attention." With the renunciation of the child and the intention to adopt one came relaxation, and with relaxation came conception.

This explanation probably reflects a powerful psychologic motive for the pregnancy. What the woman herself feels as relaxation is certainly her inner perception that the inhibition has been removed. The fear of sterility has its effects long before the problem has become real and actual, and the removal of these effects rarely has such quick and direct results. In a case observed by Orr,[2] pregnancy set in, just as in the case I observed, when the woman after several years of sterility decided to adopt a child. The preparations for receiving the adopted child were accompanied by a reorganization of the woman's external life for the sake of the child, and were doubtless the expression of an inner, emotional change.

I have earlier mentioned another case (p. 115). The sterile woman became pregnant when she saw that her husband, who

[2] ORR, D. W.: Pregnancy following the decision to adopt. Psychosom. Med., vol. 3, 1941.

previously was not emotionally ready for fatherhood, reacted with a fatherly sense of responsibility and unexpected joy to the adopted child. Obviously her sterility resulted from an inhibition that originated in her lack of confidence in her husband.

Another case of an adoptive mother who later unexpectedly conceived a child presents more complicated features. In her I made my only direct psychoanalytic observation relating to the problem under discussion. The patient was a woman of about 30 years of age, whose conscious ideas about being a mother were always associated with immense happiness. It seemed to her impossible and inconceivable that she herself should achieve such happiness. She was the next to youngest child in a very large family; her mother was a warm-hearted, loving person who spread around her a kind of aura of motherliness. All of the patient's older sisters and brothers had many children; she herself as a little girl, and also later, greatly enjoyed her role of aunt, and often helped her sisters in the care of their children. She was perhaps somewhat prematurely drawn into the atmosphere of pregnancies, confinements, care of suckling babies, etc. All her impressions relating to these activities were positive, and her own joy in the babies aroused in her the feeling that when one has one's own child, the happiness must be even greater.

She thus had the best chances of becoming a happy mother. She married a man whom she loved, and yet remained a black sheep in her family, blessed as it was with many children, because for years she was childless. After that period she adopted the child of her cook, born against the will of its parents. She remained in contact with the mother of the child, and the adoption took place without guilt feelings or jealousy, and my patient displayed great tact in it. She continued giving financial support to the mother of her adoptive child, helped her to bring up her other children, and, contrary to the usual attitude of adoptive mothers, intended to maintain the contact between the other woman and the adopted child for a long time, until severance could be achieved gradually and without friction.

It became clear at that time that with the adoption she re-established her old situation of loving aunt, with the sole difference that now she had achieved a previously inaccessible happiness—the child's mother gave her unreserved possession of the child.

During the first year of her adoptive motherhood, my patient became pregnant. However, her pregnancy was very difficult, her physicians struggled against a protracted threat of miscarriage, her delivery was long drawn out, and lactation was unsuccessful. She realized that she was not a good birth giver, and above all that her difficulties were psychogenic.

Psychoanalytic treatment clarified the nature of these difficulties only partially. My patient had vividly retained the memory of all the positive, joyful aspects of the reproductive function as she had observed it in her sisters, and thus of the great happiness of motherhood. Her idea of that happiness was greatly exaggerated; she endowed it with the character of something inaccessible. This exaggeration was the result of a psychologic process: she found the realization unattainable because she associated it with the idea that a high price must be paid for such great happiness. But this idea remained unconscious. She had repressed the negative aspects, the seamy side of the reproductive process—the toil, the pains, the renunciation, the fears, and the dangers, with which she had been abundantly confronted, had dropped from her memory. Thus two ideas were opposed to the consummation of her motherhood. The conscious one, which was almost an obsession, was: "I cannot have a child, this would be too much happiness." Her unconscious idea contained the threats and dangers.

Through adoption she learned to accept the positive aspect, the joys of motherhood, and it may be surmised that this experience influenced her anxious inhibition. She conceived, but her fear of the dangers of biologic motherhood continued to operate by creating difficulties of the reproductive functions. It must be admitted that even analytic study of such conflicts enables us only to formulate conjectures about their relation to sterility and about the part played by adoption in overcoming sterility.

Unfortunately I lost sight of this patient, and I do not know whether her treatment was successful.

It can be assumed that in all such cases of overcoming of sterility by adoption, the miraculous result is based upon the discharge of fear, of guilt feelings, and of the neurotic belief "I cannot be a mother." But this can occur only when the psychic contents have produced nothing worse than a reversible disturbance of the hormonal activity or of the direct innervation of the genital apparatus. Maternal love for the adopted child can here act like any object love, as a discharging, reconciling, healing agent. To the believer, the adopted child may seem a heavenly messenger, an angel of peace. He helps a woman to motherhood like the Madonna of Czestochowa (p. 111).

The view that adoption helps to conquer sterility enjoys great popularity among laymen, and is confirmed in scientific literature on the basis of objective observation.[3] My opinion is that the "miracle" of adoption is the result of many factors operating together against the inhibition and disturbance of the hormonal process.

[3] MENNINGER, K. A.: Somatic correlations with the unconscious repudiation of femininity in women. J. Nerv. & Ment. Dis., vol. 89, 1939. ROBBINS, L. L.: Suggestions for the psychological study of sterility in women. Bull. Menninger Clin., vol. 7, 1943. KNIGHT, R. P.: Some problems involved in selecting and rearing adopted children. Bull. Menninger Clin., vol. 5, 1941. MENNINGER, W. C.: The emotional factors in pregnancy. Bull. Menninger Clin., vol. 7, 1943.

CHAPTER TWELVE

Stepmothers

THERE is no doubt an inner kinship between adoptive mothers and stepmothers. The child in the one or the other situation may be motherless for the same reasons: he has been deserted by his mother or has lost her through death. Her place is taken by a substitute who takes care of him as his foster mother or adoptive mother, with all the rights and duties of a natural mother, or who assumes the role of mother because the widowed or deserted father marries or cohabits with her.

Even before individually determined positive and negative elements of the emotional relationship between stepmother and child enter into operation, the atmosphere of this relationship is spoiled by a kind of tradition. The idea of the foster mother, and in part that of the adoptive mother, is associated with the woman's kindly, unselfish readiness to replace the mother of the orphaned child, while the term stepmother automatically evokes deprecatory implications. This association exists in all cultural milieus. Many fairy tales give us a grim picture of the sufferings of stepchildren; their stepmothers torment them in every way and often wish to kill them. This general idea has even left its mark on our language; we speak of "God's stepchildren," etc., and innumerable proverbs of all nations embody the idea of the wicked stepmother.

In discussing the psychology of adoptive mothers, we have mentioned the psychic mechanism of the family romance. The situation of adoption often gives the child a welcome opportunity to connect his criticism of his parents with an existing reality, whereas the same criticism in relation to natural parents drives him into fantasy. Everything that in his life can arouse dissatisfaction or a feeling of slight, all his impulses of rivalry in relation to one of the parents or sisters or brothers, all his wishes for revenge and retaliation, all the devaluation tendencies, can be gratified by the fantasies of the family romance. The child's feeling that his love needs are not sufficiently gratified by his mother, or that his own aggressions are justified or excusable, are expressed in the idea "I am a stepchild" or "She does not love me, she is my stepmother."

The best loved fairy tales and stories for children give food to such stepmother fantasies. Especially the relation between stepmother and stepdaughter has been the theme of many fairy tales. In some of them, the long-suffering stepdaughter is gradually driven to despair and death by the malicious, persecuting stepmother. In others, the maltreated heroine must perform the lowliest services for her stepmother. The motive for this maltreatment is very frequently the stepmother's jealousy, and the theme of incest appears directly in many tales, when the stepmother openly accuses her husband and his daughter of harboring incestuous feelings toward each other and strives to make her beautiful rival harmless either by degrading her through dirty, menial work or by doing away with her through witchcraft. It is noteworthy that sometimes the effect of the evil magic is to make the daughter pregnant as the result of eating a bewitched, poisoned fruit, so that later she can be accused of having committed incest with her father. The association between fecundation and killing, life and death, is often clearly brought out in such stepmother tales. The eating of an apple is used with particular frequency to represent this polarity. The seeds of the apple are suitable as symbols of fecundation, and its rounded form represents motherhood.[1] Because of the spell cast by the wicked stepmother in the story of Snow White, the apple (symbol of the breast) enjoyed by the stepdaughter emanates poison instead of life-giving milk.

The interpretation of most of these tales shows that they represent the fantasies of stepdaughters who feel supplanted by the stepmother in their relation with their fathers. In these fantasies the evil mother insidiously usurps all the rights and prerogatives that should belong to the daughter. In

---

[1] RANK, O.: Inzestmotiv in Dichtung und Sage: Psychoanalytische Beiträge zur Mythenforschung. Vienna: Internat. Psychoanal. Verlag, 1922.

most of the stories the daughter first suffers painful maltreatment—a kind of preliminary punishment—but later gains her
desires. The evil woman is punished, usually with the same
kind of cruelty as she has displayed toward her stepdaughter,
and the latter enjoys complete happiness. She is united with
her father in tender love or enjoys the passionate love of a
father substitute (king, prince, etc.)

Psychoanalysis has long recognized that in these tales powerful unconscious emotional relations with a real mother strive
for expression. Elaboration and masking transform the
"wicked" mother into the wicked stepmother. The splitting
of the mother figure into the beloved tender mother (usually
dead) and the hated evil stepmother, follows the same mechanism as the theme of the witch. In the Hänsel and Gretel
story this splitting goes one step farther: the wicked stepmother is developed into an even more wicked witch, and also
serves to project the girl's own mother hatred. It is interesting
to note that the repressed pregnancy fantasy appears in the
tales in the guise of a birth brought about by the magic of the
wicked stepmother. In this way the daughter can realize the
fantasy without guilt.

The fairy tales that stimulate fantasy activity in the child,
as an outlet for his unconscious impulses, are objectivized
when a stepmother enters his life. The projection of the child's
conflicts can then take place directly, for they have a suitable
real object.

Thus the woman who assumes the role of stepmother is
immediately surrounded by the hostile atmosphere of the fairy
tales. Adults know more clearly than children that the evil
stepmother of the fairy tales is only a fantasy product. And
it is curious how easily even grownups give credence to the
story of the evil stepmother and what distrust they show of a
woman in that position. Little episodes in the life of the child
that would otherwise pass unnoticed acquire special significance
when a stepmother is involved. The surrounding persons are
inclined to take the child's side, and to regard the punished
child as a "tortured" child; on the slightest provocation they
enthusiastically and indignantly spread accusations against

the wicked stepmother. The bad reputation created for her by the fairy tales pursues her and bears witness to the fact that even though adults have gone beyond the fairy tale intellectually, they do not differ very much from children, who are full of primitive emotions. In them too the fairy tale continues as a specific psychic reality, ready to be revived at any time. Thus a stepmother by her attachment to the child may win his complete love, until the moment when the grown-up members of the family, friends, and above all other children, make the stepchild the executive agent of their own aggressions and stir him to hostility: "She is not your mother, she cannot love you," or "Don't take anything from her."

The neighbors lie in wait for this wicked stepmother, however kind she may be, and appeals made to the police to rescue mistreated children often prove very much exaggerated, especially in cases involving stepmothers. Often a somewhat older child himself calls the police and accuses his stepmother (but more frequently his stepfather) of the worst brutalities. Sometimes there is a grotesque disparity between these accusations and the actual facts of the case. Such behavior is not a proof of especial mendacity, nor does it necessarily arise from excessive hatred of the stepmother. The subjective feeling of the stepmother's injustice springs from the conscious or unconscious knowledge "She is not my own mother," and this knowledge lends to each of her actions a cruel significance, such as applies to the actions of the wicked stepmother of the fairy tales.

The stepmother herself, by virtue of her own childish impulses, once had the fantasy of the evil stepmother and was affected by the theme of the fairy tale. Her relationship to her stepchildren may still contain the same dynamic factors that were at play in her fantasies. We have seen that a woman's attitude toward her own children is greatly influenced by her earlier attitude to her mother, and we may assume that all her own feelings and fantasies about a stepmother are involved in her real stepmother situation.

There are younger or older girls who in their conscious or

unconscious fantasy activities act out cruelly masochistic stepchild roles, or who vent their aggressiveness in playing stepmother with their little brothers or sisters or with dolls. There are adult women who discover remnants of such fantasies in their great tenderness for their own children and state proudly: "There is no trace of the wicked stepmother in me."

The old fairy tale thus becomes a problem for the stepmother: the people around her, the child, her own unconscious memories are all full of these common primitive themes that originally gave rise to the fairy tales. The final result, that is, whether the woman becomes a good mother or a wicked stepmother, depends not only upon the woman's psychic orientation but also upon the environment involved. The stepmother must not be considered an isolated phenomenon; we must try to understand her psychology from the point of view of the relationships between her and the rest of the family—father, children, grandparents, dead mother, etc.

The development of her stepmotherhood is often predetermined from the beginning by her choice of a husband. There are women who, following an inner necessity, turn their interest and inclination only to men who belong to other women, and there are women who like best to marry widowers or deserted husbands. We are quite familiar with the motives that drive them to such a choice.

From similar motives, some women feel particularly attracted to men who have orphaned children. Many such women try to find positions as housekeepers for widowers who have children, and my observations suggest that theirs is a profoundly determined behavior, not merely a practical calculation or a simple compensation for having lost their chances of having children of their own.

One of the most clear-cut types is the efficient, aggressive woman who, acting out an unconscious stepmother fantasy, introduces marvelous order and discipline in the orphaned household, makes herself indispensable to the man, and forces the children into a masochistic dependence upon their "fair" stepmother.

Others want to realize a definite situation: the woman feels that the other woman's children belong to her, or she actively assuages an old guilt feeling: "I am a good, self-sacrificing mother to the other woman's children." The man's relation with such a housekeeper or platonic friend who from these or similar motives takes efficient or tender care of his orphaned children, often leads to marriage, not because of his erotic needs, but because in this situation marriage is the best form of adjustment to reality. Sexuality usually plays a very secondary role here. But in the woman, under cover of dutifulness, friendship, motherliness, there is concealed an erotic yearning that now wants to come into its own. She is disappointed when her wish is realized; instead of the hopeful fantasy that formerly endowed her relationship to the children with warmth and tender solicitude, we have now a frustration reaction, and the good foster mother is transformed into the wicked stepmother. The people around her superficially think that she is calculating and hypocritical and that she only acted the good mother until she achieved her worldly aim.

Incidentally, the situation of the nurse or governess who can expend all her motherliness on the children entrusted to her, is usually more favorable than the stepmother's. The former's role is from the beginning that of a deputy who does not claim to be a complete substitute. In her efforts to win the children's love we do not find the tendency, so powerfully active in the stepmother, to devaluate the mother in order to pre-empt the maternal role. Thus the guilt feeling toward the other woman is less intense and the child's tendency to be loyal to the mother is less severely taxed.

Because such substitute mothers make no claim upon the man's love, or repress such a claim, they do not compete with his children; above all—and this seems to be the decisive factor in the children's attitude toward them—their relation with the father is not sexual. For it is the sexual character of the relationship that principally stirs up the infantile protest and the hate impulses of the children of both sexes against the stepmother.

The psychology of the stepmother who in her infatuation for the man includes his children, is different. When the intoxication passes and is replaced by the humdrum routine of married life, she discovers in herself an increasing dislike for the other woman's children, often even before she has become conscious of having cooled off with regard to her husband. The initially tender and kind stepmother develops into an evil one; her psychology is certainly not very different from that of a natural mother who transfers her dislike for her husband to the children, but the stepmother because of her status is tagged with a different character.

The fate of a woman's stepchildren and of her own stepmotherhood is largely predetermined by the character of her love for her husband. If the tender-motherly component is predominant in it, the woman will with her tenderness easily master her own stepmotherly impulses and corresponding impulses in her children. If she is of the erotically desiring and wanting-to-be-desired type, the degree of her narcissism will determine her fate as a stepmother. If narcissism constitutes an essential part of her personality, she will either reject the child's demand for love as troublesome, or will make the father himself jealous of her tenderness toward the child. The narcissistic woman in her general desire to be loved woos the child, delights for a time in her husband's gratitude and admiration, and later, becoming aware of his negative feelings toward the child, pushes the latter away, just like a wicked stepmother. Her self-love blinds her to the mischief she has done.

In another type of narcissistic woman, the desire to make her own ego the center of her stepchild's life, to be loved and admired by him, is the condition she imposes for being a good stepmother. She wants to be considered the savior of the orphan and not an intruder. Her capacity for motherliness depends upon the extent to which she can transfer her narcissism from the idea of "fruit of her flesh" to that of the "rescued" child. To be loved, she must woo, but despite her efforts to win the love of her stepchildren, her motherliness cannot have the same effects as that of a natural mother. The children sense her wooing and perceive it as something alien.

If her love choice was inspired by the image of her father, and if she was attracted to her husband by his widowhood and his fatherly relation to his children, her stepmotherhood will be determined by her earlier father relationship. The role of oldest sister is not unfavorable, and I have observed very happy stepmothers who were successful in the upbringing of their stepchildren when they were mature enough to be free of sisterly competition.

I also observed a differently determined stepmother case which is probably one of many. A 25-year-old girl, emotionally very infantile, went with her friends to visit a widower who was the father of several still very young children. She fell in love with him at first sight. She realized that his attraction for her was based above all on his kind and understanding attitude toward his children, but she was unconscious of the fact that the determining motive of her choice was that she believed that she had found in him features of her own mother. She was very much attached to her mother, and because she could not bear the competition of her younger brothers and sisters, she had preferred since her twelfth year to live with a childless aunt in a less tense atmosphere.

After her marriage she found herself once more among little brothers and sisters, and her relation with her stepchildren was an exact repetition of her old situation. At first she was the loving, authoritative mother substitute; then her behavior went to the other extreme. The children annoyed her, she became impatient with them, and felt unfree; a rivalry for the love of the motherly man developed between her and the children, she became a malign stepmother, and in the end fell ill with a depression; she felt that she was wasting away in this life, because, as she realized during her treatment, she could find no way out of the situation of the little girl who was called a wicked stepmother in this marriage. It seems that the transference of the former father relationship to the husband creates more favorable conditions for stepmotherhood than the more infantile transference of an old mother tie. As we have seen, motherhood always requires a certain degree of maturity; this applies particularly in regard to stepmotherhood.

The age and sex of the stepchildren greatly influence the psychologic reactions of the stepmother. If a stepmother takes over a child before he is old enough to have formed a union between himself and his own mother, and if she creates the family triangle before the natural mother has left her own personal mark on it, the prospects that her stepmotherhood will develop into genuine motherhood are most auspicious, provided that she contributes sufficient motherliness to the situation.

Still another condition must be fulfilled: she must bring sufficient freedom from guilt feelings into the situation in which she becomes the mother of another woman's child. In her relation to her stepchild she has not gone through the purifying effect of suffering, and the situation itself is very apt to intensify her guilt feelings, especially when the natural mother of the child has died. I once observed the marriage of a widower with a friend of his wife, who had died shortly after bearing a child. The new wife married with the wish to save the motherless orphan, to be a good mother to him in the place of her friend. When she began to suspect that she loved her husband and that the marriage also fulfilled her erotic wishes, she fell into a state of anxiety, and for a long time refused to have intercourse with him. She could become a good stepmother only under the condition of freedom from guilt.

Another loving and motherly woman developed into a rejecting, wicked stepmother because she was willing to assume the mother role in the home of her beloved husband only if the former wife was completely excluded from its emotional atmosphere. In some women this condition may spring from an uneasy sense of guilt, in others from jealousy of the deceased wife. Photographs or the personal possessions of the dead wife are either not tolerated and treated without piety, or their presence produces a constant resentment. The stepmother's efforts to drive out the other woman are often made prematurely, before the members of the family can grant her wish for reasons of piety, and thus an atmosphere of resentment is created. In other cases, the very presence of the children prevents the woman from considering her husband's marital past disposed of, and she becomes intolerant, spiteful, a wicked stepmother. Another woman whom I observed developed a chronic neurotic condition as a result of her efforts to overcompensate a similar situation. She took active part in piously preserving the memory of the dead, collected and arranged everything associated with her, and at the same time hated her husband's ancestral home and engaged for decades in an unsuccessful search for another residence. She was an excellent stepmother, but transformed her house into a shrine of the dead to such an extent that the children found it impossible to engage in any lively games or later on in social activities. She was unconsciously taking her revenge upon them for the fact that they had had another mother.

The stepmother actually aims to win not only the children's love but also their emotional consent to her relation with their father. Otherwise this relationship may assume the character of a forbidden act; the children's consent helps the stepmother to discharge her guilt feelings and to achieve inner peace. To this end she must make a sacrifice to the children: she must be willing to share her husband's love with them. This agreement is sometimes made at once, in other cases it is achieved gradually and is subject to fluctuations. Not every stepmother is able to fight soberly day by day for her position. Hysterically predisposed stepmothers whose emotions are exaggerated, and who display an enthusiastic readiness to love their stepchildren, feel at once disappointed in their daydreams and discouraged by the distrustful attitude of the children; they withdraw from making use of their readiness to love and become negative in their relation.

A woman of the obsessional-neurotic type may have an objectively perfect ideal of child training and may display a kind of waiting indifference toward the children, which is replaced by a more emotional attitude when the children prove worthy, according to her standards, of her maternal love.

It must be said that as a rule stepmothers find it hard to win their stepchildren's affection. The latter often have a hostile attitude. They resist the stranger's intrusion with fury, bitterness, and secret malice; every time the stepmother makes a demand upon them, they feel exploited or supplanted. If the child has lost his mother by death, he must often remain loyal to her out of his own guilt feelings, and hates the stepmother who woos him, because she thus exposes him to the danger of disloyalty. On the other hand, a mother who is still living, but has no close affective bonds with her child, often creates worse conditions for transference to the stepmother than a dead mother. How can the child trust a stranger when his own mother has betrayed him?

The age of the stepchildren and their level of development are also important factors. In little children who still greatly need maternal protection, it is certainly easier to outweigh the negative forces with tenderness. If the children are beyond the phase of helplessness, they often try to dominate their step-mother, to humiliate her, and to wreak their aggressive im-pulses on her. If the stepmother has masochistic tendencies, the child's sadistic impulses acquire new strength and their development is encouraged. The stepmother's active wooing frequently strengthens the child's feeling of having been wronged and his belief that he is entitled to special favors. If he fails to receive them, he easily adopts a hostile attitude to-ward the obstructive mother. Orphaned children are usually loved and pampered by friends and relatives and their narcis-sistic demands are reinforced. Their emotional attitude to-ward a reality that must gradually limit their demands is full of disappointment and hatred. Since the stepmother often personifies this limitation, she comes to be regarded as invidious.

It is harder to overcome the infantile Oedipus complex with regard to a stepmother than with regard to the natural mother. The little girl can more easily tolerate the renunciation of intimacy with her father when the presence of the mother as a rival no longer spurs her fantasy activity. When she has a new rival in her stepmother, she feels betrayed and deserted by her father. The fairy tale is revived, the girl fantasies herself as Cinderella, and her provocative behavior often drives the best intentioned stepmother into the role of the wicked one. Or, conversely, an aggressive stepmother at once takes the traditional position of the inhibiting, forbidding, and punishing wicked stepmother. It goes without saying that this Cinderella attitude is strengthened during puberty. A stepmother who enters the family when the young girl is going through a phase of well mastered and sublimated homosexuality and is searching for a feminine object to identify with, has, if she is tactful, the best prospects of establishing a satisfactory and fruitful relation with her stepdaughter. A puberal girl's longing for a stepmother who has tactlessly rejected her is a more frequent motive for defiant rebellion and aggressive vengeance on the girl's part than the rivalry for the father. It is necessary for the stepmother to have mastered her own homosexual impulses, if she is to be capable of coping with the often violent love assault of her stepdaughter without hurting her.

In the little son, the Oedipus situation, in its infantile, naïve, instinctual form, is likewise more dangerous and intense where a stepmother is concerned than where it is centered on the natural mother. The tender love for his parents that the little boy has developed from the beginning of his life, helps him to master the difficulties of the Oedipus situation; but this is not the case where a stepmother enters the family later The competition for exclusive possession of the mother is sharper if the boy is approaching puberty, and the Oedipus complex becomes the Don Carlos conflict: father and son face each other as rivals for the love of the woman who belongs to the father and is not the son's natural mother.

This conflict of the son is mirrored in the stepmother. Her psychologic behavior greatly depends upon whether she has come into the house as a governess or nurse, an authority hired by the father to watch his little son, and has subsequently become the stepmother, or whether she is a young stepmother who is the father's new love object brought in from outside. The former has often in a sense betrayed the father in favor of the son from the very beginning, by taking the latter's side in the difficulties between him and his father. This tender understanding may arouse in the son a feeling that the father has been deceived, and this feeling is part of the strong attraction that the nurse or governess unconsciously exerts upon him. But if her role in the home changes and she becomes the father's sexual object, the previous situation, till then kept within bounds, can greatly sharpen the psychic conflict. Not only the woman's relationship with the father but the whole situation is sexualized, and the tenderness between stepmother and stepson is disturbed by a sexual admixture; the son now unconsciously counts on his previously enjoyed alliance with the stepmother against his father, and begins to hate her for having failed him. For the stepmother, the previous harmless relationship becomes taboo, and in self-defense she reacts with negative feelings to the son's hatred. Again the beloved mother substitute is transformed into the wicked stepmother.

In some cases the sexualized motherliness wins the upper hand and the stepmother lets herself be seduced by the erotic suffering of her tenderly loved stepson. She would struggle more energetically against an ardent erotic desire; but moved by her motherly feeling, she feels almost compelled to assuage the beloved boy's passion, and permits realization of his boyish fantasy. The taboo may be transgressed with the excuse that after all the boy is not her own son; yet as a result the good stepmother has played in the life of the family the part of the wicked, seducing, disloyal, unmotherly witch.

I have often had opportunity to observe Don Carlos situations in which beyond doubt the fascination of the stepmother was due solely to the fact that she was the father's wife. The taboo attracted the stepson, certainly unconsciously, but the age difference between the stepmother and the father also seemed to him to deprive her of the character of mother and helped him to disavow the Oedipus situation. For her, however, the situation had nothing in common with motherhood; a young and an old man were fighting for her love, and the term stepmother had become merely a name without meaning.

Despite the bad reputation of stepmothers, good ones are as frequent as good mothers, and wicked, aggressive mothers are perhaps just as frequent as wicked stepmothers. A feminine, motherly woman can master the most difficult stepmother situation with the help of her intuition. She feels that the most important thing is to restore, in the child's emotional and fantasy life, the parental unity broken by the mother's departure. But as long as the stepmother is merely the father's wife, or, even worse, the father's sexual object, the woman who sleeps with him, she must remain the wicked stepmother.

Under a favorable parental unity, the child or children must be accepted as full-fledged members of the family. Children are not deceived by the merely formal stress on their membership. Naturally this relation is easier to establish if the foundation of the child's security in belonging is laid at an early stage of his life, when the stepmother has all the chances of the natural mother. Later the child develops a definite social personality and mutual adjustment is necessary. If the stepmother is incapable of adjusting herself to the child, her best intentions fail. This is particularly the case with women whose personalities are rigid, congealed under a definite formula, aplastic, unintuitive. This point can be illustrated by the following case history.

Mr. and Mrs. Cohen came together to a social agency to ask for advice and help in mastering their educational problems with David, the 10-year old son of Mr. Cohen's first marriage. The father had been divorced for several years before he remarried, two years before this application. Mrs. Cohen, the stepmother, took care of David with exemplary dutifulness; she was as kind and conscientious with him as if he were her own child and felt absolutely innocent in David's difficulties. The agency was able to ascertain the truth of these statements made by the parents.

The father declared that the situation had reached a critical point; the boy and his stepmother were getting along so badly that he thought it unfair to all of them to keep David in his house. The boy stole and lied, was disobedient and disagreeable. Asked for more details about the stealing, the father said that the most the boy was known to have taken at one time was $6. He stole from his stepmother's pocketbook or from her relatives. The incident that was the last straw had occurred only a few days before, when he took a dollar from his stepmother's sister. The parents learned about it from a storekeeper, who noticed David spending money, but when they asked the boy about it, he denied it even before the storekeeper. This was typical, for the boy never admitted any misdemeanor, even when they actually found proof. He was quite apt to buy candy with the money he stole and then to give it away to other boys. This stealing had gone on periodically ever since they took the boy into their home, which was two years before, at the time of their marriage. Sometimes he would go for weeks without stealing and they would think that he had overcome his habit; then he would dash their hopes by stealing again.

The boy's home situation had been as follows. His father and mother had separated when he was 2, and from that time on until his father's second marriage he had lived in a near-by town with his paternal grandparents. When the social worker inquired whether the boy stole from his grandparents, the father said that they did not consider him a thief; but the stepmother thought that this was because the grandmother was not careful of her possessions and probably did not even know it when the boy stole something from her.

The information about David's lying was as follows. One day his father took him to a dentist. When he came home he told the neighbors that he had visited the airport, which was not true, although father and son had talked about going there. The other example was that the boy had said that his father was the head of the fire department, while actually he was only a volunteer.

The stepmother said that the boy got her into such a state

over the stealing and lying that she hardly knew what she was doing. When she had married his father, she had had the best intentions toward the boy, but he had made it impossible for them to get along together. When asked whether the boy was affectionate, she said that he occasionally was so with her; his affection for her own 1-year-old boy was very great, and he was extremely nice to the child. On this score they had no complaints.

The father was one of six children, the rest of whom were girls. He had been given his way in everything and had never had any discipline. He obviously felt that his son should be brought up differently. His marriage with David's mother had been unhappy; she had been unfaithful to him, and, as said, they had separated when David was 2 years old. For some time David's mother had kept up contact with him; but the occasions became more and more rare and she had not seen him at all during the past two years. He himself had left David's upbringing completely to his own parents, had bothered about him very little, and now reproached himself for this. The father's tie to the boy seemed to be mainly one of duty. He gave the impression that the relations between him and his wife were warm and harmonious. They were obviously very much disturbed by David's behavior, and wanted to place him. They had no clear idea of where they should send him, and were obviously disturbed in their wishes by their sense of duty.

The stepmother was a daughter of a rabbi. Her parents had come from Russia, she herself was born in this country. She had an older brother who was to become a rabbi like his father. Both she and her brother were brought up with extreme strictness. Her mother was a particularly severe disciplinarian and made high moral demands upon her children, who were compelled to obey her unconditionally. The father was very religious, softer, and entirely dominated by the mother, who ruled the home. Mr. Cohen confirmed the social worker's impression that his wife had carried over many rather rigid standards to David, and that she was an excessively careful housekeeper. She wanted everything spotless and worked her fingers to the bone to keep her home in that condition. He did not feel that she could ever change much, but he did feel that the situation was especially hard for David.

David's life in his grandparents' home had always been an easygoing one.   He could come and go as he pleased, and came in for dinner at any hour.   The grandmother was a rather lax housekeeper; people slept anywhere, the beds were not made immediately, the house was quite disorderly most of the time, but it was homelike and had a warm atmosphere that the boy now missed.   It must also be emphasized that in the home of his grandparents David had become attached to a boarder who obviously had become for him an active and solicitous father substitute.

One of the stepmother's complaints against David was that he refused to help her sufficiently with the household chores. Mrs. Cohen could not bear dirty dishes standing around in the kitchen, nor could she bear to have dishes drying in a drainer.   She liked them washed and wiped immediately after a meal.   She agreed that she was too fussy as a housekeeper; she had too high standards and was terribly upset if anything in her house was out of place.

David displayed absolute unwillingness to obey her, complained about having to do dishes three times a day, and considered dishwashing an indignity for a boy: "They are trying to make a girl out of me; it's only girls who have to do dishes."

Mrs. Cohen had been quite insistent about this chore; of course he did the dishes more willingly when he did them with his father.

Other complaints against David related to his forbidden sexual games with neighbors' children.   When he was taken to task for this, he showed himself very repentant.   Tears came to his eyes and he seemed quite upset.   Mrs. Cohen was pretty anxious about the whole situation.   She did not know that children did such things—she certainly had never done them as a child.

She was absolutely intolerant about all of David's misdemeanors, even the most trivial of them, and considered them serious crimes. She declared that she had had no contact with children at all before she married Mr. Cohen; once she took a friend's child out in a perambulator but it turned over, and so she never took care of a child again. She had gone to work at 19 and had been a bookkeeper in a store for twelve years. Her face softened and lit up as she told about her evenings. She attended lectures and courses and read scientific books. It was hard for her to marry and settle down and particularly to keep house, because she had never kept house before. She did not give up her job until she was pregnant, and then David came to live with them. Her pregnancy had been difficult, she had had numerous complaints, the baby had been sickly, etc. Mrs. Cohen's attitude did not reveal any signs of a happy motherhood.

She was very willing to receive psychologic explanations of David's behavior; she understood them and intended to follow the advice she was given. But this amelioration was probably temporary, since David's behavior too was changeable. He improved and then again was mischievous. This intelligent and charming child was gradually developing into a problem youth. He grew harder and more aggressive, protested energetically against everything that made him a "sissy," and softened up only when the subject of his own mother was broached.

Even Mrs. Cohen had the impression that his mother was on his mind more than they realized, and the father said that David showed clearly that he yearned for his mother. In the interviews it also developed that at least in fantasy he had an idealized picture of her to which he clung. He was obviously afraid of his stepmother; his father appeared to be just as much intimidated by her as he was, and they did not dare to league together against her.

It is perfectly believable that Mrs. Cohen had married with the best intentions of being a good stepmother and of treating David as her own child. But she imposed a condition that the boy could not meet: she wanted him to adjust himself to her

way of living, however alien it was to him.   For Mrs. Cohen had formed herself after the model of her own strict and cold mother, and, as her husband justly said, would hardly be able to change.   But since David could not adjust himself to the strict obsessional-neurotic order in the home, he became a stranger, a stepchild, and had to go.

Mrs. Cohen's own child would have time and opportunity to adjust himself from the beginning of his existence to the life pattern of his own mother, who was just as intolerant toward him as toward David.   He would more or less thrive under her orderly coolness.   But David came from another world, his emotional life needed the continuation of the atmosphere of his grandmother's home; he needed a feminine-motherly, intuitive stepmother, who, even without grasping the situation intellectually, would realize that David above all needed to be with his father, that he was fleeing from his own passivity, and that unless he was given a favorable opportunity to identify with a masculine father, he would inevitably become a "tough guy," and under certain circumstances even asocial.   Or he would escape more violently from the unemotional atmosphere of his new mother into the fantasy about his own hardly real and almost inaccessible mother, and develop a neurosis.

It is interesting to note that David longed for his mother in a conscious, direct manner, apparent to the persons around him.

"When God takes someone's mother, he also takes his father."[2]   David had tried to overcome his second trauma, the brutal neglect of his father, through his friendship with the boarder.   Now he had his father again and insisted upon having him in reality.   He expressed his disappointed protest by indirect means.   He lied to the effect that his father was a great and important man who took him—in a two man alliance —to interesting places.   And since the children of the neighborhood apparently disbelieved his boasts, he tried to bribe them, so to speak, and bought them candy with stolen money. By stealing from his stepmother, he recovered indirectly what she had taken away from him—his father's love.

---

[2] Lapp proverb, quoted in PLOSS AND BARTELS: Op. cit.

The good Mrs. Cohen, despite the best of intentions, became a wicked stepmother because, with her devotion to order and cleanliness and her unmotherly heart, she was incapable of sympathizing with David's needs and longings.

If David had been a girl, he would perhaps have been threatened with an even more dangerous—because frequently irreversible—stepchild fate. In face of the bleak chores of dishwashing, out of protest against the stepmother and revenge against the father, and poisoned by the apple of mutual jealousy, a daughter would have run away from home. Her next refuge would have been not Snow White's glass coffin, but a dirty room in a disreputable hotel, and the lost love of her father would have been given back to her not by a marvelous prince, but by one of the many sailors who lie in wait for young girls at various "joints." Not all girls in such situations are stepdaughters, but many accuse their own mothers of being stepmothers, using the term "wicked stepmother" to give a name to their often unconscious frustrations.

David's conflict with his stepmother (like that of many boys in similar situations) was probably sharpened by the birth of the new child. Stepchildren justly suspect that mothers prefer their own children. We know the strong slight that a child feels in the coming of a new child, even a child of his own mother, and how much jealousy and bitterness accompany the birth.

Under normal family conditions the child is expected to overcome these reactions. A good stepmother sometimes thinks that she is obliged to make a sacrifice and renounce having children of her own in order to turn all her solicitude to the stepchild. Such a fundamental sacrifice, which affects the depths of the woman's soul, usually does not bear good fruit. The good stepmother unconsciously demands a compensation from her stepchildren and husband, and since her excessive claims are not satisfied, she takes her disappointment out on the stepchildren and becomes a wicked stepmother. We know by experience that all her efforts to remain a good one under these circumstances are not very successful.

The psychologic task of the stepmother is even more complicated when she brings children of her own into her new marriage.   It seems that in such complicated family constellations,
it is above all the relationship of the parents that determines
the outcome of the numerous possible conflicts.   Especially an
illegitimate child who, through the mother's subsequent marriage, receives a stepfather and stepsisters or stepbrothers,
creates a difficult problem for the mother.   Under bad economic conditions, the psychologic conflicts are transferred to
the plane of gross economic reality.   The stepfather is burdened with the support of another man's child, a demand to
which he can relate all his hostile feelings against the child, and
the stepmother retaliates on her stepchildren in defense of her
own child.   Under more favorable social conditions, the conflicts disclose their psychologic character more clearly: the
father is spiteful against and jealous of the stepson whom he
has not begotten, and intolerant of the expressions of his
Oedipus complex.   The mother watches the expressions of the
stepfather's feelings toward her own daughter, and the emotional reproach "He does not love her as he does his own children" often conceals an unconscious fear of his erotic interest
in her daughter.   This is the fear that importunes in "Little
mirror on the wall, who is the most beautiful of all?"   And the
mother feels that the decision may be the more openly in favor
of the daughter because she is not the husband's own daughter,
protected by fear of incest.   Women often come to us to accuse
their husbands of being sexually interested in their daughters
by former unions.   Closer examination often reveals that such
unjustified accusations are not very different from those made
by young girls who express their own fantasies by unjustly
accusing their stepfathers or foster fathers of seducing them.

A situation that has such multiple emotional determinants
results in great irregularities in the relations between stepmother and stepchildren.   "An eye for an eye" will influence
her best intentions; the necessary—or purportedly necessary—
defense of her own children, and the comparison between them
and the others, makes her overcritical toward the stepchildren;

she devaluates them, and the mutual emotional reactions create an atmosphere that only a feminine-motherly woman with her intuitive tactfulness can cope with successfully. The stepmother's passive subordination or her masculine-aggressive wish to dominate the situation likewise sharpens the family conflicts, although by different means.

Attempts are being made, through theoretic discussions and on the basis of practical observations, to establish norms and rules for the best solution of the stepmother problem. On the whole, it can be said that a good mother is also a good stepmother, and the solution of this difficult problem can be left to her maternal feelings.

The Climacterium

WOMAN's capacity for reproduction normally lasts as long as menstruation is regular. With the cessation of this function, she ends her service to the species. The end of menstruation indicates that ovulation has ceased and that the whole glandular apparatus has interrupted or decreased its activity. The genital organs become atrophied and the rest of the body gradually shows symptoms of aging. This phase of woman's life is called the menopause, the climacterium, and, in a wider sense, the change of life or the critical period. It is indeed critical, and whatever influence the changes in hormonal activity may exert upon the whole psychosomatic picture, there is no doubt that the mastering of the psychologic reactions to the organic decline is one of the most difficult tasks of woman's life.[1]

Usually the climacterium has a preliminary phase, marked by certain phenomena that presage the end: menstruation becomes irregular, appears at longer or shorter intervals, and the amount of discharge increases or decreases. Vasomotor disturbances appear, with the characteristic "hot flushes," sensations of dizziness, and sweatings; these are often accompanied by headaches, neuralgias, etc. As a rule, all the subjective physical complaints of this period of life are considered as "climacterical" and are explained on the basis of the modified glandular function. The same is true of the psychologic symptoms that appear at this time—insomnia, anxiety states, excitability, and depressions. The whole course of the climacterium is undoubtedly determined by the fact that with the cessation of ovarian activity the remainder of the endocrine system is deranged in its functioning. The individual manifestations of the climacterium, however, greatly depend upon the

---

[1] DEUTSCH, H.: Psychoanalyse der weiblichen Sexualfunktionen. Vienna: Internat. Psychoanal. Verlag, 1925.

given woman's personality. Weiss and English[2] have formulated this interrelationship: "One may say that the glandular function seems to furnish an impetus to the psychologic processes, but that there must be a well-integrated psychologic structure which can do something intelligent for the emotional needs of the individual who possesses the glands."

The climacterium is under the sign of a narcissistic mortification that is difficult to overcome. In this phase woman loses all she received during puberty. With the onset of the genital retrogressive processes, the beauty-creating activity of the inner glandular secretions declines, and the secondary sex characteristics are affected by the gradual loss of femininity. The biologic process, actual or imminent, is perceived internally before the organic changes. While still organically capable of conception, woman feels the threatened devaluation of the genitals as organs of reproduction. This inner signal, combined with her perception of the first signs of old age, heightens the woman's interest in her own person. A struggle for the preservation of femininity, now in process of disappearance, sets in. This struggle fills out the preclimacterical life period before the genital function has really stopped. We can compare this period to prepuberty: just as was the case then, there is a thrust of activity, now too all the forces of the ego are mobilized to achieve a better adjustment to reality, the old values crumble, and a drive to experience something new, exciting, makes itself felt.

The thrust of activity assumes different forms in different individuals. In many women it rushes directly to the threatened sector: after several years of interruption of the reproductive service, they feel a strong urge to become pregnant and re-experience motherhood. Despite the urgency of other important life interests, despite their absorption in the problems of their grown-up children, often even against their conscious will, they give life to one or two late born children—before the closing of the gates, so to speak. One has the impression that

[2] WEISS, E., AND ENGLISH, O. S.: Psychosomatic medicine. Philadelphia: Saunders, 1942, p. 254.

even if sterility has already set in, it may yield to the woman's passionate wish still to be capable of reproduction.

In women who up until then have been completely absorbed by the reproductive function, the thrust of activity strikes out in different directions. They turn to occupations outside their homes, and those who before marriage and motherhood displayed any sort of creative urge or skill, dig up and revive long buried interests—interests that flowered for a short time during prepuberty but were lost in the conflicts of puberty.

Many of these women at marriage gave up this form of activity because of a very typical and not always understandable inhibition. This applies especially to artistic aspirations that were not sufficiently consolidated before marriage. Such women shun, as though in a phobia, the piano, palette, or whatever the instrument of their former interests is, because of a dark feeling that they must "choose." Apparently they fear that their artistic sublimations will endanger the emotional experience of marriage. Elsewhere we have mentioned the inner connection between woman's erotic experience and her creative achievement. This connection explains why, in a phase of heightened activity and of simultaneous threat to eroticism, the urge to creation is renewed. This process becomes particularly clear as it manifests itself with regard to the now ending reproductive function.

The urge to intellectual and artistic creation and the productivity of motherhood spring from common sources, and it seems very natural that one should be capable of replacing the other. A motherly woman can give up her other interests in favor of the reproductive function, and she returns to the former when she feels the biologic restriction approaching.

It is difficult to define exactly the age of the preclimacterium. Under our own cultural conditions it is increasingly delayed, for climacterical women now have greater opportunity to deny the biologic facts. Broadly speaking, the age of the psychologic preclimacterium is between 40 and 50, regardless of whether ovulation still takes place or not. And there are also many preclimacterical elements during the phase when the physiologic reduction of functions is already in full swing.

The preclimacterical thrust of activity and the return to an old psychic attitude is set in motion by several motives. Inner and outer signals play a part in this process. Among the outer ones, there is the imminent or already begun emancipation of the children from their mother, the cutting of the psychic umbilical cord on the part of the children. The aging mother's emotional situation is here very much like the little girl's in prepuberty: at that time too the tie between mother and child was loosened and the child's psychic energy turned toward new goals. Now it is the mother who experiences this loosening, although passively, and who must turn her emotional energy elsewhere. With the approach of the climacterium, new motherhood is impossible, and the frustrated activity is directed toward other goals. Simply expressed, this attitude is: "If I cannot have any more children, I must look for something else."

The more unconscious motive for the new activity is the perception of the imminent disappointment and mortification. Here the activity has the effect of a defense mechanism. At the moment when expulsion of ova from the ovary ceases, all the organic processes devoted to the service of the species stop. Woman has ended her existence as bearer of a future life, and has reached her natural end—her partial death—as servant of the species. She is now engaged in an active struggle against her decline.

The thrust of activity also expresses woman's protest, her assertion that she is not merely a servant of the species, not a machine for bearing children, that she has higher brain centers and a complicated emotional life that is not restricted to motherhood. Thus she may succeed in actively finding a way out of the biologic complications.

Despite these preparations for what we have termed partial death, no woman really renounces motherhood as long as monthly or even already irregular bleedings remind her of this possibility. Even here we may venture a comparison with puberty, during which every menstruation signifies the promise and the loss of a child. In preclimacterical women the positive component predominates: "I still menstruate, I can still have a child." In this case menstruation may have only a symbolic meaning; the woman has really renounced new children, but she still wants proof that she is biologically alive. The reactions of the woman who shortly before the climacterium must undergo a radical genital operation, show what great symbolic value the possession of these organs, soon to become useless, still has for her. Increased aggression, depressive moods, etc., are often explainable as due to the loss of the reproductive organs, a loss that for woman is equivalent to castration. For a young girl, menstruation, while it is a sign of maturity, is also an experience full of anxieties and disappointments. The sudden termination of menstruation by operation may have largely the same significance.

In contrast to this kind of reaction, such operations may have a psychologically liberating effect. Women who in protest against imminent biologic processes have developed all sorts of symptoms, often accept the operation as a *fait accompli* to which they must submit with resignation. Especially unmarried or childless women who in their eternal hope that "it may still happen" have been unable to devote themselves wholeheartedly to other things, are as though newborn after an operation that deprives them of their last chance of motherhood. They free their vital energies from the immobility of waiting and put them to use in productive occupations.

Gradually the preclimacterium changes into the climacterium. The graafian follicles cease to open and the mucous membrane of the uterus is no longer periodically replaced. For some time the ovules continue to form, but do not reach maturity; after a shorter or longer interval of time, usually after several years, all gametic traces disappear as though they had never existed, and the whole ovary assumes the character of a solid connective tissue organ. Little by little the whole female genital apparatus is transformed into a number of inactive and superfluous structures.

Similar changes begin simultaneously in the activity of the other endocrine organs. The subcutaneous layer of fat thickens, the skin loses its tension. A masculine growth of hair begins (upper lip, chin, abdomen). The changes that take place in the body of a climacterical woman have the character not only of the cessation of physiologic production but also of general dissolution. Woman's biologic fate manifests itself in the disappearance of her individual feminine qualities at the same time that her service to the species ceases. As we have said, everything she acquired during puberty is now lost piece by piece; with the lapse of the reproductive service, her beauty vanishes, and usually the warm, vital flow of feminine emotional life as well.

The psychologic processes of the climacterium seem like a call for help to enable the woman to continue to experience. The inner tension against the current leads again to the situation to which we have so often referred: the progressive movement toward biologic withering is accompanied by regressive elements. After the preclimacterium, which we have likened to prepuberty, the changes in woman's behavior clearly suggest the analogy between the climacterium and puberty. The climacterium itself can be divided into two stages in accordance with the biologic processes. The first comprises the years when menstruation is considerably disturbed or has stopped completely but when the sexual endocrine apparatus has not yet stopped functioning as a whole. The second stage is probably parallel to the definitive cessation of all life in the gamete-forming part of the organism. The first stage may continue the preclimacterical thrust of activity, but is characterized by an increase of sexual excitation, heightened sexual readiness, and, according to the life situation of the given woman, a more or less vigorous struggle against these sensations, just as in puberty. If up until then the woman has lived in the quietly contented fashion of "respectable" people, the persons around her will be very much surprised by the change in her behavior.

This second puberty, just like the first, is marked by all kinds of oddities of conduct; and although in an older woman these have a comical external effect, their profound meaning is rather tragic. Because of these manifestations, the climacterium is known as the "dangerous age," and a certain type of aging woman has become a comical theatrical type.

One type of climacterical woman displays a quasihypomanic activity. She herself has the feeling of heightened psychic vitality. If previously she avoided violent experiences, she is suddenly seized by an urge to make her life richer, more active. She feels like a young girl, and, as she says, wants to begin her life all over again. She starts a diary, as in puberty, becomes enthusiastic about abstract ideas, changes her attitude toward her family, and leaves her home from the same motives as in her adolescence. With an enthusiasm that often exceeds that of her children, she becomes interested in their ideologies. At the age of 50 she is absolutely unready to renounce anything. She vigorously continues her struggle against the biologic devaluation of her femininity by resort to psychologic means, and is pleased to discover that her chances as a woman have considerably improved in our day. Her mother, she declares, was an old lady at her age. Naturally this improvement is not due to biologic factors: probably nothing has changed in the hormonal processes. Possibly the increasing passivity of men in the prewar years partly accounts for the fact that the chances of older women, in whom men sense more active protection and lesser demands upon their masculinity, have actually improved.

Modern fashions and cosmetics help the aging woman to behave like a girl in puberty. Narcissistic self-delusion makes her painted face appear youthful to her in the mirror. Her rebellion against old age makes her forget all her experience. Even if she has previously displayed good judgment of people, she now surrounds herself with men whose level is far inferior to her own, in order to have the illusion of being admired and loved by many.

Like a pubescent girl she now brags about her personality, and after thirty years of happy marriage she may raise the problem of whether her husband is worthy of her, suggesting that her marriage was a degrading mistake. Sometimes, amidst the difficulties of existence, she begins sentimentally to go back to the first days of her marriage, trying to repeat her experiences or to make up for what she has missed. She makes friends with dubious individuals whom she now attracts as light attracts a moth. Her respectable acquaintances seem to her insignificant and boring. She shows much more interest in disreputable women, whose life now has for her the same mysterious seduction that it had in puberty.

The suggestibility of women in this life period increases markedly, their judgment fails, and they readily fall victim to evil counselors. If their activity is not sufficiently strong, or if their normal inhibitions stop them from puberal acting out, they turn to the past. Instead of having real experiences they regress to fantasying, just as in puberty. To endow their fantasies with real content they dig up old letters from their husbands or from former lovers. A woman who for a long time before her marriage was promiscuous, and escaped from this mode of life into an orderly bourgeois existence, may begin to speak of the "happy days" of which she has been ashamed for years. Another, who before her marriage had an unhappy liaison in which her lover, in her opinion, behaved like a scoundrel, now recalls him with tenderness, praises him for qualities he never had, and writes him letters that she does not mail.

One woman, who during the early stages of her climacterium was quasi-obsessed by a painful and tearful longing for a man whom she had loved platonically many years before, sought psychiatric help because she herself considered her condition abnormal. She followed the advice given her and met the man in question. At this meeting she behaved exactly as she had behaved many years before: she was coy and inaccessible. Later she praised the man for not having abused her alleged readiness to yield to him and for having spared her "purity."

A 50-year-old woman, divorced and then happily married for a second time, behaved similarly. She began inexplicably to yearn for her first husband, concerning whom she correctly reported that he had mistreated her. Realizing that her yearning was morbid, she resorted to psychotherapeutic treatment. In the course of this she discovered that in her youth she had fallen in love with this man and married him, knowing even then that he was inferior to her, because she wanted thus to realize masochistic rape fantasies typical of puberty. But her instinctual dependence upon her aggressive, sadistic husband failed to destroy her pride and dignity, and after a few years of suffering she divorced him. As might have been expected, she then married a more refined, kind, and passive man, with whom she had three children. Her second marriage was harmonious and happy up to the time of her climacterium, although she had remained frigid with her second husband (she had not been so with the first). With the approach of the definitive renunciation, her libido grew more insistent, and she yearned for her earlier gratification. Her rape fantasy reappeared, and her pride, shaken by the climacterium, was no longer strong enough to resist her yearning.

All these women who are no longer able to bridle their intensified libidinous needs, and who are driven to act out their fantasies, repeat their psychologic puberty. The impulses and wishes of that period have actually been present all the time; during the years of maturity they were successfully repressed or sublimated, and now in the climacterium they break through again. The acting-out types usually display a hysterical disposition; here the greater persistence of puberal fantasies is very characteristic. From their earliest childhood to the climacterium, these women tend to indulge in dreams, and puberty endows these dreams with definite contents. At the approach of the real frustration of the climacterium, they escape into the previously created world of fantasy, where they can remain young, beautiful, and in full possession of their femininity.

Other women, just as was the case in puberty, flee from fantasies into reality—a queer reality, as described above, or an orderly, constructive one. Some, again as in puberty, escape into an ascetic mode of life, philanthropic self-sacrifice, or religious devotion. The transformation of a vain, worldly woman into a pious bigot is very typical, as witnessed in the German proverb: "A young harlot, an old nun."

Some women overemphasize their objective evaluation of the process of aging. "I look like an old witch," they say—not only to provoke flattering protestations on the part of others but also to express their deep mortification: "What fate has done to me!"

Many women, in an attempt to strengthen their self-confidence, which is disturbed by the narcissistic mortification of the climacterium, avoid social life because it reminds them of the sad reality, and withdraw into "splendid isolation." Unlike the narcissistic women who in their climacterical fear seek new proofs of love, the solitary ones protect themselves from frustrations with a proud "I am sufficient unto myself," in the manner so typical of puberty.

Woman's relation to her own sex often undergoes a change in the climacterium. Friendships previously loyal and harmless begin to be troubled; well sublimated homosexuality is subjected to the same tests as sometimes in puberty: the sublimation is no longer sufficient, new demands are made, jealousy appears. The so-called homosexual panic is even more frequent, and as a result of their fear-ridden reaction to an unconscious danger, women break old friendships. Paranoid ideas in the climacterium usually result from an intensification of homosexuality previously latent. Two unmarried friends or sisters who have lived together for years in spinsterish seclusion, and calmly followed their respective vocations, suddenly change their behavior. They start to quarrel with each other or ally themselves in a kind of *folie à deux* against the environment—neighbors, relatives, colleagues, etc.[3] In such cases, of course, we are usually dealing with two individuals constitutionally predisposed, who even before the climacterium isolated themselves from the rest of the world and maintained a pathologic relation with each other. But in these cases too the paranoid outbreak results from the climacterical intensification of the inner conflict. It may be recalled here that we are quite familiar with such temporary paranoid reactions to the homosexual danger in puberty. Sometimes they inaugurate a chronic psychotic process.

The frequent depressions during the climacterium contain

[3] DEUTSCH, H.: Folie à deux. Psychoanalyt. Quart., vol. 7, 1938.

justified grief in the face of a declining world. Depressed moods connected with feelings of inferiority are also frequent in adolescents. And just as the depressed moods of young girls are sometimes overcome by a sudden flare-up of ecstatic feelings, so in aging women depression yields to moods of elation.

If we observe the intensified fantasy activity of climacterical women psychoanalytically, we discover that with regard to its deepest unconscious determinants it also repeats the puberal processes. In the intensified hunger to continue being loved as a woman by many, the old prostitution fantasy reappears. An elderly woman, mother of several children and a respectable grandmother, was arrested in a public park for soliciting men, and was taken to the police station. The next day she had amnesia of the events of the preceding night and was sent to the hospital for psychiatric observation. The last thing she remembered was that she had been at a party at the home of one of her friends, where she became slightly drunk, and that one man took her home. When questioned, this man stated that he had brought the woman to the door of her house, and had been a little surprised when she coquettishly extended her hand to him and said airily: "No doubt you would like to spend the night in my place?"

The patient did not remember this incident, for at this point her unconscious fantasies began to operate. It proved impossible to overcome her amnesia, and until her death she refused to believe what she was told about her behavior that night. But she gave such a clear picture of her feelings of solitude, her longings, her night anxieties, and her timidity with men, that the psychologic situation that resulted in the twilight state and the acting out could easily be reconstructed. Our knowledge of the twilight states in young girls who act out their fantasies supplied us with the key to this aging woman's psychology. In both life periods the twilight state brings to light what lies at the bottom of the soul.

The identity of the two phases goes deeper still. We know that liberation from the home milieu, and above all from the ties of the Oedipus complex and its fixations, are at the center of the puberal conflicts. After the woman's many years of good and even very good adjustment to reality, of mature femininity and motherhood, the old gods of the nether world emerge from the depths of psychic life under the assault of the climacterical excitations and take part in the events of the upper world in a new form. Freud called puberty the second edition of the infantile period because in it the old, preserved relations to the parents are remobilized in the form of a revival of the Oedipus complex. In the climacterium we find a third edition, and discover that in the course of all the years only a regrouping has taken place; the never mastered original relationships to the parents are now revived with reference to the grown-up children. The asexual, tender love that once was directed toward the parents is now directed toward the children, and the pure tenderness for them contains—as the love for the parents did in childhood—unconscious sexual admixtures. We have pointed out before that even when still awaiting the birth of her son, the mother elevates him into an ego ideal and he becomes the heir of the grandfatherly model. Everything that the little girl once found godlike in her father, all her valuations, overvaluations, and expectations, are later bestowed on the son. But even the best sublimation product is never perfect. The sexual component that once related to the father is also transferred to the son.

It is now clear that the new edition of the typical puberty fantasies that we find in the climacterium, in all possible variants, contains remnants of the relation to the father and its realization and negation.

The old rape fantasy that led our divorced woman back to her brutal husband did not at all concern him; the prostitution fantasies, now as before, express the replacement of the one and only by many. The psychic structure has been reorganized only to the extent that the place of the former tabooed object has been taken by a new one: the son now replaces the father, and not only as an ideal.

The pull at the psychic umbilical cord and the yearning for the son grow more intense. The increased need for his tender-

ness is now definitely frustrated, and the flight from the son—
just as formerly the flight from the father—results in hunger for
substitute objects. In analyses of climacterical and preclimacterical women, one can observe this reorientation in their fantasies, dreams, and symptoms. Thus a patient beset by
climacterical difficulties, the mother of an adolescent son,
fantasied that she had a woman friend who, in a spirit of heroic
and joyful sacrifice, tenderly initiated adolescent boys into the
mysteries of sensual love. This fantasy was depicted in the
most glowing colors, and it soon became clear that the friend
was the patient herself and that the adolescents were substitutes for her own son. In this connection one should recall a
dream recorded by H. von Hug-Hellmuth and utilized by
Freud.[4]

The dreamer was a 50-year-old woman "who night and day
had no other thought than concern about her child." In
her dreams she showed herself willing

> To put her person at the disposal of the military, officers, and privates, for
> the gratification of their love needs, to fulfil her patriotic obligation. But
> one condition had to be observed: age had to be taken into account; an el-
> derly woman must not be made to be with quite young boys. . . . This would
> be horrible.

The prostitution fantasy under the mask of a patriotic deed,
and the repressed relation to young boys as substitutes for the
son, are very clear here. Another patient, previously healthy,
began a neurosis with a nightmare representing coitus with her
son. Again, a 50-year-old woman who was treated for depressions disclosed the following history.

As a 40-year-old spinster she had married her 55-year-old
teacher. She was a talented musician and had previously been
living with an older woman friend for whom she felt a conscious
homosexual inclination, which, however, was not translated
into practice. She imagined that her marriage with an older
man would be a peaceful haven, and this turned out to be the
case. Her relations with her husband were not entirely pla-

[4] FREUD, S.: Introductory lectures on psychoanalysis. Transl. by Joan Rivière.
London: Allen & Unwin, 1929, lect. 11.

tonic, but were very unexciting and only slightly gratifying sexually. Before the beginning of her depression, the patient had gone through a state of excitation that was diagnosed as climacterical. As a result of hormonal therapy, her excitation ceased and was replaced by a depression.

The patient herself was able to report that her excitation had begun for a very real reason. Her husband had taken into his home a young and talented boy pupil whom she could not bear. His presence made her restless and angry, and she left her home in climacterical excitement. She confessed that she had not taken the pills that were given her to calm her nerves, and explained that she quieted down only when she learned that the young man had left the house. Then she returned, but soon fell ill with the depression that brought her to me. This depression was due to her bereavement of the young man (thirty years younger than she), with whom she had unconsciously fallen in love.

Her homosexual feeling for her older woman friend expressed a typical attachment to a mother figure under pressure of the sense of guilt; as a young girl she had fled from her father tie into an overcompensated relation with her mother. In later years she managed to engage in a relation with a man, a fatherly man, but apparently with the exclusion of sexuality. Her sexual yearning broke through only in the climacterium, transferred to a "son." It was obvious that the young musician really played the part of a son for her. Her depression covered feelings of resentment toward her husband: he had failed to give her a child, a son. But he himself, she felt, had filled out this gap in his life by taking a son into his home to teach and to love. Why did she not take part in this way out? She answered that question indirectly: she had felt sexual yearning for the boy instead of tender maternal love. In her climacterium she repeated the experience of her puberty: at that time she had fled from her father because she began to fear her love for him.

It is interesting to note that many years ago, a physician who was not a psychiatrist stated that the physical symptoms of the climacterium are strikingly reminiscent of those observed in given individuals in their puberty. J. Wiesel[5] writes:

I was struck by the fact that, for instance, the gastro-intestinal disturbances observed during puberty with extraordinary frequency also inagurate the climacterium. Furthermore, it can be established that in cases in which hyperthyreosis begins in puberty, and later vanishes without becoming manifest again, the climacterium too starts with hyperthyreosis; or if during puberty the pigmentation of the skin was modified, such modification also occurs during the climacterium. The same is true of vasomotor disturbances, eczema, anomalies of growth, etc. I am struck by the case of a patient who formed a thick strand of snow white hair during puberty; this strand later disappeared, but reappeared in the climacterium at the same spot and with the same dimensions.

Wiesel concludes: "I wanted to show to what extent the symptomatology of puberty can be likened to the events of the climacterium."

Wiesel's conclusion as to the organic symptomatology is true to an even greater extent of the psychic. Numerous observations have so thoroughly convinced me of this analogy that, basing myself on the course of puberty—especially if it has been pathologic—I make a prognosis for the climacterium and often advise psychoanalytic treatment as a preventive of disturbances.

It is not clear at present whether this analogy extends to the normal hormonal functions. But the menstrual processes, interestingly enough, often have their counterpart later: for instance, the menstrual depressions of adolescence, which disappear during the years of the reproductive service, sometimes recur in the climacterium. Although there are no bleedings, the depressions occur at regular intervals corresponding to the dates of the menses. Analysis reveals that the content of these moods is grief: "If I were still a complete woman, I would be menstruating now." With the end of menstruation the hope of a child is lost, and, just as in puberty, the idea is: "I shall have no child."

All these modes of behavior in which we can find similarities as between puberty and the climacterium may be intensified

[5] WIESEL, J.: Innere Klinik des Klimakteriums. In Handb. d. Biol. u. Path. d. Weibes.

into psychosis if there is a disposition to it—into puberal psychoses in young girls and into climacterical psychoses in aging women. The content of the delirious ideas as revealed by psychoanalysis often shows the striking kinship between the two processes.

This analogy is also unmistakable in the sexual manifestations: both the pubescent girl and the climacterical woman clearly display an increase of sexual excitation. Many aging women who were frigid during the reproductive period now become sexually sensitive, others become frigid only now, and often monogamous marriage ceases to gratify their intensified narcissism. At a time when the husband's sexual potency is usually low, the wife demands that he desire her with greater ardor. Other women, who have previously borne their frigidity well, now begin to manifest all its typical accompanying phenomena: their changing moods, lack of stability, and excitability become a painful problem both for them and for those around them. Complete absence of order and sense of responsibility alternate with extreme pedantry. The moderation of married life or the extinction of the sexual stimulus by habit is no longer tolerated, and the environmental influences thanks to which woman preserves her marital exclusiveness, have little effect now. But since reality and the acquired inhibition are very strong, the intensified sexuality usually does not go farther than self-gratification.

The obtruding sexual fantasies are connected with strong orgastic vaginal reactions, even in women who were not vaginally excitable before. Others revive the clitoris masturbation they long ago gave up; this is especially true of old maids without any direct genital experience. At any rate, sexual excitability outlasts reproductive capacity by a long time. My observations of a considerable number of women in early and late climacterium confirm the truth of Princess Metternich's witty answer to the question: "When does a woman cease being capable of sexual love?"

She replied: "You must ask someone else, I am only sixty."

We do not know whether the intensification of sexual excitability is of endocrine origin. It is difficult to assume that an involution, a somatic reduction, should begin with a real intensification of a function. Possibly this intensification is a purely psychic process, a reaction to the processes of reduction, their overcompensation. In contrast to it, we have in puberty a readiness heightened by the somatic development, but this readiness is under the pressure of the forbidding "too early." This prohibition often results in a bizarre and varied behavior characteristic of puberty.

In the climacterium, the "too late" has the same effect as the "too early" of puberty. In puberty various defense mechanisms operate to resist the sexual assault; in the climacterium they operate to negate the loss. In puberty, the defense processes serve for the construction of solid sublimations—spiritual values, social ideals, artistic and sports interests; in the climacterium the same attempt is often made with little success. Both puberty and the climacterium try to construct a present, the former with an eye on the future, the latter with an eye on the past.

The climacterium not only has a tendency to repeat the neurotic and psychotic states of puberty, using analogous defense mechanisms; in addition, neurotic features that previously appeared as character traits become intensified, just as in puberty. As we have said, eccentric actions characterize women with hysterical dispositions; this same disposition was once expressed in a charming, exuberant puberty inclined to adventurousness. The puberal obsessional-neurotic disposition stopped short of neurosis, but resulted in defense mechanisms in the form of strengthened masculine tendencies and intellectualization. The effect of symptomless obsessional neurosis on woman's development is usually very typical: it creates emotionally impoverished, intellectually unproductive, but ambitious personalities that are often outstandingly intelligent but completely unoriginal—in brief, the type to which the lines of *Faust* (vol. 1, p. 291) seem to apply so exactly. Up to the climacterium, the life of these women is under the sign of a well sublimated masculinity—well sublimated in the sense that their masculine tendencies have not led to neurotic distortions, although they have given their lives a definite character. In such women, the climacterium manifests itself in the fact that the previously unexpressed feminine tendencies now present their claims and fall into conflict with the masculine ones. These women avoided a pathologic outcome of the conflict in puberty by a good sublimation, but in the climacterium they fall ill because of their inability to gratify their new, belatedly awakening femininity. In brief, they fall ill not of the masculinity complex in puberty, but of the femininity complex in the climacterium. This process is strikingly reminiscent of the puberal processes described by Freud[6]:

It can frequently be observed that the very girls who up until the year of prepuberty have displayed a boyish nature and inclinations, become hysterical beginning with puberty. In a number of cases, the hysterical neurosis only corresponds to an excessively marked typical repression thrust that creates woman by the elimination of masculine sexuality.

The process is analogous because in both cases masculinity is given up in the attempt to become a woman, which usually fails in the climacterium.

The active, restless forms of the climacterium as I have described them do not represent exceptions. They are probably just as frequent as the depressive ones, which in their external manifestations are more "normal." Almost every woman in the climacterium goes through a shorter or longer phase of depression. While the active women deny the biologic state of affairs, the depressive ones overemphasize it. The physiologic decline is felt as the proximity of death, life begins to seem pale and purposeless; a mood of grief tones the content of the woman's psychic life even though she continues to participate in external life as before. The depression is often so mild that only the woman herself or her closest intimates notice the change. But more or less pronounced hypochondriac ideas appear, which in an overwhelming majority of cases relate to the genital organs. What was formerly a source of life now, in the hypochondriac fears, becomes a malignant growth. I have

[6] FREUD, S.: Allgemeines über den hysterischen Anfall: Kleine Schriften zur Neurosenlehre. Vienna: Deuticke, 1909.

often met women who speak of their "tumors" as though tumor were as inevitable as death. Psychologically this expresses the devaluation of the vital organ, the destruction of its function.

These "normal" depressive moods in some cases disappear, in others they develop into a morbid melancholy. It is my impression that feminine-loving women have a milder climacterium than masculine-aggressive ones.

Much naturally depends upon external conditions and the circumstances of the woman's previous life. Feminine women who have lived in a harmonious, happy, sexually gratifying marriage, enjoy the late storms in its calm haven, and many an old married couple speak of their second honeymoon. The artists in love, the women with a rich and warm erotic life, use the last urges not in panic to deny the impending loss, like ridiculous old women, but to enjoy their erotic gifts to the end. Incidentally, it is well known that women whose life content is mostly beauty and feminine charm remain young and beautiful for a strikingly long time. "Love for one's own person is perhaps the secret of beauty," says Freud. Apparently these women possess a psychic cosmetic in a certain form of feminine narcissism, a cosmetic that other, less resourceful women try to replace by rouge, massages, and youthful dress. The former remain young for a long time, the latter maintain that they feel young.

A frequently cited example of a youthful old woman is the famous French wit and beauty, Ninon de Lenclos, who is said at the age of 65 to have aroused the stormy love of a young man. He turned out to be her son and committed suicide when he learned this fact. Whether this modern Oedipus myth is true is questionable, but psychologically it is correct; the love object of the aging woman is the son. And for three generations of climacterical women with youthful hearts, Ninon de Lenclos has been the ego ideal.

Feminine-erotic women, experienced in love, accept the inevitable with greater dignity and calm than the spinsterish, frigid, ever frustrated ones. The fear of these latter before their loss also expresses their indignation at having been swindled of their femininity earlier in life. It is apparently easier to contemplate a darkening future when one can contrast it with a brilliant and pleasant past. Reference to former possessions doubtless also comforts the narcissism mortified by loss. That is why aging women talk so much about their glorious past and construct an illusory world that they themselves finally believe in.

Women who are good observers of themselves report that, confronted with the climacterium, they experience a kind of depersonalization, a split, in which they feel simultaneously young and old: "Is this aging woman really myself? Only a short time ago I was that promising young girl, whom I feel in myself still so alive." And they turn away from themselves in order to love that young being longingly as a lost object. Another, more favorable method of overcoming the disaster of the climacterium is continuous, active, warm, and successful love wooing, so characteristic of women with definite narcissistic structure. But this wooing must originate in a genuine and permanent need for being loved, in order not to become crippled under the assault of the physiologic processes. The woman wooing from an inner need and the old woman smiling with insincere friendliness are not identical.

Beautiful narcissistic women whose beauty seems to be the center of their existence, often make one wonder: "What will they do in the climacterium?" It is interesting to observe how the self-love of these women prophylactically provides for this situation. Before they are surprised by the disaster, they avert it by gradually turning to an occupation that later will supply them with a gratifying substitute. They utilize some capital they possess in the form of a modest talent, with which they can maneuver cleverly by virtue of their self-love. Thus one sees a beautiful woman suddenly becoming interested in politics, appearing as a speaker at meetings, making important contributions to an idealogic movement, or emerging as an art patroness. In brief, she makes and feels herself important and thus avoids the disaster that the physiologic process would have brought to her narcissism.

The psychic reactions to the climacterium also greatly depend upon the woman's center of gravity and upon her own opinion of the real meaning of her existence. If she has been dominated by the masculinity complex and the new thrust toward femininity does not confuse her, her climacterium is very much like the processes that affect men also at a certain age: for man's self-assurance ebbs considerably with the decrease of his potency, and his fear of the more active, daring youth and his reactions to his own decline have a typical character.

Both men and masculine women, in accordance with their personalities, can age with dignity or degrade themselves through the narcissistic mortification. Aggressive references to past and no longer recognized exploits play the same part in the psychic structure of men and masculine women as the old woman's assurance that she was once a beauty; and the appeal is evaluated by others in the same way.

In the course of woman's life, masculinity often plays the part of a rock of salvation. This is also true in the climacterium. An intellectual sublimation through a profession protects her against the biologic trauma. This applies to an even greater extent to feminine women who have not staked their feminine qualities on the single card of eroticism and motherliness, but have also invested them in good sublimations. On the other hand, if their social and professional interests have taken excessive hold of them, these women are threatened in the climacterium by the danger that I call *pseudomasculinity*. Although not really masculine like the intellectualizing woman, they have been drawn under the pressure of certain inner or outer complications into a mode of life in which neither their feminine eroticism nor their maternal love could fully blossom. Without going into details, I shall stress only one trait that differentiates such women from the masculine ones: they preserve their genuinely feminine qualities even in a masculine-active mode of life and display little envy in their characterologic personality. In the climacterium they realize their mistake and would halt the biologic process in order to be able to love more and to be maternal for a longer time. Very often they are too busy; constant exhaustion then replaces peaceful serenity, and cleverness replaces maternal wisdom.

The various typical organic symptoms of the climacterium in most cases acquire a secondary psychologic significance, and, vice versa, are also strongly determined by psychologic factors. Those who have not had an opportunity to gain a deeper insight will hardly believe how much anxiety is concealed behind the hot flushes, heart sensations, feelings of dizziness, sweatings, etc. Various new physical habits are—as in the years of early childhood—masked forms of onanism, and the numerous difficulties with elimination and their accompanying psychologic phenomena are reminiscent of the behavior of little children. The pregnancy fantasy is concealed here as in the various other organic symptoms of the climacterium. This fantasy is now as far from realization as it was in the anal birth fantasies of little children, or in the vomiting, intestinal complaints, etc., of puberty. The "too early" and "too late" meet here likewise.

Successful psychotherapy in the climacterium is made difficult because usually there is little one can offer to the patient as a substitute for the fantasy gratifications. There is a large element of real fear behind the neurotic anxiety, for reality has actually become poor in prospects, and resignation without compensation is often the only solution. And resignation is the hardest task for a human being!

In the future many difficulties of the climacterium may be avoided through influencing of the endocrine apparatus. With the modesty of a great man who realizes the limits of his own achievements, Freud left room for such possibilities in the treatment of neuroses. For the time being, however, aging women must accept the *status quo*; they are wise to base their positive life values on what they can still enjoy.

For a motherly woman, the trauma of the loss of capacity for reproduction is deeper and more important than the narcissistic mortification of vanishing beauty and youth.

Has nature really been so cruel to woman and has it prepared only disappointments for a considerable part of her life? Has it deprived her of everything that formerly constituted the deepest meaning of her existence? Let us look at the situation more closely. One of the tasks of this book has been to attempt an understanding of the nature of motherliness, not only in the direct exercise of the reproductive function, but also as a principle radiating into all the fields of life, a principle innate in woman.

Fortunately this principle outlasts the capacity of the generative organs. Without realizing it, the motherly woman knows how to save her psychologic capacity from atrophy, and reality helps her in this endeavor. The "lost" children who have emancipated themselves from their mother return to her if they have succeeded in really achieving freedom. If the mother has understood her children's aspirations to liberty, if she has not abused the methods by which she tried to attach them to herself, she has happy prospects of richly repossessing them. She must lose them in order to possess them again. Only if she has been tolerant of her children's hatred during puberty, if she has avoided exploiting their guilt feelings, if she has really deeply, and not only intellectually, understood that she must withdraw from her maternal tasks, is she fully justified in her hope that she will not lose her children. The climacterium occurs at a point when, if the development of the mother-child relationship was normal, peaceful reconciliation has already taken place; and although the emotional relations have lost their former intimacy and exclusiveness, they can be very gratifying to the aging woman.

We must not forget that a motherly woman often has the opportunity to increase the host of her children within the framework of the family without performing reproductive service herself. There are, for instance, her children-in-law, and the intense and often complicated emotional relationships resulting from this new kinship. The possibilities extend from conventional indifference and ineradicable hatred to gratifying, loving tenderness.

In *Totem and Taboo* Freud[7] has said everything that psychoanalysis has to say about the problem of the relations between the mother-in-law and the son-in-law:

[7] FREUD, S.: Totem and taboo. In The basic writings of Sigmund Freud. New York: Modern Libr., 1938, pp. 817 ff.

It is known that also among civilized races the relation of son-in-law and mother-in-law belongs to one of the most difficult sides of family organization. Although laws of avoidance no longer exist in the society of the white races of Europe and America, much quarrelling and displeasure would often be avoided if they did exist and did not have to be re-established by individuals. Many a European will see an act of high wisdom in the laws of avoidance which savage races have established to preclude any understanding between two persons who have become so closely related. There is hardly any doubt that there is something in the psychological situation of mother-in-law and son-in-law which furthers hostilities between them and renders living together difficult. The fact that the witticisms of civilized races show such a preference for this very mother-in-law theme seems to me to point to the fact that the emotional relations between mother-in-law and son-in-law are controlled by components which stand in sharp contrast to each other. I mean that the relation is really ambivalent; that is, it is composed of conflicting feelings of tenderness and hostility.

A certain part of these feelings is evident. The mother-in-law is unwilling to give up the posession of her daughter; she distrusts the stranger to whom her daughter has been delivered, and shows a tendency to maintain the dominating position to which she is accustomed at home. On the part of the man, there is the determination not to subject himself any longer to any foreign will, his jealousy of all persons who preceded him in the possession of his wife's tenderness, and, last but not least, his aversion to being disturbed in his illusion of sexual over-valuation. As a rule such a disturbance emanates for the most part from his mother-in-law, who reminds him of her daughter through so many common traits but who lacks all the charm of youth, such as beauty and that psychic spontaneity which makes his wife precious to him.

The knowledge of hidden psychic feelings which psychoanalytic investigation of individuals has given us, makes it possible to add other motives to the above. Where the psycho-sexual needs of the woman are to be satisfied in marriage and family life, there is always the danger of dissatisfaction through the premature termination of the conjugal relation, and the monotony in the wife's emotional life. The aging mother protects herself against this by living through the lives of her children, by identifying herself with them and making their emotional experiences her own. Parents are said to remain young with their children, and this is, in fact, one of the most valuable psychic benefits which parents derive from their children. Childlessness thus eliminates one of the best means to endure the necessary resignation imposed upon the individual through marriage. This emotional identification with the daughter may easily go so far with the mother that she also falls in love with the man her daughter loves, which leads, in extreme cases, to severe forms of neurotic ailments on account of the violent psychic resistance against this emotional predisposition. At all events the tendency to such infatuation is very frequent with the mother-in-law, and either this infatuation itself or the tendency opposed to it joins the conflict of contending forces in the psyche of the mother-in-law. Very often it is just this harsh and sadistic component of the love emotion which is turned against the son-in-law in order better to suppress the forbidden tender feelings.

Women who have succeeded in harmonizing the ambivalent psychic impulses find their old age enriched by an additional tenderly loved son who is the son-in-law.

Perhaps even more complex is the relation with the daughter-in-law. Renunciation of the son in favor of a stranger is a much more crucial test than relinquishment of the daughter to a son-in-law. A life and death struggle between the rivals can arise, and its outcome is always disastrous for the mother-in-law.

Marie Bonaparte, in her analysis of the famous Lefèbre case,[8] has given us an insight into the psychic life of Madame Lefèbre, who shot her hated daughter-in-law because she was unable to master her terrible hateful envy of the latter's pregnancy. The psychic processes that preceded Madame Letèbre's psychotic act of murder were fairly ordinary. A domineering, ambitious, matriarchal woman tried to attach her husband and sons to herself in a possessive manner. She succeeded in this until her son André tore himself away from her—"this was the first wound." His marriage was an even more painful wound. Madame Lefèbre

Longed increasingly for her son who no longer fully belonged to her. Night and day she brooded over the grief caused her by her daughter-in-law who separated her from her son.... During the first months of his marriage, Madame Lefèbre's hatred grew, but she tolerated her daughter-in-law.... Only upon learning that her daughter-in-law was pregnant, did she feel that the situation was unbearable and she began to conceive her crime.

Marie Bonaparte assumes, probably rightly so, that Madame Lefèbre herself had pregnancy fantasies in connection with her climacterical symptoms and could not bear the fact that her daughter-in-law should receive, particularly from her son, what she herself could no longer have—a child.

[8] BONAPARTE, M.: Der Fall Lefèbre. Imago, vol. 15, 1929.

Mrs. Z., a mother-in-law whom I observed, experienced the same murderous hatred toward her daughter-in-law as did Madame Lefèbre. She was not psychotic and did not go beyond urging her only son to abandon his beloved wife, on the ground that a physical illness prevented the latter from giving him a child and her a grandchild.

Mrs. Z. had several married daughters and a number of grandchildren. But she insisted on having a grandchild from her only son. She was obsessed by the idea of making her son divorce his wife, and tried to force the fulfillment of her wish by means of heart attacks and death threats. The son fled from his mother to the battle front, kept his relation with his legitimate and beloved wife secret, and was increasingly tormented by a feeling of guilt: "My mother will die because of me." For the mother, her son's marriage had only this meaning: since she herself could not conceive a son by him, the other woman must perform this task, and give birth to a child for her, the actual mother. She was a kind of grandmotherly Aunt Tula who was inhibited by her fear of incest and commissioned another woman to fulfill her wish for a child, while she desired to preserve her position of uniquely beloved woman. But her daughter-in-law's sterility made her a rival and fanned the mother's jealous hatred.

Many mothers endure promiscuity in their sons more easily than their monogamous love. They remind us of the daughters who assign the role of humiliated sexual object to their own mothers, only to appropriate the "better" part of their fathers for themselves. A daughter-in-law who becomes a mother herself seems to the jealous mother-in-law to endanger her tender possession of her son more than a daughter-in-law who is only a sexual object. The mother also fears that fatherhood may cause her own son, who is still a little boy in her eyes, to grow up and liberate himself from her.

However, a normal, kindly, motherly woman has different, gratifying opportunities in her relation with her daughter-in-law. In the first place, this relation, if the women involved are tender and capable of love, can develop into warm friendship without unleashing unconscious competition. In the second place, it is not true that the son's wife always takes his mother's beloved away from her. For even more than by her son's love for another woman, his mother is endangered by his fear of being too strongly tied to her. I have often observed an estranged son returning to his mother with tender feelings when he felt protected from his mother tie by his love for a wife. The daughter-in-law, in such cases, returns the lost son to his mother, and if she herself assumes the role of a tender daughter, the aging woman has acquired two new children—she has, so to speak, given birth to them in her psychic world.

The aging woman's need to have children is also intensified in those who are unmarried or have never had any children. This fact is movingly illustrated by the story of a 50-year-old employee who had led a peaceful, contented existence for many years, and who had become attached to her work. One day, while dining with friends, she heard that another employed woman was about to give birth to a child, and would be glad to take someone into her home as a mother substitute. The old spinster was asked facetiously whether she would accept this job. She laughed, but from that moment on the idea did not leave her head; she was as though obsessed by the prospect of having a child. She left her good position and sacrificed all the rest of her life to this child of another woman. It is difficult to decide whether she was driven by instinct, the power of the hormonal processes, or the suppressed eternal feminine longing for a child that was aroused by the horror of the "too late."

However, in most cases, old spinsters and childless women, when it is too late to make up for their missed motherhood, and the psychologic reaction is that of "sour grapes," become intolerant and impatient toward children, who pay them back with spiteful hate.

Despite everything, the end of woman's reproductive function does not mean that she has completely surrendered to decline. Nature shows more consideration than that. After motherhood has ceased to serve the species, it goes on serving the individual experience. Counting the two preliminary phases of motherhood, the girl's childhood and puberty, we may say that old age adds a fourth phase, which is grandmotherhood.

Even in the preliminary phases we have more or less motherly girls; later we have motherly and unmotherly women, and I have tried to describe the great variety of forms comprised in the seemingly simple term mother. The same can be done for the term grandmother. There are as many kinds of grandmothers as there are individual types and characters of mothers. Above all, there are good, motherly grandmothers and wicked, unmotherly grandmothers.

We shall first turn our attention to the good ones. Since they are seldom accessible to direct psychoanalytic observation, our remarks will of necessity be brief. Even so, we are able to discover three types.

1. For the mother who as a grandmother continues her motherhood, the grandchildren are simply the youngest among her children. After a shorter or longer interruption of her maternal joys and sorrows, she experiences her grandchildren with the same emotional reactions with which she once experienced her children. In her psychic world it is as though she has been taking a vacation from motherhood for a time, and now has come back. Sometimes she has been enriched by experience, sometimes she does not quite agree with all sorts of changes that progress has brought about, but on the whole she is a happy and solicitous mother. The main difference is that the transference tendencies in this case have an additional generation to draw upon for models. If formerly she wanted in her children to realize what she herself had lacked, she now wants to realize in her grandchildren what she was denied by her children. This time, of course, ideologies, qualities, or ambitious gratifications are rarely involved. If the aging woman had no sons, she salutes the little grandson with particular joy; if she lacked a daughter, her daughter-in-law will doubly compensate by giving birth to a girl. In brief, definite emotional needs are now expected to be fulfilled.

In the eyes of this grandmother, the grandchild means above

all and always the real return of the child, her child. For a motherly woman, in her unfulfilled longing for motherhood, returns with her wishes to the past in which she had little children. The climacterium only intensifies in her something that has always been present, ever since her children left her to pursue their own independent ways. Just as the narcissistic woman is in love with her lost past, the motherly woman is in love with the past of her motherhood, during which she really had her children, because she was indispensable to them. "Children should always remain little," thinks many a mother when her grown-up son leaves. She objectifies this longing in the grandchildren, restores the severed umbilical cord, and reconstructs her world that seemed irretrievably lost.

With her grandchildren, the motherly grandmother repeats the tenderness, the spirit of sacrifice, and the solicitous activity that she displayed toward her own children. It is true that of these three qualities of motherhood, the two first are better preserved, and that nature has wisely weakened the third. If this is not the case, if the active tendencies prove stronger than wise adjustment to new reality, conflicts arise between the daughter or daughter-in-law and the grandmother, and the latter's too active concern is felt as unwelcome interference.

2. The second type of the good grandmother presents perhaps more complicated features. The aging woman has reached that station in her life in which her own motherhood has no prospects. She no longer wants anything of this lost world, she has inwardly adjusted herself to the frustration. But she is far removed from giving up the game; she still loves life, has varied interests, and has already succeeded in filling out the great gap created by the decline of her physiologic functions. She accepts grandmotherhood as a gift of heaven, and does not experience it as a continuation of her own motherhood, but as a quite new edition of it, through identification with her daughter. She has memories and experiences of the past, but she can enjoy motherhood as a personal experience only through identification. One elderly woman, a former beauty, was very happy to accompany her beautiful daughter-in-law to public places,

theaters, concerts, etc. At the entrance she would stand a few steps behind her, and note the flattering remarks and admiring glances of which her daughter-in-law was the object. She laughingly admitted that she felt as she had in long-ago times, when she herself had been beautiful and vain. The grandmother type we are discussing now experiences her grandchildren in exactly the same way. Her daughter's worries, efforts, disappointments, and joys become her own. In her relations to her grandchildren she also experiences the world that reawakens for her through identification.

We know that the process of identification involves certain dangers. To identify also signifies to take someone else's place, and the loving grandmother can easily become a hateful and hated competitor.

In this world of motherhood, teeming with repetitions, the grandmother usually must assume the role of assistant mother, just as she did in puberty; she becomes a third party in the mother-child relationship. Then she was too young by a generation, now she is in an analogous position, because the child's own mother claims to be older and wiser by a whole generation of human experience. And the wise grandmother does not try to dispel her daughter's illusion that the experience of a whole generation is more valuable than her own personal experience. If she has preserved her feminine introspective power, she knows that her own experience too is an illusion, for she is driven by the regressive forces of the repetition compulsion and by her longing for the past, and has reached the same stage with her little grandchild in which she was when his father or mother was as little as he is now. Both these grandmother types recall the assistant mother. The anxious grandmother is even more frequent than the anxious mother. The latter may refer to her lack of experience, the former fears to apply her experience. Deep in her psychic life she feels the competing jealousy that she wants to avoid. She tries to please the other woman; this makes her uncertain, ambivalent, and anxious. Even the wisest and best grandmother is after all only the grandmother, where she wishes to be the mother. The daughter's or daughter-in-law's psychology, her attitude toward the grandmother, the whole psychologic interaction, can naturally influence the grandmother's behavior.

3. The third type is the grandmother par excellence. She has renounced everything, she does not continue anything, she does not seek repetitions, she needs no identifications, she is free of competitive feelings. In all her relations she is freer than at any other stages of life, perhaps she confronts life with the same directness as a little child. She is freed from her own passions, perhaps the conqueror of them. All she wants from the world is peace; she does not reach out for the inaccessible, she wants only what she can have. She does not suffer from the split between will and ability, her gaze is not directed to any distant goal. She is now as kind as a human being who has accepted the imminence of death and as wise as only a kind human being can be. And because she is free of all human ambivalence, the children usually love her unambivalently, with a minimum of their own typical aggressions. She represents only one danger for the mother's pedagogic efforts: she pampers the children, but this pampering when done by the grandmother is an act of wisdom, because she is moved by kindness.

> You, little grandmother, with a golden mind!
> You, little mother, with a soft heart![9]

These words from a Mordvin lamentation for the dead grandmother prove that "the grandmother's tenderness toward the grandchild and that of the grandchild toward the grandmother, must be regarded not as a product of civilization but as a general trait of the human soul."[10] This, incidentally, applies to most human relationships.

There are also wicked grandmothers, because there are wicked old women. Hence the term witch. These women do not want to be disturbed by their grandchildrem, or, like Madame Lefèbre, they want them for themselves, in burning envy of their daughters or daughters-in-law.

[9] Ploss and Bartels: Op. cit., p. 377.
[10] Op. cit.

Old age brings regressions in its train. What takes place in the sexual sphere becomes a pattern for the personality as a whole. The typical characterologic changes of involution— depressive moods, paranoid traits, increasing orderliness and pedantry coupled with avarice and fear of poverty, the emotional emphasis on excretory and alimentary processes—are the product of infantile regressions. With these, the ambivalence of emotional life increases, self-seeking egoism replaces altruistic feelings, and aggressive hatred replaces love. All these features characterize the dreaded wicked grandmother.

Whatever course a given woman's life has taken—whether it has been devoted to trivial and selfish or to noble and broadly human goals—she believes, as a grandmother, that she has fulfilled herself only if she has been rich in those experiences that constitute the essence of motherhood. This book has attempted to break down the psychologic aspect of motherhood into its numerous components and to show what rich experience and happiness woman can find in her biologic destiny. The shortest road to this goal is that of the direct biologic function. But woman can also make enormous contributions in the social, artistic, and scientific fields by drawing indirectly upon the active aspirations of motherhood and the emotional warmth of motherliness.

In the present phase of our civilization, woman's ambition to break with the old traditions of her existence is being realized more and more successfully. The advances of medicine will increasingly lighten the biologic tasks of woman, and it will be possible to divert the energies thus released to other goals. All those to whom the ideals of freedom and equality are not empty words sincerely desire that woman should be socially equal to man. The postwar generation will play its part in hastening this ן rocess. However, the experiences presented in this book show that woman's achievement of full social equality will be beneficent to her and to mankind as a whole only if at the same time she achieves ample opportunity to develop her femininity and motherliness.

Bibliography

ABRAHAM, K.: Traum und Mythus. Leipzig, 1909.

———: Koinzidierende Phantasien bei Mutter und Sohn. Internat. Ztschr. f. Psychoanal., vol. 11, 1925.

———: Selected papers. London: Hogarth, 1929.

ALEXANDER, F.: The medical value of psychoanalysis. New York: Norton, 1936.

BALINT, A.: Liebe zur Mutter und Mutterliebe. Internat. Ztschr. f. Psychoanal., vol. 24, 1938.

BARRETT, W. G.: Penis envy and urinary control, pregnancy fantasies and constipation: Episodes in the life of a little girl. Psychoanalyt. Quart., vol. 8, 1939.

BENEDEK, T., AND RUBENSTEIN, B. B.: Ovarian activity and psychodynamic processes. Psychosom. Med., vol. 1, 1939.

BIVIN, G., AND KLINGER, M. P.: Pseudocyesis. Bloomington, Ind.: Principia Press, 1937.

BONAPARTE, M.: Der Fall Lefèbre. Imago, vol. 15, 1929.

BRIFFAULT, R.: The mothers. New York: Macmillan, 1931.

BURLINGHAM, D. T.: Die Einfühlung des Kleinkindes in die Mutter. Imago, vol. 21, 1935.

CLOTHIER, F.: Problems of illegitimacy. Ment. Hyg., vol. 30, 1941.

———: Psychological implications of unmarried parenthood. Am. J. Orthopsychiat., vol. 13, 1943.

COLETTE [pseud.]: Nuit blanche. In ASWELL, M. L. (ed.): It's a woman's world, New York: Whittlesey, 1944.

DEUTSCH, F.: Studies in pathogenesis. Psychoanalyt. Quart., vol. 2, 1933.

———: Euthanasia: A clinical study. Ibid., vol. 5, 1936.

DEUTSCH, H.: Psychoanalyse der weiblichen Sexualfunktionen. Vienna: Internat. Psychoanal. Verlag, 1925.

———: Zur Genese des Familienromans. Internat. Ztschr. f. Psychoanal., vol. 16, 1930.

———: Psychoanalysis of the neuroses. London: Hogarth, 1932.

———: Motherhood and sexuality. Psychoanalyt. Quart., vol. 2, 1933.

———: Folie à deux. Ibid., vol. 7, 1938.

———: Some forms of emotional disturbances and their relationship to schizophrenia. Ibid., vol. 9, 1942.

———: Some psychoanalytic observations in surgery. Psychosom. Med., vol. 4, 1942.

DUNBAR, H. F.: Emotions and bodily changes (ed. 2). New York: Columbia Univ. Press, 1938.

———: Psychosomatic relationships between mother and infant. Psychosom. Med., vol. 6, no. 2.

EISLER, J. M.: Über hysterische Erscheinungen im Uterus. Internat. Ztschr. f. Psychoanal., vol. 9, 1923.

FENICHEL, O.: The ego and the affects. Psychoanalyt. Rev., vol. 28, 1941.

FERENCZI, S.: Das unwillkommene Kind und sein Todestrieb. Internat. Ztschr. f. Psychoanal., vol. 15, 1929.

———: Thalassa: a theory of genitality. Psychoanalyt. Quart. vol. 2, 1933; vol. 3, 1934.

FREUD, A.: Psychoanalysis for teachers and parents. New York: Emerson Bks., 1935.

FREUD, S.: Ein Fall von hypnotischer Heilung. Ztschr. f. Hypnot., Suggestionstherap., Suggestionsl., vol. 1, 1892.

———: Allgemeines über den hysterischen Anfall: Kleine Schriften zur Neurosenlehre. Vienna: Deuticke, 1909.

———: Introductory lectures on psychoanalysis. Transl. by Joan Rivière. London: Allen & Unwin, 1929.

———: Concerning the sexuality of woman. Psychoanalyt. Quart., vol. 1, 1932.

———: New introductory lectures on psychoanalysis. New York: Norton, 1933.

———: Totem and taboo. In The basic writings of Sigmund Freud. New York: Modern Libr., 1938.

———: Moses and monotheism. New York: Knopf, 1939.

———: Group psychology and the analysis of the ego. London: Hogarth, 1940.

———: On narcissism: An introduction. Collected Papers, vol. 4.

———: The taboo of virginity: Contribution to the psychology of love. Ibid., vol. 4.

FROMM-REICHMANN, F.: Notes on the mother role in the family group. Bull. Menninger Clin., vol. 4, no. 5, 1940.

GIARD, A.: Les origines de l'amour maternel. Bull. de l'Inst. gén. de psychol., vol. 5, 1905.

GREENACRE, P.: The predisposition to anxiety. Psychoanalyt. Quart., vol. 10, 1941.

GRODDECK, G.: The book of the id. New York, 1928.

HALE, N.: The season of summer. In Aswell, M. L., It's a woman's world, New York: Whittlesey, 1944.

HORNEY, K.: Maternal conflicts. Am. J. Orthopsychiat., vol. 3, 1933.

HUTTON, L.: The single woman and her emotional problems. Baltimore: Wood, 1937.

IRVING, F. C.: Safe deliverance. Boston: Houghton Mifflin, 1942.

JACOBSSOHN, E.: Beitrag zur Entwicklung des weiblichen Kinderwunsches. Internat. Ztschr. f. Psychoanal. vol. 22, 1936.

KARDINER, A.: The individual and his society. New York: Columbia Univ. Press, 1939.

490 BIBLIOGRAPHY

KASANIN, J., AND HANDSCHIN, S.: Psychodynamic factors in illegitimacy.
Am. J. Orthopsychiat., vol. 11, 1941.
KAUFMAN, M. R.: Old age and aging: the psychoanalytic point of view.
Am. J. Orthopsychiat., vol. 10, no. 1.
KNIGHT, R. P.: Some problems involved in selecting and rearing adopted
children. Bull. Menninger Clin., vol. 5, 1941.
———: Functional disturbances in the sexual life of women. Ibid., vol. 7,
no. 1, 1943.
KRAMER, S. N.: Bull. Am. Schools Oriental Research.
KUBIE, L. S.: The ontogeny of anxiety. Psychoanalyt. Rev., vol. 28, 1941.
LAMPL-DE GROOT, J.: Problems of femininity. Psychoanalyt. Quart., vol.
2, 1933.
LEVY, D. M.: Maternal overprotection. New York: Columbia Univ. Press,
1943.
LORAND, S.: Contribution to the problem of vaginal orgasm. Internat. J.
Psycho-Analysis, 20: 432, 1929.
LULL, C. B., AND HINGSON, R. A.: Control of pain in childbirth. Phila-
delphia: Lippincott, 1944.
MALINOWSKI, B.: Sex and repression in savage society. New York: Har-
court, 1927.
MARCINOWSKI, J.: Zwei Entbindungsträume einer Schwangeren. Internat.
Ztschr. f. Psychoanal., vol. 7, 1921.
MEAD, M.: Sex and temperament. New York: Morrow, 1935.
MENNINGER, K.: Man against himself. New York: Harcourt, 1938.
———: Somatic correlations with the unconscious repudiation of femininity
in women. J. Nerv. & Ment. Dis., vol. 89, 1939.
———: Love against hate. New York: Harcourt, 1942.
———: Psychiatric aspects of contraception. Bull. Menninger Clin.,
vol. 7, no. 1, 1943.
MENNINGER, W. C.: The emotional factors in pregnancy. Bull. Menninger
Clin., vol. 7, no. 1, 1943.
MIDDLEMORE, M. P.: The nursing couple. London: Hamish Hamilton
Med. Bks., 1941.
MOULTON, R.: Psychosomatic implications of pseudocyesis. Psychosom.
Med., vol. 4, 1942.
ORR, D. W.: Pregnancy following the decision to adopt. Psychosom. Med.,
vol. 3, 1941.
PAYNE, S. M.: A conception of femininity. Brit. J. M. Psychol., 1936.
PLOSS, H., AND BARTELS, M.: Das Weib. Berlin: Neufeld, 1927, vol. 2.
RADO, S.: An anxious mother: A contribution to the analysis of the ego.
Internat. J. Psycho-Analysis, vol. 9, 1928.
RANK, O.: Myth of the birth of the hero. Nerv. & Ment. Dis. Monog. 18.
New York: Nerv. & Ment. Dis. Pub. Co., 1914.
———: Psychoanalytische Beiträge zur Mythenforschung. Vienna: Inter-
nat. Psychoanal. Verlag, 1919.

Rank, O: Inzestmotiv in Dichtung und Sage: Psychoanalytische Beiträge zur Mythenforschung. Vienna: Internat. Psychoanal. Verlag, 1922.

———: The trauma of birth. New York: Harcourt, 1929.

Read, G. D.: Childbirth without fear. New York: Harper, 1944.

Reik, T.: Probleme der Religionspsychologie: die Couvade. Vienna: Internat. Psychoanalyt. Bibliot., vol. 5.

Ribble, M. A.: The rights of infants. New York: Columbia Univ. Press, 1943.

Rickman, J. (ed.): On bringing up of children. London: Kegan Paul, 1938.

Robbins, L. L.: Suggestions for the psychological study of sterility in women. Bull. Menninger Clin., vol. 7, no. 1, 1943.

Sachs, H.: One of the motive features in the formation of the superego in women. Internat. J. Psycho-Analysis, 10: 50, 1929.

Siegler, S. L.: Fertility in women. New York: Lippincott, 1944.

Thompson, L. J.: Attitudes of primiparae as observed in a prenatal clinic. Ment. Hyg., Apr., 1942.

Warburg, B.: Suicide, pregnancy, and rebirth. Psychoanalyt. Quart., vol. 7, 1938.

Weiss, E., and English, O. S.: Psychosomatic medicine. Philadelphia: Saunders, 1942.

Wiesel, J.: Innere Klinik des Klimakteriums. In Handb. d. Biol. u. Path. d. Weibes.

Wittels, F.: Mutterschaft und Bisexualität. Internat. Ztschr. f. Psychoanal., vol. 20, 1934.

Wittkower, E.: New developments in the investigation and treatment of sterility. Proc. Roy. Soc. Med., vol. 36, 1943.

——— and Wilson, A. T. M.: Dysmenorrhea and sterility: Personality studies. Brit. M. J., vol. 2, 1940.

Wolf, A.: The parents' manual. New York: Simon & Schuster, 1943.

Yates, S. L.: An investigation of the psychological factors in virginity and ritual defloration. Internat. J. Psycho-Analysis, 1930.

Zilboorg, G.: Malignant psychoses related to childbirth. Am. J. Obst. & Gynec., vol. 15, 1928.

———: The dynamics of schizophrenic reactions related to pregnancy and childbirth. Am. J. Psychiat., vol. 8, 1929.

———: Some observations on the transformation of instincts. Psychoanalyt. Quart., vol. 7, 1938.

———: Masculine and feminine. Psychiatry, vol. 8, no. 3, 1944.

Index